ENCYCLOPEDIA OF
Cesar Chavez

IA OF

Cesar Chavez

*The Farm Workers'
Fight for Rights and Justice*

Roger Bruns

Movements of the American Mosaic

GREENWOOD

AN IMPRINT OF ABC-CLIO, LLC
Santa Barbara, California • Denver, Colorado • Oxford, England

Library of Congress Cataloging-in-Publication Data

Bruns, Roger A., 1941–
    Encyclopedia of Cesar Chavez : the farm workers' fight for rights and justice / Roger Bruns.
        pages cm — (Movements of the American mosaic)
    Includes bibliographical references and index.
    ISBN 978–1–4408–0380–2 (alk. paper) — ISBN 978–1–4408–0381–9 (ebook)
1. Chavez, Cesar, 1927–1993. 2. Labor leaders—United States—History—20th century.
3. United Farm Workers—History—20th century. 4. Mexican American migrant agricultural laborers—History—20th century. I. Title.
HD6509.C48B79   2013
331.88'13092—dc23   2012036347
[B]

ISBN: 978–1–4408–0380–2
EISBN: 978–1–4408–0381–9

17 16 15 14 13   1 2 3 4 5

This book is also available on the World Wide Web as an eBook.
Visit www.abc-clio.com for details.

Greenwood
An Imprint of ABC-CLIO, LLC

ABC-CLIO, LLC
130 Cremona Drive, P.O. Box 1911
Santa Barbara, California 93116-1911

This book is printed on acid-free paper ∞

Manufactured in the United States of America

Contents

Introduction

In March 1968, Senator Robert Kennedy, shortly before his tragic assassination, declared to a group of farm workers in California,

> And when your children and grandchildren take their place in America—going to high school, and college, and taking good jobs at good pay—when you look at them, you will say, "I did this. I was there, and the point of difficulty and danger." And though you may be old and bent from many years of labor, no man will stand taller than you when you say, "I marched with Cesar." (Kennedy 1968)

Cesar Chavez was an unlikely hero. Born into a poor family of Mexican Americans outside Yuma, Arizona, in 1927, faced with an early life doing hard labor as a migrant farm worker in the harvest fields, without money or influence, Chavez took on a personal crusade that seemed a foregone failure. He would attempt to organize a labor union of farm workers, the *campesinos* among whom he grew up.

The men, women, and children in those fruit and vegetable fields faced stifling days in the heat, worked in contorted positions with inferior tools that made back injuries routine and lasting, made little in wages, had no benefits, and lived mostly in shacks. In the orchards and fields of the American Southwest and California, they worked a grueling routine, day after day, always without enough food and faced with constant danger of disease or accident. By the time most of the children were 12 years old, they joined their parents in the fields and attended school only when there was no work.

With little more than grit and uncommon instincts of leadership, Chavez took on a seemingly quixotic fight against American agribusiness and formidable political enemies. With the help of extraordinary allies such as Dolores Huerta, he made possible what seemed to most observers a fanciful dream—the United Farm Workers of America (UFW).

His story comes from the profound upheaval and discontent of the 1960s—the divisive Vietnam War, political assassinations, the civil rights movement, and the drive of Mexican Americans and other Latinos to gain equal rights. It is a story of young people and old thrust into situations demanding exceptional bravery; of marches, labor strikes, and boycotts; of violence in the streets; and of putting into action the organizing techniques that could bring together people without power to enable them to achieve it.

"La Causa," or "The Cause," was never a typical union. It was a movement for dignity as well as higher pay; it was for Latino self-identity as well as for bargaining rights. It had a profound national impact. The sparks of protest lit by Chavez in the tiny town of Delano, California, showed to the world the plight of the farm worker. The union's boycott calling on consumers not to buy grapes produced by growers who exploited farm workers, for example, raised awareness of the issue to such an extent that millions of Americans responded to Chavez's call.

He was an admirer of both Mohandas Gandhi and Martin Luther King Jr. On a number of occasions, Chavez decided, as part of strikes and boycotts, to go on fasts to demonstrate his commitment to nonviolent protest. Huerta, the cofounder of the infant union of farm workers, remarked that a number of long-time members of other unions had no idea what the leader of this new union was accomplishing by not eating. They were used to using clubs and baseball bats during strikes, not fasting:

> Well you can imagine what these tough, burly labor leaders from New York thought when we told them our leader, our president, was fasting. "What's wrong with him? Is he crazy?" I mean they were just—they went ballistic. Because in New York, especially during that time, they'd go into a place and wreck it up. They would wreck it all up to get a contract and here we had our leader who was *not eating*. All he would do was take Holy Communion every day. (Huerta 2004)

But if those workers had the mistaken impression that Chavez was merely a meek ascetic, they simply did not as yet know the man—a fiery battler, commanding and determined.

During a grape boycott in 1969, Chavez declared, "We are militant. You have to be militant to stand on a picket line with a gun pointed at your head. You have to be militant to keep the pressure on the growers all the time, pushing them back from one barrier to the next. . . . We have found prayer important in nonviolent work, but it's most effective accompanied by lots of hard picketing" (Warman 1969).

A half century after the first strike of Chavez's farm workers union, the debate in the United States about illegal immigration, border security, and undocumented workers rages, affecting state legislation from Arizona to Alabama. Throughout its history, the UFW has wrestled with the immigration issue. Ironically, Chavez himself fought against the importation of illegal workers from Mexico because those workers, who could be paid extremely low wages, were used by growers as scabs to replace members of Chavez's union in the fields. The UFW policy on immigration has since changed. But in the story of the UFW are the dilemmas and contradictions of a seemingly intractable issue that continues to defy solution.

Although farm workers in California and in other agricultural areas of the West and Southwest continue to labor under poor working conditions, and although the actual numbers of members of the UFW are far lower than in earlier years, Chavez and those who marched with him made indelible marks on American cultural and political history. Many reformers, activists, and other Americans committed to various causes trace their work and drive to the farm workers movement. Many coalitions between labor, student groups, and religious organizations devoted to social justice have been inspired by the movement. They and their children and others newly inspired carry on their own march with Cesar.

Roots

Chavez was the second of six children of Librado and Juana Chavez. His fraternal grandfather, Cesario "Papa Chayo," had crossed the border into Arizona from Mexico in 1888, settling on a farm in the North Gila Valley desert along the Colorado River. It was here that the extended family worked the land, cared for horses and cows, and opened a small grocery store.

In 1937, unable to make tax payments on their farm during the Great Depression, the Chavez family left Arizona. Loading their few possessions in a dilapidated car, the family joined other Depression-era families on the road to California to its harvest lands and the faint promise of work.

For a time, Brawley, California, became a home base. They traveled north each spring from job to job, gaining knowledge about the harvests and job opportunities. They picked peas, lettuce, tomatoes, figs, prunes, grapes, and apricots. Many times the family spent the night under bridges or in tents. And, as did other Mexican Americans, they faced the constant reminder that they were a minority race and culture. From his earliest childhood days, Cesar, as did other Hispanic children in the United States, learned limitations rather than possibilities.

In 1943, the Chavez family settled in Delano, California, in the center of the crop-rich San Joaquin Valley. The young Chavez began to sport the *pachuco* or "zoot suit" look—a flowing coat; tapered pants; a broad, flat, wide-brimmed hat; and long ducktail hair. Nurtured in Los Angeles, the style was one of rebellion, anger, and frustration of Mexican American youth.

Cesar's father joined the National Farm Labor Union. Organized by Ernesto Galarza, a Mexican American sociologist and labor organizer, the union organized a number of strikes in the 1940s, but they were short-lived and relatively ineffective. Nevertheless, Cesar admired the union's purpose if not its success.

At an early age, Chavez faced racial humiliation. He faced signs that proclaimed "White Trade Only" or "We Don't Sell to Dogs or Mexicans." He later remembered the time in Indio, California, when his father was turned away from a small restaurant along the road when he tried to buy coffee, and the time when, as a youngster, Cesar tried to get a hamburger at a diner and was told to go to "Mexican town."

He fought back at the racism. While at a movie in Delano with a young woman named Helen Fabela, Chavez refused to sit in the section of the theater reserved for Latinos. "The assistant manager came," Chavez recalls. "The girl who sold the popcorn came. And the girl with the tickets came. Then the manager came. They tried to pull me up, and I said, 'No, you have to break my arms before I get up.'" Chavez was hustled off to the jail for a lecture from the chief of police on proper behavior in a segregated place of business ("The Little Strike . . ." 1969).

In 1946, Chavez enlisted in the Navy. After two years, he returned to Delano. On October 22, 1948, he married Helen Fabela. They would eventually have eight children. He was 21 at the time of his marriage—thin, 5 feet 6 inches tall, with a shock of jet-black hair, his body muscled from years of grinding work in the fields. But like most farm workers, he was plagued by back pains, the result of daily stooped labor.

In 1952, Chavez moved with others of his family into a barrio in southeast San Jose with the uninviting name of Sal Si Puedes ("Get Out If You Can"). When a young Catholic priest named Father Donald McDonnell traveled to Sal Si Puedes to help establish a community organization among the farm laborers, Chavez soon became a close friend.

The two men were nearly the same age, and both were excited about working for change. For Chavez, it was coming together now—the lessons from his father about not accepting as fate the conditions in which you found yourself and about working with others in unions to improve those conditions; the teachings of his grandmother about spirituality and the elements of Catholicism that inspired one to reach out to help those in need; and also the example of his mother, who, on many occasions, asked her children to go out by the railroad tracks and ask a hobo to come for dinner.

He read biographies of individuals whose leadership made a difference, such as labor organizers John L. Lewis and Eugene V. Debs. He read about Gandhi, the Indian politician and spiritual leader who had preached and practiced the philosophy of nonviolent social change. He was particularly struck by the power unleashed strategically by campaigns of civil disobedience and even the spiritual ritual of fasting to unleash the power of redemption. He was young and poor but had in him a fire to help change the lot of his family and of the thousands of others who worked painstakingly in the fields. He decided to become a community organizer.

Organizing

In Chicago's tough neighborhoods of the 1930s, Saul Alinsky, a graduate of the University of Chicago and a man who had grown up in the city's Jewish ghetto, began his life's work of helping ethnic groups, unions, and others to organize themselves to take on governments and corporate interests that had wielded power over them. In 1936 Alinsky cofounded the Back-of-the-Yards Neighborhood Council (BYNC), his first effort to build a neighborhood citizen reform organization.

In 1939, Alinsky established the Industrial Areas Foundation to help reform other declining urban neighborhoods. His approach was to unite and organize ordinary, aggrieved citizens. He taught them techniques such as house meetings, marches, and communication strategies to help them become effective forces for change. Other organizations traced their own strategies to Alinsky's work; one of those was the Community Service Organization (CSO). Its leader was Fred Ross.

A graduate of the University of California and a former worker with the Farm Security Administration (FSA), one of President Roosevelt's most notable New Deal programs, Ross helped found the found the CSO, a Latino civil rights group that became highly successful in registering new voters and in establishing citizen involvement in social issues. By building Mexican American voter strength, Ross believed, politicians would be forced to improve services, streets, parks, sewage systems, garbage removal, and especially schools. A self-help, civic-action agency, the CSO worked to improve living and working conditions, to promote educational and youth programs and community outreach, and to protest violations of human and civil rights.

Deeply distrustful of Anglos, Chavez hesitated when the lanky Ross, in wrinkled clothes and with a beat-up car, walked up to Chavez working in the fields on a day in 1952 and asked if he could have a house meeting with him and some of his friends. A dubious Chavez agreed, but almost as a lark. "I had hatched a plan with some of my Pachuco buddies to scare him away. At a prearranged signal from me, they'd start insulting him; that way, we thought, Fred would leave" (Chavez and Stavans 2008).

At the meeting, the plan never worked because Chavez never gave the signal. When one of the friends in the room interrupted, Chavez demanded silence. What Ross was saying made sense. This was the beginning of a remarkable friendship and a historic collaboration. Ross later recalled,

> I just talked quietly about what I had done helping the people of Riverside and Redlands, in the Casa Blanca and El Modena barrios, do away with seg-regation in the schools and skating rinks and schoolbuses. And how, on the eastside of Los Angles, the people built their own civic-action organization

(the C.S.O.), which went to work on their problems as well as registering neighbors to vote and turning them out to the polls. (Ross 1989, 3)

Ross saw immediately in Chavez the burning desire to change the plight of farm workers. For two months, Chavez showed up at the meetings Ross held for the workers, displaying the kind of urgency and determination that Ross had not seen in others. Chavez decided to join the organization. "I was an apricot picker," he said. "I liked what they were doing, a real big program, fighting police brutality and discrimination and things like that" (Berman 1966).

Chavez agreed to help organize a voter-registration drive in San Jose. Still working as a field laborer to make ends meet, he conducted house meetings at night, talking with fellow field workers about their constitutional rights and showing them how to register to vote. Chavez recruited friends from the barrio to help with the work and by the end of the campaign had signed up several thousand new voters.

California Republicans charged that many of the first-time Mexican American voters were actually illegal aliens or had criminal backgrounds. When they began to intimidate voters at the polls, a furious Ross wired the U.S. Attorney General in Washington asking that the federal government investigate this voter harassment. Chavez added his name to the letter. For the Department of Justice and the Federal Bureau of Investigation (FBI), however, the letter was less an alarm against voter fraud than a signal that this group in San Jose might be tied to some kind of communist conspiracy.

The FBI sent agents to follow the activities of this young activist Chavez and his comrades. Who was this new face of protest, and what were his links to communism? It was not long before they rounded up Chavez for interrogation. Suddenly Chavez was the talk of the area. Everywhere he went, he said, people asked whether he was a communist.

The file on Chavez at the FBI headquarters in Washington grew over the years, filling up with information about his friends, work, speeches, philosophy, and family. As the FBI tracked Chavez with increasing intensity, it found no evidence of his implication in communist activities. Instead, the file bulged with evidence of Chavez's strong commitment on behalf of Latino farm workers.

Ross and the CSO decided to hire Chavez as a full-time organizer at $35 a week. In his entire career, he would never earn more than $6,000 a year. In the 1950s, Chavez organized over 20 CSO chapters. Workers came to him with their problems. For them he wrote letters to government agencies and intervened in misunderstandings with the police or with physicians or welfare departments.

Huerta

In the mid-1950s, Chavez befriended Dolores Huerta. She, too, was a recruit of Fred Ross. Born in New Mexico to a farm worker and raised in Stockton,

California, Huerta, like Chavez, spent time in the fields picking cherries and tomatoes. She managed to attend Stockton College and took night classes at the University of the Pacific, earning a teaching credential. After a short stint in the classroom, she became disillusioned attempting to help students who did not have enough clothing or food. She joined the CSO to organize a chapter in Stockton. Attractive and gregarious, Huerta became an effective representative for CSO in its meetings with local government leaders and took on lobbying efforts with members of the California legislature on such issues as assistance to agricultural workers.

Huerta had heard of Chavez, about his extraordinary energy and his ability to gather people together. She had imagined a powerful figure with gifted abilities as an orator. Yet when she met him in person, he seemed shy, almost retiring. Yet she soon realized that he had keen intelligence, a fiery disposition, and a firm determination to make a difference.

In the summer of 1958, Chavez was in Oxnard, a town north of Los Angeles, to establish a local office of the CSO. He realized that the federally funded Bracero Program that brought workers from Mexico for temporary employment in the fields damaged the prospects for local workers. Although sympathizing with the plight of the Mexican workers brought into the United States in the harvest seasons and then sent back, Chavez realized that the system severely jeopardized the wages of Mexican American workers already in the country. Not only were the braceros used by the growers as strike-breakers, the low wages they received and the conditions under which they worked set a grim standard of wretchedness.

Chavez and his lieutenants doggedly rallied the farm worker community to his cause. By the end of 1959, they had set up at a local CSO headquarters, a so-called hiring hall from which many of the growers agreed to find workers. Chavez had essentially turned the local CSO in Oxnard into a union hall. It was here that he began to see clearly in his mind the exciting potential of organizing the farm workers of California into a union. He proposed to the board members of CSO that they found such a union.

Although Ross and others at CSO shared the belief that some kind of activism was necessary to improve the lot of the field workers, they did not agree to take the CSO in a direction that might adversely affect the work they were already undertaking, principally as a social service organization. After all, the possibility of forming a successful union of such diverse, oft-moving, and unskilled workers seemed fanciful at best.

Ross agreed to have the Chavez proposal presented at the convention to the full membership. The vote lost. When the vote was announced, Chavez quietly rose in the hall and said that he had an announcement. It was two words—"I resign."

He had little money, no property, and no job. What he did have was a burning wish to form a union and a determined will to succeed. He soon asked Huerta to join him in his seemingly quixotic quest and she accepted. So did another of the CSO members, Gilbert Padilla, a former harvest worker foreman and army veteran. They would move to Delano, California, hometown of a number of relatives, and attempt to start a farm workers organization.

Union

Soft-spoken, with jet-black hair; liquid-like, heavy brown eyes; and, oftentimes, a wry grin, Chavez was almost boyish-looking at 35 years old when he arrived in Delano with his family in the spring of 1962. He had a natural instinct to gather around him many loyal friends.

At first, the growers were totally skeptical of any attempts to rally farm workers as a group. Workers knew their place, the growers believed, and would never be able to muster the coordination or commitment to endanger the system in place. In addition, all the local institutions, from the police to business owners and political leaders, could be expected to react defensively, protecting the status quo.

But Chavez and Huerta settled in Delano to try to make U.S. labor history. With the help of friends and relatives, they went from house to house setting up small meetings with farm workers. On Sunday, September 30, 1962, in an abandoned theater in Fresno, California, nearly 300 workers gathered to show solidarity and celebrate a new organization. They called it the National Farm Workers Association (NFWA).

They held a convention in Fresno on January 21, 1963. Chavez became president of the new organization; vice presidents were Dolores Huerta, Gilbert Padilla, and Julio Hernandez, a field worker from Corcoran, California.

They gathered together a close knit set of "co-fanatics," as they called themselves, including Jim Drake, a graduate of Occidental College and Union Theological Seminary.

Although their relationship was sometimes contentious given their mutual headstrong beliefs and self-confidence, Chavez and Huerta worked closely together. Huerta began to take charge of various administrative matters. Padilla and others continued working in the fields while secretly passing out literature to the workers. But even when workers agreed to sign up, some would soon change their minds; others simply moved to other areas and lost interest.

But Chavez and his lieutenants looked forward to the time when the union could seriously challenge the growers with a strike. Nevertheless, they did not feel that the time had yet arrived. They knew well the tactics they would face from the growers as soon as they called a strike. The owners would approach the courts for rulings to prevent the union from boycotting or picketing. They would hire goons and thugs from other parts of the valley to beat up strikers. They would bring in undocumented foreign workers to help to replace picketing workers. They would enlist the efforts of police to arrest picketers and protesters for causing mayhem. They would plant stories in the media that the strikers were violent, un-American, and probably communists.

Committed strongly to the idea of nonviolent protest, Chavez knew how difficult it would be to embolden strikers to stand tough against these kinds of threats and intimidation, against actual assaults, and against the loss of wages during the protests. They knew that for the workers to stand up to the roughhouse methods and to be nonviolent in response, they would need outside support, solid commitment, and great dedication.

By 1964, Chavez, Huerta, and other lieutenants had signed up over 1,000 families. They were able to create a credit union and begin to provide services such as immigration counseling and voter registration. For the first time, Chavez could go on a salary from union dues. The organization also began publishing its own newspaper called *El Malcriado* (The Unruly One).

In the spring of 1965, Chavez and his union engaged in its first small-scale, localized strike actions—a wage protest by rose grafters in McFarland, California, and a protest against a rent increase at a labor camp. Rose grafters were skilled workers whose job entailed many rigorous physical demands. Crawling on their knees for miles, the grafters slit mature rose bushes and inserted buds. If the workers were careless, many of the bushes could be ruined. For this labor, the workers had been promised $9 for a thousand plants. They had not received their full wages. Instead, they had received less than $7 per thousand plants. The largest company, Mount Arbor, employer of nearly 100 workers, became the union's first target.

On a Sunday prior to the strike, the workers gathered in a formal ceremony, with Dolores Huerta holding a crucifix, and pledged not to break the strike. Early Monday morning, Chavez and Huerta drove around the camps watching for any of the workers who might have changed their minds. Only a few had balked and were gently dissuaded from heading off to the fields. When a couple of workers decided to go to work later in the week, Huerta was in front of their house in her green truck and refused to move.

The strike was not entirely successful. The company brought in a group of Mexican workers as scabs. Nevertheless, the company did agree to increase the wages of the workers for the remainder of the season.

At about the same time, the Tulane County Housing Authority, located in nearby Porterville, California, decided to raise the rents in two farm labor camps whose facilities lacked running water and whose flimsy tin shacks had been built during the Great Depression and were near collapse. Jim Drake and Gilbert Padilla persuaded the workers to strike for lower rental costs. The summer-long picketing prompted the Tulane County Housing Authority to tear down the tin shacks and replace them with modest but livable cottages.

Strike

As the summer of 1965 drew to a close near Delano, California, and grapes ripened on the vines, farm workers began moving through the rows of the harvest fields expecting to make 90 cents an hour plus 10 cents a basket. But members of a mostly Filipino group called the Agricultural Workers Organizing Committee (AWOC) decided to go on strike, demanding higher wages.

The Filipino farm workers, many of whom were single men in their fifties, had lived most of their adult lives in ranch housing along back-country roads east of Delano. After joining the strike en masse, they were evicted. Led by Larry Itliong (a friend of Dolores Huerta), Andy Imutan, and others, the Filipinos realized that any success they might have in Delano depended on an alliance with Chavez's new labor union.

On Mexican Independence Day, September 16, 1965, the mostly Latino membership of the union met in Delano. Chavez had sent out word through local disk jockeys on Spanish radio and in *El Malcriado* that something big was in the works. Dressed in an old sport shirt and work pants, Chavez, in a halting and somewhat shaky voice, rallied the men and woman to what he called "La Causa." The union voted unanimously to go forward with the strike.

On September 20, 1965, NFWA workers joined a winding picket line in the dawn's fog alongside a farm east of Delano. As workers pulled up to go to work, picketers challenged them to join the strike. Many responded. Soon, foremen in trucks sped along the dirt road throwing dust in the faces of the strikers, demanding that they leave the area. Nevertheless, in the chaos of the first days of the strike, the workers remained disciplined and controlled.

On October 16, 1965, the Kern County sheriff issued an announcement that picketers who called out to the scab workers over loudspeakers would be arrested. It did not take long for the NFWA to take on the threat. The Rev. David Havens, a minister of the Christian Church in Visalia, California, was arrested for disturbing the peace by Kern County deputy sheriffs for reading in a loud voice the words of novelist Jack London describing a strike-breaker: "After God had finished the rattlesnake, the toad and the vampire, He had some awful substance left with which He made a strikebreaker" (Bernstein 1965).

On October 19, nine clergymen joined Helen Chavez and 34 strikers in going to jail for shouting "Huelga!" on the picket line. On December 13 and 14, 11 national religious leaders, Protestant and Catholic, visited Delano. It was not long before Protestant denominations across the country struggled over whether and how deeply the church should be involved in the events unfolding in the fields of California.

Chavez recruited LeRoy Chatfield, a young teacher from Bakersfield who had earlier visited Delano to see what the farm worker movement was all about.

Chatfield was studying at the University of Southern California for his Ph.D. Chavez asked Chatfield to change his plans. Would he join Cesar to help raise funds and supplies to support the families on strike? Chatfield agreed and became a resourceful ally.

From the outset of the strike, Chavez preached the message of nonviolence and the spiritual quality it invested in the social movement. Martin Luther King Jr., an apostle of nonviolent social protest, sent a telegram to Chavez commending the labor and civil rights activist on his "commitment to righting grievous wrongs forced upon exploited people." King wrote, "We are together with you in spirit and determination that our dreams for a better tomorrow will be realized" (Bogater 2009).

Like King, Chavez was deeply religious. The union often held religious services, and Chavez surrounded himself with Christian religious leaders from various denominations. The catalyst for the clerical involvement in the beginnings of Chavez's work was the California Migrant Ministry (CMM), and its leader, Chris Hartmire. The CMM had migrant ministry programs in many states providing nursing care, educational and recreational activities, day care, and other services. Speaking to synods, conventions, assemblies, and other kinds of religious gatherings, Hartmire clearly laid out, in terms understandable both to clergy and laity, the origins of the farm workers movement, its deep connections to ideals of Christian charity, and the religious impulses that drove Chavez in his quest for social justice.

Chavez was emotionally moved by the relationship of ministers to the farm laborers. He often used the example of Hartmire and his group to persuade other religious organizations, including the Catholic Church, to send more representatives to the fields and barrios. As in the black civil rights movement, Christian clergy and laity became ever more omnipresent in the farm workers struggle, recruiting volunteers through their own ministries and lobbying legislatures at all levels of government. And they gave to the movement a legitimacy that helped deflate rumors and innuendo that somehow Chavez and his allies were bent on violence and posed a threat to American values and way of life. "The churches *had* to get involved," Chavez said. "Everything they had taught for two thousand years was at stake in this struggle" (Day 1971, 53).

Valdez

Luis Valdez and Chavez had similar backgrounds. Both were born in Arizona to farm worker parents; both moved to California. By the age of six, Luis joined his nine brothers and sisters in the fields of the San Joaquin Valley. He became interested in plays and acting at an early age and earned a scholarship to attend San Jose State College. After his graduation, Valdez joined the San Francisco

Mime Troupe. When Chavez began his movement in southern California, Valdez found a perfect vehicle for his political and social protest instincts. Two months into the strike, he joined Chavez in Delano.

Valdez created a theater company of actor-laborers not only to raise funds and to publicize the farm worker strike but to energize the workers. On Friday evenings, Chavez began to hold two-hour meetings to bolster the camaraderie of the strikers. With songs, testimonials from families and friends of the strikers, and presentations by guests from religious, social, and labor organizations, the meetings forged greater union.

It was here, in one of these Friday meetings, that Valdez included the first performances of El Teatro Campesino. It combined Mexican folk theater, comedy, and mime and offered comic reflections on laborers and bosses. The actors themselves were campesinos. The performances were morality plays brought to work sites. "I learned how to create something out of nothing," Valdez said later. But of Chavez, he said, "The man created a movement out of nothing" (Rubiano 2007).

The growers fought the new union with every weapon at their disposal. Company lawyers persuaded the courts to issue injunctions against picketers, restrict organizers' access to the fields, and evict strikers from their shelters at the labor camps. Growers also turned to undocumented immigrants as scabs to fill the slots abandoned by the strikers, fully confident that the police would not interfere.

After absorbing the first round of volleys from the growers, Chavez decided to raise the level of the protest. He decided to employ a boycott. He would try to convince citizens not to buy grapes until the industry instituted humane work practices and paid fair wages. He would turn the Delano strike and the cause of the farm workers even more intensely into a national movement.

Schenley

In early December 1965, Chavez called a boycott of the large grape producer Schenley Industries. Recruiting volunteers from churches, community organizations, labor organizations, and universities, the union began to set up boycott centers in various cities across California, attempting to persuade citizens, as part of the farm worker protest, to stop buying grapes. Soon, volunteers fanned out across the United States to major cities. With little money, the volunteers hitchhiked to New York, Chicago, St. Louis, and other major cities. They carried signs imploring the public to "Help Farmworkers—Do Not Buy Grapes." As the protest moved from the fields to the urban areas, it began to attract additional national attention.

Young and old, Mexican Americans, other Latinos, whites—the volunteers arrived in Delano wanting to be a part of the fight. They went to work for no wages and for barely enough to eat. They took on various tasks. One youngster agreed to jump freight cars to keep track of where grape shipments were headed and then rode the rails back to Delano to report to Chavez and the other leaders. Others formed student groups to picket at universities and university towns and to organize rallies.

Delano became increasingly the center of a major unfolding drama. On December 13, 1965, a delegation of 10 church leaders—four Roman Catholics, one Jew, and six Protestants—arrived to meet the strikers and issue a statement of support:

> The suffering of farm workers and their children cries to heaven and demands the attention of persons of conscience. Farm workers are worthy. Their labor is important to the agricultural industry. It is both natural and just that they should participate in the decision-making process about wages, working conditions, and automation. (Ganz 2009, 142)

On December 16, 1965, United Auto Workers (UAW) president Walther Reuther visited Delano to pledge his support of the strike. Nearly 1,000 farm workers and others joined in a spirited rally. For Reuther to have made this visit was an enormous boost to Chavez at this critical time, giving powerful national visibility to the movement. Reuther announced that the AFL-CIO and the UAW would provide a cash contribution for organizing activities and would allocate $2,500 per month to support the strike.

The movement began to elicit increasing fear and contempt from California growers. The pressure on the strikers increased. The local Delano sheriff and his deputies, inextricably tied to the owners, did their own part. At one point, a decree went forth that picketers would no longer have the right to shout at scabs because it was disturbing the peace. Quieting the strikers was no small order, but it did add another annoyance to the labors of those on the lines. The no-shouting order, however, proved to be a near perfect foil for Chavez.

In order to test the mettle of the sheriff, Chavez carefully created a special picket line filled with women and children. Over 40 mother protestors were hauled off to jail; Chavez asked his aides to take the 76 children of the incarcerated mothers to a nearby park, where they ate and played games. The following day, a massive protest, including the children, surrounded the jail. On the third day, the American Civil Liberties Union posted bail, and the strikers emerged to great cheering. The Delano sheriff and his men were now suitably tainted with the same kind of ignominy as the Birmingham, Alabama, police and others in the South who wielded hoses and thrust dogs at black demonstrators.

On occasion, strikers floated helium balloons with the word "Huelga" prominently displayed. At a railroad loading dock where growers brought their grapes for shipment, the union set up a 24-hour picket line. On one occasion, a truck drove into the picket line, seriously injuring one of the protestors. Angered and frightened, the picketers nevertheless kept up the line day and night.

When the season ended, the growers claimed that despite the strike they had enjoyed a bumper crop, that the efforts of the union had been futile. However, the Federal Marketing Service Commodity Report told a different story. It showed one-half million fewer grapes sold in 1965 than in 1964. In truth, the California growers had suffered from the strike, and many were anxious about the future.

SNCC

More than any other civil rights organization, the Student Nonviolent Coordinating Committee (SNCC) recognized early on that Chavez's efforts in behalf of Mexican American farm workers were strikingly similar to the efforts of Martin Luther King Jr. and others to combat racial and ethnic prejudice and to improve the lives of people living on the edge of the United States' capitalist system. Founded in 1960, the SNCC, comprised primarily of college students, stood for multiracial equality, not just the equality of blacks and whites.

The SNCC's strong belief in multiracial equality and cooperation made possible the first major coalition between a civil rights organization and the drive for Mexican American workers and civil rights. The SNCC was not only helpful in the farm workers' battle against Schenley but also encouraged other civil rights organizations to tie their own causes to those of the farm workers.

One of the first SNCC representatives to arrive was Marshall Ganz from the San Francisco office. Fluent in Spanish, he joined Chavez in 1965 and became a chief strategist and organizer.

In March 1966, the strike received unexpected and welcome publicity. The U.S. Senate Subcommittee on Migrant Labor, including Senator Robert Kennedy (D-NY), scheduled a visit to Delano to investigate conditions in the farm labor sector. The subcommittee toured the union offices with large numbers of curious farm workers trailing the group with cameras flashing and reporters taking down notes.

Angered by what he saw and mightily impressed by Chavez, Kennedy embraced the farm workers movement. Chavez later recalled, "By the time the hearing ended Kennedy was like a thousand percent behind us endorsing our efforts . . . when he came, and came totally and completely on our side, this gave the people a real . . . well, jacked them up" (Chavez 1970).

Shortly after the visit from Senator Kennedy, Chavez announced a major plan that would, in the end, have historic consequences for La Causa. The NFWA would begin a 300-mile pilgrimage or *peregrinación* from Delano to the state capitol of Sacramento. The march, Chavez said, would end on the steps of the capitol on Easter Sunday.

Peregrinación

Chavez realized that the day-by-day grind of the strike and boycott was taking a toll on the union members. A stalemate was not acceptable, and he searched for a way to jolt the protest, to gain greater national publicity, and most of all to lift the spirits of the protestors to a new high. He decided to adopt another tactic that had been successful in the civil rights movement—a long march. It would cover a route from Delano to the state capital of Sacramento, through such towns as Madera, Fresno, Modesto, and Stockton.

Chavez was following a Mexican custom of walking to historic shrines to do penance during the season of Lent. Its theme would be pilgrimage, penitence, and revolution. The striking farm workers—the *huelgistas*—would march to do penance for the ills they might have committed during the strike. The march would help cleanse their feelings, Chavez felt, for any violent actions either committed or planned.

On the morning of March 17, 1966, Chavez gathered the marchers in Delano. A line of 68 chosen *peregrinos* began by walking east onto Highway 99 toward Ducor, then Porterville, and other small towns in the rich agricultural areas in which they had worked. As they marched, some carried pictures and waved banners of the Virgin of Guadalupe, the patron and symbol of Mexico, representing the fusion of the Aztec and Spanish cultures. As Catholic and Episcopal bishops voiced support for the *peregrinación* and as rabbis appeared along the march route, it was clear that Chavez, now limping badly on his swollen feet and using a cane, had succeeded in framing the march in religious as well as cultural terms. He had also succeeded in making the strike a fight for justice.

In an attempt to connect even further the union movement with the history and culture of Mexico, Chavez asked Valdez to help write a "Plan of Delano" to be read in each town through which they marched. Valdez said it was inspired by the "Plan of Ayala," a document written by Emiliano Zapata and his supporters in 1911 during the Mexican Revolution. It talked of seeking an end to the suffering of farm workers; of their determination to be heard; and of their resolve to follow their God. It promised unity with people of all faiths and races and a revolution for "bread and justice."

As the marchers neared Sacramento, with approximately a week to go before they would reach the edge of the city, Chavez answered a phone call. It was from a representative of Schenley Industries. Already stung economically and suffering from negative press attention, the company decided to limit the damage and enter into a contract to formally recognize the NFWA. This was the first time in U.S. history that a grassroots farm labor union had achieved recognition by a corporation. Schenley agreed to a substantial increase of wages and to an improvement of working conditions.

On Saturday afternoon, the day before Easter, the marchers gathered on the grounds of Our Lady of Grace School on a hill looking across the Sacramento River and held a rally. They had covered over 300 miles; some 51 "originales" had walked the entire distance.

On Easter Sunday, April 10, 1966, led by some supporters on horseback carrying the NFWA flag and many others wearing sombreros, to the sound of trumpets and the rhythm of guitars keeping the beat, they crossed the bridge, paraded down the mall, and ascended the capitol steps. A weary but jubilant Chavez stood before the 10,000 supporters and told them that Schenley had bowed before the pressure of the union and before the will of the campesinos. His words were nearly swallowed in thunderous cheers.

In the spring of 1966, Chavez and his team purchased a piece of land that would become the union headquarters. Richard Chavez said later, "it was forty acres.... This would be great ... it was just far enough out of the city ... [that] we could really build something" ("Forty Acres" 2008).

Chavez's vision was of a center where farm workers could find products and services normally hard to reach for lower-income, Spanish-speaking migrants. Soon there would be a gas station, a grocery, a health clinic, a credit union and other banking and legal services, and even a small retirement home for aging Filipino farm workers. They called the headquarters "The Forty Acres."

DiGiorgio

In the spring of 1966, the union launched a boycott against DiGiorgio Fruit Corporation, a company controlling vast citrus fields in the San Joaquin Valley. By 1946, the company was the largest grape, plum, and pear grower in the world and the second largest producer of wine in the United States. It controlled S&W Fine Foods, TreeSweet Products, and the White Rose food distribution business in greater New York.

In fighting the strike and boycott, DiGiorgio, already known for its ruthless strike-breaking methods, tried a new strategy. DiGiorgio's officers turned to the International Brotherhood of the Teamsters union, whose leadership was open to the idea of incorporating farm workers among its membership. DiGiorgio knew that the Teamsters would be a much less demanding organization with which to deal than the upstart but spirited NFWA. The grape grower and the Teamsters would try to use each other to defeat Chavez and his union. DiGiorgio invited the Teamsters to organize company workers.

In the summer, the company reported the results of a hastily held election, announcing that the farm workers had chosen to be represented by the Teamsters. After reports of numerous cases of voter irregularity, an investigation by the California state government proved that the election had been rigged. The company agreed to a new election to be held on August 30, 1967.

A few weeks before the election date, Chavez unexpectedly employed an effective strategic gambit. He agreed to merge the NFWA with the AWOC, the mostly Filipino union with whom he had been working in the Delano strike. On August 22, 1966, the NFWA and the AWOC became the United Farm Workers

Organizing Committee (UFWOC) under the umbrella of the AFL-CIO, the national labor federation. Chavez and his union would now receive organizing funds from the AFL-CIO.

As the new election among workers at DiGiorgio approached, Chavez turned to Fred Ross to head up the election drive. His team grew to include not only farm workers but students, labor organizers, and the clergy. But could this infant union pull it off—could it beat the established Teamsters? The Las Vegas betting line gave odds of 3–1 against the UFWOC. And yet, on election day, August 30, 1966, the farm workers marched to the polls and voted overwhelmingly for Chavez's union. In Delano, they celebrated long into the night. Soon afterward, DiGiorgio agreed to sign a three-year contract.

Giumarra

In August 1967, Chavez, Huerta, and other union leaders turned their sights on Giumarra Vineyards Corporation north of Bakersfield, California, the largest producer of table grapes in the United States. Giumarra officials dismissed the union as a socialist movement aided and abetted by anti-American leftists.

Giumarra responded with a well-coordinated effort to import a large influx of Mexican labor from across the border. Also, the Kern County Superior Court issued an injunction restricting picketing to one person per hundred feet. The injunction also banned the use of bullhorns.

Chavez responded to the setback by resuming the nationwide boycott on table grapes with even more intensity. The answer to the continuing roadblocks faced by the union, Chavez believed, was increased nationwide visibility.

In 1967, Chavez hired a young lawyer named Jerry Cohen as general counsel. Cohen, who had worked briefly for the California Rural Legal Assistance program, would play a pivotal role not only in the strike and boycott but in numerous contract signings and legal and political matters involving the California state legislature. During the strike against Giumarra, Cohen tackled the bullhorn prohibition in court and won.

When the UFWOC decided to intensify the nationwide boycott of table grapes, many questioned whether they could muster the funds, support troops, and solutions to communications challenges to pull it off. Chavez found enough individuals willing to take on the daunting task with little or no financial assistance. Some did it by hitchhiking to their destinations and taking part-time jobs. They shared food, housing, and whatever savings they on hand. One group left for New York in old school buses.

Eliseo Medina led the boycott in Chicago. He was, as he often said later, scared. Born in a small Mexican town called Huanusco, he had worked alongside his family in the grape fields. And now he was an enthusiastic "Young Tiger" of the movement, pictured on the cover of *El Malcriado*. Boycott leaders like Medina enlisted civic groups, labor organizations, churches, and student and women's groups; they made speeches, printed out literature on street corners and in front of grocery stores; and managed to get media attention. Many people across the country gradually refused to buy grapes.

Meanwhile, in Delano, Chavez and his staff worked mightily to bring new services to their dues-paying members. By 1967, the farm workers union numbered about 8,000 members.

From his tiny two-bedroom house in Delano, Chavez, Helen, and eight children lived on $10 a week from the union and on food from a communal kitchen in the nearby union headquarters. As the union began completely to dominate his time and energy, he had almost given up casual socializing. He no longer smoked or drank alcohol. Invariably, for the large Chavez family, the union—its work and battles—was the central focus of their lives.

Fasting

As the battles along the picket lines grew increasingly tense, Chavez despaired that his nonviolent protest campaign was in jeopardy. Profoundly disappointed by the reports of violence, Chavez, in mid-February 1968, called a meeting in Delano to announce his decision to engage in a fast until union members recommitted themselves to nonviolence. For this student of Gandhi, his reaction to these unfolding events was not totally surprising. It was what Gandhi had taught; it was what Gandhi himself had practiced.

On February 14, 1968, Chavez stopped eating. He believed the fast would emphasize the dimensions of his movement for social justice—nonviolent, spiritual, a willingness to sacrifice for the greater good. Most of his fellow lieutenants, although very worried about the health of their leader, also saw that his extreme sacrificial gesture, religious in nature, was his own way to rededicate the cause to nonviolence.

As far as generating publicity and support, the fast gained remarkable attention. At one point during the fast, Chavez was forced into court to defend himself against an injunction. In many of its legal struggles with the growers, the UFWOC often used the courthouses as stages to publicize the cause. Often, UFWOC protestors and their supporters, much like the civil rights demonstrators in the South, surrounded courthouse proceedings with vigils, songfests, and pray-ins.

For 21 days Chavez fasted, losing much weight and drawing dire warnings from his doctor. He finally decided to end the fast on March 10, 1968. After making the decision, Chavez received word that Robert Kennedy would join him.

As a crowd of several thousand watched, Chavez sat with his wife, his mother, and Kennedy. At the open-air Mass, several priests and nuns distributed bread to the crowd. Addressing the 8,000 onlookers, Senator Kennedy heaped praise not only on Chavez but on the workers themselves who had, through nonviolence, achieved profound victories in asserting the rights of Mexican Americans and of farm workers.

As the grape boycott continued, the Giumarra Vineyards had been able to avoid financial losses by shipping its grapes under various labels, thus making it impossible for consumers to target its products. Faced with this new tactic, the union decided in early 1968 to expand the boycott to the entire table-grape industry. The UFWOC had soon placed organizers in 20 strategic cities. Their job was to gain cooperation from wholesalers and retail outlets, to picket those who were uncooperative, and to get publicity for the boycott in local news media.

In 1968, Huerta headed the New York City boycott and was instrumental in developing a model strategy for building community support. It reflected much of what she had learned from Fred Ross and the CSO years earlier.

The boycott spread to other cities such as Los Angeles and Detroit and even to Canada. The mayor of Toronto proclaimed November 23, 1968, as "Grape Day" in honor of the boycott.

Assassinations

When Robert Kennedy announced his candidacy for president on March 16, 1968, he knew that the state of California would be critical in his uphill battle for the Democratic nomination. Running on a promise of ending the war in Vietnam and leading a return to the generous impulses of the nation in fighting for equal rights for minorities and help for the poor, Kennedy was fighting against much of the Democratic Party establishment.

Chavez asked Marshall Ganz to be the chief organizer of a UFWOC campaign to help elect Kennedy to the presidency. With much political acumen and deft strategies for mobilizing the Latino vote in California, Ganz gathered together a team of organizers that zealously saturated selected Mexican American communities to register new voters and get them to the polls for the election scheduled for June 6.

On one fateful night, however, the election frenzy among the union faithful came to a sudden pause. On the evening of April 3, 1968, Martin Luther King Jr. gave a dramatic speech in Memphis, Tennessee, on behalf of striking sanitation workers who planned a march the following day. On the morning of April 4, as King prepared to leave the Lorraine Motel to meet with march organizers, he stepped from his room on the second floor. An assassin's rifle bullet ended his life at age 39.

Chavez was stunned and profoundly saddened by King's assassination. The civil rights leader was not only a heroic figure to many Americans; he was also in Chavez's mind a great teacher and role model.

Yet, in the wake of King's assassination, the work of Chavez and his union to elect Kennedy continued apace, canvassing door to door encouraging residents to vote. An unusually large outpouring of Mexican American votes was the difference in the election. On June 5, Kennedy pulled off the victory. Late that night, at the Ambassador Hotel in Los Angeles following his victory speech, he, like King, fell to an assassin's attack.

All of it seemed incomprehensible. In the space of two months, Chavez and the farm workers union had lost two towering and inspirational supporters. Devastated by the two assassinations, they nevertheless carried on their fight for farm workers.

In late 1968, the grinding stress, the years of long hours, and the fast at last took their physical toll. So painful was his back that Chavez was forced into traction and spent several months bedridden much of the time. Instead of spending long hours driving around the state, he began to receive a constant stream of visitors at his bedside.

The tragedy of losing Kennedy was much more than personal to Chavez, Huerta, and other leaders of the La Causa as well as to the thousands of its members. It was also a terrible political cataclysm. The hopes of the presidency for Kennedy, an ardent supporter of the union and its works, crumbled in the assassination and the subsequent election of Republican Richard Nixon in the November 1968 elections. A Californian with close ties to the growers and their supporters, Nixon would unquestionably lead an administration unfriendly to the growing power and influence of the UFWOC.

Its opponents now savored the opportunity to use all possible leverage on the administration and its friends in California to put Chavez in his place, to marshal the forces of agribusiness and defy the impudence of a union that dared take on their power and threaten their profits. The Republican establishment in Sacramento regarded Chavez and his union, with its ties to Democratic politicians and the civil rights movement, as a noxious force in the state that had to be repelled politically and legally.

California Governor Ronald Reagan was especially contemptuous toward Chavez. Reagan and his allies mocked the farm workers grape strike, the governor often popping a grape into his mouth before photographers and offering grapes to reporters and visitors in the governor's mansion.

The boycott continued. Throughout 1969, shipments of California table grapes were stopped by strikes in Boston, New York, Philadelphia, Chicago, Detroit, Montreal, and Toronto. In some British ports, dockworkers refused to unload grapes. In New York, Huerta was like a mobilizing machine, sweeping through the offices and meeting halls of political activists and union leaders, Latino associations, religious groups, peace organizations, and consumer organizations.

By the summer of 1969, the Chavez family still lived in a small two-bedroom house on $10 a week from the union and on food from the communal kitchen.

Early in his career, writer Peter Matthiessen visited Chavez and described his office:

> The walls . . . are decorated with photographs of Martin Luther King and Mahatma Gandhi; beside them is a blood-red poster of Emiliano Zapata, complete with mustachio, cartridge belts, carbine, sash, sword, and giant sombrero, under the exhortation "Viva la Revolucion." . . . There are also portraits of John Kennedy and Robert Kennedy, black-bordered and hung with flowers, as in a shrine. Here and there is the emblem of U.F.W.O.C., a square-edged black eagle in a white circle on a red background, over the word "Huelga." (Matthiessen 1969)

Sufficiently recovered from his back condition in September, Chavez once again was on the road for a seven-week tour across the country. It had been nearly four years since Chavez called the strike against the table-grape growers of California.

In 1969, Chavez and his union gained the support from another civil rights group—the Black Panther Party (BPP). In many ways, the alliance of the two groups was unlikely. The BPP was African American, militant, and urban, and the UFWOC was largely Mexican American, nonviolent, rural, and religious in orientation. But the two organizations also had much in common: the fight for racial and economic justice and labor solidarity.

Victory

By 1970, it was clear that the grape boycott was having a profound economic impact. Coachella grower Lionel Steinberg lamented that a number of distributors in such cities as Boston, New York, Chicago, and Toronto had drastically stopped handling table grapes. In early April 1970, Steinberg signed a contract with Chavez's union, telling fellow entrepreneurs in the grape industry that the boycott could wreck their own companies. He said, "I had a high regard for Cesar—he was an honest man." Yet he remained perplexed by his adversary. "He was running the union with priests and nuns and Ivy Leaguers on sabbatical. It was more like a political crusade than a trade union effort" (Oliver 1999).

Later that summer, after a speaking engagement on the night of July 25, 1970, Chavez returned home to find a message from John Giumarra Jr., nephew of the founder of the Giumarra company. After five years of La Huelga, Giumarra was also ready to deal with the UFWOC.

The union responded with a demand that the Giumarras bring the growers who still were holding out with them to the bargaining table. Giumarra managed to persuade the others to agree. On July 29, the union and 29 growers signed contracts that brought an end to the table-grape strike. Almost an entire industry was now under union contract. For the first time, more than 70,000 farm workers had gained legal protection of their basic rights to fair wages and benefits, fair hiring systems, job security measures, and safe working environments.

As the farm workers celebrated their new labor contracts in the summer of 1970, Chavez faced another major challenge. It was from the lettuce growers and, once again, the Teamsters union. Knowing they would get more favorable treatment from the Teamsters, the growers began to sign contracts. Although he had not planned to take on the lettuce growers so quickly after the grape boycott, Chavez responded forcefully to the collusion between the Teamsters and the companies.

On August 23, some 6,000 UFWOC workers struck the Salinas Valley growers. Within three days, an estimated 10,000 workers had walked out of the fields. The strike turned violent with Teamster heavies attacking union picketers across the valley. Nevertheless, some of the growers backed down and signed UFWOC contracts. When local courts responded with injunctions against the union to prohibit picketing, the union responded with a national boycott. Refusing to back down, Chavez was jailed in early December in the town of Salinas. Released on Christmas Eve pending appeal, Chavez called for additional strike action. The "Salad Bowl Strike" finally ended in March 1971 with a jurisdictional agreement between the farm workers union and the Teamsters. Through it all, the UFWOC had once again proved its muscle and determination against establishment power.

It had been the largest farm labor strike in California history. Within the first week after it ended, InterHarvest, the largest lettuce grower, granted a 30 percent wage increase bargained by Huerta. Not only did the increase in wages to $2.10 far exceed anything that the Teamsters had been able to offer farm workers, but Huerta also negotiated an agreement by the company to eliminate the use of DDT and other dangerous pesticides.

The victories in several strikes and the increased union membership convinced Chavez that the Delano facility was too small to encompass all of the union's activities. In 1971, Cesar, his family, and most of the union's administrators moved the union's headquarters from Delano to the site of a former tuberculosis sanatorium in Keene, California, located in the foothills of the Tehachapi Mountains. Chavez called it "La Paz," a shortened version of "Nuestra Senora Reina de la Paz" or "Our Lady, Queen of Peace."

The union expanded benefit programs and established medical clinics. By the middle of 1972, some 300 staffers in 25 field offices from California to Florida carried on union work. No longer merely an organizing committee, Chavez and his colleagues had turned the organization into a full-fledged, successfully functioning union. Leaders of the national AFL-CIO decided to recognize the farm workers union, offering it a full charter as the United Farm Workers of America,

AFL-CIO (UFW). Chavez, Huerta, and all the others who in Delano had set out to establish such a union no longer seemed like dreamers.

Arizona

In 1972, the Arizona governor Jack Williams signed a bill highly prejudicial against farm workers. The Arizona law prohibited farm workers from unionizing or engaging in boycotts. Shortly after the passage of the legislation, Governor Williams, when asked to meet with representatives of the farm workers, said, "As far as I'm concerned these people do not exist" (Levy 2007, 463).

Chavez launched a campaign to recall the governor. He again conducted a fast. Union members began a massive voter-registration drive. At one of the union meetings, some of the participants said of the recall drive, "no se puede" (it cannot be done). Dolores Huerta insisted that from now on they would never say it could not be done. From now on, they would say "si se puede" (yes we can do it). "Si se puede" became a battle cry for the Arizona fight and others that followed.

Union volunteers swelled the ranks in Arizona, fanning out across the state encouraging Mexican Americans, Native Americans, and others to register. In only four months, 100,000 new voters had put their names on recall petitions and, most importantly, registered to vote.

Although the Republican attorney general eventually blocked the recall election through legal maneuvering, the UFW had changed the electoral demographics of Arizona. Its brief registration drive paved the way in succeeding elections for Mexican Americans and Native Americans to win several seats in the Arizona state legislature. When Raul Castro became the first Mexican American governor of Arizona in 1974, his margin of victory was 4,100. The UFW drive had made a powerful impact.

In 1972, California's growers, aligned with the state Republican Party, attempted to put the UFW out of business. As Republicans had done with many other issues over the years in California, they set out to weaken farm workers' rights with a ballot initiative. The so-called Agricultural Labor Relations Initiative, known as Proposition 22, was an attempt to curtail workers' rights to organize and collectively bargain.

With the help of the state Democratic Party, the AFL-CIO, and various charitable and religious organizations, the UFW prevailed, despite the deep pockets of agribusiness to run an intense advertising campaign. From those thousands of men and women whose hands they shook, whose voices were on the phones, and who honked from their cars when passing the campaigners, thundered a resounding vote of support. The 58 percent vote against Prop 22 was a testament to the dedication of thousands of individuals who, most for the first time in their lives, immersed themselves in political action. The victory marked a significant turning point in Latino voter participation in California and became a model of grassroots organizing that would spawn increasing numbers of electoral successes in coming years.

Despite its victories, UFW leaders realized that consolidating the union's gains and growing its power were major challenges. The Teamsters remained eager to oust farm workers from the UFW. They had the support of growers, California politicians, and, of course, President Richard Nixon, who in the 1968 election had been supported by the Teamsters.

On April 14, 1973, over 30 three-year contracts that Chavez had signed with growers in Coachella Valley expired. Only two growers decided to renew those contracts. Thirty others signed with the Teamsters. A bitter Chavez charged that the agreements "weren't contracts, they were marriage licenses. Tomorrow you will see the growers and the Teamsters skipping hand in hand into the fields on their honeymoon" ("Again, la Huelga" 1973).

George Meany, president of the AFL-CIO, blasted the Teamsters campaign to smash Chavez's union. The Teamsters, he said, were doing more than fighting a union; they were also suppressing Mexican Americans. The AFL-CIO urged its constituent unions and their families to support the UFW in any strike or boycott activities.

The move triggered a series of strikes by Chavez and his union that started in Coachella and moved into the San Joaquin valley. Again, the strikers faced tough strong-arm tactics. Many were arrested or beaten. It was not the attackers, however, that went to jail. Throughout the summer local judges, with close personal and political ties to the growers, issued injunctions limiting legitimate strike activity. More than 3,500 farm workers were jailed in 1973.

The local police, especially in Kern and Tulare counties, turned especially aggressive against the strikers. These were echoes from the deep South and the civil rights movement. At the Giumarra vineyards, protestors, kneeling to pray, were beaten and sprayed with mace. In Arvin, California, a farm worker named Juan de la Cruz was shot down and killed. As in the civil rights movement, the protestors filled the jails to until jails choked to the breaking point. In Fresno, over 3,500 protestors were arrested; nearly 2,000 went to jail, including 70 priests and nuns.

Many growers expressed not only their fierce anger and frustration with the union protestors but also their ingrained racial attitudes. "Those people were made to suffer," one grower said to a *New York Times* reporter. God had made them to work in the fields and now Chavez has made "those people think they're something better" (Griffith 1974).

The heated battle between the UFW and the growers and Teamsters continued in the late summer of 1973. Chavez decided on a new move. Five hundred farm workers left in caravans of cars headed to destinations in every part of the country. They were on the move to increase the intensity of the boycott. In a letter distributed in cities across the United States, Chavez pleaded for consumers to back the union in this critical time.

But Chavez faced formidable and determined enemies and a growing belief among even some of his closest supporters that the union could not ultimately prevail in a protracted war with the growers. Asked how he could continue such a hectic pace day after day and not be physically drained, Chavez said to a reporter, "I don't usually get tired . . . the strikes, the boycotts that is never tiring. I don't ever get tired of fighting the Teamsters. That is what you are here for, and so it's not work and you don't get tired" (Powers 1974).

As the growers began to feel the impact of the boycott, Chavez sought to deepen its impact by expanding its influence to Europe. In the fall of 1974, he planned a trip to Europe to visit various leaders in the European labor movement. Financed by gifts from the World Council of Churches, private charities, and several European labor unions, Chavez, Helen, and others left the United States on September 16.

In talks with various union heads in London, Oslo, Stockholm, and other European cities, Chavez gained assurances that their organizations would assist in the boycott. On September 25, 1974, Chavez met at the Vatican with Pope Paul VI, who praised Chavez and his dedication toward Christian social teaching.

After eight years of dealing with the intractable opposition of Governor Ronald Reagan, Chavez and his union looked forward to the election of 1974. Here was an opportunity to help elect a man and a party to the executive mansion in Sacramento that could help the union legislatively in a major way.

The Democratic candidate was Jerry Brown. With an unusual educational background, including Jesuit studies as well as a Yale Law School degree, Brown had been elected California's secretary of state in 1970. In 1974, he visited La Paz to seek Chavez's endorsement for his gubernatorial campaign. "The place was totally off the beaten path," Brown remembered later, "yet there were hundreds of people around—mostly young and with infectious vitality and enthusiasm. It was clear that the United Farm Workers was a movement . . . from my point of view, the UFW was on the forefront of working for genuine social change—not merely its illusion—and that required precisely the dedication and sacrifice which Chavez inspired" (Brown 1993).

Chavez and his lieutenants were ready to mobilize forces to help Brown; nevertheless, they wanted specific assurances that, if elected governor, he would support legislation favorable to California's farm workers, a law that would protect the rights of those working in the harvest fields freely to exercise collective bargaining and other activities enjoyed by other labor unions to protect their workers

With the help of the union's vigorous work on the campaign trail, Brown triumphed in the November election. For the first time in the history of his union, Cesar Chavez now had a friend in the governor's mansion.

El Cortito

To the farm worker in the field, one of the great enemies was a simple tool that growers provided to the workers. It was a short handled hoe called "El Cortito" (the Short One). Lettuce growers, insisting that the implement was the fastest and most efficient, demanded that the workers use it. Even when the UFW provided testimony from numerous workers and physicians that the tool caused ruptured spinal disks and other serious back injuries, the lettuce growers would not allow other equipment.

Farm worker Roberto Acuna remembered the tool. "The hardest work would be thinning and hoeing with a short-handled hoe," he said.

> The fields would be about a half a mile long. You would be bending and stooping all day. Sometimes I wouldn't have dinner or anything. I'd just go home and fall asleep and wake up just in time to go out to the fields again. There were times when I felt I couldn't take it anymore. It was 105 in the shade and I'd see endless rows of lettuce and I felt my back hurting I felt the frustration of not being able to get out of the fields. (Terkel 1974, 35)

Some laborers called it "the Devil's instrument." One field worker told attorney Mo Jourdane, who conducted an intensive lobbying effort against the use of the short-handled hoe, "Just like the Southern plantation owners had whips to keep the black slaves in line, the corporations have short-handled hoes to keep control over their brown-skinned slaves. It's their symbol of power" (Jourdane 2007, 21).

On January 1, 1975, after intense lobbying by the UFW through Jourdane and the support of Governor Brown, the short-handled hoe was finally outlawed. Thus, the victory was not only a giant step forward in protecting the health and well-being of farm workers; it was also profoundly symbolic. The Mexican Americans who worked the fields would from this day forward stand taller.

Legislation

In early 1975, Chavez was ready to push strongly for state legislation to grant farm workers legal rights they had heretofore lacked—ready to put pressure on Governor Jerry Brown to back up his words of support for the union. The tactic would be a march to Modesto, the headquarters of the E&J Gallo winery.

On February 22, 1975, several hundred members of the UFW began the 110-mile march from San Francisco to Modesto. Other contingents of the march headed out from Stockton and Fresno. Thus, they would approach Gallo from the north, south, and west in a kind of siege on the winemaker. Although just a few hundred marchers left San Francisco and the other locations, more than 15,000 people had joined them by the time they reached Modesto on March 1. They stretched over a mile long, with farm workers singing labor songs, waving the union flag, engaging in conversations with onlookers along the route, and chanting slogans: "Chavez *si*, Teamsters no; Gallo wine has got to go!"

After this show of strength, Chavez met with Brown. Now was the time, Chavez asserted, that farm workers legislation must become a reality and not merely a campaign promise. After a succession of meetings, proposals, and counterproposals, Brown, his assistants, and union representatives, especially Jerry Cohen, shaped the outlines of a bill that would represent a significant step in establishing bargaining rights for farm workers in California.

After the bill was crafted, Brown spoke with an array of interested parties—bishops and religious groups that supported Chavez, supermarket executives, and union officials. Later, Brown said, "I saw my role as a catalyst. I wanted that bill, and I brought all the forces together and constantly mixed them and made them interact in a way that made things possibly more propitious for solution" (Levy 2007, 531).

Legislators reached agreement, and Brown signed the legislation into law on June 4, 1975. Chavez was joyous. For farm workers, the passage of California's Agricultural Labor Relations Act (ALRA) was a legislative triumph of profound consequences, not necessarily for the economic gains it immediately afforded the workers but the power it confirmed on them—protecting the right of farm workers to unionize and boycott and guaranteeing secret ballots in farm workers' union elections. When the individual elections at the companies ended, the UFW had prevailed in 214 companies; the Teamsters in 115.

On March 10, 1977, the Teamsters and the UFW reached a five-year jurisdictional agreement granting Chavez's union exclusive rights to represent the field workers covered by ALRA. The UFW agreed that the Teamsters would have labor jurisdiction in industries surrounding agricultural production such as canneries, packing sheds, and frozen food operations.

Thus, in the spring of 1977, Chavez enjoyed victory. Nevertheless, he knew as well as anyone that the union must press ahead with as much fire and ingenuity as it could muster. Enemies of the union lurked, and political fortunes were always uncertain. But this was a giant victory for Chavez. *Newsweek* ran a story entitled "Cesar's Triumph."

Turmoil

By January 1978, the UFW had brought 25,000 new workers under contract. The benefits for farm workers were impressive: wages rose significantly, and many received health and pension benefits for the first time in their lives. At its height two years later, the UFW had over 50,000 members under contract and as many as 50,000 more affiliated farm workers.

But in the late 1970s, at a time of the great ascendancy of the UFW, internal pressures began to crack its foundation. Chavez seemed preoccupied with consolidating the gains the union had already achieved at the expense of aggressively continuing to recruit new members and of keeping up the organizing fervor that had so characterized the early years. Increasingly, he became involved with establishing cooperatives and expanding medical services and other projects to help the poor.

When such union leaders as Eliseo Medina, Marshall Ganz, and Jerry Cohen began to express views on union strategy and direction that diverged from those of Chavez, the union leader reacted defensively, exerting even more strongly his control over almost all organizational activity. Some of his closest colleagues began, among themselves, to criticize his strong-armed administration of union policy.

The first serious fracture erupted over a request by Jerry Cohen and his legal team for a reasonably slight increase in the low salaries each received from the union. To Chavez, the request for additional salary seemed a failed test of purity. Although Chavez and Cohen continued to work together for a time under strained relations, within a few years the entire legal team would depart—individuals who had steered the union through rough waters and had, in most cases, prevailed in the courts. Their departure was a staggering loss.

Chavez repeatedly rejected the suggestions by several of his closest confidants that he involve the rank and file of the union, the farm workers themselves, in decision making, keep them more informed, and give their views more consideration. He refused.

La Paz now seemed like a refuge for Chavez against his own union members. As personal disagreements became increasingly combustible between Chavez and other of his colleagues, he dug in his heels even more stubbornly. Always with an ascetic bent, Chavez suddenly became infatuated with a strange drug-rehabilitation organization called Synanon and its leader Charles Dederich and demanded that his lieutenants engage in some of the practices of the cult-like group in order to receive purification. Whether from growing fatigue or depression, Chavez thus became increasingly detached from some of his associates. Gripped by a sense of paranoia, he even began to suspect that communists were infiltrating union activities and that the union would become compromised by leftists in its midst. He began to distrust even his closest aides and to suspect that they were attempting to change union policies against his wishes, to sabotage his plans, or even to take over the union.

Suddenly the union was gripped by a series of arguments and misunderstandings and a growing sense of betrayal. Chavez accused a number of boycott leaders and other union workers of being communists, an ironic and sad twist considering the early FBI investigations into whether Chavez himself was a communist. A number of men and women who were not, in fact, communists were forced out of the UFW, unable to convince Chavez and other UFW leaders that they were not plotting nefarious activities.

Thus, the UFW in the mid-1970s began to lose talented people, either by their own decision to leave or by being pushed out by Chavez himself. The word *purge* began to enter the lexicon of many members.

In the summer of 1978, after being elevated to second vice president, Eliseo Medina planned an ambitious organizing drive. But Medina, along with others, became gradually disillusioned with the direction from the top, which seemed scattered, suspicious, and lacking clear direction. Convinced that the union had abandoned most of its organizational zeal and was moving in the wrong direction, Medina left Chavez in late 1978. He would move on to a highly successful career with the Service Employees International Union (SEIU).

Other internal disagreements battered the union. Chavez seemed totally unwilling to sacrifice any of his personal control over union affairs. Within the next few years, other organizing leaders in the union left to find other avenues to fight for social justice. Philip Vera Cruz, a long-time Filipino supporter of the movement, said later, "I'm afraid, now as I look back, that this kind of attitude that was perpetuated by Cesar really came out of a fear of losing power" (Vera Cruz 2000, 102). Cesar's old friend Gilbert Padilla began to question Chavez's emotional state. "I knew Cesar was the man, el jefe," he said later, "but I didn't think the movement belonged to him. I thought it belonged to the workers." Padilla also left the union (Pawel 2006).

In succeeding years others departed—Marshall Ganz, Chris Hartmire, Jim Drake, LeRoy Chatfield, and others. Ganz said later, "Something happened in the course of those years that just really shattered something within him. I don't know exactly what. It was an accumulation of many things. But he sort of lost his soul there. And became a very different person" (Bardacke 2011, 562).

The organizational chaos and disruption ensuing from the loss of such key union figures left the UFW severely wounded and some of his closest friends of the early years at a loss to understand why Chavez was acting in such a domineering fashion. Hartmire, for example, was forced out after Chavez suspected that he was shielding another union member who was pilfering funds. When Eliseo Medina heard of Hartmire's ouster, he called to express his regrets. Hartmire wrote to him, "Thanks for your call, Eliseo, and your concern. It has not been an easy year but we are on our feet and doing well" (Pawel 2009, 325). He was not well, but understandably crushed.

In January 1979, despite the turmoil within his ranks, Chavez decided to launch a strike against 11 lettuce growers in the Imperial and Salinas Valleys. At the onset of the strike, the UFW workers displayed much precision and discipline. But on February 10, 1979, the strike turned deadly. Shortly before noon on day 22 of the strike, 28-year-old UFW member Rufino Contreras and a half-dozen fellow strikers attempted to speak with a crew of scab laborers. Three armed foremen suddenly appeared and opened fire. As the strikers scattered back towards the road, one was lying face down in the mud. It was Contreras. He died at the hospital.

On Wednesday, February 14, the Contreras family, joined by 9,000 farm workers and others including Governor Jerry Brown, attended the funeral. Chavez called February 10, 1979, "a day of infamy for farm workers" (Jourdane 2007, 253).

Led by counsel Jerry Cohen, the union won several contracts with lettuce growers as a result of the strike. The new agreements provided for company-paid ranch union representatives, workers akin to shop stewards in factories. Although Chavez first went along with the arrangement, he had little confidence that the workers could do a credible job because they had too little training. He also feared that such arrangements would diminish his own control. Once again, Chavez asserted his command and reduced the power that the workers themselves had in union administration.

In November 1982, Republican George Deukmejian, a champion of growers who contributed hefty sums to his campaign, became governor of California. Soon, Deukmejian packed the Agricultural Labor Relations Board with representatives who supported the interests of the growers. Under the new leadership of the board, enforcement of election law became mired in delay and inaction. Gradually, the UFW over the next several years lost most of its contracts with growers.

Realizing that seeking redress of grievances through the farm labor board under Republican control was futile, Chavez made plans to boycott certain broccoli and lettuce growers. Looking down the road two or three decades, Chavez was still optimistic. The new boycotts and marches, he said, would drive home to Americans the continuing need to reform the harvest fields of California and the farm labor areas in the rest of the United States. And it would be the Latino community in California that would turn the page on state and national politics.

Pesticides

In 1986, Chavez decided to increase the pressures on the growers in another controversial area—the use of pesticides. As part of the grape boycott, he launched a campaign called "Wrath of Grapes"—a wordplay takeoff on John Steinbeck's famous novel about the tribulation of farm workers in California.

In the summer of 1988, Chavez, determined to draw attention to the pesticide issue, once again began a fast. He called it "The Fast for Life." This time, Chavez decided to involve his supporters and those who agreed with his stance. Picket lines formed in various cities comprised of volunteers, some of whom agreed to join Chavez in his water-only fast.

After 36 days, a weary and malnourished Chavez gave in to the entreaties of his family and doctors and ended the fast. On August 21, 1988, more than 6,000 people gathered to celebrate, including Chavez's 96-year-old mother, Juana.

Yuma

In 1992, Chavez and his son-in-law, UFW vice president Arturo Rodriguez, orchestrated walkouts in vineyards in the San Joaquin and Coachella valleys. They succeeded in winning pay hikes. Most importantly, the victories demonstrated to younger activists that nonviolent protest was still a potent force. Not only in California but in cities in the Midwest, young activists took on such industrial giants as Campbell Soup, and young labor leaders took their places in Hawaii, Oregon, Pennsylvania, New Jersey, and other states.

In April 1993, Chavez traveled back to the tiny southwest Arizona town of San Luis, near Yuma, where the Chavez family settled a half century earlier. He was there to help UFW attorneys defend the union against a lawsuit brought by Bruce Church Inc., the giant Salinas, California–based lettuce and vegetable producer. After testifying in court, Chavez was driven around Yuma by a long- time friend, David Martinez. They passed the playground where Cesar and his brother Richard had played stickball. When he retired for the evening, he took with him a book about Native American art and went to sleep. On April 23, 1993, he died during the early morning hours. He was only 30 miles from the spot where the Immaculate Conception Church once stood, where he had been baptized. At age 66, he died young. His father lived to 101, his mother to 99.

Forward

In the rise of the farm workers movement, Chavez, Huerta, and the other leaders melded strong passion, commitment, and belief from various elements: religious heritage anchored in Christian social justice; militant, nonviolent social protest principles exemplified in the U.S. civil rights movement and in the teachings of Gandhi; and the community-organizing skills developed by Saul Alinsky, Fred Ross, and other leaders of community organizations fighting for equal rights and justice for the workers and others left on the outside of the American dream.

Yet in 2005, the magazine *Economist* ran an article describing the wretched conditions endured by farm workers in the Giumarra family's vineyards in California's San Joaquin Valley. Mostly illegal immigrants from Mexico, they labored for a wage of $7 an hour and 30 cents for each box. Many worked for 10-hour shifts. Here, in Giumarra's fields, it was as if the great movement launched by Chavez had never occurred.

The dissension in the ranks of the leaders of the union had unquestionably been a root cause of thc decline of the union in the fields; so had Chavez's reluctance to delegate authority. With its internal divisions and dissensions and its loss of organizational focus and drive, the UFW had thus become less of a labor union and more of an advocacy group for farm workers. Its membership rolls dropped dramatically. Chavez and other union leaders who replaced those who had left under duress turned much of their attention to a variety of political causes and fund-raising activities.

In addition, the immigration issue became an increasingly corrosive influence on union power. In the last years of Chavez's life and beyond, illegal immigration by Mexicans to the United States increased dramatically. For members of the UFW and union organizers, the appearance of hundreds of thousands of new arrivals anxious to work for wages less than those earned by union members became a profound threat. During his own leadership of the union, Chavez insisted that the union must support efforts to close the influx of new workers.

At the beginning of the new century, the UFW began to change its position on immigration, becoming a leading voice inside the AFL-CIO in favor of ending employer sanctions and legalizing unauthorized foreigners. But as the fields continued to be filled by undocumented workers, the rolls of UFW members paled by comparison to the dues-paying membership of the union in its heyday. Nevertheless, the influence of the movement begun by Chavez, Huerta, and others had produced profound changes.

In 2006, looking back over the accomplishments of the UFW, Huerta talked about

> . . . the millions of people we have helped . . . knowing that we have secured laws requiring toilets in the field, drinking water, rest periods and unemployment insurance is a great feeling. People that work under farm worker contracts now have medical plans that cover their entire families . . . so it's really quite wonderful to reflect on that. (Aledo and Alvarado 2006)

And, as many of the older farm workers testified, there were the emotional and psychological triumphs of challenging head-on an established order with little more weaponry than grit and commitment. These were triumphs of spirit and endurance difficult to measure but impossible to underestimate. One of the most enduring legacies from the battles in the fields of the 1960s and 1970s is the abiding influence that Chavez and other UFW leaders had on a successive generation of organizers.

When 21-year-old Eliseo Medina arrived in Chicago in 1967, carrying with him $20 and a bag of UFW buttons, he began union's boycott effort in the Windy City. Although he left the UFW in 1978, he never stopped his zealous organizing efforts. In 2006, he was executive vice president of the SEIU, overseeing locals across the country that organized janitors and health care workers.

After leaving the UFW in 1978, Jim Drake organized woodcutters in Mississippi and worked with an organization in Texas to help provide adequate water and sewage facilities. Later, he organized churches in New York City's South

Bronx area in a campaign to build 800 units of affordable housing and to open a model public high school.

Jose Cortez worked with his parents in the fields laboring with a short-handled hoe and later marched with Chavez. Later he joined an organization called Chicanos Por La Causa, dedicated to empowering the Latino community in acquiring education, affordable housing, and jobs. He said that Chavez gave him the inspiration to help and to be an advocate and that the feeling would probably be there until he died.

Chavez's movement, with its energy and appeal to the religious and cultural heritage of Mexican Americans, sparked among workers in the harvest fields an idea that life could improve, that the system holding down the workers was not so powerful that it could not be changed.

The UFW movement also contributed to a more general movement for civil rights among Mexican Americans during the 1960s and 1970s. It helped inspire a new generation of urban Mexican American youths to organize their communities and become active in social and political programs. As the Chicago movement grew, the picture of Cesar Chavez became, along with others, one that hung in the homes of Latino homes.

On March 31, 2010, President Barack Obama, in declaring that date "Cesar Chavez Day," said, "To this day, his rallying cry—'Sí, se puede,' or 'Yes, we can'—inspires hope and a spirit of possibility in people around the world. His movement strengthened our country, and his vision lives on in the organizers and social entrepreneurs who still empower their neighbors to improve their communities" (White House 2010). President Obama took the slogan close to heart. In 2008, he used the words in his campaign for president.

What the UFW accomplished will never be forgotten by the workers themselves or by the thousands of social activists who have been inspired and energized by the farm workers struggle. Chavez's movement, with its energy and appeal to the religious and cultural heritage of Mexican Americans, had lit a spark in the harvest fields that consumed old notions that life could not improve, that the system holding down the workers was too intractable and too powerful that it could not be changed. Through grit, stubbornness, and a deep commitment to purpose and to making a difference, Chavez and his lieutenants had struck away at the stereotypes and the defeatism and convinced large numbers of people that they could fight back.

Chavez said many times that his motivation for attempting to form a union of farm workers had first come from watching the struggles of his father and mother and his own early experiences in the fields and the realization that the system and the socicty was fixed against them in such a profound way that they were made to feel more like farm implements or cows and horses than like humans.

The UFW did not ultimately become a successful labor union. Yet the movement stirred passions and commitments to action for countless Latinos, passions that continued to resonate long after Chavez's death. People who had shared common humiliations and shattered pride now fought back. People who had never before considered joining social movements now became activists. La Causa had never been simply an effort to found a union; it had been a battle for self-respect —standing up, at last, against a system that destroyed dignity.

La Causa proclaimed that the beginnings of progress to gain that dignity came in organizing, educating, and coalescing around common dreams and aspirations. Not only for farm workers but for other Mexican Americans, the movement became an exciting struggle. People for the first time in their lives joined picket lines in front of grocery stores, passed out leaflets, registered others to vote, sang the songs and chants of protest, and gained a new awareness that they could actually make a difference. La Causa was a fight for empowerment and self-determination.

Chavez said that history would be on the side of the workers, especially the Mexican Americans who were taking their proper place in American society despite the formidable opposition they faced. The reactionaries saw the future, Chavez said, and they were afraid. Latinos and their children were on the rise.

In those towns such as Salinas, Delano, Fresno, Bakersfield, and Modesto, those towns that had been the battlegrounds of the farm workers, it would be the children and grandchildren of those workers who would be in the majority, not the children and grandchildren of the growers. And from the lessons learned in the farm workers' fights, they could seize the power. There will in the end, he said, be triumph.

In recent years, a number of Chavez's fellow union members have written articles and books about their experiences. Organizations have gathered and made available for research letters and other documents about the strikes, boycotts, and marches; about the strategies and tactics employed and discarded; and about some of the inner turmoil plaguing the union. Through this first-person testimony and original documentation, we can see now more clearly the missteps and human weaknesses of Chavez along with his triumphs, the driving forces behind the movement, and its lasting influences. The encyclopedia entries that follow provide a glimpse into the lives of the men and women, events, organizations, and themes that touched the life of Cesar Chavez.

Further Reading

"Again, la Huelga." 1973. *Time*. May 7, 85.

Aledo, Milagros, and Maria Alvarado. 2006. "Dolores Huerta at Seventy-five: Still Empowering Communities: Interview with Cofounder of United Farm Workers of America." *Harvard Journal of Hispanic Policy*, 13.

Bardacke, Frank. 2011. *Trampling Out the Vintage: Cesar Chavez and the Two Souls of the United Farm Workers*. New York: Verso.

Berman, Art. 1966. "Chavez a Modern Zapata to Grape Strikers." *Los Angeles Times*, May 6, A1.

Bernstein, Harry. 1965. "Minister Arrested in Grape Strike." *Los Angeles Times*, October 19, 3.

Bogater, Julian. 2009. "King, Chavez Shared Social Justice Spirit on Road to Change." *The University Record Online* (University of Michigan), January 22. http://www.ur .umich.edu/0809/Jan19_09/20.php.

Brown, Edmund G. 1993. "Chavez Based His Life on Sharing and Frugality." *San Francisco Examiner*, April 25, 2.

Chavez, Cesar. 1970. Oral history interview. January 27. Robert F. Kennedy Oral History Program, John F. Kennedy Library, Columbia Point, Boston, MA.

Chavez, Cesar, and Ilan Stavans, ed. 2008. *An Organizer's Tale*. New York: Penguin Classics.

Chavez Jailed First Time, Urges Union to Press Boycott," 1970. *Los Angeles Times*, December 5, A1.

Chavez's Charisma Still Flourishes," *Arizona Republic*, March 23, 4.

Day, Mark. 1971. *Forty Acres: Cesar Chavez and the Farm Workers*. New York: Praeger Publishers.

"Forty Acres: National Historic Landmark Nomination." 2008. http://www.nps.gov/nhl/ designations/samples/CA/FortyAcres.pdf.

Ganz, Marshall. 2009. *Why David Sometimes Win: Leadership, Organization, and Strategy in the California Farm Worker Movement*. New York: Oxford University Press.

Griffith, Winthrop. 1974. "Is Chavez Beaten?" *New York Times*, September 15, 258.

Huerta, Dolores. 2004. Interview. Veterans of Hope Project. http://www.veteransofhope. org/show.php?vid=51&tid=42&sid=69.

Jourdane, Maurice. 2007. *Waves of Recovery*. Mountain View, CA: Floricanto Press.

Kennedy, Robert. 1968. "Statement on Cesar Chavez, March 10." http://www.archives .gov/research/arc/, ARC identifier 194027.

Levy, Jacques E. 2007. *Cesar Chavez: Autobiography of La Causa*. Minneapolis: University of Minnesota Press.

"The Little Strike that Grew to La Causa." 1969. *Time*, July 4, 20.

Matthiessen, Peter. 1969. "Profiles: Organizer-II." *The New Yorker*, June 28, 43.

Oliver, Myrna. 1999. "Lionel Steinberg: Grower Signed 1st Pact with Chavez's Union." *Los Angeles Times*, March 10, 15.

Pawel, Miriam. 2006. "UFW: A Broken Contract." *Los Angeles Times*, January 8, A1.

Pawel, Miriam. 2009. *The Union of Their Dreams: Power, Hope, and Struggle in Cesar Chavez's Farm Worker Movement*. New York: Bloomsbury Press.

Powers, Charles. 1974. "Chavez and the State of His Union." *Los Angeles Times*. June 23, d3.

Ross, Fred. 1989. *Conquering Goliath*. Keene, CA: El Taller Grafico.

Rubiano, Sherry Anne. 2007. "Valdez Recalls Chavez's Inspiration for Activism." *Arizona Republic*, March 31, 18.

Terkel, Studs. 1974. *Working*. New York: Avon Books.

Vera Cruz, Philip. 2000. *Philip Vera Cruz: A Personal History of Filipino Immigrants and the Farmworkers Movement*. Seattle: University of Washington Press.

Warman, C. S. 1969. "Chavez Asserts Grape Sales Off 20 Per Cent Here." *Tucson Daily Citizen*, December 4. Clipping in the Arizona History Museum, Tucson, AZ.

White House. 2010. "Presidential Proclamation—Cesar Chavez Day." http://www.whitehouse.gov/the-press-office/presidential-proclamation-cesar-chavez-day.

A

Agbayani Village

In 1973, the United Farm Workers (UFW) began construction of a retirement home for aging Filipino farm workers at the union's headquarters at Forty Acres in Delano, California. It was called Agbayani Village, named after Paolo Agbayani, a Filipino who had died of a heart attack while on a picket line in Delano during the union's early grape strike. The idea of a communal retirement facility originated during a series of meetings with Cesar Chavez and Filipino leaders such as Larry Itliong and Philip Vera Cruz in the late 1960s. It had been the Filipino-led Agricultural Workers Organizing Committee (AWOC) that had first launched the grape strike in 1965 and persuaded Chavez and his infant farm workers union to join forces. Agbayani Village was to be a place that could accommodate at least 60 elderly Filipinos at reasonable rents—a place where they could live out their days in a setting far different from the debilitating and grungy atmosphere of farm labor camps where they had spent most of their adult lives.

During the 1920s and 1930s, thousands of Filipinos immigrated to the United States, almost all of them young, single males. The great influx followed the passage of anti-Asian immigration laws that barred continued importation of Japanese laborers to work in the harvest fields. Growers responded by sending recruiters to the Philippines, at that time an American territory exempted from the immigration laws. Lured by the stories of jobs and a good life in the United States, the Filipinos saved enough money to board steamships, left their families with promises to send money home, and landed at ports such as Seattle and San Francisco. Many found their way across the country to major cities such as Chicago and New York, where they worked mostly as bellhops, waiters, domestic workers, and busboys; others found work on farms in California and canneries and farms in Washington.

The racial hatred and bigotry faced by young Filipino workers was fierce, often coming from those who benefited the most from their work. A Chamber of Commerce official in California called them "worthless, unscrupulous, shiftless. . . . " On several occasions, bombs were tossed into Filipino labor camps. In California, antimiscegenation laws made it illegal for Filipinos to marry white women. Restrictive immigration laws prevented them from bringing brides from the Philippines. "We became an entire generation that was forced by society to find love and companionship in dancehalls," wrote Vera Cruz (Scharlin and Villanueva 2000, 13).

In 1975, a retirement community for aging Filipino farm workers opened in Delano, California, at the headquarters of the United Farm Workers (UFW). A new resident, wearing a pin on his collar featuring the UFW logo, is pictured in his room. (Cathy Murphy/Getty Images)

Disillusioned by their treatment in the United States, especially after the hopeful stories they had been told by their teachers in the Philippines, they did not encourage other family members from back home to join them. Most tried, as they could, to send some money back to their families, but for the most part, they remained cut off, isolated, embarrassed by their situation, and secure only in the company of other Filipino workers.

For the field laborers, it was a day-by-day, year-by-year grinding existence in backbreaking work in the fields and vineyards, living in labor camp shacks, and relieved only by the occasional pool-hall visit. When the AWOC, led by Filipino farm workers, began the celebrated Delano strike, it was not the first time the Filipinos had fought the repressive existence under which they worked. As early as the 1930s, they struck lettuce fields in Salinas, California, and in the decades following, they organized labor actions in other parts of California and the Pacific Northwest. But it was the Delano strike for which Filipino labor activists would be remembered and for which the UFW owed much.

For Chavez, the Agbayani Village was not only a charitable enterprise, it was a sign of appreciation and respect. One aging Filipino worker, on hearing about the plans for a retirement home, told Catholic priest Mark Day, "We are looking forward to a time when we can have a place of our own." He looked back at the months in which all they had to eat was boiled cabbage and rice. "We have been through some rough times," he said. "It would be wonderful to have a place to live when we get old" (Day 1971, 181).

After the farm workers union had won contracts from grape growers, ending the five-year strike that began in Delano, Chavez and other union leaders, including Itliong and Vera Cruz, were now in a position to make the vision of the retirement home a real project. UFW volunteer Ramona Holguin and Vera Cruz were able to recruit Chicano architect Luis Peña to make the drawings for a 60-unit village that would be located at the east side of Forty Acres, now consisting of offices, a hiring hall, a health clinic, and the Huelga gas station.

For farm workers who had lived in the conditions of the labor camps, Agbayani Village would be palatial. It would have individual rooms, a recreation hall with pool tables, a central kitchen and dining room, an outside garden, and even air conditioning.

Construction of Agbayani Village became a team effort of volunteers not only from California but from many states. As word spread of the project, hundreds of individuals from as far as Switzerland, Germany, France, and Japan offered to help, as well as many from the Philippines.

Agbayani Village opened in 1975. Vera Cruz was asked to head its operations. At one time, Chavez envisioned expanding the complex. Nevertheless, internal disputes ensued over such matters as the amount of rent to be paid and whether preferential treatment should be given to those Filipino workers who loyally stayed with the strike during its toughest times.

Many aging Filipinos and a few Mexican American residents benefited over the years from Agbayani Village. In time, the few aged veterans of the 1960s labor battles became valuable sources of information for students and researchers interested in the Filipino experience in the United States. One of these was Fred Abad, who passed away in 1993 at age 87. In 1929, at age 17, Abad arrived in California, hoping to get a college education. Instead, he labored in the fields. In his room at Agbayani Village were letters and photos from individuals who had visited him in his later years. A junior high school student named Juan Martinez wrote, "I am honored to have met the people that set a ground for the Filipinos in the United States" (DeParle 1993).

Further Reading

Abarquez-Delacruz, Prosy, and Enrique Delacruz. 2011. "The Birthplace of Labor Rights Becomes a Historic Landmark." *Asian Journal*, February 26. http://www.asianjournal .com/dateline-usa/15-dateline-usa/9084-the-birthplace-of-labor-rights-becomes-a -historic-landmark.html?tmpl=component&page.

Cruz Lat, Emelyn. 1997. "Filipinos Began Historic Grape Strike of 1965: Cesar Chavez Joined Them 11 Days Later," *San Francisco Chronicle*, October 19. http://www .sfgate.com/cgi-bin/article.cgi?f=/e/a/1997/10/19/METRO15295.dtl.

Day, Mark. 1971. *Forty Acres: Cesar Chavez and the Farm Workers*. New York: Praeger Publishers.

DeParle, Jason. 1993. "Last of the Manongs: Aging Voices of a Farm-Labor Fight Find an Audience." *New York Times*, May 11. http://www.nytimes.com/1993/05/11/us/last-of -the-manongs-aging-voices-of-a-farm-labor-fight-find-an-audience.html?pagewanted= all&src=pm.

Scharlin, Craig, and Lilia Villanueva. 2000. *Philip Vera Cruz: A Personal History of Filipino Immigrants and the Farmworkers Movement*. Seattle: University of Washington Press.

Agribusiness of California

In 1939, progressive writer Carey McWilliams coined the phrase "Factories in the Field" in describing the agricultural industry in California. The term has remained an apt characterization of California's agribusiness—a word used to describe the commerce and business involved in the production of food, from farming and wholesale and retail distribution to other aspects of agriculture, especially the relationship of grower interests with farm labor. California produces about one-half of the United States' fruits, nuts, and vegetables produced each year on approximately 75,000 farms and ranches, less than 4 percent of the nation's total. In other words, the state is home to extraordinarily large farm tracts owned by wealthy and influential growers. Over the years, they have drawn to their side powerful policy-makers, federal government support, and the loyalty of local civic organizations such as the Chambers of Commerce, boards of supervisors, churches, school boards, and, most importantly, law enforcement officials and the courts. Agriculture was and remains the state's most dominant industry. And it was agribusiness—this intimidating, powerful coalition of interests—that had broken any attempts at unionization of farm workers. It was this coalition that faced Cesar Chavez as he began his own quest to organize workers to challenge the systemic abuses of their labor—low wages, intolerable working conditions, lack of medical care, political powerlessness, and demeaning ethnic discrimination.

Since the late 1900s, Californian agriculture was dominated by large landholders and speculators. The vast industrial-type farms benefited from a number of developments, many of which were promoted by the U.S. government, that made California a robust oasis of farmland. Railroads that made possible extensive commerce, dams that diverted water for irrigation, homesteading policies that enabled vast land grabs, improved mechanization of farm equipment, research that paved the way for crop diversification, and soils receptive to a wide array of fruits and vegetables—all of this combined to define California's topography and establish the economic and financial terrain that made possible the state's unprecedented agricultural development over the course of only a few decades.

By the beginning of the twentieth century, many of California's wheat farmers, aided by modern equipment and recognizing the commercial possibilities of a vast market across the country, turned to the production of fruit and vegetables. The Imperial, Central, and Coachella Valleys would in the not-too-distant future become the most important vegetable-producing areas of the nation, and they would be dominated by vast conglomerates and wealthy landowners. The DiGiorgio Fruit Corporation. the largest distributor of citrus in the nation, had an enormous ranch in Arvin, California, near Delano. One owner, J. G. Boswell, controlled over 100,000 acres of California farmland.

Early in the twentieth century, California growers began to organize cooperatives. Citrus growers started the California Fruit Grower's Exchange, a marketing cooperative that, from its inception, became a driving force in selling fruit to the wholesale trade, an enterprise bringing greater and greater profits to growers. The exchange soon became known as Sunkist, and it came to control two-thirds of the California citrus marketplace. The fruit and vegetable industry was becoming a bonanza. But it was a bonanza dependent on a large workforce at harvest time.

The laborers in the fields had been mostly foreigners, except for the Depression-era whites who migrated from the Dust Bowl agricultural horrors in Oklahoma and Arkansas and other states in the late 1920s and early 1930s. The foreigners included the Chinese in the late 1900s, then Japanese, and later Filipinos and Mexicans. The availability of these foreign-born farm workers kept wages low and allowed growers to spend a pittance on improving living conditions and providing medical help or other needs of the migrants. The overwhelming assumption by government and the local citizenry was that such a lifestyle for nonwhite immigrants was acceptable and expected. If workers protested their wages or the treatment meted out to them by the growers, if they engaged in any kind of strike activity, they could be replaced by importing more foreign laborers. Over the years, California's growers had turned back labor organizing with ruthless and often violent means.

In the early 1960s, when Chavez began to hold house meetings to convince farm workers that they could band together to force change in their lives, agribusiness in the southern San Joaquin Valley around Delano was especially centralized. There were approximately 70 grape ranches in the immediate area with an estimated 38,000 acres of land.

Almost all of the growers were politically conservative, and most of them saw the nascent farm workers movement as communist inspired, whatever that appellation seemed to mean. At the least they saw the Mexicans and Filipinos in the fields as an ignorant lot, susceptible to communist or un-American persuasion.

Agriculture was the lifeblood of the region, and all parts of the Delano community depended on its success. Any threat to that lifeblood had to be stamped out. Churches, both Catholic and Protestant, were loyal to the growers and their financial contributions. If the field workers made meager wages and lived and worked in wretched conditions, at least they were better off than they would have been in Mexico or in the Philippines. Law enforcement officials had no patience for troublemakers, especially those who came from outside the Delano area to foment trouble and labor unrest. Judges, accountable to their neighbors and with no farm labor laws on the side of the workers, found little reason, legal or otherwise, to rule against the ruling class. Local political leaders as well as those who represented the area in the state legislature were all agribusiness allies, dependent on the industry's support in times of elections. Business interests of every kind, affected by the upturns or downticks of agriculture's fortunes in the area, shuddered at the possibility that the system might be adversely affected by groups of foreign workers who had no cause to complain and certainly no right to organize as a union.

These were the forces that faced Chavez, a young organizer with no money, as he set out to improve the lives of farm workers. It was no wonder that his chances of any kind of success seemed remote at best.

Further Reading

Dunne, John Gregory. 1971. *Delano: The Story of the California Grape Strike*. Berkeley: University of California Press.

Galarza, Ernesto. 1977. *Farm Workers and Agribusiness in California, 1947–1960*. Notre Dame, IN: University of Notre Dame Press.

McWilliams, Carey. 2000. *Factories in the Field: The Story of Migratory Farm Labor in California*. Berkeley: University of California Press.

Walker, Richard. 2004. *The Conquest of Bread: 150 Years of Agribusiness in California*. New York: New Press.

Agricultural Labor Relations Act of 1975 (ALRA)

In 1975, the California state legislature passed and Governor Jerry Brown signed the California Agricultural Labor Relations Act (ALRA). With a preamble that promised justice for all agricultural workers, it was the first law in the United States guaranteeing the rights of California farm workers to organize for collective bargaining purposes and providing for secret-ballot elections for those workers to

On June 5, 1975, Governor Jerry Brown of California signed the landmark California Agricultural Labor Relations Act granting farm workers the right to organize and to bargain collectively. It created a state-run Agricultural Labor Relations Board that oversaw union elections and settled disputes between employers and employees. (AP/Wide World Photo)

select the union of their choice to represent them. It guaranteed farm worker unions a seven-day turnaround for the elections, important for a highly mobile workforce, and gave workers remedies for employer violations. The legislation was not only a landmark in the history of labor law, but it was also a signal accomplishment for Cesar Chavez and the United Farm Workers (UFW). The law would not have been possible without the decade-long fight in the harvest fields by the union—the strikes and boycotts and the political pressures exerted by the UFW in taking on the interests of agribusiness and the political enemies arrayed against the union.

When Jerry Brown was elected governor in 1974, Chavez at last had a Democratic Party ally with whom he could work in crafting a farm workers bill. The UFW had campaigned vigorously for Brown's election and now pressured the new governor into acting quickly. In order to give a public face to UFW demands that the legislature and the governor act quickly on farm labor legislation, the union organized a 110-mile march from San Francisco to the E & J Gallo Winery in Modesto. More than 15,000 individuals participated en route. By the time the march reached Modesto on March 1, Chavez and the union had garnered significant media attention to the cause of farm worker legislation. Brown and the legislature responded.

At one point in the negotiations in mid-May, which lasted several days, a number of interest groups, meeting in separate rooms, hammered out the details of the bill, often in the early hours of the mornings, as Brown himself walked from room to room to bring the parties closer together. In one room were representatives of the growers; in another were leaders of the Teamsters, the union that would vie for contracts against the UFW; and in another room were Chavez and his lieutenants, most notably UFW counsel Jerry Cohen.

At Brown's side during the negotiations was his campaign manager and advisor, LeRoy Chatfield, who knew the UFW and its interests from a close perspective. After finishing religious training in college, Chatfield had worked with Chavez and the UFW for several years until branching out into politics. He had been a campaign manager for Brown and was now a close assistant. He was thus in a unique position to aid Brown during the talks.

Years later, Chatfield still felt the aching tension surrounding the final day of negotiations. Brown, Cohen, and others were finally gathered in one room with growers, Teamsters, and legislators—about 30 people in all, some sitting on the floor—to put the final touches on the bill. Chavez was not in the room at the time. When Brown, who was "the ringmaster," as Chatfield recounted, saw that everyone appeared to have reached a tentative agreement on the final bill, he decided, at about midnight, that the time was right to call Chavez to see if he was amenable to the terms. Brown made the call. Chavez's voice came on the speaker phone, and the crowd listened intently as Brown went over the provisions of the bill that had been put in place. Brown asked what Cesar thought. Chatfield recalled that Chavez then said that he would agree on one condition. And what was that? He would agree, he said softly, if not one comma were changed. Chavez said later that he was told that the growers sitting at the edges of their seats listening to the loudspeaker "broke into smiles and applause" (Levy 2007, 533).

On May 26, 1975, the California State Senate passed the bill; the State Assembly passed it two days later. On June 4, Governor Brown signed the law. It went into effect on August 28, 1975.

Cohen said later that the legislation had been made possible by the 10 years of organizational strife inflicted by the UFW upon the status quo. The energy and dedication of the picketers and boycotters who had waged a war of civil disobedience and the aggressive tactics employed by Chavez had shaken the establishment. All of it, Cohen said, had "dealt me a strong hand which I simply played out. The coalition of forces which came together to support the law was extraordinary: growers sick of strikes, stores tired of boycott lines, and county officials who no longer wanted their jails filled with farm workers" (Cohen 2008).

Though none of the parties affected by Brown's compromise bill was fully satisfied by the outcome, all found reasons to agree to it. The Teamsters officials were confident that, in a head-to-head battle with the UFW in the elections mandated in the legislation, they could prevail. The growers saw the deal as the blessed end of a disastrous assault of strikes, and especially the boycotts, that had turned their businesses into war zones. And for the UFW—although the legislation would require intense struggles with the Teamsters and a change of focus from protest and civil disobedience to administration and political development, the ALRA was, after all, an enormous victory, one that could not have been forecast or even imagined by most observers with any knowledge of the history of farm worker labor.

With the passage of the act, the UFW and the Teamsters would go head to head in elections at various California vineyards and ranches. It was an unprecedented opportunity to demonstrate that the majority of workers preferred Chavez's union to that of the Teamsters or to no union at all. They prepared to take on the challenge with as much determination and doggedness as had marked the strikes and boycotts that had made possible this historic achievement.

Jerry Brown said later that the enactment of the farm-labor relations law was the greatest accomplishment of his administration. Jerry Cohen, reflecting on the final passage of the legislation, said that "the law came from ten years of organizing, boycotting, striking, people going to jail. . . ." It was the product, he said, "of all the work that those folks did and Cesar . . . was crucial in organizing that" (Gordon 2005).

Further Reading

Bardacke, Frank. 2011. *Trampling Out the Vintage: Cesar Chavez and the Two Souls of the United Farm Workers*. New York: Verso.

Cohen, Jerry. 2008. "Gringo Justice: The United Farm Workers Union." Jerry Cohen Papers, Amherst College. https://www.amherst.edu/media/view/314670/original/Gringojustice.pdf.

Ferriss, Susan, and Ricardo Sandoval. 1997. *The Fight in the Fields: Cesar Chavez and the Farmworkers Movement*. New York: Harcourt Brace & Company.

Gordon, Jennifer. 2005. "Law, Lawyers, and Labor: The United Farm Workers' Legal Strategy in the 1960's and 1970's and the Role of Law in Union Organizing Today." *Pennsylvania Journal of Labor & Employment Law*, 1 (2005).

Levy, Jacques. 2007. *Cesar Chavez: Autobiography of La Causa*. Minneapolis: University of Minnesota Press.

Martin, Philip. 2003. *Promise Unfulfilled: Unions, Immigration, and Farm Workers*. Ithaca, NY: Cornell University Press.

Shaw, Randy. 2011. *Beyond the Fields: Cesar Chavez, the UFW, and the Struggle for Justice in the 21st Century*. Berkeley: University of California Press.

Agricultural Workers Organizing Committee (AWOC)

In 1959, the AFL-CIO decided to undertake a program in California to organize a segment of American labor that it had in the past ignored—farm workers. It chartered the AWOC, provided it seed money, and hired a few professional organizers. It set out to explore the possibility that these harvest laborers, so vital to American agriculture and yet so ill treated, could be organized into a force effective enough to convince the agribusiness industry to provide them with decent wages, adequate working conditions, and a modicum of dignity. Although the AWOC in its brief existence would be hamstrung by organizational inadequacies and strategic miscalculations and would fall short in its goals of gaining union recognition and collective bargaining rights from the growers, it would play a pivotal role in influencing the early history of Cesar Chavez's own farm workers movement. Its strike of grape growers near Delano, California, in 1965 and its successful entreaties to Chavez to ally his own organization in the protest became a turning point in farm labor history.

George Meany, head of the AFL-CIO, had never been particularly keen to attempt to organize farm workers. He knew the history of the failed efforts of other unionization drives. He knew the many difficulties inherent in attempting to organize workers from other countries, most of whom had no permanent homes and very little money. Yet, faced with pressure from some other union organizers, reformers, and church leaders who reminded him that his organization had trumpeted its goal of "organizing the unorganized," Meany relented and went ahead with the project. He allocated $200,000 for an organizing drive. It aimed at improving wages and working conditions of farm workers and also at supporting AFL-CIO lobbying efforts to convince Congress and the president to overturn the Bracero Program that allowed growers to hire foreign nationals, mostly from Mexico, as temporary workers. Bracero workers had often been used by growers as scab laborers to replace striking local workers in times of labor disputes.

For the headquarters of the AWOC, the AFL-CIO leadership chose Stockton, California, an area in which Filipino workers had settled in large numbers to work the fruit, asparagus, and tomato fields and also in the canneries. It was also an area in which braceros had hampered the growth of a local workforce. AWOC's first director, Norman Smith, a former United Auto Workers (UAW) leader, was not familiar with California's agricultural industry and did not speak Spanish. Although most of the AWOC leadership was Anglo, Smith did choose as one of his top organizers the highly respected and aggressive Filipino leader Larry Itliong, who was intimately acquainted with the competing agribusiness interests in California, especially in the Stockton area, and had already worked on numerous labor drives. Smith also brought in community organizer Dolores Huerta, a Stockton native, who, like Cesar Chavez, had worked with the Community

Service Organization (CSO). She would, for a short time, become the union's secretary-treasurer.

In 1960, the AWOC launched a number of strikes throughout California, most of which resulted in higher wages but not contracts or union recognition. In 1961, the union took on lettuce growers in the Imperial Valley. Although the strike hurt growers financially, they did not yield to union demands. Indeed, the strike led to the arrest of over 50 strikers and cost the AFL-CIO a hefty price in legal bills.

Meanwhile, in Delano, California, Cesar Chavez, with the help of Huerta, who became frustrated with the inability of the AWOC to organize Mexican American workers, launched a new farm workers movement they called the National Farm Workers Association (NFWA), the forerunner of the United Farm Workers (UFW). Chavez, Huerta, and a growing group of volunteers began their dedicated, grueling task of convincing farm workers, one by one, to join their cause of forming an effective force to challenge the power of agribusiness interests.

In 1962, C. Al Green, a former Plasterers Union official, became the new head of the AWOC. Even more than Norman Smith, Green seemed unable to understand the dynamics of California's agricultural system and the forces that kept the workers mired in poverty. Instead of attempting a vigorous campaign to organize the workforce itself to build a base of power, he began to organize labor contractors, the middlemen who supplied laborers to the growers. The approach did little to improve the lives or working conditions for the farm workers.

But in 1965, after a long hiatus from actual strike activity, the AWOC once again was forming picket lines, demanding higher wages, and attempting to exert power in the fields. It was not Al Green who ignited the AWOC strike but Larry Itliong, leader of the Filipino workers in the union. Itliong, along with Ben Gines, first directed AWOC strikes against asparagus growers in the Stockton area in March 1965. When the strikes achieved wage gains, they decided to launch an even greater effort. They moved south to the Coachella Valley where the season's first table-grape harvest was beginning and where growers were depending on both Filipino and Mexican migrants.

On May 3, 1965, approximately 1,000 Filipino workers went on strike, an action that began to send shock waves through California's agricultural industry. When some vineyards agreed to increase wages, Itliong and other emboldened AWOC leaders escalated their efforts. As the seasonal labor moved from Coachella to the Delano area, the AWOC strike moved with it. The grape battle was now about to send shock waves to another farm workers organization in the area—Chavez's NFWA.

On September 8, 1965, Filipino farm workers in Delano met at the Filipino Community Hall and voted to call a strike. Unlike those in Coachella, the growers in Delano were ready to fight the strike action and began to import scab labor from Mexico to replace the Filipino strikers. Strategically stymied, Itliong realized that he needed the support of Mexican workers to join in the strike. He turned to Chavez to ask that his union join forces.

Although his NFWA had untaken two minor strike actions, Chavez was uncertain whether his supporters could muster the necessary resources and commitment to undertake what he saw correctly as a major battle, one that might be bitter, violent, and protracted. After discussions with Huerta and others, however, he realized that he must go forward. This was the time, they concluded, to act decisively.

On September 16 at Our Lady of Guadalupe Church in Delano, members of the NFWA voted unanimously to join with the AWOC in the strike. The Delano grape strike would be long, divisive, and historic. It would take five years of picketing, boycotts, arrests, violence, and strategic maneuvering, but the farm workers movement would emerge with union recognition, collective bargaining rights, and much national attention. It would be the greatest farm workers union success in American history.

By the end of the strike, the AWOC would no longer be a separate union. In August 1966, AFL-CIO leaders and Chavez merged their organizations into the United Farm Workers Organizing Committee (UFWOC). Chavez was its first president; Itliong was elected one of the vice presidents. Although the AWOC had lasted independently only a few years, its actions in launching the grape strike in Delano stands as a decisive moment in the struggle of farm workers and in the life and work of Chavez and his farm workers movement.

Further Reading

Bardacke, Frank. 2011. *Trampling Out the Vintage: Cesar Chavez and the Two Souls of the United Farm Workers*. New York: Verso.

Ferris, Susan, and Ricardo Sandoval. 1997. *The Fight in the Fields: Cesar Chavez and the Farmworkers Movement*. New York: Harcourt Brace & Company.

Ganz, Marshall. 2009. *Why David Sometimes Wins: Leadership, Organization, and Strategy in the California Farm Worker Movement*. New York: Oxford University Press.

Levy, Jacques. 2007. *Cesar Chavez: Autobiography of La Causa*. Minneapolis: University of Minnesota Press.

Alinsky, Saul

Cesar Chavez became one of the most successful community organizers in U.S. history. He learned the techniques from Fred Ross, who learned them from Saul Alinsky, the man who is often credited with laying the foundation for post–World War II grassroots political organizing. When Chavez was a young child, Alinsky was entering the University of Chicago. Born to Russian Jewish immigrant parents

Saul Alinsky, regarded as the father of community organizing and modern protest tactics, is shown in Chicago, where he founded the Back-of-the-Yards Neighborhood Council that trained activists to fight on behalf of a declining section of Chicago's South Side. Alinsky helped found the Community Service Organization in which Cesar Chavez learned organizing techniques in California. (AP/Wide World Photo)

in Chicago on January 30, 1909, Alinsky, from his earliest days as a teenager, was interested in social causes. At the University of Chicago, he organized a group of students who traveled to southern Illinois to help coal miners.

After two years of graduate work, he took a job with the Illinois Division of Criminology, working with delinquent youths. In 1933, Alinsky joined the staff of the Illinois State Penitentiary at Joliet. It was there, he said later, that he gained insight into the causes of criminal behavior—poor housing, unemployment, discrimination, disease, and economic deprivation.

In 1936, Alinsky cofounded in Chicago the Back-of-the-Yards Neighborhood Council (BYNC), an effort to build a citizen reform organization in a largely Irish Catholic Southside neighborhood near the Union Stockyards. Working with the United Packinghouse Workers Union, the BYNC, through self-help methods of organizing, enabled workers to gain union recognition, collective bargaining rights, and improved working conditions and helped citizens fight for better schools and housing. Through Alinsky's leadership and his evolving organizing techniques such as local house meetings, the movement, which gradually gained outside support from some Catholic clergy, Democratic Party leaders, and other unions, gave individuals a growing sense of power and collaboration to take on the establishment forces holding them back.

In 1939, aided by the Marshall Field Foundation, Alinsky established the Industrial Areas Foundation (IAF) to help reform other declining urban neighborhoods. He worked to unite citizens in vigorous protest movements to improve their condition and taught them communication strategies to help gain power through combined economic and political force. They held meetings; sought partners; organized marches, boycotts, and rent strikes; and slowly brought together tough, sustained, and committed groups willing to fight for their rights. They registered voters, protested against discrimination policies and police brutality, and demonstrated how working-class ethnic groups and blacks could work together for their common interest. Since the formation of the IAF, hundreds of community and labor organizers have attended its workshops.

Alinsky inspired the organizing methods of groups in numerous cities, modifying his techniques to fit the situation. He and his organizers became despised threats to corporate and political interests. He spent numerous days in jails after violating local ordinances prohibiting protest actions. It was while in jail in 1946 that he wrote *Reveille for Radicals*, a manifesto laying out his vision for "People's Organizations" and outlining principles and practices of recruiting and training indigenous organizers to take the lead in local communities.

Many organizations adopted his organizing techniques across the country. One of those was the Community Service Organization (CSO). After World War II, Alinsky met Fred Ross, who had worked to better conditions in migrant work camps in California. In 1947, Alinsky agreed to back a plan to organize the CSO in Mexican American communities. Introducing many of Alinsky's organizing techniques, Ross built a network of CSOs in California and tutored young recruits such as Cesar Chavez, Dolores Huerta, and Gilbert Padilla. The CSO sought to make Mexican Americans aware of their civic rights and responsibilities, encouraged voter registration and political participation, and organized Mexican Americans to demand redress of grievances.

As one of Ross's proteges, Chavez traveled the state helping developing CSO chapters. It was in the early years of Chavez's organizing career that he tried out the various methods taught by Alinsky—house meetings, organizational structures, and stirring local collaboration and political participation. Like his mentors Alinsky and Ross, Chavez became more and more determined to make a difference, relentless in his day-to-day drive to inject commitment and common purpose to the communities in which he worked. Impressed with the energy and effectiveness of Chavez, Alinsky summoned Ross and the young organizer to a meeting in San Francisco in 1958 to discuss the creation of a CSO chapter in Ventura County.

Although Alinsky did not work with Chavez in his later unionizing activities among the farm workers of California, it was his methods that inspired Chavez and that worked so successfully in the seemingly impossible task of organizing a union.

In the late 1950s, Alinsky formed several organizations such as the Woodlawn Organization and the Northwest Community Organization to help impoverished areas of Chicago and to help local residents deal with inferior housing and sanitation problems. In 1965, Alinsky went to Rochester, New York, to organize poor African Americans in fighting for greater job opportunities at Eastman Kodak Company. He organized similar groups in Detroit, Michigan, and Buffalo and Syracuse, New York. When he died on June 12, 1972, in Carmel, California, Alinsky was generally recognized as "the Father of Community Organizing."

Alinsky's teachings influenced a young community organizer in Southside Chicago named Barack Obama. In the mid-1980s, Obama worked for the Developing Communities project organizing initiatives ranging from job training and school reform to improving public housing conditions. He gave training classes to young organizers on Alinsky's methods. In the election of 2008, Obama borrowed a winning slogan for his campaign that had been adopted by Cesar Chavez and Dolores Huerta in their organizing work for the UFW—"Si, Se Puede" or "Yes We Can." From Saul Alinsky to Cesar Chavez to Barack Obama, community organizers changed the face of American politics.

Further Reading

Alinsky, Saul. 1989. *Reveille for Radicals*. New York.

Bailey, Robert, Jr. 1974. *Radicals in Urban Politics: The Alinsky Approach*. Chicago: University of Chicago.

Horwitt, Sanford D. 1989. *Let Them Call Me Rebel: Saul Alinsky, His Life and Legacy*. New York: Random House.

Von Hoffman, Nicholas. 2010. *Portrait of Saul Alinsky*. New York: Nation Books.

Arizona Fast, 1972

In May 1972, a decade after Cesar Chavez had launched the farm workers movement, Republicans in his native state of Arizona pushed through a bill denying farm workers the right to strike and boycott during harvest seasons. Republican governor Jack Williams signed it. Aimed mainly to protect the giant lettuce industry in southern Arizona, the bill essentially prohibited farm workers from creating a union. When members of Chavez's union asked to meet with Governor Williams, he arrogantly refused with the demeaning comment, "As far as I'm concerned, these people do not exist" (Levy 2007, 463). Alerted to the legislation and the governor's actions, Chavez decided to travel from California to take on Arizona's agribusiness and political interests. For the second time in his leadership role in the farm workers union, Chavez would use an unorthodox move to challenge the law—a fast.

Chavez now had considerable national support and recognition. He saw an opportunity in the Arizona struggle to energize a statewide mobilization of farm workers not only to highlight the injustices wrought by the political and business leaders and possibly affect future state legislation but also to help workers gain a sense of power that, working together, they could change the dynamics in the state that held them down socially, culturally, and economically. Chavez called it a "fast of love" and remarked that it was done "out of a deep conviction that we can communicate to people, either those who are for us or against us, faster and more effectively spiritually than we can in any other way" (Levy 2007, 465).

Chavez's close confidant LeRoy Chatfield later talked about the difference between the 1968 fast in Delano and the fast four years later in the Santa Rita Center in Phoenix. In 1968, Chatfield said, "the fast seemed like navigating a rickety boat over a shoals in uncharted waters." No one had ever done it before. No one seemed to know whether this was a personal act of religious penance by Chavez or a public act of protest or a combination of the two. They had no idea how the fast would be perceived either by the farm workers themselves or by those who held power over them or by the public at large. On the other hand, Chatfield recalled the Arizona Fast as:, "dusting off the badge, strapping on the holster, mounting up, and riding into Phoenix, I felt like the retired marshal who was called back to duty to restore law and order" (Chatfield, n.d.).

As in 1968, as the fast became national news, famous visitors began to arrive in Arizona—Joseph Kennedy, son of Robert Kennedy; folksinger Joan Baez; Coretta Scott King; Senator George McGovern, who was running for President; and others. When Arizona politicians mocked Chavez's actions, and when growers charged that it was nothing but a publicity stunt, Chavez, as he had done in 1968, became an increasingly sympathetic figure, and the 1972 fast became a media bonanza.

Chavez's room in the Community Center was small. In the evenings, hundreds of people would sit on metal folding chairs and stand along the walls in the building's main hall for nightly Masses as Chavez sat on a rocking chair. Union leaders read messages of support from around the country. There were speeches and music. The protest gained momentum. As the days of the fast wore on, Chavez agreed to a campaign suggested by Chatfield and others that would, in Chavez's words, "make the governor who signed the bill pay for it" (Shaw 2011, 149).

The union would launch a campaign to recall the governor through a massive voter-registration drive. Latino leaders in the state pointed out that the grower lobby and Republican legislature were so powerful that a recall effort seemed futile. In response to some at one of the meetings who said "no se puede" (it cannot be done), Dolores Huerta insisted that from now on they would never say it could not be done. From now on, they would say "si se puede" (yes we can do it). "Si se puede" became a battle cry for the Arizona fight and others that followed.

In early June, Chavez became so weak that he was hospitalized. On June 4, he ended the fast. A mass attended by thousands included a statement by Chavez, read for him: "The greatest tragedy," he said, "is not to live and die, as we all must. The greatest tragedy is for a person to live and die without knowing the satisfaction of giving life for others" ("Statement by Cesar Chavez").

Following the fast, the UFW mobilized thousands of labor, religious, and community activists in the recall and voter-registration campaign. Led by Chatfield and other Chavez lieutenants including Jim Drake and Marshall Ganz, the campaign drew volunteers into Arizona from states around the country. Organizers fanned out from county to county encouraging Mexican Americans, Native Americans, and others to register. They also worked with community leaders, union officials, and Democratic Party politicians to ignite further the organizing activities.

On makeshift tables and even ironing boards, volunteers set up registration sites in heavily trafficked areas across Arizona, especially shopping centers. They marched from door to door. In only four months, 100,000 new voters had put their names on recall petitions and, most importantly, registered to vote.

Although the Republican attorney general eventually blocked the recall election through legal maneuvering, the UFW had changed the electoral demographics of Arizona. Its brief, overwhelmingly successful registration drive paved the way in succeeding elections for Mexican Americans and Native Americans to win several seats in the Arizona state legislature; others won local council and school board races; and a few became judges. When Raul Castro became the first Mexican American governor of Arizona in 1974, his margin of victory was 4,100. The UFW drive had made a powerful impact.

Ethnic political division in Arizona remains seemingly intractable well into the twenty-first century over issues surrounding immigration. Yet Cesar Chavez's historic fast and the UFW's activism transformed Arizona to the present day, when Latino voting power can make a significant impact. And the rallying cry of "Si Se Puede!" has reverberated through the years to other social-justice activists and even all the way to the presidency. President Barack Obama used the slogan ("Yes We Can!") as the theme for his 2008 presidential campaign.

Further Reading

Chatfield, LeRoy. n.d. "Cesar Chavez and the Farm Worker Movement." Farm Worker Documentation Project. http://farmworkermovement.com/essays/essays/008 %20Chatfield_LeRoy.pdf.

Levy, Jacques. 2007. *Cesar Chavez: Autobiography of La Causa.* Minneapolis: University of Minnesota Press.

Shaw, Randy. 2011. *Beyond the Fields: Cesar Chavez, The UFW, and the Struggle for Justice in the 21st Century.* Berkeley: University of California Press.

"Statement by Cesar Chavez at the End of his 24-Day Fast for Justice, Phoenix, Arizona, June 4, 1972," http://chavez.cde.ca.gov/ModelCurriculum/teachers/Lessons/resources/ documents/EXR1_Cesar_E_Chavez_Statements_on_Fasts.pdf.

B

Boycotts

In his battles on behalf of farm workers, Cesar Chavez's favorite weapon became the boycott. Although forms of consumer boycotts can be traced for centuries, the term itself derives in the English language from one Captain Charles Boycott, an Irish soldier for a time and then a land agent for the Earl of Erne in County Mayo, Ireland. In 1880, in times that were particularly rough on tenant farmers, Captain Boycott refused to reduce rents, even temporarily, and instead opted for forced evictions. His actions created united protest among the locals, and he soon found himself isolated. Workers in his fields, stables, and house put down their tools and equipment. Local businessmen banded together to stop offering him services and trade. Even the local postman left his mail in the post office. So determined were his neighbors to fight back that they were even able to convince potential workers to avoid replacing those that had ceased their labors. The protest cost Boycott dearly. He and his family left Ireland and moved to England. By November 1880, the *Times* used his name in describing the action of his neighbors as organized isolation. Eventually, the word made its way into English argot as a concerted action by a group of people to avoid purchasing the goods or services of a company or business.

Chavez was familiar with the use of the boycott from his reading of the life and work of Mahatma Gandhi and of the early days of the American civil rights movement. In the early 1920s, as a leader of the Indian independence movement against Great Britain, Gandhi urged the Indian people to boycott British products, educational institutions, and courts. He urged them not to accept any British titles or honors. One of the central focuses of the boycott was that the people wore home-spun cloth instead of British-made textiles. He succeeded in convincing many women and men to spend time spinning their own cloth as a nonviolent form of protest. Chavez said of Gandhi, "When we apply Gandhi's philosophy of nonviolence, it really forces us to think, really forces us to work hard. . . . Violence only seems necessary when people are desperate; frustration often leads to violence" (Levy 2007, 93).

In December 1955, at a time when Chavez was working with the Community Service Organization (CSO), black citizens led by Martin Luther King Jr. conducted a year-long boycott of the Montgomery, Alabama, city buses. The boycott, which involved masses of black citizens walking and sharing rides to avoid using

19

the bus system, was in protest of racist seating laws that reserved the front seats of buses for whites. The Montgomery boycott was one of the early successful campaigns that set in motion the modern civil rights movement.

Chavez realized that the grape strike, begun in the harvest fields of Delano, California, was a local protest that had limited potential to mobilize large numbers of protesters and to make substantial gains. Although the farm workers and those other supporters who came to Delano to participate were an inspired group along the picket lines, the growers had money, time, law enforcement, and political friends on their side. The infant farm workers union needed a new tactic that could rouse a larger base against agribusiness, one that could truly shake the foundations of the large industry against which the union was pitted. Chavez decided on a boycott.

He would call a boycott on grapes. He would appeal to the public to participate in an issue of social justice, not just labor rights. He would attempt to capitalize on the heightened civil rights consciousness already on the march across the nation. He would try to enlist students, the clergy, activists, labor officials—all who could make themselves part of a movement to make things right by the workers in the harvest fields. He called the boycott "a gate of hope" (Peterson and Diaz n.d.).

In the case of the UFW, there was an irony that worked to the union's advantage. When the National Labor Relations Act (NLRA) became law in the 1930s, pressure from agribusiness had exempted farm labor from the benefits the law provided to the U.S. labor force, most notably the right to organize. Nevertheless, the law itself prohibited the practice of so-called secondary boycotts. A secondary boycott is one that targets a business that is not a primary source of a labor conflict. Because farm labor was not covered by the NLRA, the UFW was not prohibited to engage in secondary boycotts. Chavez was free, for example, to send boycotters to such retail chains as A&P and Safeway, businesses that were only secondarily associated with the labor action against grape growers. By selling products produced by grape growers in Delano, the retail grocers also became targets. Activists surrounded their stores imploring customers to avoid shopping at retailers who aided and abetted growers who exploited farm workers.

At first, the effort to launch a nationwide boycott was, as Chavez said, "helter skelter" (Shaw 2008, 19). The farm workers union first concentrated on Schenley Industries, Inc., a company whose liquor products were distributed through outlets across the country. Chavez picked 13 major cities in which to establish boycott centers. Gathering together a staff of young activists willing to hitchhike or hop freight trains, Chavez organized a team that had no money or experience. But they made progress, using their wits and instincts to start the undertaking. To New York, Chicago, Detroit, and other cities they traveled, visiting churches, labor organizations, and others that might be willing to help. Soon, in most of the cities, volunteers were handing out leaflets on street corners and in front of stores. The boycott leaders raised some money, convinced some grocery and liquor stores to cooperate, recruited others interested in helping the cause, and made a boycott out of nothing.

The writer John Gregory Dunne remembered walking out of a supermarket in Los Angeles and finding on his car a leaflet that had the endorsement of the entertainer Steve Allen. It asked simply that consumers not buy Schenley products and Delano grapes. "A few days later," Dunne said, "the supermarket put up a sign: 'We do not handle Delano grapes' " (Dunne 2008, 129).

Franciscan priest Father Mark Day remembered a day in Toronto: "We had a balloon-in at several supermarkets. Helium-filled balloons with 'Boycott Grapes' painted on them would be released in the stores" (Day 1971, 71).

The use of the boycott would bring many successes to the farm worker movement. Through the years, UFW boycotts affected decisions not only by consumers and retailers but by executives in the board rooms of American agribusiness.

Further Reading

Day, Mark. 1971. *Forty Acres: Cesar Chavez and the Farm Workers*. New York: Praeger Publishers,.

Dunne, John Gregory. 2008. *Delano: The Story of the California Grape Strike*. Berkeley: University of California Press.

Friedman, Monroe. 1999. *Consumer Boycotts: Effecting Change through the Marketplace and Media*. New York: Routledge.

Ganz, Marshall. 2009. *Why David Sometimes Wins: Leadership, Organization, and Strategy in the California Farm Worker Movement*. New York: Oxford University Press.

Levy, Jacques. 2007. *Cesar Chavez: Autobiography of La Causa*. Minneapolis: University of Minnesota Press.

Peterson, Claire, and Susana Diaz. n.d. "Exploring the United Farm Workers' History." http://l3d.cs.colorado.edu/systems/agentsheets/New-Vista/grape-boycott/History.html.

Shaw, Randy. 2008. *Beyond the Fields: Cesar Chavez, the UFW, and the Struggle for Justice in the 21st Century*. Berkeley: University of California Press.

Smith, Syndey. 1987. *Grapes of Conflict*. Pasadena: Hope Publishing House.

Bracero Program

As the United States entered World War II, damaging labor shortages affected many areas of the economy, especially agriculture production and the workforce necessary to pick crops in the harvest fields. On July 23, 1942, the United States and Mexico signed an agreement that became Public Law 78 to enable temporary workers to cross the border into the United States during harvest seasons and then be returned to Mexico. It was called the Bracero Program.

Mexican migrant farm workers registering for the Bracero Program at a processing center at Hidalgo, Texas, June 18, 1959. At the processing centers in Texas, California, and Arizona, laborers were given medical exams, disinfected with DDT, photographed, and fingerprinted. (AP Photo)

A boon to American growers, the system was fraught with harsh treatment to the migrant workers. Mexican nationals, eager for work, were willing to take harsh jobs for meager pay, and many looked back on the experience as an opportunity they would not have otherwise had in Mexico. Yet many often felt as if they were treated like cattle. Cecilio Santillano, an ex-bracero, remembered the trip to the United States: "They brought them in trucks and some in trains and not passenger trains but cargo trains . . . like sheep, up to El Paso." One government official in the U.S. Department of Labor later called the Bracero Program a "system of legalized slavery." From his earliest days as an organizer, Cesar Chavez fought the program and its damaging effects on his dream of founding a farm workers union (Smithsonian).

Originally expected to last the duration of the war, the Bracero Program would last for 22 years and would comprise nearly 4.5 million contracts offered to nearly 2 million Mexican men. On paper, the agreement originally stipulated that the workers would be provided with sanitary housing and access to medical care, and be paid a wage typical of that paid to workers in the United States for the same type of labor. Those rules were soon left to the individual states to administer. As many studies and investigations revealed during the program and after it had ended, the system did not live up to any of those original guarantees.

Most braceros were experienced farm workers from regions such as Coahuila and other lush agricultural regions in Mexico. At the border towns, especially El Paso, Texas, the braceros were registered, given medical exams, fumigated, and shipped to farms mostly across the Southwest and especially to California. Contracts with the braceros were controlled by independent farmers associations and written in English. Most braceros did not fully understand their conditions of employment. For example, braceros could return to their native towns in Mexico in case of emergencies only with written permission from the grower.

They picked lettuce, grapes, cotton, tomatoes, and other crops that enabled extraordinary growth in agribusiness. At first a wartime measure, the Bracero Program was codified into law and expanded, especially in California.

In his work with the Community Service Organization (CSO) in the late 1950s, Chavez was in Oxnard, a town north of Los Angeles, to establish a local office of the CSO in one of the leading citrus-growing areas of the state. Early on in his work to help farm workers, Chavez realized that the Bracero Program was fraught with problems. Because of the financial advantages that the Bracero Program afforded the growers, many of the local California Mexican American workers and other migrant laborers frequently went without jobs. By the late 1950s, Mexican American field workers had been to a large extent replaced by the braceros. Signs declaring "No Pickers Wanted" increasingly greeted those looking for work. And after the war ended, growers continued to lobby the federal government to continue the program, falsely claiming that there was still a labor shortage.

Celedonio Galaviz came to the United States as a bracero in 1951. Without money to make the trip to the border, his family sold their cow for 80 pesos. In his time in the United States, Galaviz had two contracts, the first in Texas and the second in California. His son later said, "He did faced [sic] racial discrimination . . . like having to use the back entrance at restaurants to eat and drinking out of a water hose instead of a fountain. He didn't mind or complain much. He was just glad to be working and making money to help support his family in Mexico" (Galaviz, n.d.).

Increasingly, Chavez had little sympathy for the personal plight of braceros; he saw the issue more in terms of the deleterious effects it had on his farm worker movement. After he began to organize his farm workers union in the early 1960s and after engaging in the early grape strikes, he became increasingly frustrated and enraged over the obstacles to organizing caused by the Bracero Program. It severely jeopardized the wages of Mexican American workers already in the country. Not only were the braceros used by the growers as strikebreakers, the low wages they received and the conditions under which they worked set a standard of wretchedness. The growers were treating these guest workers like the lowest peons, and it was all being undertaken under a government-sanctioned program.

The dilemma was extraordinary. Mexican American workers could not protest wages or working conditions for fear of losing jobs to braceros. The braceros, on the other hand, could not protest their treatment for fear of being returned immediately to Mexico.

Attacked by organized labor, church organizations, and others, the Bracero Program formally ended in 1965. It had been a lucrative source of scab laborers for growers, and its demise encouraged Chavez and his leadership of the farm worker movement. Nevertheless, California's growers would continue to use Mexican labor to break strikes. They would use workers who crossed the border illegally.

Further Reading

Cohen, Deborah. 2011. *Braceros: Migrant Citizens and Transnational Subjects in the Postwar United States and Mexico*. Chapel Hill: The University of North Carolina Press.

Ferriss, Susan, and Ricardo Sandoval. 1997. *The Fight in the Fields: Cesar Chavez and the Farmworkers Movement*. New York: Harcourt Brace & Company.

Galarza, Ernesto.1964. *Merchants of Labor: The Mexican Bracero Story: An Account of the Managed Migration of Mexican Farm Workers in California 1942–1960*. San Jose, CA: Rosicrucian Press.

Galaviz, Sal. n.d. "The Promised Land." Bracero History Archive. http://braceroarchive.org/items/show/3227?view=full.

Ganz, Marshall. 2009. *Why David Sometimes Wins: Leadership, Organization, and Strategy in the California Farm Worker Movement*. New York: Oxford University Press.

Smithsonian Institution, National Museum of American History. "Bittersweet Harvest: The Bracero Program 1942–1964." http://americanhistory.si.edu/exhibitions/exhibition.cfm?key=38&exkey=1357.

Brown, Jerry

In Governor Jerry Brown's long and accomplished political career in California, he and the United Farm Workers (UFW) have been mutual friends and supporters. From his early days in state government as secretary of state, he helped pave the way for UFW strides forward. Most notably, in his first years as governor, Brown helped draft and then signed the California Agricultural Labor Relations Act (CALRA) of 1975, the first legislation in the nation guaranteeing the rights of farm workers to form a union and to conduct collective bargaining. In return, Cesar Chavez and the UFW became Brown's stalwart political supporters, providing organizers, precinct workers, and ground forces in his political campaigns.

There was much of politics and religion in Jerry Brown's background. He was born in San Francisco on April 7, 1938, the son of Edmund (Pat) Brown, who was California's governor from 1959 to 1967. In 1956, he entered Sacred Heart Novitiate, a Jesuit seminary. Later, he received an undergraduate degree from the University of California at Berkeley and a law degree from Yale Law School. After returning to California, he worked for a time as a law clerk at the state Supreme Court and then traveled and studied in Mexico and Latin America. By 1970, back in California, he was on the career path of his father and was elected California's secretary of state. In was in this position that he began his interaction with the UFW.

In 1972, California's agribusiness interests launched a fierce attack against the UFW with a legislative initiative designed to ban nearly every effective weapon available to the union, including the boycott. Known as Proposition 22, the ballot initiative was well financed and coincided with the national presidential election in which President Richard Nixon was heavily favored to win reelection. With Nixon leading the ticket, farm and business leaders anticipated that his coattails in California would help drive Proposition 22 to a decisive win.

Chavez countered the threat with an intensive political operation that included much door-to-door canvassing by volunteers. By now, the UFW, which had been through rugged strikes and boycotts, could muster the kind of political muscle that could make a difference. Chavez concentrated heavily on the election as a must-win contest, one that, if lost, could immediately diminish the union's power.

Chavez not only relied on his own lieutenants in the campaign, he also enlisted the support of Secretary of State Brown, the only high-ranking Democratic state official at the time. Impressed by the goals and accomplishments of the farm workers movement, Brown spoke out often in favor of the UFW.

The UFW presented Brown with affidavits from many individuals who testified that they had been tricked into signing the Proposition 22 petitions that had forced the issue onto the ballot. Based on the information the UFW provided, Brown decided to threaten lawsuits and probe possible criminal activities based on the evidence of voter fraud. Although the lawsuits and criminal investigations did not proceed, the threats had been politically brilliant moves. Discredited by negative publicity, Proposition 22 did not pass, despite the landslide victory of President Richard Nixon in the presidential race. Brown had thus ingratiated himself with Chavez. It was the beginning of an enduring political alliance.

In 1974, aided by an all-out political organizing effort by the UFW, Brown won election as governor of California. No longer would Chavez and the UFW have to deal with the intractable opposition of Republican governor Ronald Reagan.

In 1975, Brown, UFW counsel Jerry Cohen, and others crafted legislation that became a milestone in the history of farm workers—Agricultural Labor Relations Act. Brown's role was crucial. He spoke with an array of interested parties—bishops and religious groups that supported Chavez, supermarket executives, and union officials. He sent out thousands of letters to enlist the broadest base of support. Later he said that he saw his role as a catalyst bringing the forces together to reach a solution. Brown signed the legislation into law on June 4, 1975. The act went into effect on August 28, 1975. Chavez was joyous. For farm workers, the passage of ALRA was a legislative triumph of profound consequences, protecting the right of farm workers to unionize and boycott, and guaranteeing secret ballots in farm workers union elections.

After his two terms as governor ended in 1983, Brown embarked on international lecture trips, studied Spanish in Mexico and Japanese and Buddhist culture in Japan, worked with Mother Teresa in India at the Home for the Dying, and traveled to Bangladesh to assist after the tragic floods of 1987.

Brown ran unsuccessfully for the U.S. presidency three times—in 1976 and 1980, while he was governor, and in 1992. At the 1976 Democratic Convention in New York, Cesar Chavez delivered a nominating address for Brown.

Remarkably, Brown began an unprecedented comeback in California politics at the turn of the century. In 1999, he became mayor of Oakland, a position he held until 2007. He was attorney general of California from 2007 to 2011. And, once again, he was elected governor of California, taking office in 2011.aIn 1993, at Chavez's funeral, Brown helped carry the casket. He said of Chavez:

> He had an overwhelming sense that modern life was disordered and that human beings were being cut off from the soil and a harmonious balance of friendship and nature. He recoiled from the pervasive waste and poisoning that we call our affluent modern life. Cesar Chavez ended his life as he began it, close to those who toil with their hands. In a mechanical age full of plastic and loneliness, he stood against the crowd: unbossed, undoctored and unbought. He kept the faith to the end. We won't find another like him. I will miss him (Brown 1993).

Further Reading

Brown, Edmund G, Jr. 1993. "Chavez Based His Life on Sharing and Frugality." *San Francisco Examiner*. April 25, 2.

Ferriss, Susan, and Ricardo Sandoval. 1997. *The Fight in the Fields: Cesar Chavez and the Farmworkers Movement*. New York: Harcourt Brace & Company.

Pawel, Miriam. 2009. *The Union of Their Dreams: Power, Hope, and Struggle in Cesar Chavez's Farm Worker Movement*. New York: Bloomsbury Press.

Shaw, Randy. 2008. *Beyond the Fields: Cesar Chavez, the UFW, and the Struggle for Justice in the 21st Century*. Berkeley: University of California Press.

Bruce Church, Inc.

Bruce Church, Inc., one of the nation's largest lettuce producers, was for Cesar Chavez an unshakable nemesis. In Chavez's youth, it was this company that took over the ranch of Chavez's grandfather near Yuma, Arizona, forcing the family to become migrant laborers and head to California. When Chavez died in 1993, he was back in Yuma fighting a lawsuit filed in Arizona by the same company over a lettuce boycott that it claimed had been waged illegally by the United Farm Workers (UFW) and had cost the company millions of dollars. The beginning and end of Chavez's remarkable life had come full circle back to Yuma, and, once again, there was Bruce Church, Inc.

Born in 1900, the founder of the company, Bruce Church, studied business economics at the University of California—Berkeley and then worked for a produce shipper. With the backing of a financial partner, Church began a company to ship head lettuce, also known as roundhead or crisphead, to Eastern markets covered in ice. Company legend attributes this method of shipping head lettuce as the source of the term "iceberg lettuce."

Church's company boomed, leading to the creation of Bruce Church, Inc., based in Salinas, California. It became one of the state's largest vegetable producers and shippers and one of the major lettuce companies in the country, with large fields not only in California but in southwest Arizona.

Church died in 1958, while Chavez was still working with the Community Service Organization (CSO) and nurturing dreams of making the lives of farm workers hired by companies such as Bruce Church more humane. With the death of the company founder, his son-in-law Edward "Ted" Taylor took over the company. It was under Ted Taylor's leadership that the company introduced packaged shredded lettuce and further grew Bruce Church's power and influence. And it was with Ted Taylor that Chavez would cross labor swords for over a decade.

In the summer of 1970, Chavez's UFW, fresh from victories in a grape strike and boycott, launched an effort to force growers in the vegetable fields in and around the Salinas Valley to sign contracts. Unnerved by the success of UFW in the vineyards, most Salinas Valley growers turned to the Teamsters Union, which offered sweetheart union contracts to the growers much more favorable than those offered by the UFW. Just as in the grape strike in the late 1960s, the UFW struggle with the vegetable growers, through both strikes and a boycott, would be protracted, often violent, and fought in the courts as well as in the fields.

By 1979, many large California vegetable companies, including SunHarvest, the nation's largest lettuce producer, succumbing to the strike and boycott pressure of the UFW, turned away from the Teamsters Union and signed UFW contracts. Bruce Church, Inc., was not one of those companies. Chavez called for a nationwide boycott of nonunion lettuce, principally that produced by Bruce Church, Inc. In taking on company, the UFW became one of the first advocacy groups to make use of computers and direct mail to reach consumers. In November 1979, Chavez was in St. Louis while touring the Midwest in support of a boycott against Red Coach Lettuce, a brand marketed by Bruce Church, Inc. Expressing confidence in the boycott, Chavez said simply that supermarket chain owners should not sell Red Coach Lettuce until the company decided to negotiate in good faith.

Some of those supermarket chains listened and acted, including Lucky Grocery and even McDonalds. With the boycott obviously damaging Bruce Church sales, Ted Taylor and the company decided to do something about it. In 1984, they filed suit in the state of Arizona, where the political atmosphere toward the UFW was less favorable than in California. They claimed that the UFW had violated Arizona's statutes that prohibited "secondary boycotts," those directed against parties other than the principal company, and also that the union had defamed the company.

For four years the litigation crawled through the judicial system until, in 1988, a superior court in Arizona ruled in favor of the company. It ordered the UFW to pay $5.4 million in damages.

Through the appellate courts the case proceeded. In April 1993, Chavez returned to Arizona to face the Bruce Church lawyers in defense of the lettuce boycott. After his second day of testifying in Yuma County Superior Court, he spent the late afternoon driving through Latino neighborhoods east of Yuma that he had known so well as a child. In San Luis, in the home of a former farm worker and longtime friend, Dofla Maria Hau, Chavez and other UFW leaders arrived for their lodging. Chavez passed away during the night.

As the legal maneuvering proceeded after Chavez's death, a number of unions came to the aid of the UFW in mounting the appeal, including the International Brotherhood of Electrical Workers (IBEW), the United Mine Workers (UMW), and the American Federation of State, County and Municipal Employees (AFSCME). The UFW ultimately prevailed in the courts with the appellate court deciding that the case should never have been tried in Arizona but in California, where the major boycott activity took place.

In May 1996, after nearly 18 years of boycotts, strike violence in the fields, and legal warfare, Bruce Church, Inc., finally agreed to a five-year contract with the UFW providing for increased wages and other negotiated terms favorable to the workers. The contract, something of a peace treaty, was signed in a library in Salinas that had already been named after Cesar Chavez. "Cesar gave his last ounce of strength defending the farm workers in this case," stated his successor, UFW President Arturo Rodriguez, who was with him in Arizona during the trial. "He died standing up for their First Amendment right to speak out for themselves."

The lettuce strike and boycott between the UFW and Bruce Church, Inc., had been one of the longest-running farm labor disputes in American history (United Farm Workers n.d.).

Further Reading

Bardacke, Frank. 2011. *Trampling Out the Vintage: Cesar Chavez and the Two Souls of the United Farm Workers*. New York: Verso.

Ferriss, Susan, and Ricardo Sandoval. 1997. *The Fight in the Fields: Cesar Chavez and the Farmworkers Movement*. New York: Harcourt Brace & Company.

Stevenson, Richard. 1988. "Farm Workers Union Is Told to Pay $5.4 Million in Boycott." *New York Times*, April 8, A20.

United Farm Workers. n.d. "The Story of Cesar Chavez." http://www.ufw.org/_page.php ?inc=history/07.html&menu=research.

C

California Migrant Ministry (CMM)

From the earliest days of the farm workers movement, Cesar Chavez emphasized the need to involve religious organizations. The California Migrant Ministry (CMM) was with Chavez from the beginning.

In 1920, the National Migrant Ministry, an interdenominational program, began to serve the needs of migratory farm workers. The organization, affiliated with the National Council of Churches, provided health care, vocational training, recreational activity, and religious services at New Deal labor camps across the country. The organization exemplified the belief that Christian charity is not ministering only to the souls of individuals but also caring for the needs of the oppressed and poor. By the 1950s, 38 states had migrant ministry programs, including California.

Under the leadership of director Doug Still, the CMM established a rural ministry in the San Joaquin and Imperial Valleys. The organization set up camps for children during harvest periods, classes to teach English and other remedial education both to parents and children, classes on personal hygiene, day care centers, food for the particularly needy, and other activities aimed to make life more tolerable for the field workers and, if possible, to help their assimilation into the larger society. Also in the 1950s, with the help of a Schwarthaup Foundation grant, the organization introduced its staff members to the work of the Community Service Organization (CSO) under the direction of Fred Ross. It was through this training that a number of CMM members learned firsthand the work of community organizing and also met a young organizer named Cesar Chavez.

From their association with the CSO, members of the Migrant Ministry began to question whether the organization's commitment to charitable service was the most effective way to help the distressed farm worker communities. The system under which the workers labored struck at their dignity and self-respect. Perhaps the long-term answer, many came to believe, was to help these workers, through their own initiatives, become more self-sufficient—to fight for higher wages, to find ways to fight against job discrimination, and to gain increasing economic and political power.

In 1961, Chris Hartmire, an ordained Presbyterian minister and a graduate of Princeton University and Union Seminary, replaced Rev. Still as head of the

CMM. In 1963, the CMM sent organizers to Tulane County, north of Delano, to begin building an organization of farm workers that would begin to press public agencies to be more responsive to their needs. They set up recreational and tutorial programs to demonstrate to school officials and others that the workers were not only eager to improve their condition but were gaining confidence and aspiration to work together effectively.

When the Delano grape strike began in 1965, the CMM was thus already on the road toward community organizing and building efforts at self-determination. When Chavez approached Hartmire to assist in the strike, he eagerly agreed to join in La Causa.

CMM leaders soon called on other church leaders in the area to try to persuade them to join in the fight for social justice and invited religious leaders outside of California to visit Delano. They began collecting food and money for the strikers and became a visible presence on the picket lines. When strikers were arrested and jailed for violating local ordinances prohibiting picketing, they helped secure their release. They spoke with reporters covering the strike about the economic and political powerlessness suffered by farm workers and the religious duty that called CMM members to join this nonviolent social movement. The CMM made La Causa its own, concentrating its ministry on the aspirations and struggle of farm workers to gain not only better working conditions but also a measure of dignity that had been wrongfully denied.

When the growers and their allies realized the impact church involvement on the side of the workers might engender, they mounted a campaign to discredit the CMM and to pressure religious groups not to follow its example. When those opponents of Chavez appealed to church officials to steer their congregations against the union, Hartmire and other CMM leaders spoke to synods, conventions, and church boards to plead the opposite case.

Although most religious organizations came slowly to the side of Chavez, the CMM example began to stir others to action. For Chavez, the willingness of this religious organization to back this infant union of farm workers in what seemed an impossible challenge to Californian agribusiness interests was an invaluable commitment. To Chavez, the movement toward a farm workers union was from the beginning steeped in religious feeling and symbols. The CMM gave the union a legitimacy it desperately needed in its early years.

The farm workers movement would increasingly seem to many outsiders as well as to the farm workers themselves as much a religious experience as a social protest drive toward the creation of a labor union. Religious symbols and trappings abounded—picketers on their knees in prayer, masses held during strike actions and marches, flags emblazoned with the Virgin of Guadalupe, fasts for penance, marches that were pilgrimages, prayer vigils at strike and boycott sites, and speeches invoking scripture and moral imperatives.

Hartmire later recalled that when the boycott became the focus of the union's strategy, the CMM sent volunteers to various cities across the country. Gradually, other religious leaders and organizations joined the movement—national and world councils of churches and individual denominations, Catholic organizations, the Central Conference of American Rabbis, and the Union of Hebrew Congregations.

By March 1968, Chavez had generated such national attention that he appeared on the cover of *Time* magazine. In the story about the grape strike, Chavez lauded the work of the CMM in the camps and fields. They were Protestants and the workers were Catholics, Chavez pointed out, but the cause of the farm workers had exerted a mighty force of common religious commitment.

The decision of the CMM early in the farm workers movement to join in common cause was not only an invaluable contribution in establishing the UFW, but it also made a profound impact on the Migrant Ministry itself. In 1971, the National Migrant Ministry became the National Farm Worker Ministry and redefined its mission as supporting farm workers as they organize themselves to seek equality, freedom, and justice. Their message and their work of faith continue to this day.

Further Reading

Griswold del Castillo, Richard, and Richard Garcia. 1995. *Cesar Chavez: A Triumph of the Spirit* Norman: University of Oklahoma Press.

Smith, Sydney. 1987. *Grapes of Conflict*. Pasadena, CA: Hope Publishing House.

Watt, Alan. 2010. *Farm Workers and the Churches: The Movement in California and Texas*. College Station: Texas A & M University Press.

Wells, Ronald. 2009. "Cesar Chavez's Protestant Allies: The California Migrant Ministry and the Farm Workers." *Journal of Presbyterian History*, Spring/Summer, 5–16. http://www.farmworkermovement.us/essays/essays/cec.pdf.

Chatfield, LeRoy

From both inside Cesar Chavez's farm workers movement and from outside its formal organization, LeRoy Chatfield made unique contributions. In the early years of its organizing work and its strikes, boycotts, and other nonviolent protest actions, Chatfield became a close Chavez confidant, entrusted with numerous critical responsibilities. When he left after over a decade of dedicated service, he continued working on behalf of progressive causes. He also launched a nonprofit enterprise—the Farmworker Movement Documentation Project—that is preserving for future generations historical materials that tell the remarkable story of the United Farm Workers (UFW).

In late February 1968, Cesar Chavez, now in the 13th day of a fast, is helped into the Kern County Superior Court in Bakersfield, California, by his close confidant LeRoy Chatfield. Chavez was charged with contempt for refusing to obey an antipicketing injunction during a grape strike against Giumarra Vineyards. (AP/Wide World Photo)

Chatfield was born in 1934 in Arbuckle, California, where his family worked in agriculture. Immersed in strong Catholic teachings, he joined a Catholic boarding school in Sacramento and later entered St. Mary's College, where he earned a degree in philosophy in 1956. He became a member of the Christian Brothers, a Catholic order of teachers, and was known as Brother Gilbert. From 1957 to 1965, he taught in Catholic high schools in San Francisco and Bakersfield. In 1963, while Chatfield was in Boston attending a National Catholic Social Action Convention, he heard activist Father Philip Berrigan speak about the nascent farm workers movement beginning in Delano, California. When he returned to Bakersfield, Chatfield made the short trip to Delano to visit Chavez.

In October 1965, in the early days of the historic grape strike, Chavez asked Chatfield to join La Causa. Strongly drawn to a movement that seemed particularly grounded in Christian social commitment, Chatfield became one of Chavez's close advisors. Among those advisors, he was easily recognized—tall and angular like Fred Ross but with blond hair.

Chatfield was at the center of many of the most significant events of the early years of the National Farm Workers Association (NFWA). Chavez asked him to develop the union's Co-Op movement to provide services for the farm worker members and their families. Under his direction, a gas station and social services center was developed in Delano. He also raised and administered funds and provided legal services.

In March 1968, he coordinated activities surrounding Chavez's celebrated fast, ensuring that the event maintained a religious posture. Cordoning off the area around the farm worker union's headquarters at Forty Acres, he turned the scene into a kind of sacred pilgrimage center, including a chapel. Hundreds of people traveled to the site to spend days in tents. Images of the Virgin of Guadalupe, the patron saint of Mexico, were everywhere. For over a week, Chavez greeted visitors quietly. Chatfield later said that many of those visitors left as newly committed organizers. The fast became one of the greatest organizing efforts ever accomplished by the farm workers movement.

Chatfield developed the Robert F. Kennedy Farm Workers Medical Plan. When the union first won contracts, they included funds for self-insured preventative health care including maternity benefits, medicine, and short-term hospitalization.

In 1972, Chatfield, with his keen political acumen, became the chief strategist of the farm workers union its fight to combat a nefarious effort by agribusiness interests and the Republican Party to weaken farm workers' rights through a statewide ballot initiative. The Agricultural Labor Relations Initiative, known as Proposition 22, was a ballot measure to block farm workers from organizing unions, to forbid them to bargain collectively with employers, and to curtail strike activity. Chatfield plunged into the election challenge with much ingenuity and tactical skill.

Union workers fanned out into major cities, especially in Latino communities, passing out flyers. In some strategic locations, they stood on the side of heavily traveled intersections holding billboards encouraging voters to reject the attack on farm workers. They set up phone banks, canvassed neighborhoods, and enlisted the help of unions, religious groups, charitable organizations, student activists, and even media celebrities to carry out a relentless grassroots campaign to defeat the initiative. Also, Chatfield's wife, Bonnie, led researchers in discovering that a large number of the petitions originally submitted to get the initiative on the ballot were fraudulent, a discovery that helped crush the opposition.

Proposition 22 went down to ignominious defeat. Led by Chatfield, the victory marked a significant step forward in Latino voter participation and organizing success that would lead to increasing numbers of other electoral victories. In reaching out to individuals who had never previously voted, mobilizing phone banks, pursuing door-to-door canvassing, gaining access to the press, and dissecting the voting blocs of the state district by district, Chatfield and his colleagues had created a model for the union and for other labor and Latino political organizers.

In 1973, Chatfield, who was asked to stand for the position of secretary treasurer of the UFW, decided instead to leave his formal attachment to the union and move on to other work. In 1974, California prepared to elect a new governor. Since the inception of the farm workers movement, California's governorship had been held by Ronald Reagan, a man entirely hostile to Chavez and his cause. Now, in 1974, the Democratic candidate was Jerry Brown, son of former governor Pat Brown and a supporter of the UFW. Impressed with Chatfield's political work in helping defeat Proposition 22, Brown hired Chatfield as one of his campaign leaders. Helped by the backing of the UFW and by Chatfield's work on his campaign team, Brown triumphed in the November election. For the first time in the history of his union, Cesar Chavez now had a friend in the governor's mansion, and, once again, Chatfield had played a decisive role in a political fight vital to the interests of the UFW.

For five years Chatfield served in the Brown administration, including a stint as a member of the Agricultural Labor Relations Board (ALRB), the state body with responsibility for enforcing the 1975 Agricultural Labor Relations Act (ALRA), the milestone farm labor law that, for the first time, recognized the right of farm workers to organize.

Chatfield worked with numerous other organizations whose goals were to help the powerless overcome intractable forces that held them in poverty and degrading circumstance. In 1987, he founded Loaves & Fishes, an all-volunteer, private-sector charity dedicated to feeding the hungry. In 2001, Loaves & Fishes began the Golden Day Project that acquired property in Sacramento County to develop low-cost housing for disabled homeless people.

In 2009, Chatfield teamed with former UFW general counsel Jerry Cohen to launch a national initiative called LABOR JUSTICE, a campaign to encourage legislators to include farm workers and domestic laborers under the protections of the 1935 National Labor Relations Act, from which they were excluded when the law was first signed into law.

In 2010, Chatfield revived a literary journal that he had started many years earlier called *Syndic*. He publishes it online. Also online, he continues to expand the Farmworker Movement Documentation Project. Nearly 40 years after he visited Cesar Chavez in Delano and joined the movement, Chatfield, in 2003, began to gather original source material on La Causa from those who partici-pated in its work and others affected by it. The material includes numerous essays written by UFW organizers and volunteers as well as video clips, music, oral histories, manuscripts, and photographs. Through his monumental project, Chatfield is still providing historians, students, and progressive reformers with the facts, insights, and strategies, along with the successes and shortcomings, that make up the story of the most significant farm labor movement in American history.

Further Reading

Chatfield, LeRoy. n.d. "Farmworker Movement Documentation Project." http://farmwork ermovement.com.

Chatfield, LeRoy. 1991. "Meeting Cesar Chavez and Becoming a Disciple." Farmworker Movement Documentation Project, August. http://farmworkermovement.com/ category/commentary/leroy-chatfield-recalls/.

Ganz, Marshall. 2009. *Why David Sometimes Wins: Leadership, Organization, and Strat-egy in the California Farm Worker Movement*. New York: Oxford University Press.

Levy, Jacques. 2007. *Cesar Chavez: Autobiography of La Causa*. Minneapolis, University of Minnesota Press.

Shaw, Randy. 2008. *Cesar Chavez, the UFW, and the Struggle for Justice in the 21st Century*. Berkeley: University of California Press.

Chavez, Helen

She first met Cesar Chavez in a malt shop in Delano called, as Cesar later remem-bered it, La Baratita. Helen Fabela was with a group of friends, all about 15 years old, and she wore a flower in her hair. She also attended Delano High School and worked part time at a grocery store where Cesar, also about 15 years old, suddenly became a frequent visitor.

She was born on January 21, 1928, in Brawley, California, the eldest child of parents who had immigrated to the United States—her father from San Jacinto, Mexico, and her mother from Sombrete, Mexico. Both worked as migrant laborers in the San Joaquin Valley. After her father's death when Helen was 15, she quit high school to support the family, which included her mother, two sisters, and four brothers.

In 1944, Cesar joined the U.S. Navy and served two years as a deck hand in the Western Pacific. When he returned in 1946, Helen and Cesar continued their rela-tionship, and on October 22, 1948, they married in Reno, Nevada. The two then returned to San Jose for a church wedding. On their honeymoon they visited California missions from Sonoma to San Diego.

They made their first home in Delano. Over the course of their married life they would have eight children and 31 grandchildren.

The two began their married lives as agricultural workers, picking strawberries in Greenfield, California. Later, they moved to Crescent City in northern California, where Cesar worked for a time in the lumber mills. By 1952, they were in a barrio of San Jose called Sal Si Puedes. It was in the San Jose area that Cesar, at Helen's urging, met Fred Ross, a founder of the Community Service Organization (CSO), a grassroots Latino civil rights group. Under Ross's tutelage, Chavez became a community organizer, a path that would lead both him and Helen to their remarkable journey of forming a union of farm workers.

While caring for her children, she also devoted time assisting with CSO business. She taught literacy classes for migrant workers, helped them gain U.S. citizenship, and worked in voting drives. She even managed to write the daily logs of her husband's CSO activities.

When Cesar resigned from the CSO in 1962 to form a union of farm workers, Helen helped the family's meager finances by working part time picking grapes and assembling cardboard boxes at a local factory. She took on various administrative jobs for the union, especially helping prepare for chapter meetings. She became an accountant for the union and then the administrator for the United Farm Workers Association's (UFWA) credit union.

Although Helen's more circumscribed roles as mother and wife frequently prevented more public forms of activism, she was never far from the labor fight and, on a number of occasions, at the center of strike activity.

In 1966, she was arrested for shouting "Huelga" on a picket line at the W. B. Camp Ranch, one of the early targets of the grape strike. In 1975, Helen and her daughter Linda were arrested for attempting to organize field workers at the Jack Pandol & Sons grape ranch near Delano. They were eventually released when the state courts upheld a regulation that allowed labor organizers to meet with workers outside of work hours.

She was arrested again in 1978, this time along with Cesar, for challenging an Arizona ban on picketing. Her public acts of defiance encouraged more women in the union to step forward in roles to which they had heretofore been unaccustomed—open displays of labor activism.

After her husband's death in 1992, Helen continued her work with the union. In 1993, she traveled to Washington, DC, to accept on behalf of Cesar the Presidential Medal of Freedom from President Bill Clinton at the White House. The Medal of Freedom is the nation's highest civilian award.

In 2010, the United Farm Workers (UFW) dedicated the National Chavez Center in the Tehachapi Mountain town of Keene in honor of Helen Chavez. In 1971, Cesar decided to purchase an abandoned tuberculosis sanitarium and move the UFW's main headquarters from Delano to this new compound he would call Nuestra Señora

Reina de la Paz (La Paz), a place more ascetic and peaceful, he envisioned, than the complex at Forty Acres. At first, Helen had not been enthusiastic about the venture. In fact, when she had been a child, her parents had placed Helen for a time in that sanitarium, in a section called a "preventorium," where fragile or underweight children as well as those who had been exposed to tuberculosis were isolated for their protection. Helen had hated the time she had spent in the facility. But now, in 2010, she proudly accepted the honor. She made La Paz her home, worked with full heart for the union cause, and remained there in the mountain setting after Cesar's death.

In a 2012 interview for the International Museum of Women in San Francisco, Dolores Huerta, cofounder of the UFW and close friend of the Chavez family, spoke forcefully about the immense contribution made by Helen Chavez in the creation of the union, in its struggles to stay afloat financially, and in the emotional support necessary to sustain a prolonged fight to survive. Huerta spoke of Helen's working in the grape vineyards while managing a household with eight children and of accepting the union's plea for her to become the head of the credit union despite all of her other responsibilities. Most of all, she said, Helen was Cesar's "fortress" and his "foundation."

Further Reading

Ferriss, Susan, and Ricardo Sandoval. 1998. *The Fight in the Fields: Cesar Chavez and the Farmworkers Movement*. New York: Harcourt Brace & Company.

Levy, Jacques. 2007. *Cesar Chavez: Autobiography of La Causa*. Minneapolis: University of Minnesota Press.

Rose, Margaret. 2002. "Traditional and Nontraditional Patterns of Female Activism in the United Farm Workers of America, 1962 to 1980." In *Chicana Leadership: The Frontiers Reader*, edited by Yolanda Flores. Lincoln: University of Nebraska Press.

Chavez, Juana

Cesar Chavez credited his mother with teaching him nonviolent protest long before he ever read about Mahatma Gandhi. Born in Mexico in 1892, Juana Estrada moved to Arizona with her parents when she was six months old.

Like her future husband, she had little formal schooling but had done much practical work with her parents on a small family farm. She also had a strong Catholic upbringing. In 1924, she married Librado Chavez, who had also moved with his parents to an area in southwestern Arizona in the North Gila Valley near the Colorado River. The two would become the parents of six children: three girls (Rita, Helen, and Vickie) and three boys (Richard, Librado, and, in 1927, Cesar).

The extended Chavez family, especially with many of Librado's relatives living in the area, managed to maintain a small family farm with a few horses and cows and to open a grocery store. In 1938, however, burdened by debt after a devastating drought hit the area, the family eventually lost their land and were forced to pack up whatever belongings they could fit in an old Studebaker and head for California in search of work.

For a time, they settled in a San Jose barrio called Sal Si Puedes ("Get Out If You Can"), an apt name for the uninviting location. Then they hit the road as migrant laborers, seeking work picking a variety of crops. Through these extraordinarily challenging days, Cesar later said, it was his mother's strong spirit that kept the family together.

Cesar later talked about the times when his father was injured or sick and his mother would join other family members in the fields, sometimes beginning as early as 3:30 in morning and not returning until 7:00 in the evening to keep the meager earnings coming in. He talked about how his mother sold crochet work by the roadside to pay for gas money for the car.

One of Juana Chavez's predominant religious faiths was her devotion to St. Eduvigis, a Polish duchess who gave up all her possessions and distributed them among the poor. Juana Chavez taught her children the tradition of *religion casera*, the spirit of charity at the heart of many of the lives of Catholics of Mexican descent.

Cesar, for example, talked about his mother asking him and his brother Richard during the days of the Great Depression to go to the railroad yards and along the tracks and invite hobos to dinner. He talked about the days on the road in California as migrant workers when Juana Chavez would never pass up a family in trouble without trying to help. He talked about her inviting many homeless families to share their tents or whatever small spaces they had available. He talked about the lesson of charity she taught all of the children—that in helping the needy you are doing God's work and will be rewarded with friendships. Many of the family's lifelong friends, he said, were people whom his mother had assisted in their most troubled times.

Cesar often talked about a rainy night in a farm labor camp in Mendota when a young girl, unable to get to a doctor, gave birth to her first baby in the camp; Juana Chavez rolled up her sleeves and delivered the child. He talked about the many times that farm workers came to her for herbal medicines, especially manzanilla.

Juana Chavez was also not intimidated by labor contractors, who often used unscrupulous methods to reduce even further the immensely unfair wages for farm workers. On a number of occasions she would sharply question the methods and practices of the contractors. Her defiance angered the contractors but impressed her children greatly.

She welcomed the strike battles and the chance to stand up and fight injustice. Nevertheless, she always emphasized that the workers had to resist violence.

It not only was morally wrong, she said, but self-defeating. Much of this instruction came from *dichos*—Mexican folk sayings.

In February 1975, UFW members gathered in San Francisco's Union Square to begin a 110-mile march to Modesto protesting the Gallo Wine Company's contract with the Teamsters Union and push for a state farm labor law. Cesar Chavez, wearing a leather jacket in the early morning chill of northern California, was photographed with an 83-year-old woman holding his hand and offering support. It was his mother.

On August 21, 1988, Cesar Chavez ended a 36-day fast in Delano, California, to protest the use of pesticides in the fields and the refusal of growers to bargain in good faith with the UFW. At his side, holding his hands, were his wife and his mother, now in her mid-nineties.

Juana Chavez passed away in December 1991 at the age of 99. At her funeral, Cesar Chavez eulogized her as a woman of courage and compassion, one who taught him and others not to accept prejudice and injustice but to fight back with methods short of violence. He said, "We are here today because our lives were touched and moved by her spirit of love and service. That spirit is more powerful than any force on earth. It cannot be stopped" (Chavez 1991).

Further Reading

Chavez, Cesar. 1991. "Eulogy for Juana Estrada Chavez." Cesar Chavez Foundation, December 18. http://www.chavezfoundation.org/_cms.php?mode=view&b_code=001008000000000&b_no=18&page=1&field=&key=&n=10.

Dunne, John Gregory. 1997. *Delano: The Story of the California Grape Strike*. Berkeley: University of California Press.

Ferriss, Susan, and Ricardo Sandoval. 1997. *The Fight in the Fields: Cesar Chavez and the Farmworkers Movement*. New York: Harcourt Brace & Company.

Levy, Jacques. 2007. *Cesar Chavez: Autobiography of La Causa*. Minneapolis: University of Minnesota Press.

Chavez, Librado

In the early 1880s, a family named Chavez crossed the border at El Paso, Texas, into the United States, seeking opportunities. Cesario Chavez, with his wife, Dorotea, and their children, fled slave-like working conditions on a hacienda in Chihuahua, Mexico, made their way to Arizona, acquired a small section of land in the North Gila Valley, and began farming. One of those children, Librado, would become the father of Cesar Chavez, who would be named after his grandfather, Cesario.

A labor activist and his labor activist son. Cesar Chavez visits his father, Librado Chavez, in San Jose in the 1970s. (Cathy Murphy/Getty Images)

Cesario, named Papa Chayo by the family, and his sons and daughters built a farm near what is now Yuma, Arizona. Librado later bought a small grocery store with a pool hall while he continued to help his parents farm their 160 acres. He even became postmaster in the area.

On June 15, 1924, Librado married Juana Estrada, whose family was also from an area in Chihuahua. Librado and Juana Chavez would have five children, one whom, Cesar, was born in the store on March 31, 1927.

Thus, generations of Chavez family members clustered in the sparsely settled desert area along the Colorado River, one of the hottest spots of land in the United

States. Cesar Chavez not only had nearby his father Librado and his mother Juana but brothers and sisters, grandfather and grandmother, and uncles and aunts and cousins that numbered well over 100 relatives. Centered in a Roman Catholic faith, Chavez's family taught the children the rituals and trappings of religious life.

In the early 1930s, Librado, unable to pay off debt on loans, was forced to sell the store, move his family for a time into the adobe house of his parents, and work the farm. By this time Cesario had died, and Dorotea, known as Mama Tella, was over 90 years old. With no electricity and no running water, and one room for Librado's family, life on the dry, parched Arizona frontier, amid the mesquite and assorted cactus, was a testing struggle.

Cesar Chavez, from his earliest days, admired his father's resilience, charity, and ethic of hard work. Rita, Cesar's sister, later said that her brother was the "right hand of my father's arm," chopping wood, taking care of the animals, and working "like a man, because that's the way father taught him" (Levy 2007, 20).

While in Arizona, Librado became an influential member among the Mexican American community, organizing fund-raising events and supporting local political candidates. Yet as the years of the Depression wracked millions of other families, Librado Chavez did not escape. When a severe drought dried the Gila River and brought barren fields, the family was unable to pay bills for irrigation water. Local officials foreclosed the farm and sold it at auction.

Librado sold the farm only after a vigorous struggle to convince political figures to intervene when the local banks would not loan money to Mexican Americans. He even traveled to Phoenix to petition the governor. It was to no avail, and in the late 1930s, the family loaded a few possessions in their dilapidated car and joined other Depression-era migrants on the road to California, to its harvest lands where they might find work.

From valley to valley, from harvest to harvest, they kept moving. For a time, Brawley, California, became a home base. Later it would be Delano. Traveling northward each spring from job to job, they gained knowledge about the rotation of crops and the successive harvests.

They endured the grueling days in the fields with little water, no toilet facilities, and tough labor. At night they survived in wretched shacks.

They picked peas, lettuce, tomatoes, figs, prunes, grapes, and apricots. They were exploited by labor contractors, and many times the entire family made little more than a dollar a day. But Librado kept them moving from one labor camp to another, from one harvest field to another, never pushing the children too hard but never giving up.

On many occasions, Librado, often with some of his family members in tow, would be turned away from restaurants or faced signs that said "No Dogs or

Mexicans Allowed" or "White Trade Only." His children were often isolated in segregated schools. As he chafed at the senseless discrimination and never lost his self-respect, he taught his children, by example, invaluable lessons about dignity, justice, and honesty.

Always fighting against long odds, Librado Chavez joined a number of small labor unions for brief periods of time. He participated in *huelgas* (strikes) that were almost always unsuccessful, plagued by disorganization, lack of money, and general lack of awareness of effective protest tactics. It was during a strike in the Tulane County cotton fields near Corcoran in 1946 that Cesar Chavez first carried a picket sign alongside his father. Cesar would later quip that the Chavez family was probably one of "the strikingest families in California" (Levy 2007, 78). At the first mention of the word "Huelga," he said, the Chavezes would leave the fields.

The most successful of the early attempts to gain power for farm workers was the advent of the National Farm Labor Union (NFLU), led by Ernesto Galarza, a Mexican American writer and sociologist with a doctorate from Columbia University. Librado Chavez eagerly joined the NFLU, anxious to see if this new union could overcome the enormous obstacles facing farm workers attempting to assert their rights.

In the late 1940s, the union struck the DiGiorgio Corporation, one of the largest fruit growers in the country. Through the use of scab workers, charges of communist infiltration, and assorted other antilabor tactics, DiGiorgio managed to overcome the union's two-and-a-half-year fight. Nevertheless, watching his father and his fellow union members in action gave much insight to the young Cesar Chavez. Little did he or anyone know it, but the DiGiorgio Corporation had not seen the last of farm worker unions or the Chavez family.

Librado Chavez would eventually join the Agricultural Workers Organizing Committee (AWOC), a union mostly of Filipinos who, in 1965, asked that a young organizer of an infant union join their strike against grape growers in Delano. That young organizer, of course, was Librado Chavez's son.

Librado Chavez died on October 12, 1982, after a long, noble journey. He lived to see his son a giant in the history of American labor.

Further Reading

Ferriss, Susan, and Ricardo Sandoval. 1998. *The Fight in the Fields: Cesar Chavez and the Farmworkers Movement*. New York: Harcourt Brace & Company.

Griswold del Castillo, Richard, and Richard A. Garcia. 1995. *Cesar Chavez: A Triumph of Spirit*. Norman: University of Oklahoma Press.

Levy, Jacques. 2007. *Cesar Chavez: Autobiography of La Causa*. Minneapolis: University of Minnesota Press.

Chavez, Manuel

He was Cesar's *primo hermano*, his first cousin. Manuel Chavez was born in Yuma, Arizona, in October 1925. Two years older than Cesar, he grew up with Cesar's family in Arizona after his own mother passed away when he was 12. Cesar and Richard Chavez now had what amounted to another brother. The three of them, close in age and in spirit, were a tightly knit trio during their teenage years. Later remembering those years, Manuel said of Cesar: "We were teenagers working in the fields and living in a labor camp. We were cold, hungry, angry, and had not been paid. We said, 'someday if we can, we will change how this works'" (Ybarra 2010).

Manuel was a hustler and schemer, even in his early days living with Cesar and Richard. He was also a street fighter, an activity that landed him in jail on a number of occasions. But he was highly likable and jocular, a storyteller with an infectious sense of humor. He joined the Navy and left just as Cesar joined. For a time, when Cesar himself left the service, the three again reunited for a time in Crescent City, California, to work in the lumber mills. But then Manuel was off again, a rolling-stone wayfarer on the look for action. At the Mexican border he repeatedly found himself in trouble—assault, auto theft, and, finally, dealing marijuana, an offense that landed him in federal prison for nearly two years.

When he regained his freedom, he took an honest job as a car salesman in San Diego. During a Fourth of July holiday, Manuel visited Cesar in Delano. It was then that Cesar, determined to start a farm workers movement, convinced a reluctant Manuel to quit the car business, move to Delano, and join the improbable organizing effort.

It was Manuel, in September 1962, who found and rented the abandoned theater in Fresno for the first convention that brought nearly 300 workers to create the National Farm Workers Association (NFWA). They adopted a union motto: *Viva la Causa!* or "Long Live the Cause!" They also waved a new flag sewn by Manuel bearing the organizational symbol—an Aztec eagle, emblematic of pride and dignity. A white circle in the flag signified the hopes and aspirations of the farm laborers; the black represented the plight of the workers; and the red background stood for the hard work and sacrifice that the union members would have to give. When they showed off the flag at the meeting, Manuel leaped to his feet and shouted, "When that damn eagle flies, the problems of the farm workers will be solved" (Altman 1994, 64). The union created a newspaper it called *El Malcriado* (the unruly one). The name could have applied to Manuel Chavez.

Although Manuel moved in and out of Delano, sometimes for months at a time, he participated in most of the strike and boycott actions that made national news. Much of the time he lived near the Mexican border, acting as a kind of liaison between Cesar, Mexican unions, and government officials. Although some of Cesar's organizers regarded Manuel as something of a thug, Cesar greatly appreciated his native abilities and valued him deeply not only as family but as a helpmate in La Causa. Manuel kept Cesar informed about all sorts of labor-management issues dealing with farm laborers near and across the border and about any issues that threatened to give the United Farm Workers (UFW) problems.

In the early 1970s, Manuel traveled to a number of locations outside California where the union was beginning to make an impact. In Florida, where the sugar, citrus, and watermelon agricultural industries still had a feeling of the old plantation days and where farm workers, mostly blacks, were in virtual slavery, Manuel and other organizers, especially Eliseo Medina, made an impact. They first targeted Minute Maid orange juice, a subsidiary of Coca-Cola, an international organization that did not welcome negative publicity. In the spring of 1972, the UFW became a certified union for the Coca-Cola Minute Maid's 1,200 harvesters.

In October 1973 in San Luis, Arizona, near Yuma where Cesar was born, nearly 1,500 lemon pickers led by UFW organizers left the fields protesting low wages and poor working conditions. As growers tried to bring in scab labor from Mexico, the UFW, led by Manuel, set up a 600-man Lemon Striker Border Patrol to cajole and threaten illegal immigrants against crossing the border. At some of the usual border crossings, the patrol stationed men as close as 100 yards apart around the clock. Sometimes, the cajoling and threatening turned ugly and violent.

The UFW, under Manuel's direction, was thus running a vigilante operation to prevent illegal immigration, not a suitable or pleasant image for an organization devoted to helping poor Mexican-born farm workers. Although recoiling from the rumors of violent actions on behalf of his own union members, Cesar Chavez nevertheless did not stop the operation on the border. Imported scab labor was placing the UFW in a fight for its existence. The scab laborers themselves were being exploited by the growers with low pay and horrendous working conditions. Chavez pleaded with the U.S. Immigration and Naturalization Service (INS), the U.S. Border Patrol, and Mexican officials to stop the importation of illegal immigrants. The flow of scab labor continued. Manuel then took over. Much of the traffic stopped, at least during the time the Lemon Striker Border Patrol was on the scene.

Manuel Chavez died on May 30, 1999, about six years after the death of his cousin. He was 73. UFW President Rodriguez said of Manuel: "He and Cesar did the impossible. They built the organization for poor people that stands as a tribute to their work" ("Manuel Chavez . . . " 1999).

Further Reading

Altman, Linda. 1994. *Migrant Farm Workers: The Temporary People*. New York: Franklin Watts.

Bardacke, Frank. 2011. *Trampling Out the Vintage: Cesar Chavez and the Two Souls of the United Farm Workers*. New York: Verso.

"The Desert Strike: Dispute Enters Seventh Week."1974. *El Malcriado*, October 18, 1.

Griswold del Castillo, Richard, and Richard Garcia. 1995. *Cesar Chavez: A Triumph of Spirit*. Norman: University of Oklahoma Press.

Levy, Jacques. 2007. *Cesar Chavez: Autobiography of La Causa*. Minneapolis, University of Minnesota Press.

"Manuel Chavez: Older Brother of Late UFW Cesar Chavez Dies after Battle with Pancreatic Cancer." 1999. UFW Press Release, May 31. http://www.ufw.org/_board.php ?mode=view&b_code=news_press&b_no=694.

Ybarra, Richard. 2010. "Quien Era Cesar Chavez?" *La Voz*, April, 5. http://www .lavoznewspapers.com/La_Voz_de_Austin_April__2010.pdf.

Chavez, Richard

When his older brother, Cesar, began a quest to form a union of farm workers and a drive for social justice, Richard Chavez also made La Causa his own life's work. Born on November 12, 1929, in Yuma, Arizona, Richard Estrada Chavez, like his brother, experienced early on in his life working long days in the sweltering harvest fields, the relentless drudgery, the indignities, and the dawning realization that his life seemed destined for limitations rather than promise. From one town to another, he followed his family to California's rich agricultural fields and vineyards. He spent short periods of time in one school after another. Nevertheless, from his parents, Librado and Juana Chavez, he gained a strong family bond, a sense of self-respect, and a religious duty of charity for those in need.

Later, Chavez worked in lumber mills in California and became a skilled carpenter. He entered a carpenter's union apprenticeship program in San Jose and worked as a framer building suburban housing tracks before moving to Delano, California. There, he worked on both commercial and residential projects, including schools and freeway overpasses.

In 1952, he became president of the local chapter of the Community Service Organization (CSO), the same organization in which Cesar, Dolores Huerta, and others learned the community organizing techniques that would serve them in their work establishing the United Farm Workers (UFW).

When Cesar made Delano the headquarters of the infant union, Richard, while continuing to work as a carpenter building schools and homes, began to donate his free time to his brother's efforts.

In 1962, shortly after the formation of the union, Richard helped design the iconic black Aztec eagle that came to symbolize the UFW on flags and union labels. In 1963, Richard mortgaged his home for $3,700 to help the union establish a small credit union to make loans to members who formerly had been spurned by banks or preyed on by unsavory loan shysters.

In 1966, at the urgent request of Cesar during the early days of the union's first major grape strike, Richard quit his relatively prosperous outside work and committed himself as a full-time member of the farm worker movement. He quipped later that he was Cesar's most reluctant recruit.

When the infant union moved its headquarters to an area west of Delano they named Forty Acres, it was Richard Chavez who led the building of many of the offices, clinics, and service centers. He cleared the land, dug a well for the complex, and planned and helped construct most of the structures on the property. At one of the corners of the Forty Acres complex he erected a large cross; he constructed it out of telephone poles.

In 1966, Chavez became the first director of the National Farm Workers Service Center. The center, later known as the Cesar Chavez Foundation, helps build affordable housing for farm workers and operates Radio Campesina, a radio station heard in parts of Arizona, California, and the state of Washington.

During the grape strike against DiGiorgio Corporation in 1967, Cesar decided on a new picketing tactic, one that would help defuse the growing hostility between the men, women, and children on the picket lines and law authorities. He asked Richard to construct an altar that could be placed on the back of a pickup truck. The union thus held prayer services at labor rallies, a move that tapped into the religious nature of the movement and also flustered their opponents anxious to break up the gatherings at strike sites.

From 1972 to 1984, he served as one of the vice presidents of the union and participated in numerous negotiations, helped administer collective bargaining agreements, and helped direct grape and lettuce boycotts. In Detroit in 1973, Chavez turned an unorganized and floundering boycott into an effective volunteer force. In eight months' work, the boycotters convinced numerous chain stores to stop handling grapes and turned a nine-picket-line operation into one that amassed volunteers in over 60 locations. A year later, Chavez was in New York City, helping administer the grape boycott in that city.

In 1981, he headed the union's negotiations department that handled 130 contracts affecting about 30,000 members.

Richard Chavez was not reluctant to give advice to his brother. When the union moved its headquarters to the more isolated La Paz, California, Richard warned that the leadership would become more removed from the workers and less in touch with their needs. It was, unfortunately for the UFW, a prophecy fulfilled.

In 1983, Chavez retired from his full-time work with the union to resume his career in building, but he stayed active in the Cesar Chavez Foundation and the Dolores Huerta Foundation. He was Huerta's domestic partner for over 40 years. Together, they had four children as well as 13 other children from previous marriages.

In 1993, after Cesar's death, Richard built the simple pine coffin that carried his brother to rest in La Paz. At the funeral, a short-handled hoe was placed on top. It was through the work of the union that the dreaded tool, which Cesar, Richard, and thousands of farm workers had been forced to use, had been outlawed.

On Cesar Chavez Day in March 2010, Richard traveled to Washington, DC, with UFW president Arturo Rodriguez, Dolores Huerta, and other union and family members. At the White House, they met President Barack Obama. In February 2011, Forty Acres was designated a national historic landmark. Richard stood next to U.S. Secretary of the Interior Ken Salazar at the formal dedication. Chavez passed away a few months later in Bakersfield, California, on July 27, 2011. His funeral was held at Forty Acres.

On Chavez's passing, President Obama released a statement from the White House on July 28, 2011:

> Throughout his years of service, Richard fought for basic labor rights but also worked to improve the quality of life for countless farm workers. And beyond his work, Richard was a family man. I was honored to have Richard visit the Oval Office last year on Cesar Chavez Day with other family members, and will never forget the stories they shared. Richard understood that the struggle for a more perfect union and a better life for all America's workers didn't end with any particular victory or defeat, but instead required a commitment to getting up every single day to keep at it. ("President Obama . . .")

Further Reading

Bardacke, Frank. 2011. *Trampling Out the Vintage: Cesar Chavez and the Two Souls of the United Farm Workers*. New York: Verso.

Ferriss, Susan, and Ricardo Sandoval. 1997. *The Fight in the Fields: Cesar Chavez and the Farmworkers Movement*. New York: Harcourt Brace & Company.

Griswold del Castillo, Richard, and Richard Garcia. 1997. *Cesar Chavez: A Triumph of Spirit*. Norman: University of Oklahoma Press.

Levy, Jacques. 2007. *Cesar Chavez: Autobiography of La Causa*. Minneapolis: University of Minnesota Press.

"President Obama Statement on the Passing of Richard Estrada Chavez." July 28, 2011. http://www.whitehouse.gov/the-press-office/2011/07/28/president-obama-statement-passing-richard-estrada-chavez.

Chicano Movement

The 1960s were a time of the burgeoning civil rights movement and its protest marches, its beatings and jailing of protestors, and its violent clashes in the streets but also with its steadily growing support; a time of great social and political divide over the escalating and deadly war in Vietnam; a time rocked by assassinations. It was also a time that witnessed a drive to secure social and political justice on behalf of Mexican Americans. This was called the Chicano movement.

Most scholarly studies trace the derivation of the word *chicano* to the early 1900s, when it was associated in the American public's mind with poor, unskilled, uneducated, backward immigrants from Mexico who were considered no more than tramps or bandits. In the 1960s, the word took on a totally different aspect. The word came to signify to Mexican Americans a rejection of the discrimination meted out to their ancestors; it was now a word of cultural and ethnic pride, a harkening back to their ancient Aztec past, and an emblem of the determination of those in the movement to secure their rights, liberties, and equal opportunity in American society. Cesar Chavez's efforts toward creating a farm workers union, although not strictly part of the Chicano movement, became one of the rallying cries for those individuals of Mexican descent who now demanded liberation, dignity, and social justice.

Jose Gutierrez of Texas and Rodolfo "Corky" Gonzales, leaders of the Raza Unida Party, a dominant organization in the Chicano movement, at a national convention in El Paso, September 4, 1972. For many Chicano movement leaders, Cesar Chavez was an inspirational figure. (AP Photo/Fred Kaufman)

In New Mexico in 1963, Reies Lopez Tijerina, a former preacher and head of a commune, founded the Alianza Federal de Mercedes Libres, a group dedicated to an improbable fight to reclaim Spanish and Mexican land grants held by Mexicans and Indians before the U.S.-Mexican War. His militant organization led marches, started a newspaper, and later, in its quest to claim a part of a national forest reserve for Mexican American inheritance, invaded and occupied a courthouse, inflicting a gunshot wound on a deputy sheriff—an action that led to Tijerina's incarceration. His movement, quixotic and hopeless, nevertheless gained much notice and support among many Mexicans and Mexican Americans across the Southwest.

In Denver, Colorado, in 1965, during the period in which Cesar Chavez was launching a major strike of grape growers in the area around Delano, California, Rodolfo (Corky) Gonzales, an ex-prizefighter, wrote an epic poem called *I Am Joaquin/Yo Soy Joaquin*, in which he eloquently spoke about the historical struggles faced by Mexican Americans in the United States. In the mid-1960s, he founded an urban civil rights and cultural movement called the Crusade for Justice. Gonzales was also an organizer of the Annual Chicano Youth Liberation Conference, which brought together large numbers of Chicano youth from throughout the United States and provided them with opportunities to express their views on self-determination. The first conference in March 1969 produced a document, "El Plan Espiritual de Aztlan (The Spiritual Plan of Aztlan)," which developed the concept of ethnic nationalism and self-determination in the struggle for Chicano liberation.

In 1967, in San Antonio, Texas, Jose Angel Gutierrez, while a student at St. Mary's University, cofounded the Mexican American Youth Organization (MAYO), an activist group dedicated to inspiring militant affirmation of the rights of Mexican Americans, to attacking discrimination in the schools and in local and state government, and to developing a political agenda. In 1970, Gutierrez and other MAYO members organized a political drive in Crystal City, Texas, and nearby towns that successfully ran candidates in local elections. They christened a political party called La Raza Unida (The United People) that two years later convened more than 1,000 delegates at a national convention. Gutierrez was named party chairman. The party was later outlawed by the Texas legislature. Gutierrez himself often made virulently anti-Anglo attacks.

In 1966, in East Los Angeles, David Sanchez and other Chicanos founded the Young Citizens for Community Action. As its members began donning brown berets, the organization became popularly known by their hats. The Brown Berets were established as a group whose main function was to address social problems such as police brutality and the lack of social programs for activities among Latinos. By September, the group had opened chapters in cities across the country. They quickly attained a militant aura even though their aim was to prevent violence against Latinos. In 1969, the Brown Berets produced a newspaper called *La Causa*, the same rallying cry Cesar Chavez and his UFW members had used for a number of years.

Throughout the late 1960s and early 1970s, the Chicano Movement, inspired by its various groups, worked to increase ethnic pride and labor activism and sought to remedy, through social and political action, the educational and community needs of Latinos. The movement produced a new generation of activists and leaders who brought to national attention a variety of issues vital to the Mexican American community.

As Cesar Chavez often pointed out, his labor union and his crusade in behalf of farm workers was not, as such, a Chicano movement. From the beginning his work included Filipinos, blacks, and other minorities—laborers who suffered under oppression and in whose behalf Chavez sought to mobilize their strength, energy, and most importantly their power to change the conditions under which were forced to work. And many of his closest supporters and workers were whites—ministers, lawyers, student activists, community organizers, and others. Indeed, Chavez rejected the attacks on whites as exemplifying the same kind of racism that had been targeted toward Mexicans and other minorities. "When La Raza means or implies racism we don't support it," he said. "But if it means our struggle, our dignity, or our cultural roots, then we're for it" (Levy 2007, 123).

And so one of the heroes of the Chicano movement was Chavez. His own drive for social justice for farm workers, steeped in Mexican American culture, with the symbol of the Aztec eagle on its flag, speaking to the rights of ethnic minorities and demonstrating the power of community and political organization, stood as a towering symbol. The Chicano movement's supporters saw in Chavez's efforts for farm workers a deep measure of pride in being a Mexican American.

Further Reading

Garza, Humberto. 2012. *Organizing the Chicano Movement: The Story of CSO*. Kindle Edition. BookBaby.

Griswold del Castillo, Richard, and Richard Garcia. 1995. *Cesar Chavez: A Triumph of Spirit*. Norman: University of Oklahoma Press.

Levy, Jacques. 2007. *Cesar Chavez: Autobiography of La Causa*. Minneapolis: University of Minnesota Press.

Lopez, Ian. 2004. *Racism on Trial: The Chicano Fight for Justice*. Cambridge, MA: Belknap Press.

Rosales, Francisco. 1997. *Chicano! The History of the Mexican American Civil Rights Movement*. Houston, TX: Arte Publico Press.

Steiner, Sam. 1970. *La Raza: The Mexican Americans*. New York: Harper.

Coachella Strike, 1973

In 1973, the lush Coachella Valley, southeast of Los Angeles from the San Bernadino Mountains to the Salton Sea, became a battleground of protest and violence, a showdown between Cesar Chavez's union of farm workers and the Teamsters Union over contracts with the many growers who farmed the region. In this rich desert agricultural region with its robust harvest fields of grapes, avocados, date palms, grapefruit, melons, sweet corn, peppers, and other products, Chavez had been able to make progress in the late 1960s with strikes and boycotts that paved the way for over 30 contracts between his union and the growers. Now, however, those contracts had reached their end and, once again, the United Farm Workers (UFW) had to fight the increasingly aggressive Teamsters, who were determined to wipe out Chavez's union and take over the unionization of California's farm workers despite earlier jurisdictional agreements between the two unions.

The Teamsters, led by its president Frank Fitzsimmons, now had friends in high places. It had been the only major union to support Richard Nixon his 1968 campaign for president, and now Nixon's team in the White House was eager to help out the Teamsters in its battle in California against the UFW, a union, Fitzsimmons charged, that was run by revolutionaries and radicals. In 1972, Charles Colson, one of Nixon's advisors, sent a memo to several federal departments emphasizing the administration's desire that the Teamsters prevail in their struggle with Chavez. "The Teamsters Union is now organizing in the area," he wrote, "and will probably sign up most of the grape growers this coming spring and they will need our support against the UFW" (Ferris and Sandoval 1977, 180–81).

In mid-April, 1973, the contracts with the UFW expired, and only two growers decided to renew those contracts. One of the growers who re-signed with Chavez was Keene Lersen. In the late 1960s, Lersen had been one of the spokesmen for the growers and had given speeches around the country maintaining that the workers did not actually want a union. Finally persuaded to allow a vote at his farm, the workers proved him wrong by a whopping vote of 78 to 2. Lersen accepted a contract in the 1960s and did not join the others in abandoning the UFW in 1973.

Although almost all of the growers and the Teamsters insisted that the workers did not support the UFW, they would not allow a vote. Monsignor. George Higgins, a consultant to the U.S. Bishops' Committee on Farm Labor, led a delegation of 25 church and civic leaders into 31 fields to get their own sense of the wishes of the workers. Their poll results: 795 favored the UFW; 80 favored the Teamsters; 78 wanted no union. But polls mattered little. There would be no elections.

Bitter over the audacious move by the Teamsters in reneging on the earlier jurisdictional agreements and angered by the growers who eagerly and quickly signed sweetheart deals with the Teamsters that provided far less benefits to the farm workers, Chavez decided once again to launch a series of strikes. Supported by financial aid from the AFL-CIO, approximately 10,000 farm workers walked out of the fields.

Shortly after the strike began, 19-year-old Alicia Uribe and a number of picketers were waving their UFW flags with its Aztec eagle when a truck pulled alongside, driven by a plump man wielding a .38. He swerved the pickup inches from the picketers, spewing sand in their faces. Right behind the pickup, four men in a white sedan nearly ran over some of the picketers, and one of the men reached outside from the back window of the car and smashed a set of brass knuckles into the face of Uribe, fracturing her face. The Teamsters and its thugs had sent a message.

They would soon send many more such messages. Soon, a shirtless, growling Teamster enforcer was much obliged to have his picture taken by news photographers as he stomped on an effigy of Chavez. On one day in June, a group of Teamsters charged into a picket line along an asparagus field and chased down strikers with pipes, tire irons, and sticks. One thug, called "Cat Man," dragged down a 14-year-old boy and whipped him with a stick. Five UFW members were hospitalized; 20 others were treated and released. On another occasion, a 300-pound Teamster goon walked into a restaurant where a priest who supported the UFW was eating and broke his nose.

With California government officials and local law enforcement clearly united against the UFW and its strikers, many were arrested or beaten. Throughout the summer, local judges, with close personal and political ties to the growers, issued injunctions limiting legitimate strike activity. On April 20, 1973, for example, 135 picketers were arrested for violating a court injunction and sent to jail. One of those arrested was Linda Chavez, Cesar's daughter.

In late June 1973, two cars drove next to a trailer in which Francisco Campos lived with his wife and young daughter, and the cars' occupants burned down the trailer. Fortunately the family survived. Campos, who had joined the UFW a few months earlier, told investigators that the Teamsters had warned him that they were going to burn down his home if he did not back off his strike activities. They stuck to their word. He stuck to his commitment to La Causa. It was a mission, he said, that he would never abandon.

As the strikers followed the harvest season north, the assaults against them continued, aided by the local police and the legal system. In Fresno, the courts in four months issued many injunctions against the strikers and filled the jails with protestors, including 70 priests and nuns. In Lamont, protestors, surrounded by Kern County deputies and strikebreaker thugs hired by the company, kneeled down to pray. Undeterred, the police and goons charged the kneeling group, beat them with clubs, and sprayed mace.

In August the violence turned deadly. Two strike supporters—Nagi Daifullah and Juan de la Cruz—died of their injuries at the hands of Teamster thugs. Devastated by the deaths and with union funds depleted from the strike, Chavez decided once again to shift tactics. He would again take his case to the country with a boycott. Five hundred farm workers left in caravans of cars headed to destinations in every part of the nation.

Further Reading

Bardacke, Frank. 2011. *Trampling Out the Vintage: Cesar Chavez and the Two Souls of the United Farm Workers*. New York: Verso.

Chavez, Cesar. 1974. "A Letter from Cesar Chavez," *New York Review of Books, October 31*, http://www.nybooks,com/articles/9359.

Ferris, Susan, and Ricardo Sandoval. 1977. *The Fight in the Fields: Cesar Chavez and the Farmworkers Movement*. Harcourt Brace & Company.

Harris, David. 1973. "The Battle of Coachella Valley." *Rolling Stone*, September 13. http://www.farmworkermovement.org/essays/essays/MillerArchive/053%20The%20Battle%20of%20Coachella%20Valley.pdf.

Cohen, Jerry

In the tumultuous and challenging early years of the farm workers movement, Cesar Chavez needed a brilliant and imaginative lawyer to negotiate the treacherous legal pitfalls on the road to challenging California's agribusiness interests. He found his man: he was Jerry Cohen.

Born in Chicago in 1941, Cohen graduated from Amherst College in 1963. While earning a law degree from the University of California—Berkeley, he was an active participant in the free speech and anti–Vietnam War protests. He also spent a summer at the Meiklejohn Civil Liberties Library cataloguing civil rights cases, a job that further fueled his passion for progressive social movements.

His first year of legal practice was in McFarland, California, for California Rural Legal Assistance, Inc. (CRLA), a nonprofit services program that provided legal assistance for the state's rural poor. During his brief time with CRLA, Cohen saw firsthand some of the tactics being used against the new farm workers union organizers. One day in Bakersfield in early 1967, he saw Jim Drake and other protesters thrown off a parking lot. He struck up a conversation about laws protecting free speech.

Soon he met Chavez; the two were mutually impressed, and Cohen agreed to be the United Farm Workers (UFW) Organizing Committee's first general counsel. Aggressive and deft in arguing cases, he would play a critical role in the union's organizing drives, boycotts, and strikes in California and other agricultural states and, for the next 14 years, would use the law as an offensive weapon in fighting for the goals of the union and building its power. His work led the way not only in winning numerous lawsuits in behalf of the union but also in securing the passage of the most vital state law to protect farm workers in the nation. He also negotiated a jurisdictional accord with the Teamsters union, ending years of struggle between the two unions, and helped negotiate contracts with growers.

Tall, with a shock of unruly hair, Cohen took up his duties in 1967. He was 26 years old, and the infant union was in its sixth year. His new "law office" was the kitchen of a pink house in Delano rented by the union, in which Chavez's office was a back bedroom.

After hiring a few young assistants, Cohen led a legal team that tackled a daunting workload, especially defending picketers who were stopped with injunctions or even arrested. The lawyers and paralegals worked for small stipends, the paralegals acting almost as volunteers. All of them—from Cohen to his small staff—could have easily found other jobs if they had been interested in money; they were, instead, involved in a unique historical enterprise in the middle of California's harvest fields, and they relished the challenge.

Soon, Cohen and the legal team were not only fighting against the growers themselves and their experienced lawyers but also against a number of organizations that suddenly sprouted to fight off the union—Mothers Against Chavez, Agricultural Workers Freedom to Work Association, Mexican American Democrats for Republican Action, and others.

In 1969, for example, Fresno grape growers brought a lawsuit against the union arguing that the grape boycott violated antitrust law. Against the legal armies of several companies, the Chavez team fought for several years. The growers and their allies eventually abandoned the lawsuit.

By 1970, as the grape boycott continued to wreck the economic well-being of California growers, a number of those companies decided to deal with Chavez. Coachella grower Lionel Steinberg signed a contract with Chavez's union in early April. But it was the Giumarra company that was the biggest fish for the union. Until Giumarra came around, the victory was still not complete. In July, 1970, Chavez received a message that John Giumarra Jr. was ready to deal. Chavez and Cohen decided to put additional pressure by insisting that Giumarra bring with him to the meeting all the other local growers. He agreed. On the night of July 25, 1970, at 2:30 AM in room 44 of the Stardust Motel in Delano, Chavez and Cohen met with the Giumarras and other growers and signed contracts that brought an end to the table grape strike. Almost an entire industry was now under union contract.

Following the victory in the grape strike and boycott, the union immediately faced formidable pressure from lettuce growers that decided to sign contracts with the Teamsters Union to avoid the UFW. As the union fought off this new challenge with additional strikes and other labor actions, Cohen provided masterful legal guidance. He was responsible for negotiating a number of jurisdictional agreements between the union and the Teamsters. In 1973, Cohen and Chavez and a number of other union leaders went to see the movie *The Godfather* in Bakersfield. From that day forward, Cohen became known as "The Consigliere."

In 1975, with a Democratic administration at the helm in Sacramento, the UFW was ready to push for state legislation of a farm labor law. It was Jerry Cohen who worked closely with Governor Jerry Brown to craft the outlines of a bill that would represent a significant step in establishing bargaining rights for farm workers in California. Brown signed the Agricultural Labor Relations Act (ALRA) into law on June 4, 1975. The law protected the right of farm workers to unionize and boycott, guaranteed secret ballots in farm workers' elections, and provided for other legal remedies for farm workers never before codified.

The passage of the ALRA spurred an explosion of over 400 elections within months of its passage. The UFW won the majority of these elections, and, with the fine work of Cohen and his legal team, the union successfully defended the victories against litigation. Cohen handled a few appellate cases in the U.S. and California Supreme Courts.

After turmoil and personal disagreements and misunderstandings within the union in 1979 and 1980, Cohen resigned from the UFW. For a time, he stayed on to complete the negotiations on a few contracts. Later, he moved on to serve as legal counsel to a number of organizations and causes, especially Neighbor to Neighbor, founded by Fred Ross Jr., a group that organized key constituencies to pressure members of Congress on progressive legislation.

When Cohen looked back on his long service and friendship with Chavez, he said he preferred not to think of the times of the fractures within the union. Instead, he thought of the moments of triumphs, especially the night in 1970 when he and Chavez met in the early hours at Delano's Stardust Motel to work through contract arrangements with the Giumarras and other growers.

Further Reading

Bardacke, Frank. 2011. *Trampling Out the Vintage: Cesar Chavez and the Two Souls of the United Farm Workers*. New York: Verso.

Cohen, Jerry. 2008. "Gringo Justice: The United Farm Workers Union, 1967–1981." https://www.amherst.edu/media/view/314670/original/Gringojustice.pdf.

Gordon, Jennifer. 2006. "Law, Lawyers, and Labor: The United Farm Workers' Legal Strategy in the 1960s and 1970s and the Role of Law in Union Organizing Today."

Fordham University School of Law Legal Studies Research Series. https://www
.amherst.edu/media/view/69454/original/Law_Lawyers_Labor_Gordon.pdf.

Levy, Jacques. 2007. *Cesar Chavez: Autobiography of La Causa*, Minneapolis: University
of Minnesota Press.

Community Organizing

Community organizing is a grassroots strategy of converting one person at a
time, one after another after another, to a cause in order to gather together a
force strong enough to challenge entrenched power and authority. It comes
from the belief that societies must be transformed from within by mobilizing
individuals and communities. The origin of the term *community organizer* has
been credited to Saul Alinsky, who in 1936 cofounded in Chicago a reform
organization called the Back-of-the-Yards Neighborhood Council (BYNC). In
the South Side Irish-Catholic community near the famous Union Stockyards,
Alinsky's group was able to apply enough pressure on Chicago's city hall to
gain significant assistance in restoring a rapidly declining neighborhood. In
1939, aided by the Marshall Field Foundation, Alinsky established the Industrial Areas Foundation to help reform other declining urban neighborhoods.
His approach was to unite ordinary citizens around immediate grievances and
stir them to vigorous protest—to enable them to organize effectively for reform. He taught empowerment techniques to help them become effective in
bringing about solutions to their problems, whether those problems stemmed
from racial and religious bigotry, poverty, homelessness, or just the lack of
street lights in a slum area. One of Alinsky's recruits was Fred Ross, who
helped found the Community Service Organization (CSO). It was Ross who
recruited Cesar Chavez.

There had been other efforts and organizations that had helped poor, especially
immigrant, groups in many cities, especially in the late 1890s and the early twentieth century. Neighborhood improvement associations, various social betterment
movements, and settlement houses all attempted to close a growing income gap
between the middle and lower classes that accompanied increased industrializa-
tion. The organizations delivered services to neighborhoods including vocational
education, employment assistance, nursery care, and recreational programs. But
it was Alinsky who, through his work and writings, taught a generation of community organizers specific techniques to bring together individuals and groups to gain
power and change their lowly status in society.

Fred Ross and his grassroots CSO served the Mexican American community in
helping to fight discrimination in housing, employment, and education;

Community organizer Fred Ross with Dolores Huerta, cofounder of the United Farm Workers (UFW), at a press conference in Livingston, California, ca. 1975. Ross was a close mentor to both Huerta and Cesar Chavez. (Getty Images)

promoting self-reliance and political involvement; setting up citizenship classes; establishing self-help programs; and providing a variety of services including low-cost medical care and job referral. It fought for better education for the children of Mexican descent, worked for civil rights issues, and campaigned for voter registration.

Alinsky, Ross, and other community organizers saw their work as a war against evils that caused suffering among the powerless. It was a banding together of the oppressed and downtrodden to help themselves overcome poverty, discrimination, injustice, and other social ills that held them down. It was a crusade for fair play against the economic and political forces aligned against them.

When Chavez joined the CSO in the early 1950s, he learned the techniques of community organizing from one of the most vigorous and effective practitioners of the work—Ross himself, a master organizer. On a number of occasions, Chavez spoke about the work of community organizing, and he always centered his message on the quest for power—building the necessary commitment from the highest possible number of people to build political and economic strength to force change.

The basic building block of the organizer was the simple house meeting. One person invites five or six friends, neighbors, or relatives to his or her home for a motivational meeting to air grievances and discuss the value of joining together as an organization to fight for their rights. Those five or six in turn invite five or six others for other similar meetings. After this chain of meetings would come a large organizational meeting at which the entire group could not only gain a sense of commitment to the rest of the group but could also begin to lay out plans and strategy.

Chavez's single-minded purpose and drive was evident to all those small groups of people he gathered in the house meetings—the fellow workers he recruited from the fields, many of whom would stay with him and his cause for years. In the 1950s, Chavez organized over 20 new CSO chapters in such California towns as Madera and Hanford. During his years with the CSO, the young organizer met a whole range of public and private authorities who were involved with labor issues and social problems involving Mexican Americans. With worker after worker, Chavez intently listened to their problems. To him they came singly or in groups; for them he wrote letters to government agencies and intervened in misunderstandings with the police, with physicians, or with welfare departments. This was the grinding work of a community organizer, the kind of work that proved to be invaluable training for the enormous undertaking that lay ahead for him beginning in the early years of the 1960s as he began to organize a union of farm workers.

Chavez often said that the organizer had to work harder than anyone else in the group. That message had been told to him time and again by Fred Ross. Later, Chavez remembered the early days trying to build this organization of farm workers. "We had hundreds of house meetings," he said. "Sometimes 2 or 3 would come, sometimes one. Sometimes even the family that called the house meeting would not be there" ("Cesar Chavez Talks . . ."). It was from this beginning that Chavez and other organizers built the United Farm Workers (UFW).

Scores of organizers who learned strategies and tactics employed by the UFW went on to make important contributions to other progressive organizations. Eliseo Medina, for example, was elected in 2010 as the International Secretary-Treasurer of the 2.1-million-member Service Employees International Union (SEIU). The field of community organizing has produced a wealth of dedicated individuals committed to making a difference in the lives of those in need.

In 1985, for example, a 24-year-old graduate of Columbia University became a community organizer and first executive director of the Developing Communities Project (DCP) on Chicago's South Side. His name was Barack Obama.

Further Reading

Alinsky, Saul.1989. *Reveille for Radicals*. New York: Vintage.

Betten, Neil, and Michael J. Austin. 1990. *The Roots of Community Organizing, 1917–1939*. Philadelphia: Temple University Press.

"Cesar Chavez Talks about Organizing and the History of the NFWA." 1965. *The Movement*, December. http://www.farmworkermovement.com/essays/essays/MillerArchive/009%20Cesar%20Chavez%20Talks%20About%20Organizing.pdf.

Fisher, Robert, and Peter Romanofsky. 1981. *Community Organizing for Urban Social Change: A Historical Perspective*. Westport, CT: Greenwood Press.

Levy, Jacques. 2007. *Cesar Chavez: Autobiography of La Causa*. Minneapolis: University of Minnesota Press.

Ross, Fred. 1989. *Conquering Goliath: Cesar Chavez at the Beginning*. Keene, CA: El Taller Grafico Press.

Community Service Organization (CSO)

In 1947, community organizer Fred Ross and Ed Roybal, an executive with the California Tuberculosis Association and an aspiring political figure, formed the Community Service Organization (CSO). Established under the auspices and financial support of the Chicago-based Industrial Areas Foundation, headed by organizer Saul Alinsky, the CSO served the Mexican American community as a grassroots civil rights organization helping to fight discrimination in housing, employment, and education; promoting political involvement; setting up citizenship classes; and establishing self-help programs. One of its early major successes was a 1949 massive get-out-the-vote drive in Latino neighborhoods that not only gave the Mexican American community heightened political power but also propelled Roybal, CSO's first president, to an election victory to the Los Angeles City Council. He was later elected to the U.S. House of Representatives, the first Latino to serve in the U.S. Congress since 1879. For a young farm worker named Cesar Chavez, the CSO would open a world that would define a life's commitment.

It was Fred Ross who recruited Chavez into the CSO. After managing a camp for Dust Bowl migrants outside of Bakersfield, Ross began working with the Los Angeles office of the American Council for Race Relations. Alinsky, with his close ties with activists across the country, befriended Ross, and through the efforts of Ross and Roybal, the CSO by the early 1950s had become an increasingly effective organization. It established branches across the state. It began to draw in thousands of men and women determined to change the lives of Mexican American citizens for the better, individuals who would hold house meetings, carry on voter-registration drives, fight against police brutality, and bring to community groups the education and tools to battle for true citizenship.

In 1952, Ross met Chavez and persuaded the young farm worker to join the fight against injustice. "Fred did such a good job of explaining how poor people could build power," Chavez said later, "that I could even taste it. I could really feel it" (Meister n.d.).

Starting in San Jose, then north to Oakland and on to the San Joaquin Valley, young Chavez did what Ross had envisioned him doing—house by house, meeting by meeting, he emboldened Mexican Americans to buy in to the fact that they could assert themselves politically. He registered them to vote, helped them negotiate government bureaucracies on such issues as immigration status, and arranged, in some cases, to find volunteer legal counsel to defend them in court. From Madera to Bakersfield to Hanford, he signed up hundreds of individuals for the CSO.

Ross once wrote, "To carry on a hard-hitting program of civic action and militancy, you must have people who are of a certain temperament, who just cannot live with themselves and see injustice in front of them. They must go after it whenever they see it, no matter how much time it takes and no matter how many sleepless nights of worry" (Levy 2007, 95). In Chavez, Ross had found such a man.

In six years, Chavez organized CSO chapters in many parts of California. Meanwhile, the CSO organization, through the use of volunteers and some paid staffers, became an increasingly influential force in promoting self-reliance and providing a variety of services including low-cost medical care and job referral to communities that sorely needed support. It fought for better education for the children of Mexican descent, worked for civil rights issues, and encouraged voter registration.

In 1955, Ross recruited for the CSO a young, dynamic former school teacher named Dolores Huerta to run the Stockton chapter. Attractive and gregarious, Huerta would be an especially effective representative for CSO in face-to-face meetings with local government leaders and with potential donors. Huerta also took on lobbying efforts with members of the California legislature in Sacramento for such issues as the expansion of state disability assistance to agricultural workers. During her years with the CSO, Huerta would cross paths with Chavez and begin a friendship and working relationship that would, for Chavez, last a lifetime.

In the summer of 1958, Chavez was in Oxnard, a town north of Los Angeles, to establish a local office of the CSO in one of the leading citrus-growing areas of the state. In Oxnard, many of the farm workers in Chavez's house meetings asked what the CSO could do to prevent *braceros* from taking most of the jobs. The Bracero Program, the federally funded means by which workers from Mexico were brought to the United States for temporary work in the fields, afforded growers much financial advantage over hiring locals. In Oxnard, many Mexican American workers found themselves at farms greeted by signs saying "No Pickers Wanted." The braceros were being exploited with little pay, poor working conditions, and no benefits, and then were shipped back to Mexico after the growing seasons nearly penniless. And it was all at the expense of local workers who could not find jobs.

This was the issue—the Bracero Program—on which Chavez honed his sights. Braceros were supposed to be used only when there were no local laborers. The program, he began to demonstrate through group protests, was now a fraud being perpetrated on local Mexican Americans. He began to draw big crowds at the CSO meetings as local workers felt that this young organizer could perhaps make a difference in their lives. It was in Oxnard that Chavez began to see clearly in his mind the exciting potential of organizing the farm workers of California into a union. This was the way, he believed, they could challenge the Bracero Program and other impediments holding down the local laborers.

Encouraged by the backing of the 1,500 workers at Oxnard, he proposed to the CSO that they found a union. The proposal was turned down. The organization, the CSO Board of Directors insisted, was by nature a social service program, not a union. Disappointed by the decision but determined to move ahead with his idea, Chavez resigned from the CSO. He would move forward with his plans to start a farm workers union. The CSO would continue its laudable work for the Mexican American community.

For Chavez, the CSO had been a source of invaluable training that he took with him into his new venture. And it was the training ground for others who committed themselves to the union. Dolores Huerta joined him in his quest as the union's cofounder.

It was in the CSO that Chavez recruited Gilbert Padilla, a farm worker who would become one of the union's most successful organizers. It was also in the CSO that Juan Govea, a Santa Fe Railway worker, became an active member and encouraged his daughter, Jessica, to join the march toward justice for the farm workers. Jessica Govea, a "CSO kid," would also become a formidable leader of the union. In the history of the United Farm Workers (UFW), the CSO played a crucial part.

Further Reading

Bardacke, Frank. 2011. *Trampling Out the Vintage: Cesar Chavez and the Two Souls of the United Farm Workers*. New York: Verso.

Community Service Organization. n.d. "CSO Project." http://www.csoproject.org/Organizers.html#GP.

Dunne, John Gregory.1971. *Delano: The Story of the California Grape Strike*. Berkeley: University of California Press.

Griswold del Castillo, Richard, and Richard Garcia. 1995. *Cesar Chavez: A Triumph of Spirit*. Norman: University of Oklahoma Press.

Levy, Jacques. 2007. *Cesar Chavez: Autobiography of La Causa*. Minneapolis: University of Minnesota Press.

Meister, Dick. n.d. "A Trailblazing Organizer's Organizer." http://www.dickmeister.com/id73.html.

Ross, Fred. 1947. *Community Organization in Mexican-American Communities.* Los Angeles: American Council on Race Relations.

Smith, Sydney. 1987. *Grapes of Conflict.* Pasadena, CA: Hope Publishing House.

Constitutional Convention of United Farm Workers, 1973

On September 21, 1973, approximately 350 delegates gathered in Fresno, California, officially to establish through a constitutional convention the birth of the United Farm Workers of America, AFL-CIO (UFW). Chartered by the AFL-CIO in 1972, the union members met formally to approve a constitution and to elect a board and officers. But the meeting was also a celebratory gathering of those who had fought with such determination and against such overwhelming odds to form such a unique organization. The playwright Luis Valdez, who had joined the farm workers movement and created El Teatro Campesino (the Farmworkers Theater), once said that Cesar Chavez had created something from nothing. Indeed, here in Fresno, a decade after Chavez set out with no money and few friends to begin to organize oppressed and powerless laborers, the UFW would conduct the formal proceedings necessary to set administrative rules and delegate authority as part of the AFL-CIO. The delegates wore badges that read "I'm a delegate." They regarded them as badges of honor.

The convention opened during uncertain times for the union. There had been brutal days on the picket lines in the Coachella Valley, with scores of beatings, over 3,000 arrests of picketers, and the deaths of two workers in strike-related violence. Because of continued aggressive moves by the Teamsters and their political allies, many growers had turned away from Chavez and the farm workers movement for more favorable Teamster contracts. In a letter to the delegates before the convention, Chavez and Dolores Huerta, cofounder of the union, wrote: "It is a time when growers and their allies in Government and business are making a concerted and vicious effort to destroy our Union. But farm workers, arising from generations of suffering and exploitation, are more determined than ever before to have their Union" ("Convention Call . . .").

Despite the assaults against the union, its national boycott was hurting agribusiness interests. As the convention convened, Chavez hoped that the event would raise the spirits of hundreds of men and women who arrived in Fresno, many from boycott outposts far from California.

Welcoming the delegates in Fresno's cavernous convention center, Chavez stood before a giant mural depicting a violent assault on a union picket line.

Declaring that forces of evil were challenging the union's right to exist, Chavez attacked the Teamsters and their friends in Richard Nixon's Republican administration in Washington. He slowly read from the preamble to the new UFW constitution that began: "We, the Farm Workers of America, have tilled the soil, sown the seeds and harvested the crops. We have provided food in abundance for the people in the cities, the nation and world but have not had sufficient food for our children. . . . "

For three days the delegates, most of whom had never attended any kind of convention in their lives, sat through hours of official administrative business—the reading and ratification of the constitution, votes on various proposed resolutions, and the selection of officers. Unlike attendees at conventions held by most organizations, almost all of the UFW delegates stayed at the homes of local farm workers, not at hotels. The lack of hospitality suites and the other accoutrements of other conventions gave the Fresno gathering a proper sense of the organization itself. Instead, the delegates often chanted slogans, clapped, and listened attentively to the speeches of guests such as Senator Ted Kennedy of Massachusetts, whose brother Robert F. Kennedy had been so close to Chavez, Huerta, and the union before his tragic assassination after his victory in the Democratic presidential primary in California in 1968. They also sang and danced, especially to the music of folk singer Joan Baez, who attended the convention. And they prayed. The last session opened with an ecumenical mass in honor of the farm workers who had died since the beginning of La Causa.

Chavez, drinking glass after glass of carrot juice instead of his usual diet colas, presided over nearly all the sessions. The nine-member executive board selected by the delegates, almost all of whom were Latinos, also included Philip Vera Cruz, a Filipino who had worked with Chavez since the early days of the grape strike; Mack Lyons, a Texas-born African American organizer who had worked in boycotts for Chavez in New York City and Cleveland; and Marshall Ganz, son of a Brooklyn rabbi who had become one of Chavez's closest strategists and advisors.

The delegates passed numerous resolutions to unite the union in its struggle. They pledged to reject violence of any form in their aggressive quest for social justice. They pledged to fight for the unrestricted right to strike, boycott, and engage in other nonviolent means to ensure union recognition and collective bargaining rights. They even, at the suggestion of a member from the Texas delegation, voted to stamp out on the convention floor scab cigarettes that were being smoked by a few of the attendees—a gesture certain to warm the feelings of any AFL-CIO trade unionist.

After several days of meetings, Chavez seemed pleased with the convention. The organization of the UFW, he believed, was stronger, with a more clear understanding of the roles of its leadership and the members in the field. After the final proceedings had ended, Chavez boarded a plane for Washington, DC, to engage in talks with AFL-CIO officials. The rank and file of the UFW, along with others of its leaders, returned to their respective locations and duties to carry on the fight. They returned to convince American consumers and store owners that the only grapes and lettuce they should purchase should arrive in packing boxes bearing the union label of an Aztec eagle.

Further Reading

Bardacke, Frank.2011. *Trampling Out the Vintage: Cesar Chavez and the Two Souls of the United Farm Workers*. New York: Verso.

"Convention Call to the First Constitutional Convention." n.d. http://www.farmworkermovement .com/ufwarchives/DalzellArchive/UFW%201973%20Convention.pdf.

Levy, Jacques. 2007. *Cesar Chavez: Autobiography of La Causa*. Minneapolis: University of Minnesota Press.

Meister, Dick. 1973. "KPFW Commentary." September 26. http://farmworkermovement .com/ufwarchives/meister/37%20KPFA%20Septem%2026,%201973.pdf.

Pawel, Miriam. 2009. *The Union of Their Dreams: Power, Hope, and Struggle in Cesar Chavez's Farm Worker Movement*. New York: Bloomsbury.

Contract Signings, 1970

July 29, 1970, was a day of triumph for the farm workers union. The long Delano grape strike and boycott had begun five years earlier with Filipino and Mexican Americans working together. It had been launched with little resources beyond a steely determination to fight against the unjust treatment and unfair pay received by the workers for their grueling labor in the fields. It had now come to this. Nearly 30 grape growers, financially crippled by the nonviolent protest of the United Farm Workers Organizing Committee (UFWOC), headed by Cesar Chavez, gathered to sign contracts with the union in Delano. The union's supporters were poised for celebration.

A week earlier, Chavez had learned that several of the growers, fearing additional economic setbacks from the strike and boycott, had reluctantly decided to sit down with UFWOC officials to hammer out a possible agreement. At a Holiday Inn in Bakersfield, the union's negotiating team of Bill Kircher of the AFL-CIO, Chavez, Larry Itliong, Dolores Huerta, and lawyer Jerry Cohen began to face grower representatives, including John Giumarra Jr., son of the largest table grape grower, and their chief negotiator, Philip Feick. Accompanying the bargaining teams were prominent Catholic Church leaders of a special committee from the National Conference of Catholic Bishops—Bishop Joseph Donnelly, Monsignor George Higgins, and Monsignor Roger Mahoney.

As had been expected, this meeting, as others in the following days, was tense. Growers had never imagined themselves to be in this situation. The UFWOC submitted its proposals, which were countered at nearly every turn. After days of contentious parrying, the discussions moved from the hotel to a grammar school auditorium in Delano. With the preliminary negotiations completed, the talks now were led by John Giumarra Jr. and Cohen. On and on the discussions continued over a range of issues—wage proposals, working conditions at labor camps, election processes, safety regulations for farm workers against the ill effects of pesticide use, and even the possible unionization of companies producing lettuce and other crops. And then the discussions temporarily broke down.

But, unexpectedly, after a late-night call from the Giumarras, Chavez and Cohen met John Giumarra Jr. and also his father at the Stardust Motel in Delano. There, they hashed out a temporary agreement. Cohen and Chavez agreed to the tentative proposals only if the Giumarras were able to gain the support of all the other growers in the region. At another round of negotiations at the school, the growers were all there, ready to join the Giumarras in acceding to contracts with union.

The terms included an immediate base pay increase from $1.65 to $1.80 an hour. Growers would use a union hiring hall for the employment of all pickers. The two sides agreed to set up a committee made up of growers and unions representatives to regulate the use of pesticides. The employers would also contribute 10 cents for every hour worked to a union medical plan named after Robert F. Kennedy. And so the preliminaries had been completed. It was now July 29—signing day.

The word had spread. Union volunteers who had been manning picket lines and boycotting stores arrived in buses from Los Angeles and San Francisco. The UFWOC hall in Delano was soon jammed with spectators. Outside, hundreds of farm workers and volunteers mixed with newspaper and television reporters and camera crews, all jockeying to see any action.

Cesar's brother Richard recalled:

And there were . . . hundreds, thousands, outside . . . And you could see the growers coming in here. . . . And it was a really *great* moment. I mean . . . knowing that it was over. . . . Knowing that we had *successfully* beaten them, that we had successfully defeated them with the boycott, was a great feeling. They knew it, we knew it, and everybody knew it. So it was a great feeling. (National Park Service 2008)

Chavez, wearing an embroidered, high-collared Filipino shirt that he donned only on special occasions, spoke to those assembled about the sacrifices the workers and volunteers had made. He said that many in the long five-year struggle had lost most of their worldly possessions. But in that struggle, he said, they had found in themselves a dedication and commitment to service. He talked of the hopes of farm workers that, finally, through coordinated effort they could achieve social justice, dignity, and fair treatment.

Larry Itliong, the Filipino leader of the Agricultural Workers Organizing Committee (AWOC) that had first struck the grape growers in Delano and had persuaded Chavez to join in the fight, was now a top leader in the new farm workers union. He briefly recounted the struggle of Filipino farm workers who for decades had struggled to find a better life. This day, he said, was a new beginning.

After the 29 contracts were signed, the younger Giumarra sounded conciliatory —relieved, he said, that peace had come to the valley. "It has been a mutual victory," he said. "With the power of the union, the power of the people and the ability of the men in this valley to grow the finest crops in the world, we can get these products into the marketplace where they can bring a higher return to the farmers, so that they can sit down at some future time and negotiate to give a higher return to the workers" ("The Black Eagle Wins" 1970, 14).

For the first time, more than 70,000 farm workers had gained legal protection of their basic rights to fair wages and benefits, fair hiring systems, job security measures, and safe working environments. On this day, as they jubilantly sang *Nosotros venceremos*—the civil rights song of *We Shall Overcome*—and as they shouted the slogan of *Viva La Huelga*, they were asserting newly won respect.

Further Reading

"The Black Eagle Wins." 1970. *Time*, August 10, 14.

Day, Mark. 1971. *Forty Acres: Cesar Chavez and the Farm Workers*. New York: Praeger Publications.

Ferriss, Susan, and Ricardo Sandoval. 1997. *The Fight in the Fields: Cesar Chavez and the Farmworkers Movement*. New York: Harcourt Brace & Company.

Levy, Jacques. 2007. *Cesar Chavez: Autobiography of La Causa*. Minneapolis: University of Minnesota Press.

National Park Service. 2008. "National Historic Landmark Nomination: Forty Acres." http://www.nps.gov/nhl/designations/samples/CA/FortyAcres.pdf.

Pawel, Miriam. 2009. *The Union of Their Dreams: Power, Hope, and Struggle in Cesar Chavez's Farm Worker Movement*. New York: Bloomsbury Press.

Contreras, Rufino

On February 10, 1979, in the midst of a bitter strike against lettuce growers in the Imperial and Salinas Valleys, a 28-year-old member of the United Farm Workers

(UFW) named Rufino Contreras was shot to death at Mario Saikhon Farms, Inc., near Holtville, California. Rufino, who along with his father and brother had worked for many years at the Saikhon farm, was attempting to talk to scab laborers in the field as he was gunned down by security guards. With his death, he left his wife, Rosa, and two young children, Julio, age 5, and Nancy, age 4. The day before the shooting, Contreras had received papers informing him that he and his wife were now eligible for the union's medical insurance, and he had shown the papers to several of his friends. He was a proud union member.

Since the inception of the farm workers union in 1962, three others had lost their lives during the union's strike actions—Nan Freeman, a 19-year-old college student killed in a strike in Florida in 1972; Nagi Daifallah, a 24-year-old farm worker from Yemen killed in Kern County California in 1973; and Juan De La Cruz, age 60, a native of Mexico, killed on a UFW picket line near Arvin, California, in 1973. Now the killing of Contreras filled Cesar Chavez, who had preached non-violent social protest, not only with searing anger but also with dread that the deadly violence would somehow burst completely out of control, that his own union forces might, against all of his entreaties, retaliate in kind with unquestioned dire consequences. Nevertheless, the union would not retreat. Rufino Contreras's murder would become a union rallying cry for carrying on the drive for social justice.

The violence at the Saikhon farm erupted shortly before noon on the 24th day of the strike that had shut down much of the harvesting by Arizona and California growers, who produced about 40 percent of the nation's winter lettuce. Determined to fight off the demands of the striking farm workers, grower Mario Saikhon had brought in scores of mostly Filipino workers to act as scabs and had lined his ranch with armed guards to keep the striking workers out of the fields. On this day, the strikers who attempted to talk with the scabs were met not only with the usual bullying and thuggery common in strike actions but also with bullets flying in a crossfire from several angles. Hit in the face, Contreras collapsed face-down while his fellow workers scattered. When his father and brother attempted to reenter the field to help Contreras, the guards forced them away. It took an hour for the sheriff to arrive and for Contreras to be taken to the hospital. He died shortly thereafter.

Three security men from the Saikhon farm were taken into custody, arrested on suspicion of murder, and released on bail provided by Mario Saikhon. As word of the death of Contreras spread among the workers, they gathered at a place they called *El Hoyo* (the hole), a barren depression near the Mexican border where they would gather on normal workdays at 4 AM, climb into buses, and be driven to lettuce fields in the Imperial Valley. On this evening, 4,000 gathered. Black union flags waved; thousands of candles flickered in the twilight, and they held a vigil for their friend. This was only the first of several rallies held in honor of Contreras in the coming days. For the union members, the killing was a call for even more aggressive strike action against the growers and the law enforcement agencies that protected them.

On February 14, the Contreras family, joined by 9,000 farm workers and others including Governor Jerry Brown, attended the funeral north of Calexico. Chavez called February 10, 1979, "a day of infamy for farm workers. It was a day without hope. It was a day without joy. The sun didn't shine. The birds didn't sing. The rain didn't fall. Why was this such a day of evil? Because on this day greed and injustice struck down our brother, Rufino Contreras" (Chavez 1979).

The three men arrested on the day of the shooting were soon set free by a local judge. He claimed that there was a lack of evidence that any of the three had actually fired the bullet that killed Contreras. The family had feared that there would be no justice for Rufino Contreras. Their fears were justified.

Chavez later invited a group of religious and labor leaders to come to the Imperial Valley to investigate the events that had led to the tragedy. Led by Monsignor George Higgins of the U.S. Catholic Conference, the group met for two days with eyewitnesses and law enforcement officials. Local growers refused to meet. The members recommended a system of access by union representatives to the strikebreakers in the field and the elimination of all firearms and dogs by security forces as well as of the acts of violence against strikers that had escalated on February 10 to murder. Growers largely ignored the recommendations.

Nevertheless, the lettuce strike gained greater fervor after the death of Contreras. By the middle of the summer, as the harvest moved from the Imperial Valley into Salinas, the strikers took on the enemy with renewed purpose. Finally, many of the growers, financially devastated by the strike, decided to settle. If Contreras' death had not been avenged in the court, it had, to some degree, been avenged by the strike. As Chavez said in his eulogy of Contreras, "true wealth is not measured in money or status or power. It is measured in the legacy that we leave behind for those we love and those we inspire. In that sense Rufino is not dead. Wherever farm workers organize, stand up for their rights and strike for justice, Rufino Contreras is with them" (Chavez 1979).

Further Reading

Chavez, Cesar. 1979. "Eulogy for Rufino Contreras." February 14. http://www.ufw.org/_page.php?menu=research&inc=history/11.html.

Ferriss, Susan, and Ricardo Sandoval. 1997. *The Fight in the Fields: Cesar Chavez and the Farmworkers Movement.* New York: Harcourt Brace & Company.

Pawel, Miriam. 2009. *The Union of Their Dreams: Power, Hope, and Struggle in Cesar Chavez's Farm Worker Movement.* New York: Bloomsbury Press.

Shaw, Randy. 2008. *Beyond the Fields: Cesar Chavez, the UFW, and the Struggle for Justice in the 21st Century.* Berkeley: University of California Press.

"UFW Martyrs." n.d. http://www.ufw.org/pdf/Martyrs.pdf.

D

de la Cruz, Jessie

In 2003, the acclaimed author and radio broadcaster Studs Terkel, most noted for his oral histories compiled over decades, published his book *Hope Dies Last*. The theme of the book, as he explained in the introduction, came from a retired farm worker who recounted the days before Cesar Chavez founded the United Farm Workers (UFW). Jessie de la Cruz said to Terkel, "With us, there's a saying, '*La esperanza muere ultima*. Hope dies last.' You can't lose hope. If you lose hope, you lose everything." Terkel said that Jessie de la Cruz's words were a metaphor for much of the twentieth century (Terkel 2003, vii).

Jessie de la Cruz was born in Anaheim, California, in 1919. After her father left the family when she was very young and then her mother died of cancer a few years later, she lived with her grandparents. She and others in the extended family became migratory workers, traveling up and down the harvest fields of California and living in tents on mustard greens, rice, beans, and potatoes. She later remembered dragging a burlap sack and picking and cleaning cotton in a field near Bakersfield and remembered trying to avoid groups of white migrants who openly taunted Mexican Americans.

In 1938, at the age of 19, she married a farm worker. Arnold and Jessie de la Cruz would have six children. As they struggled to survive in unsanitary labor camps, with health care unavailable and little to eat, one baby daughter died.

In 1964, she and Arnold were at a house meeting in Fresno where she met Chavez. She later remembered his soft-spoken words to the group, spoken as if they were all part of a family. She listened to his message about the new farm workers movement that had started in Delano, one that sought higher wages, better working conditions, educational opportunities, and dignity for Mexican Americans. She soon joined the National Farm Workers Association (NFWA), and in 1967, after displaying much enthusiasm and a robust desire to convince others of the efficacy of the movement, she became a union organizer.

She energetically approached worker after worker, telling them about opportunities to join the movement. She held meetings at her house. She spoke before various groups, explaining the union's mission. She carried banners in protest marches and participated in boycott activities. When supporters of the growers and their thugs would call her names, she would shout, "Viva Cesar Chavez!"

She later remembered with much delight an incident at a Safeway store in Fresno where she and other union supporters were boycotting grapes. When three Anglos began taunting de la Cruz and her friends, chomping down grapes and then throwing some at the protestors, one of the men asked with much disdain and implying that the farm workers movement was un-American: "How do you say communist in Spanish?" Undaunted, de la Cruz answered "Ustedes ganaran." The three then began to chant at the protestors "Ustedes ganaran, ustedes ganaran, ustedes ganaran!" Little did they know that the words in English meant "You will win" ("Interview with Jessie de la Cruz" 2003).

Until joining the UFW, de la Cruz had not been involved with politics. She had never voted until 1968 when she registered and voted in the California Democratic primary election for Robert Kennedy in his ill-fated run for the presidency. With Chavez continually offering encouragement, she became a vigorous activist in voter registration drives and even a registrar.

Confident and gregarious, she was, by the late 1960s, running a union hiring hall, matching members of the UFW with requests from Christian Brothers Winery. She also became a fierce advocate in presenting arguments on behalf of social protest causes. At one of the state government hearings that led to the banning of the dreaded short-handled hoe (*el cortito*) in the fields of California, de la Cruz invited both state and federal officials to get out their seats, stand up and hold the tips of their shoes and then walk up and down the room and see how many times they could keep doing it. She told one grower that she had under such cruel, backbreaking conditions "measured his land inch by inch."

Jessie de la Cruz soon became highly visible in activities beyond the UFW. She spoke at city council meetings, became a strong advocate for bilingual education in the public schools, and voiced those beliefs before meetings of various school boards. She argued vigorously and passionately before a number of investigatory committees on the dangers of pesticides.

Soon she was on various boards. She even hosted her own local television program teaching farm workers how to communicate effectively in their visits to such places as shopping centers, government agencies, and doctors' offices. In 1972, she served as a delegate to the Democratic Party National Convention in Florida. It was the first time she had ever been out of the state of California.

In the late 1970s, Jessie and her husband, along with five other families, established a small, six-acre cooperative farm near Fresno where they grew and marketed cherry tomatoes. Later, she went on several speaking tours relating her early struggles as a farm worker, her experiences in cooperative land ownership, and the need for others in similar circumstances to band together to work toward social and economic justice.

She remained active in volunteer work for the UFW and continued to fight for farm worker causes and the rights of Mexican Americans. Her life remains an inspiration for young activists who see in her struggles and successes ways to challenge seemingly intractable and unfair economic and political systems.

Further Reading

Cantarow, Ellen, ed. 1993. "Jessie de la Cruz: The Battle for Farmworkers' Rights." In *Moving the Mountain: Women Working for Social Change*. New York: The Feminist Press at CUNY.

"Interview with Jessie de la Cruz." 2003. Farmworker Documentation Project, November 29–30. http://www.farmworkermovement.org/essays/essays/010%20De%20La%20Cruz_Jessie.pdf.

O'Farrell, Brigid, and Joyce Kornbluh, eds. 1996. *Rocking the Boat: Union Women's Voices*. New Brunswick, NJ: Rutgers University Press.

Rose, Margaret Eleanor. 1988. "Women in the United Farm Workers: A Study of Chicana and Mexicana Participation in a Labor Union, 1950 to 1980." Ph.D. dissertation, University of California, Los Angeles.

Soto, Gary. 2002. *Jessie de la Cruz: A Profile of a United Farm Worker*. New York: Persea Books.

Terkel, Studs. 2003. *Hope Dies Last: Keeping the Faith in Troubled Times*. New York: New Press.

DiGiorgio Fruit Corporation

When John Steinbeck published *The Grapes of Wrath* in 1939, a fictional portrayal of the indignities and hardships forced on farm workers by California's agribusiness interests, the name he used for one of the harshest growers was "Gregorio." Steinbeck was certainly using the fictitious name to represent the DiGiorgio Fruit Corporation, a major grower in the Delano, California, area. Founded in 1920 by Giuseppe DiGiorgio, an immigrant from Sicily, the company, located in the San Joaquin Valley, became the largest fruit-packing plant in the nation. Soon it ventured into the winery business, and by the late 1930s, it had also become a vast producer of grapes, plums, and pears. The company became a family conglomerate, with sons and nephews of the founder carrying on the work. It had been the target of early strikes by farm workers, including one in the late 1940s by Ernesto Galarza's National Farm Labor Union (NFLU), a union whose membership included Cesar Chavez's father. And now, in the spring of 1966, Chavez's own union, fresh off a victory in the grape strike when Schenley Industries signed a contract, squared off against DiGiorgio.

The eminent novelist and screenwriter John Gregory Dunne was in Delano during the days of the grape strike and later wrote a stirring account of the farm workers' struggle. As no other grower, Dunne recalled, DiGiorgio got under Chavez's skin. Some of Chavez's ire toward the company undoubtedly came from the

Robert DiGiorgio, president of DiGiorgio Fruit Corporation, shortly after he became president of the immense grape-growing conglomerate in 1962. In his bitter battles against Cesar Chavez's United Farm Workers (UFW), DiGiorgio would enlist the help of the Teamsters Union. Nevertheless, the company would suffer a humiliating defeat in 1966. (John Loengard/Time Life Pictures/ Getty Images)

earlier failures in strikes against the company in which DiGiorgio had used violent means to intimidate striking farm workers. But the disgust had also come from the few personal dealings he had had with the company's management and the derision in which DiGiorgio held Chavez's new union. Chavez said this about the company: "They're animals. You can't trust them. The other growers tell you something and you can be fairly sure they'll do it. Not DiGiorgio" (Dunne 1971, 140). Chavez braced to take them on.

After Schenley's capitulation to the union, DiGiorgio's leadership decided on a strategy. They would announce to the public and to Chavez that they would agree to an election among their workers on whether they preferred a union. As Chavez expected, the gesture was not what it appeared to be on the surface. Instead, DiGiorgio turned to the International Brotherhood of Teamsters union. The Teamsters wanted to sign up new workers and would offer DiGiorgio more favorable terms than would the farm workers union. The company soon announced that they had held elections and that the workers wanted the Teamsters to represent them. The entire exercise was a fraud. After the union officials appealed to California Governor Pat Brown, the American Arbitration Association was asked by state officials to undertake an investigation. The so-called election was voided, and a new election was set for August 30, 1966.

The action in the field leading up to the election turned especially ugly as Teamster heavies, swinging clubs and carrying pistols, tried to enforce their will along picket lines. Chavez responded with a unique, nonviolent counterattack that included a small Catholic shrine erected on the back of his pickup truck. As workers in the field were lured to the truck for prayers, the United Farm Workers Organizing Committee (UFWOC) did some electioneering. Teamster thugs found it awkward to attack workers praying at the shrine.

Chavez also managed to convince some of the workers still employed at DiGiorgio to strike from within—to instigate slowdowns, or what workers called "turtle plans" (*planes de tortuga)*. He also managed to develop an inside network of a few informers among DiGiorgio's foremen who would relay information to the strikers. Nevertheless, the brutality increased on the lines. At one point, when a number of union members had been attacked, Chavez tried to intervene at a DiGiorgio field at Borrego Springs, only to be arrested and briefly jailed by local police.

Chavez ratcheted up the campaign against the company by instituting a boycott aimed at such DiGiorgio products as TreeSweet brand juices and S&W canned foods. From new student recruits to clergymen and farm worker leaders, picketers soon appeared in front of stores and warehouses at the company's headquarters in San Francisco and at retail outlets in other cities. This was not the kind of opponent that the company had faced over the years. Chavez later commented: "They met with a very different brand of unionism when they met us" (Levy 2007, 222).

As the new election among workers at DiGiorgio approached, Chavez turned to Fred Ross, who had mentored the union leader in his days with the Community Service Organization (CSO), to head up the election drive. Ross employed a structured, coordinated system that became a model for future union election campaigns: frequent meetings, scrupulous accounting, and strict reporting from the various coordinators. The organizing team included union leaders, students, clergy, and farm workers.

Meanwhile, with the interference of the Teamsters Union severely clouding the potential of the new farm workers union to compete, Chavez and his lieutenants decided on another strategic move. William Kircher of the AFL-CIO, the national labor federation whose president, George Meany, detested the Teamsters, had been encouraging Chavez to initiate an official merger between the National Farm Workers Association (NFWA) and the Agricultural Workers Organizing Committee (AWOC), with whom they had joined in the Delano grape strike. The new union could then affiliate with the AFL-CIO and enjoy increased national support for its battles against the Teamsters. Although reluctant, Chavez decided this was the most sensible course. He persuaded other NFWA officials and leaders of the AWOC to merge, and they formed the UFWOC.

As election day approached, Chavez travelled to Chicago to attend the AFL-CIO Executive Council meeting at which the merger was formally approved. The UFWOC would now have the power of the AFL-CIO at its back. The merger gained national news. Senator Robert Kennedy sent his congratulations, as did officials of other unions.

Nevertheless, on election day eve, August 29, 1966, predictions for the UFWOC about the election were glum—from Las Vegas bookies to political pundits. But the meticulous campaign operation headed by Fred Ross and the tireless work of the union forces, Chavez hoped, might carry the day. As Teamster officials arrived in San Francisco in big limousines for the announcement of the results, Chavez sat by his phone awaiting a call from union cofounder Dolores Huerta. The news brought jubilance: the vote was 530–331 in favor of the UFWOC. In Delano they celebrated. For Fred Ross, the result was easy to explain. The Teamsters, he said, had underestimated their opponents: "They underestimated our willingness to work and to win" (Ganz 2009, 198).

Further Reading

Bardacke, Frank. 2011. *Trampling Out the Vintage*. New York: Verso.

Dunne, John Gregory. 1971. *Delano: The Story of the California Grape Strike*. Berkeley: University of California Press.

Ferriss, Susan, and Ricardo Sandoval. 1997. *The Fight in the Fields: Cesar Chavez and the Farmworkers Movement*. New York: Harcourt Brace & Company.

Ganz, Marshall. 2009. *Why David Sometimes Wins: Leadership, Organization, and Strategy in the California Farm Workers Movement*. New York: Oxford University Press.

Levy, Jacques. 2007. *Cesar Chavez: Autobiography of La Causa*. Minneapolis: University of Minnesota Press.

Matthiessen, Peter. 1969. *Sal Si Puedes (Escape If You Can): Cesar Chavez and the New American Revolution*. Berkeley: University of California Press.

Drake, Jim

From the earliest days of the farm workers movement, Cesar Chavez had at his side allies from the California Migrant Ministry (CMM), an organization dedicated to alleviating the lives of migratory workers. One of Chavez's closest advisors and confidants was Jim Drake, an ordained United Church of Christ minister.

Born on December 25, 1937, Drake grew up in Oklahoma and moved with his family to the Coachella Valley in California when he was 10 years old. After graduating from Occidental College and receiving his religious training from the Union Theological Seminary, Drake scrapped his plans of becoming a pastor for the National Park Service and instead, at the request of Chris Hartmire, leader of the CMM, joined the organization in 1962 and immediately made the cause of the farm workers movement his own.

In Porterfield, California, Drake founded a small farm worker association. After meeting Cesar Chavez, he merged his infant organization into that of the National Farm Worker Association (NFWA) in 1965.

Soon after joining Chavez, he became a trusted ally, helping the new organization weather daunting challenges of communication and fund raising. Early on, Drake did everything from distributing union fliers and newsletters to various communities to raising money to pay rent and buy food for strikers. He recruited union members. Over the next two decades, Drake took on numerous important responsibilities with the United Farm Workers (UFW) not only in California but also in Texas and Arizona while remaining formally connected with the Migrant Ministry.

Soon after the onset of the Delano grape strike, Drake was at the center of a union decision to launch a consumer boycott of Schenley Liquor, a prominent national company that used large quantities of California grapes. The goal was to educate consumers about the unfair working conditions in the San Joaquin Valley grape fields and to convince buyers, as a protest, to avoid purchasing any of the company's products, especially table wines.

Along with Mike Miller of the Student Nonviolent Coordinating Committee (SNCC), Drake spearheaded the boycott. Using such methods as aggressive leafleting, pledge cards, and picketing of stores that sold Schenley products, Drake and Miller pulled off a surprisingly effective attack plan that began to arouse serious concern in the company's corporate offices. The boycott tactic, along with other union actions, caused Schenley to recognize the NFWA and to sign a union contract.

The use of the boycott early in the farm workers movement convinced Chavez and other union leaders to use the tactic nationwide against grocery chains and other companies that used or sold nonunion grapes, lettuce, and other commodities. Under Drake's leadership, boycott workers enlisted the help of civil rights and other protest groups such as the Students for a Democratic Society, various union affiliates, and church organizations. They approached union, political, civic, and church leaders for endorsements as well as other figures in the world of entertainment. The boycotts became national causes.

Drake became a lead union organizer and senior strategist, a kind of ambassador at large, as Dolores Huerta once said. Tall, with a handlebar mustache, Drake was quiet and self-effacing but extraordinarily effective in devising tactics and coordinating union activities. He was a genial crusader helping to organize strikes, marches, fasts, and political activities. In 1971, he led a drive to organize grape workers in the Lodi area. He was often on the picket lines, especially in battles with the Teamsters Union. He worked in Arizona to help the union attempt to recall the state governor, Jack Williams, whose administration staunchly opposed the unionizing of farm workers.

A firm believer in nonviolence, Drake nevertheless sometimes found himself the target of assaults. He stood up to goons carrying shotguns. He was clubbed a number of times. During a strike in the Stockton, California, tomato fields, members of a right-wing "posse comitatus," a kind of vigilante mob, tackled Drake and tried to rip off his mustache by its roots. On another occasion, he permanently lost some of his hearing when a Teamster thug blew an electronic bullhorn into his ear as he tried to talk to farm workers.

In 1978, Drake left the UFW in the midst of disagreements and increasing fracturing of the organization. He took with him, however, his driving commitment to economic and social justice and the lessons and tactics he had learned in his long partnership and the leadership roles he experienced with Chavez and other colleagues in the farm workers movement. Like many other veteran UFW members, he continued to play a vital role in bringing to community organizing and to worthy causes new organizers who would carry on the spirit of the UFW.

In 1978, starting with a handful of experienced organizers who followed him from the UFW, and joined by a group of college students, many from Brown University, Drake moved to Mississippi to organize woodcutters, establishing a woodcutters association that engaged in strikes and various work actions to force companies to increase pay. Much like the UFW, the new association, the first interracial organization of the working poor in that state, established a credit union and a co-op to help members buy food, equipment, legal aid, and medical assistance.

In 1979, he moved to South Texas. Working with the Industrial Areas Foundation, he helped organize the Valley Interfaith Organization, a group that sought to improve the conditions for local Latinos. The organization worked to help those who lived in substandard housing known as *colonias*, which lacked both running water and plumbing.

In 1987, Drake organized South Bronx Churches, a coalition of more than 40 churches that joined forces to build 800 housing units and persuade the city to build a new high school, the Bronx Leadership Academy. He trained a generation of neighborhood activists in Harlem, Brooklyn, and the South Bronx to shift political power to their own communities.

In 1994, he helped form the Greater Boston Interfaith Organization (GBIO)—a regional coalition of 100 religious and community organizations. Drake passed away in September 2001 in Pittsfield, Massachusetts, still active in its work.

The mission of the GBIO is to "to coalesce, train, and organize the communities of Greater Boston across all religious, racial, ethnic, class and neighborhood lines for the public good. . . . to develop local leadership and organized power to fight for social justice. . . . We cross neighborhood, city, racial, religious, and class lines to find common ground and act on our faith and democratic values" (Greater Boston Interfaith Organization 2012). It is a mission that defined the life of Jim Drake.

Further Reading

Ganz, Marshall. 2009. *Why David Sometimes Wins: Leadership, Organization, and Strategy in the California Farm Worker Movement*. New York: Oxford Press.

Greater Boston Interfaith Organization. 2012. http://www.gbio.org/.

Griswold del Castillo, Richard, and Richard Garcia. 1995. *Cesar Chavez: A Triumph of Spirit*. Norman: University of Oklahoma Press.

Pawel, Miriam. 2009. *The Union of Their Dreams: Power, Hope, and Struggle in Cesar Chavez's Farm Worker Movement*. New York: Bloomsbury.

Smith, Sydney. 1987. *Grapes of Conflict*. Pasadena, CA: Hope Publishing House.

E

El Malcriado

The infant union of farm workers needed a newspaper to spread not only the word of its activities but also its message of fire and determination. They called it *El Malcriado*. Cesar Chavez explained that the term in English meant "malcontent" or "unruly one," an apt characterization of a movement that would not be tamed and would not remain docile but would challenge authority. *El Malcriado* would be the voice of the farm worker.

In preparing to launch the paper, Chavez selected in late 1964 a young activist named Bill Esher to head its production and distribution. Esher had attended Syracuse University for a couple of years before succumbing to the lure of social protest politics. Arriving in San Francisco, he worked for a time driving a bus for the Catholic worker movement that had a project in a farm labor community in Oakland. Later, Esher was hired by the administration of California Governor Pat Brown to take a job picking melons in Kern County as part of an effort to document wage and labor violations among farm workers. Wendy Goepel, who at that time was working for the Brown administration in Sacramento, hired Esher for the state job, and it was she who introduced him to Chavez. Both Esher and Goepel would become part of Chavez's farm worker movement.

In addition to Esher, Chavez persuaded Andy Zermeno, a talented young Chicano artist, to create a series of characters who would appear regularly in the paper and sometimes on its cover. Zermeno assembled a cast that in many ways resembled the characters that Luis Valdez would use in his Teatro Campesino, the farm workers theater company. There was "Don Sotaco," the humble and abused farm worker, a kind of Charlie Brown character who constantly drew the short end of the straw and whose tribulations were ones with which farm worker readers could identify. There was "Don Coyote," the slimy, devious labor contractor and field boss, ever loyal to the whims and wishes of the boss man, the grower. And there was the grower himself, "Patroncito," the fat, cigar-chomping, boot-wearing tyrant who owned the harvest fields.

Esher and Zermeno worked brilliantly together, exchanging information and ideas. Manuel "Fats" Sanchez served as the in-house photographer. With penetrating satire, salty humor, and information gleaned from tough, scrupulous research, *El Malcriado* became everything that Chavez had hoped it would be from the beginning—a publication that helped unite the farm worker community toward a common purpose. In addition to its spirited and aggressive reporting, it was also valuable in providing readers with information about new contracts, details of the health insurance plan, and other issues important in their lives.

Circulated throughout the agricultural valleys of California via a network of farm worker movement activists, the paper was originally printed only in Spanish, but an English edition was soon added. Offered by subscription and also sold in barrio stores for a dime, the list of subscribers gave the National Farm Workers Association a clear base of support in helping to organize. Within a year of its inception, the paper's circulation reached 3,000.

In the early days of the grape strike, *El Malcriado* printed Jack London's famous description of a scab laborer as a creature with a "corkscrew soul," a backbone of "jelly and glue," and, in place of a heart, "a tumor of rotten principles." When the Rev. David Havens of the California Migrant Ministry began to read the prose from a copy of the paper on a Delano street, he was hurried off to jail for disturbing the peace.

El Malcriado not only raised the spirits of farm workers and the ire of its targets; on some occasions it provoked action. Jimmy Hronis, a labor contractor notorious for cheating sugar-beet workers out of their pay, became the target of a state investigation after several stories about his nefarious dealings ran in the paper. After almost a year of court action, Hronis, caught lying during one of the hearings, was forced by California's labor commissioner to pay workers back the monies that he had defrauded from them.

In many of the issues, *El Malcriado* linked the farm workers movement to the peasant uprising during the Mexican Revolution. The paper ran woodcuts and ink drawings that the staff found in their research, and an early cover featured the figure of Emiliano Zapata, the champion of the underclasses and enemy of the serfdom under which they suffered. The paper ran such slogans from a half-century earlier as "The land, like the water and the air, should belong to the people," sayings that the union believed had currency in California in the 1960s.

El Malcriado also linked the civil rights movement and such figures as Martin Luther King Jr. with the struggles of the farm workers. A black Madonna and child appeared on one of the covers.

In 1966, Bill Esher moved on to other positions with the union and was replaced as editor by Doug Adair, a young activist who had been enrolled as a graduate student at the University of California—Berkeley when he joined Chavez and the movement. Adair had been in charge of much of the work on the English-language edition of the paper.

For the next several years, Adair, Peace Corps veteran David Fishlow, and Catholic priest Mark Day took responsibility for the paper, helped by an infusion of new assistants. At one point the paper had a circulation of over 10,000 copies. It continued its aggressive reporting, sometimes to the point of provoking lawsuits, which the legal team had to fend off. On some occasions, Chavez himself complained about the content that it was sometimes off-message. Yet *El Malcriado* lasted a full decade, finally replaced by other UFW publications in the mid-1970s. For the growing new union, it had indeed been a powerful voice of the farm worker.

Further Reading

El Malcriado. Farm Worker Documentation Project. http://www.farmworkermovement.us/ufwarchives/.

Ferriss, Susan, and Ricardo Sandoval. 1997. *The Fight in the Fields: Cesar Chavez and the Farmworkers Movement*. New York: Harcourt Brace & Company.

Frank. Bardacke. 2011. *Trampling Out the Vintage: Cesar Chavez and the Two Souls of the United Farm Workers*. New York: Verso.

F

Fasts

One of the portraits that hung in the small office of Cesar Chavez at his head-quarters in Delano was of Mohandas Gandhi, the leader of the Indian independence movement. One of Gandhi's expressions of nonviolent resistance to tyranny on behalf of civil rights and freedom was the use of the fast. Although hunger strikes and fasting had been used for hundreds of years around the world in various social and political conflicts, it was not a tactic familiar to American organizers attempting to build unions. In 1968, Chavez, fearful that the pressures of the strike breakers and goon squads assembled by the growers in the grape strike were beginning to erode the determination of the farm workers movement to maintain their nonviolent crusade, Chavez began a fast that would not only inspire his followers with renewed determination but would also help make the protest of farm workers in this small California town a national cause.

For Gandhi, physical abstinence was not only a spiritual and soulful expression of faith and determination but was also a tool given by God in times of apparent helplessness that could be used for political action. Gandhi used it on several occasions with great success, frustrating his bewildered enemies, who were uncertain how to respond.

Chavez was a man of strong religious belief. Many clergy across a variety of faiths were often deeply impressed not only by his daily devotional acts but also the manner in which he infused the farm worker movement with a sense of religious passion and symbolism. The 1966 peregrination to Sacramento, for example, ended on Easter with prayers and a procession under the banner of the Catholic icon Our Lady of Guadalupe. And now in early 1968, with reports of violence erupting among strikers and protestors, Chavez announced to assembled union members that he was beginning a fast.

The fast, he explained to those gathered in Delano at a meeting, would not be directed against the growers but would be an act of personal penance. It would emphasize the nature of the fight for social justice—spiritual, nonviolent, with a willingness to suffer for a greater cause. This was a sacrificial gesture, religious in nature, a way to bring the drive toward justice for the farm workers back into focus, to rededicate the movement, and to ward off any self-defeating acts of violence by the strikers.

Chavez's reaction to escalating violence was not totally surprising to those who knew well his instincts. This was what Gandhi had taught; it was what Gandhi himself had practiced. On February 14, 1968, Chavez stopped eating.

Soon, supporters began to pitch tents in the area to show support. Each night there was a Mass at the gas station at Forty Acres. Chavez took Communion each day. When some strikers began to question the wisdom of such an act, Cesar told his friends that the farm workers would, because of their faith, understand.

On February 26, two weeks after he had begun the fast, a weakened Chavez had to appear in a Bakersfield courthouse to face contempt-of-court charges from a previous incident in the strike. Hundreds of supporters gathered around their leader singing *De Colores*, an old Spanish hymn, and praying. Newspaper reporters and photographers strained to get a view of Chavez as he entered the courtroom. Quickly, the judge postponed the trial because of the possible mayhem. The charges were later dropped.

As far as generating publicity and support, the fast gained remarkable attention. From Martin Luther King Jr. and from Senator Robert Kennedy of New York, now in the race for president of the United States, came words of support.

Many questioned the fast from the beginning. For example, Dolores Huerta, who had helped Chavez found the union and who was in close contact with labor leaders around the country, later said many of them just could not understand what was going on. New York union men, she said, used to fighting off strike-breaking attacks with baseball bats, were puzzled by this union leader who was fighting back by refusing to eat.

Nevertheless, as the fast continued, most of farm workers, as Chavez had predicted, began to understand. And as news stories on radio, television, and in print daily reported bulletins from California about Chavez's condition, it was clear that the fast was becoming a dramatic organizing tool for the union. Letters and donations arrived in Delano. People across the country began voicing support for the farm workers.

Some of Chavez's friends became increasingly concerned about his health. As the days wore on, Helen Chavez was alarmed about his ebbing strength. Often, she would remind him that everything they were working toward—the union, the betterment of the lives of the farm workers, the demand for dignity toward Mexican American workers—would be jeopardized if he lost his health and perhaps his life.

For 21 days he fasted, losing about 35 pounds and drawing dire warnings from his doctor. On March 10, 1968, Chavez gave in to the entreaties and ended the fast.

A crowd of several thousand watched as Chavez, seated with his wife and mother, broke bread with Senator Kennedy, who had flown in for the event from a political dinner in Des Moines, Iowa. At an open-air Mass in Delano's Memorial Park, several priests and nuns distributed bread to the crowd. The Mass was ecumenical. A Jewish physician read a passage from the Old Testament, a Protestant minister followed with the second reading, and a Catholic priest read the third. At the end of the ceremony, although Chavez was too weak to read his speech, his friend and supporter Rev. James Drake read the words, "It is how we use our lives that determines what kind of men we are. . . . I am convinced that the truest act of courage, the strongest act of manliness, is to sacrifice ourselves for others in a totally nonviolent struggle for justice. To be a man is to suffer for others. God help us be men" (Griswold del Castillo and Garcia 1995, 76).

The fast garnered great attention for his union, gave it new political strength, and was instrumental in forging the coalition of labor and religious groups that led to the success of the grape boycott.

Chavez would fast again, most notably in 1972 for 24 days, and again in 1988, this time for 36 days. Fasts had worked for Gandhi; they also worked for Chavez.

Further Reading

Cohen, Jerry. 2008. "Gringo Justice: The United Farm Workers Union, 1967–1981." https://www.amherst.edu/media/view/314670/original/Gringojustice.pdf.

Day, Mark. 1971. *Forty Acres: Cesar Chavez and the Farm Workers*. New York: Praeger Publishers.

Dolores Huerta. n.d. Interview with Vincent Harding. Veterans of Hope Project. http://www.veteransofhope.org/show.php?vid=51&tid=42&sid=69.

Griswold del Castillo, Richard, and Richard Garcia. 1995. *Cesar Chavez: A Triumph of Spirit*. Norman: University of Oklahoma Press.

Smith, Sydney. 1987, *Grapes of Conflict*. Pasadena, CA: Hope Publishing House.

Federal Bureau of Investigation (FBI) Surveillance

In the mid-1960s, in the days of the Cold War, the Federal Bureau of Investigation (FBI), under the direction of J. Edgar Hoover, tracked with extreme diligence all reports of possible communist infiltration of the United States and its institutions. One of its targets became a young community organizer in the harvest fields of California. Could this Cesar Chavez be a subversive with anti-American schemes and connections?

In late October 1965, an informant telephoned Hoover at FBI headquarters in Washington suggesting that the table-grape strike in Delano, California, was possibly led by a number of individuals who were likely affiliated with communist groups or their fellow travelers. The informant passed along the names of Larry Itliong, a Filipino leader of a small union who had joined with a young organizer named Chavez and his partner, Dolores Huerta, of the Agricultural Workers Organizing Committee (AWOC) to foment a strike. The informant mentioned others, including David Havens, a member of the California Migrant Ministry (CMM). There was trouble brewing against the growers of southern California, and much of it might be at the hands of leftists intent on causing at the least mayhem, and at the worst subversive violence aimed at overthrowing the established order.

Soon FBI investigators arrived in Delano, and Chavez suddenly found himself in a car driven by an agent headed for a meeting that included members of the California Republican Central Committee. Chavez said later that in that meeting he did something that he had never before done in his life—shout back at Anglos. Suddenly, he said, the meeting became the talk of the Delano area. Everywhere he went, people asked whether he was a communist. A local newspaper story asked the same question. The FBI interrogation in 1965 was not the only confrontation Chavez had with FBI agents. It was also not the end of the agency's probe of all of the young leader's associates and connections. Year after year, through the presidencies of Lyndon Johnson, Richard Nixon, Gerald Ford, and Jimmy Carter, the shadowing of Chavez and the United Farm Workers (UFW) by Hoover's FBI continued.

Back in Washington, the FBI had created a file called COMINFIL (an acronym for "Communist Infiltration) to monitor antiwar activists, civil rights organizations, and other assorted groups tied to leftist organizations and causes. The information from the files on hundreds of groups and individuals was designed to protect against foreign attacks and infiltration; often, however, it became useful ammunition, in the hands of some political figures, to discredit their enemies.

And so the file on Cesar Chavez and the UFW began to fill up with reports, observations, telephone memoranda, tips and hunches, outright false charges, and aroused suspicions. This unlikely ragtag coalition emerging in California without money, power, or influence had to be, it seemed to many, the brainchild of a subversive front organization. There was, of course, the Saul Alinsky connection to Chavez, Huerta, Fred Ross, and others of the Community Service Organization (CSO). But however obnoxious Alinsky was to right-wing interests and corporate power, he was not a communist. What about his disciples and others?

The observations of dozens of field agents and informants, and numerous anonymous sources, not only from California but from other states and even from Mexico, poured into Washington relating to Chavez and the UFW. Eventually the dossier, which included materials furnished by other government agencies, grew to an astonishing bulk of over 1,500 pages.

Not-so-well-disguised FBI agents trailed along in the marches and hung around picket lines along the harvest fields or near boycott sites, and FBI information specialists checked out leads and compared notes in various files. Agents amassed a trove of information on individuals connected in almost any way with Chavez— their birthdates, addresses and telephone numbers, marriages, immigration status, criminal infractions, organizational memberships, and friends and acquaintances. They followed Chavez's daily routine, his travels and speeches and meetings.

They assembled daily reports from the field during marches. They were especially interested in his dealings with such civil rights groups as the Students for a Democratic Society, the Student Nonviolent Coordinating Committee, and the Congress of Racial Equality.

After all of this mammoth effort and expense and after a decade of intrepid snooping, the FBI had to conclude that Chavez and his supporters were not communists or Soviet spies or pro-Cuban plotters. Instead, they turned out to be farm workers and their families, students, priests, ministers, civil rights proponents, social workers, union members, liberal Democratic leaders, and others who saw a chance to help a struggle for justice. And as for Chavez, they found no subversive ties, no financial irregularities in the operation of the union, and no disloyalty, either to his country or in his personal life.

A totally one-sided investigation, the FBI shadowing of Chavez was meant for only one purpose—to discover any un-American activities that might be part of the UFW and its movement. There were no corresponding inquiries about the other side of the employer-labor divide—about the hiring of goons by growers to disrupt protest meetings, about inciting violence, about unfair labor practices, about civil rights violations, or about the corruption of local law enforcement by companies.

The last report in this formidable file, impressive in dead weight if not in revelation, was dated in 1975. There is not much threatening conspiracy in those pages—except to the status quo in farm worker rights and in the concerted efforts by dedicated workers and their supporters fighting for social justice.

Further Reading

ABC-CLIO. 2011. "FBI Surveillance of Cesar Chavez, File #100-444762, Section 6 (Part 6)." History and the Headlines. http://www.historyandtheheadlines.abc-clio.com/Content-Pages/ContentPage.aspx?entryId=1665653&currentSection=1665275&productid=41.

Federal Bureau of Investigation. n.d. "FBI Records: The Vault: Cesar Chavez." http://vault.fbi.gov/Cesar%20Chavez.

Street, Richard Steven. 1996. "The FBI's Secret File on Cesar Chavez." *Southern California Quarterly* 78, no. 4. http://farmworkermovement.com/ufwarchives/FBI-CEC/fbi_chavez.pdf.

Forty Acres

In the spring of 1966, amid the battles of the grape strike, Cesar Chavez and his fellow members of the farm workers movement began to plan for their union headquarters. A woman from Pasadena, California, had inherited a 40-acre piece of land west of Delano and had decided to sell it. Chavez's brother Richard and

On April 24, 1993, after the death of Cesar Chavez, a band sings union and sacred songs during a rosary at the United Farm Workers' union hall at 40 Acres in Delano, California. (AP Photo/Reed Saxon)

LeRoy Chatfield, a former teacher and doctoral student at the University of Southern California and now a close Chavez confidant, checked out the location. Near the U.S. Information Agency "antenna farm" used to transmit *Voice of America* and *Armed Forces Radio* broadcasts, the area for sale was overgrown with weeds, littered with debris, and near a city dump. Richard Chavez and Chatfield did not pay much attention to the weeds, debris, and the dump. What they saw was the future home of the farm workers union. It would be called simply and fondly "The Forty Acres."

Chavez envisioned a center where farm workers could find products and services usually hard to find for Spanish-speaking migrants—a gas station, health care, banking services, legal assistance, child care, and other necessities that would make life easier for those laboring in the fields. As Chatfield and other leaders of the movement raised money to help make the vision a reality, Richard Chavez, a builder and carpenter by trade, took over the construction of the site.

Chavez asked Chatfield to develop his idea for the National Farm Workers Service Center, Inc., (NFWSC). The center would serve as the umbrella for the newly formed farm worker cooperative and the other educational, health, and service programs that would develop in the farm worker movement, whose administrative offices would be housed at Forty Acres.

In 1967, union workers finished the first building at Forty Acres—a combined gas-oline station and automobile repair shop. In front of the adobe building with a gable roof and clay tiles would soon be six gas pumps that dispensed "Huelga Co-op Gas."

In early 1968, Chavez conducted his first fast. It was at the gas station at Forty Acres. Although the construction of the building itself had been completed, it was not ready to open because the gas pumps were not as yet installed. So Chavez set up a cot in one of the empty storage rooms and began the fast. It was here that he began to receive a stream of visitors. Media began to swarm around the gas station to get daily reports on Chavez's condition. During the fast, Walter Reuther and Paul Schrade of the United Auto Workers gave the union $50,000 to pay for the construction of a new office building for Forty Acres. It would be called the Roy L. Reuther Memorial Building, named after Reuther's brother, who had been a frequent participant in United Farm Worker Organizing Committee (UFWOC) organizing activities. Reuther Hall became the administrative center for the union's activities.

When Mark Day, a Catholic priest, first visited Forty Acres, he noticed a large, 15-foot cross lying face down in a far corner of the complex. Richard Chavez had constructed the cross from telephone poles. One Easter Sunday, the union workers decorated the cross with roses and celebrated a sunrise Mass at Forty Acres. Two days later, in the middle of the night, someone cut down the cross and burned part of it with gasoline. Union leaders left it there to bleach in the sun, a reminder of the bigotry and hatred faced by the union in its fight for justice.

Once, after visiting Forty Acres, Walter Reuther, seeing the *Voice of America* transmitter close by, said that it was ironic that the United States' farm workers had to struggle for basic dignity in the shadow of a broadcast tower that told enslaved peoples of the world about the "land of the free and the home of the brave."

In the summer of 1969, Chatfield learned that the Kern County Welfare Department was planning to demolish some of its older administrative buildings. Moving quickly, he acquired one of the buildings and made arrangements for it to be cut in half, loaded onto trucks, and moved to Forty Acres. After some ingenious design work, the union's health center soon opened to provide services to farm workers, many of whom, before the opening of the clinic, had little or no access to health care.

By the end of 1970, the UFWOC had negotiated contracts covering nearly 70,000 farm workers. With the increased membership and the realization that Forty Acres was too small to encompass all of the union's activities, Chavez decided that the union needed larger administrative quarters. Union officials selected a site in Keene, California, located southwest of Bakersfield in the foothills of the Tehachapi Mountains. Shortly after the union's reorganization as the United Farm Workers of America (UFW) in 1971, the union opened its new headquarters at the site of a former public tuberculosis sanatorium. Chavez called the new facility "La Paz," a shortened version of "Nuestra Senora Reina de la Paz" or "Our Lady, Queen of Peace."

Nevertheless, important union services would be still be housed at Forty Acres, including a retirement center. In 1971, Chavez asked Philip Vera Cruz, a member of the union's board and one of the Filipino leaders who had been with movement from its beginning, to take charge of the planning of the retirement center project. Many Filipino immigrants found themselves without money, family, or public resources after they were unable to continue working in the fields. The retirement center would help at least some of these individuals. Construction began in April 1973, and the first residents moved into their units in February 1975. It was called the Paolo Agbayani Retirement Village, commonly known as "The Village." It was named after a Filipino union member who had died from a heart attack while on a picket line.

Many UFW officials and members have very fond memories of Forty Acres and the role it played in the early years of the farm workers movement. Chatfield said, "this 40-acre parcel was the pride and joy, the future and the permanence of the farmworker movement" (Chatfield n.d.).

In 2011, Forty Acres was dedicated as a national historic landmark. At the dedication ceremony, Secretary of the Interior Ken Salazar declared:

Cesar Chavez is an American hero and one of the great civil rights icons of our country's history. His leadership, tireless work ethic and selfless sacrifice helped forge a new era of justice for millions of farm workers and gave them hope for a better future, both for themselves and for their children. Recognizing The Forty Acres site as a National Historic Landmark will help ensure that Cesar Chavez's story, and the story of all who struggled with him, is remembered, honored and passed along to future generations. ("America's Great Outdoors . . . " 2011)

Further Reading

"America's Great Outdoors: Secretary Salazar, UFW President Rodriguez, and the Chavez Family Honor Life and Legacy of Cesar Chavez at National Historical Landmark Dedication Ceremony." 2011. National Park Service Press Release, February 22. http://home.nps.gov/news/release.htm?id=1122 "National Park Service Press Release.

Chatfield, LeRoy. n.d. "Commentary." http://farmworkermovement.com/essays/essays/The%20Union%20of%20Their%20Dreams.pdf.

Day, Mark. 1971. *Forty Acres: Cesar Chavez and the Farm Workers*. New York: Praeger Publishers.

Matthiessen, Peter. 1969. *Sal Si Puedes: Cesar Chavez and the New American Revolution*. New York: Random House.

National Park Service. 2008. "National Historic Landmark Nomination: Forty Acres." http://www.nps.gov/nhl/designations/samples/CA/FortyAcres.pdf.

Founding Convention, National Farm Workers Association, 1962

On September 30, 1962, about 300 farm workers gathered at an old theater in Fresno, California. They were there at the invitation of Cesar Chavez to establish officially the National Farm Workers Association (NFWA). This founding convention would launch a seemingly quixotic dream of Chavez's to establish a union of farm workers. On this day, Chavez stood before this group of workers and promised to fight with fierce determination to grow this new organization. Through their own organizing and nonviolent protest, he said, they could empower themselves to defy agribusiness and its allies and make better their own lives and those of their families.

On his 35th birthday, March 31, 1962, Chavez had cleared out his desk at the headquarters of the Community Service Organization (CSO) in Los Angeles. With his wife Helen and their eight children, he drove to a small beach town near Santa Barbara and talked of their plans. They would go to Delano, California, to start a union. A town of 12,000 in 1962, Delano was in the center of the nation's table grape industry. He had worked in its vineyards when he was a boy. It was Helen's hometown. Two of her sisters lived in Delano, and two brothers were nearby. It was also the town that Chavez's brother, Richard, had made his home. After filling the tank of their beaten-up Mercury, they headed north.

Chavez knew that an effort to create a full-scale union of farm workers was a daunting prospect, especially with no money and the need to take care of his family. He later said that it was the first time in his life that he was truly frightened.

Organizing farm laborers presented overwhelming hurdles. Mostly poor, many illiterate, and all divided culturally from mainstream America, farm workers usually did not remain very long in one locality. Most had no economic power and no success in strikes and other activities in which unions engaged. If they refused to work, growers could replace them with cheaper bracero labor or illegal immigrants from across the Mexican border.

As he began his adventurous, if unlikely, dream, to build a union, Chavez had about $1,200. He also had the help of his friend Dolores Huerta, a strong leader of the CSO who had decided to join Chavez in Delano to be a part of this extraordinary quest.

Chavez set up office in the garage of the house of his brother Richard. Helen began to earn extra money by returning to work in the fields. As he, Huerta, and other allies such as Gilbert Padilla, another CSO veteran, made the rounds of Delano and nearby fruit-growing areas, they avoided using the term "union" because to most of the workers that meant "strikes," through which some of them had already suffered through firings and blacklistings. From one labor camp to another, they canvassed the San Joaquin Valley, talking about the potential of a social movement or "movimiento."

The workers listened because of the conditions under which most of them lived. Not only were most of them poor, but many did not even have tap water in their homes or refrigerators. Many lacked even the most basic health care.

In the first six months, Chavez crisscrossed the valley in a 1953 Mercury station wagon that, like Chavez himself, never quit. The car lasted over 300,000 miles. For a time, he and his family lived on food given to him by family and friends in Delano and on the road. He and his growing number of supporters fanned out across the farming areas, passing out cards for the workers to fill out if they were interested in the association and leaflets providing information. The leaflets were made possible by a mimeograph machine loaned by the California Migrant Ministry (CMM), a Christian organization dedicated to helping poor farm workers. The CMM would become over the years a dedicated source of support.

In one farm area after another, Chavez and his allies began holding house meetings as they had done while working with the CSO. They talked to the possible recruits about the possibilities of growing so powerful that they might force growers to engage in collective bargaining. They spoke about the possibilities of gaining enough political leverage that they might be able to lobby the governor and the state legislature for a state minimum wage and the right to unemployment insurance. They talked about better working conditions and about plans for an association-run credit union and a hiring hall to help workers locate jobs.

Slowly the interest grew. Farm workers began to show up at Richard's garage with all kinds of questions, not only about their jobs but also about health care, schools, citizenship, and many other issues. The number of cards filled out by interested workers began to grow.

In the early fall of 1962, Chavez decided the time had come to hold a convention that would officially establish the new organization. Manuel Chavez, Cesar's cousin, found an old theater in Fresno to hold the gathering. On Sunday, September 30, workers gathered to show their solidarity and celebrate a new union. They adopted a union motto: "Viva la causa!" or "Long Live the Cause!"

They also waved a new flag bearing the organizational symbol—an Aztec eagle, emblematic of pride and dignity. A white circle in the flag signified the hopes and aspirations of the farm laborers; the black represented the plight of the workers; and the red background stood for the hard work and sacrifice that the union members would have to give. The flag was designed by Chavez's brother Richard and sewn by his cousin Manuel Chavez.

Further Reading

Bardacke, Frank. 2011. *Trampling Out the Vintage*. New York: Verso.

Dunne, John Gregory. 1976. *Delano: The Story of the California Grape Strike*. New York: Farrar.

Ferriss, Susan, and Ricardo Sandoval. 1997. *The Fight in the Fields: Cesar Chavez and the Farmworkers Movement*. New York: Harcourt Brace & Company.

Griswold del Castillo, Richard, and Richard A. Garcia. 1995. *Cesar Chavez: A Triumph of Spirit*. Norman: University of Oklahoma Press.

Levy, Jacques. 2007. *Cesar Chavez: Autobiography of La Causa*. Minneapolis: University of Minnesota Press.

Fresno County Jail, 1973

In the summer of 1973, a jail in Fresno, California, became the scene of one of the most dramatic acts of civil disobedience in the history of the farm workers movement. The United Farm Workers (UFW) union was in a desperate struggle with the Teamsters Union over contracts with growers. The fight had turned violent against UFW protestors at the hands of Teamster thugs and local police wielding billy clubs, metal pipes, baseball bats, and tire irons and many yelling racial and ethnic insults. Cesar Chavez turned to a tactic that had proven successful in the civil rights movement in the South. The union would fill the jails of Fresno with supporters willing to get themselves arrested in order to make a personal testament against injustice. At a rally, he declared that Fresno would become another Selma. The reference was to the 1965 voting-rights campaign in Selma, Alabama, by the Southern Christian Leadership Council, in which Dr. Martin Luther King Jr. and his fellow protestors did indeed fill the Selma jail and thus garnered nationwide attention to the unjust laws prohibiting blacks from voting. Chavez called on supporters across the country to come to Fresno to take part in mass arrests to demonstrate the plight of the farm workers union in facing not only Teamster violence but also the aggressive stance of local politicians, law enforcement, and judges in restricting picketing and other protest activities. UFW supporters answered the call; they did come to Fresno, not only from nearby towns in California and adjacent states but from cities across the nation. As they reached Fresno, one of the central staging areas for organizing the mass protests and arrests was in a small town near the city of Fresno. It was Selma, California.

A large number of religious figures arrived in Fresno—nuns, priests, and members of various religious orders. One of the most prominent was Dorothy Day. She was now 77 years old and had been a social activist her entire life. In 1933 she, along with Catholic social activist Peter Maurin, had founded the Catholic Worker Movement that not only built houses across the country to serve the homeless but also published an influential newspaper. She worked tirelessly for women's rights and workers' rights and had become very supportive of the work of Chavez. She began picketing on August 1, carrying a folding chair for rest breaks, chatting with the police and other guards, and offering to read to them the Sermon on the Mount.

She wrote in her diary: "Today many Jesuits were arrested. Also sisters who had been attending a conference in San Francisco. Mass in the evening ... singing, chanting, marching—and when the Mass began there were so many people that it was impossible to kneel, but there was utter silence" (Day 1973). Day was incarcerated for over a week. Over her lifetime, she had been arrested a number of times in protests, she later recalled. In the first one, she said, she had been the youngest; in this one she had been the oldest.

Juan Romero, director of PADRES, the national Chicano priest movement, was in Fresno for the protests. His organization, dedicated to easing the racial divide that permeated the church's ministry, was founded in 1969 and became a force for change for two decades, working within ministries in poor Mexican American parishes. Romero remembered Chavez: "In his powerful and quiet way, Cesar can truly move a crowd. He is honest, tough, and straightforward." Chavez spoke about putting Fresno "on the map" as the place where the UFW made a valiant effort to assert the rights of freedom of assembly and speech (Romero 1973).

Union organizer Rey Huerta had already barely escaped the violence near Fresno with his life. On June 27, shots had been fired into his house. Huerta remembered the chaos in the Fresno County fields, the injunctions against picketing handed out by local judges, and the arrests, but he also remembered being amused by one particular scene. The folk singer Joan Baez had come to Fresno to offer support. Huerta recalled seeing her on one of the picket lines singing "God Bless America" while, across the street, counterdemonstrators were yelling and screaming and calling the UFW protestors communists. Baez, with a guitar strapped around her shoulders, just kept singing.

In Fresno that summer, the police arrested over 3,500 protestors. Nearly 2,000 went to jail, including 70 priests and nuns. On August 13, 1973, Fresno authorities decided to release all of the strikers. The bureaucratic nightmare facing the courts of Fresno would have been too daunting to continue.

Rosemary Cooperrider, the daughter of a father who had worked as a farm worker during the Great Depression in the San Joaquin Valley, had been a lifelong supporter of efforts to ameliorate conditions in the harvest fields. Along with her husband, Verne, she had helped organize the Oregon Farm Worker Ministry and had also worked with the Washington State Council of Churches on migrant worker issues. After moving to Palo Alto, California, her home became a kind of haven for UFW workers where they could have house meetings and other activities. Cooperrider spent 13 days in jail. In the end, she said, "We so filled all the jails that farmworkers could picket all they wanted to and shout 'Huelga' and use the bullhorn. In other words, we broke the 'Injunction'" (Cooperrider 2003).

One of those freed was Father Eugene Boyle of San Francisco, who had been in jail for over two weeks. At a meeting on the lawn in front of the courthouse, Father Boyle told hundreds of farm workers, "This is the greatest number of religious persons ever jailed in the United States. I hope it says something about our deep and profound belief in your cause. We know you will overcome" (Levy 2007, 505).

Further Reading

Cooperrider, Rosemary. 2003. "Rosie's 36-Year Saga to Try to do Something to Help Farm Workers." 'http://www.unionoftheirdreams.com/PDF/Rosie's_36yr_saga.pdf.

Day, Dorothy. 1973. "On Pilgrimage—September 1973." *The Catholic Worker*, September 1, 2, 6. http://www.catholicworker.org/dorothyday/daytext.cfm?TextID=533.

Huerta, Rey. n.d. "The Most Memorable Times of Our Lives." http://farmworkermovement.com/essays/essays/053%20Huerta_Rey.pdf.

Levy, Jacques. 2007. *Cesar Chavez: Autobiography of La Causa*. Minneapolis: University of Minnesota Press.

Romero, Juan. 1973. "UFW Civil Disobedience Campaign." http://farmworkermovement.com/essays/essays/JUAN%20ROMERO%20PADRES.pdf.

G

Galarza, Ernesto

From the early part of the twentieth century, beginning with the Industrial Workers of the World (IWW), there had been efforts to unionize farm workers. Faced with the power of agribusiness interests, lacking financial backing, and intimidated by the organizational difficulty of drawing together transient workers into an organized force for social protest, all of the efforts were short-lived. The most effective of the early attempts to organize migratory workers, and one that was embraced by Cesar Chavez's father, involved an unlikely figure in a labor movement—Ernesto Galarza.

Born in 1905 in Jalococotan in the Mexican state of Nararit, he immigrated with his mother and two uncles to Sacramento, California, when he was 10. For a time he worked in the fields as a farm laborer. A superior student in high school, he earned a scholarship to Occidental College in Los Angeles and then went to Stanford University, where he graduated with a master's degree in history in 1929.

In 1936, he began work as a research director with the Pan-American Union (which later became the Organization of American States) in Washington, DC, where he engaged in studies on labor and educational issues relating to Latin America. Later, he earned a Ph.D. in economics from Columbia University. His doctoral dissertation was on the electricity industry in Mexico.

Something of a renaissance man—a skilled writer and poet, a master researcher, and historian—he was also driven to action as one who harbored instincts to fight for social justice against the systems he discovered in his academic work. Returning to California, he joined the National Farm Labor Union (NFLU) that had been chartered in 1946 and funded by the American Federation of Labor. Led by H. L. Mitchell, who had headed the Southern Tenant Farmers Union, the new farm workers union focused its attention on California and its rich agricultural areas whose success depended on migrant farm workers and where such groups as the Associated Farmers, a collective of the largest growers in the state, had worked tirelessly to discourage union organizing.

Working alongside union organizers Hank Hasiwar and William Becker, Galarza orchestrated in the fall of 1947 a coordinated campaign and strike against the DiGiorgio Fruit Corporation, the largest private distributor of citrus fruits in the United States, a company whose operations included packing facilities in such major cities as New York, Chicago, and Pittsburgh. DiGiorgio's 22,000-acre farm in Arvin, California, in the San Joaquin Valley, hired in peak season about 2,000 workers.

The strike would last 30 months and entangled the company in lawsuits for the next 15 years. It was, however, crushed with astonishing force, including the use of hired company goons wielding chains. A number of picketers were hospitalized, and one of the strike's organizers escaped an attempted assassination. Nevertheless, the strike had been the most aggressive on behalf of California's migrant farm workers until the son of one of the union's members, named Chavez, would attack the DiGiorgio giant in the 1960s. Cesar's father participated in a number of strikes in these years. As a young man, Cesar admired his father's efforts toward the union's purpose—to face indignities and injustice against long odds—even if he was frustrated and angered by its inability to combat effectively the organized agribusiness and political powers set against it.

After the DiGiorgio strike, Galarza, Hasiwar, and the others conducted other, smaller strikes in California. Although some of the actions did lead to temporary wage increases in a few of the industries such as tomatoes and other summer crops, the NFLU effectively ceased operations in the early 1950s.

Any attempt at unionizing farm workers, Galarza recognized early on, was hurt by the Bracero Program, established as a wartime measure to help growers withstand the loss of employees. This system, which brought to the United States temporary guest workers from Mexico at low wages and then returned them at the end of the harvesting season, jeopardized the permanent workforce already in the United States. Not only did attempts at unionizing farm workers face legal hurdles and strike-breaking violence, the efforts faced the nearly intractable obstacle of the use of braceros as scab labor.

In 1956, Galarza published a study he called *Strangers in Our Fields* that detailed the exploitation of the contract laborers from Mexico. It provided much insight into immigration and labor history and the controversies surrounding the farm workers in California.

In 1959, Galarza, for a short time became an assistant director in a new union, another attempt by the AFL-CIO to organize farm workers. It was called the Agricultural Workers Organizing Committee (AWOC). It was this union that in 1965, as it began a strike in the grape fields near Delano, California, asked Cesar Chavez and his own infant farm workers union to join forces.

As the AWOC struggled to forge an effective organization in the early 1960s, Galarza began to research the small communities of Mexican American citizens, mostly farm workers, where many spoke little or no English and had almost no contact with the social or political structures in the state. In these communities, which he called "colonies," were people who, with the right approach and message, could perhaps be mobilized. There was potential in these areas, he argued, to organize a movement of the powerless and excluded into a political force. This was research and a message that Cesar Chavez would take to heart.

Galarza also worked feverishly to educate farm workers and others about the Bracero Program. In 1964, he published a major book entitled

Merchants of Labor, a study that followed up on his 1956 report. Galarza exposed the scandalous abuses of the program, not only showing how the program hurt domestic workers but also detailing the dangers, harassment, and racial indignities faced by the workers; the transportation accidents caused by overloading trucks with workers; and, even more scandalous, the occasional physical abuse by those in charge in the fields.

As the oppression surrounding the Bracero Program became known and publicized and the need for a continuing supply of Mexican laborers lessoned, the program was officially ended in late 1964.

Galarza died in 1984. In his work, he had formulated a rationale for organizing Mexican American farm workers and at the same time, through his research and writing, provided much factual groundwork and ammunition about labor conditions that activists and organizers, especially Cesar Chavez, used to carry forward the farm workers movement.

Further Reading

Galarza, Ernesto. 2011. *Barrio Boy*. South Bend, IN: University of Notre Dame Press.

Galarza, Ernesto. 1964. *Merchants of Labor: The Mexican Bracero Story*. Charlotte: McNally and Loftin.

Galarza, Ernesto. 1956. *Strangers in Our Fields*. Washington, DC: Joint United States-Mexico Trade Union Committee.

Ganz, Marshall. 2009. *Why David Sometimes Wins: Leadership, Organization, and Strategy in the California Farm Worker Movement*. New York: Oxford University Press.

"Testimony from a 'Bracero.'" n.d. http://www.farmworkers.org/testmony.html.

Gallo Wine Company

The E&J Gallo Vineyards, based in the Modesto, California, the nation's most well-known wineries, signed a contract with Cesar Chavez's farm workers union in July 1967 after the Delano grape strike. In June 1970, however, Gallo joined a number of California growers in signing a four-year contract with the Teamsters Union, whose leadership continued to rebuff Chavez's attempts to unionize farm workers. Indeed, Teamster goons had recently attacked picket lines, injuring 25 strikers. Infuriated, Chavez retaliated with a strike and boycott of all Gallo wines. The boycott would be protracted and would gain nationwide notice. It would also play a part in the efforts of the farm workers union to push for a state law regulating the treatment of California's farm laborers.

The brothers Gallo, Ernest and Julio, were sons of an immigrant Italian father who had a business in the early 1900s buying wine from small wineries and selling

On September 11, 1975, Cesar Chavez meets with supporters at Gallo Wineries in Livingston, California. Three months after the passage of the Agricultural Labor Relations Act, Chavez and teams of union organizers visited various wineries encouraging workers to vote for representation by the United Farm Workers. (AP Photo/Raimondo Borea)

it to bars in Oakland and San Francisco. After the end of Prohibition in the United States, the sons turned the business into an extraordinarily profitable enterprise emphasizing inexpensive wines. Wine industry experts praised Gallo's achievement in bringing new wine drinkers into the field.

By the 1970s, Gallo produced 45 percent of California wines and 37 percent of all U.S. wines. It also fought hard to convince the public through press announcements, television, and mass mailings that the company was dealing in good faith with its workers in fighting off the United Farm Workers (UFW). In fact, the company would have preferred no union at all, not even the sweetheart deal it signed with the Teamsters.

The UFW sent out its own mailings refuting many of the public statements made by Gallo's spokesmen and in its advertising. "Ernest Gallo is disturbed about the 'rights of the workers' under a UFW contract," one the UFW mailings said. "It's a strange concern coming from an employer who has turned his workers over to a Teamsters Union in which farm workers have no meetings, elect no representatives, have no say about dues policies, have no contract enforcement committee, no seniority, no job security, no health and safety committee, no rights!" ("Cesar Chavez Calls . . . " n.d.).

The early years of the 1970s were especially challenging for the union. With President Richard Nixon in the White House and Ronald Reagan in the governor's chair in Sacramento, the union did not have friends in high places. In 1973 alone, state law enforcement proved especially harsh on strikers—over 3,500 were arrested. The scenes in the fields were eerily similar to the iconic images of the black civil rights movement—local police armed with clubs, snarling dogs on leashes, antistrike agitators swinging tire irons and metal pipes while screaming obscene racial and ethnic taunts, firebombs thrown at the union supporters, and the jails filling with protestors. Although most of the cases were dismissed in the courts, the atmosphere for the union was fearful and intimidating. UFW membership fell during this period from 40,000 to 6,500.

In 1974, Chavez was in Boston to cheer on supporters. Gallo was in trouble, he declared. The boycott was having pronounced effects as evidenced by the fact that the company had cut back from three daily working shifts to two.

A 1975 poll conducted by Louis Harris indicated that the public favored Chavez's farm workers union over the Teamsters by a six-to-one margin in the struggle over Gallo and other companies. The poll also confirmed what Chavez had maintained—that the boycott was persuading many Americans to support the boycott of nonunion wines. Eleven million individuals, the poll found, had stopped buying Gallo wines.

When Jerry Brown, a supporter of the UFW for whom the union had spent time and resources in supporting his campaign, was elected governor of California in November 1974, Chavez and his leadership team now had a key backer who could wield significant influence on the union's fortunes. Indeed, Brown had even hired LeRoy Chatfield, a former high-level UFW staffer, as one of his key aides.

In early 1975, Fred Ross Jr., the son of Chavez's mentor and a committed member of the UFW, suggested that the union, as it had before, show its strength through a march. A march, he said, would garner more nationwide support for the Gallo strike and would defy stories that the UFW was in serious decline. At first skeptical, Chavez soon warmed to idea. In addition to the national publicity that would be gained by such a move, it would also help encourage Governor Brown to act quickly on his campaign promise to push for a state farm workers law.

On February 22, 1975, several members of the UFW began a 110-mile march from San Francisco to Modesto and Gallo's headquarters. As the march proceeded, there were rallies in several towns and cities, including Hayward, Livermore, Tracy, and Oakland. Marchers stayed in the homes of fellow workers and in churches that supported the UFW.

By the time the march reached Gallo, over 15,000 had joined the protest. They stretched over a mile long, with farm workers singing labor songs, waving the union flag, engaging in conversations with onlookers along the route, and chanting slogans: "Chavez *si*, Teamsters no; Gallo wine has got to go!" An ebullient Chavez met the marchers in Modesto and declared to the boisterous crowd that Gallo must now realize that the union was not going away.

Indeed, so effective was the march that the Gallo brothers decided to endorse the UFW's push for a farm labor law. In response to Gallo's support on the initiative, Chavez stopped the Gallo boycott. On June 4, 1975, after weeks of tough negotiating by Jerry Brown and with the advice of UFW leaders, the governor signed into law the Agricultural Labor Relations Act (ALRA), the first legislation protecting farm workers and providing for collective bargaining.

Further Reading

"Cesar Chavez Calls for a Boycott of All Gallo Wines until Elections Are Held." n.d. http://www.farmworkermovement.com/ufwarchives/DebbieMillerArchive/GalloStrike1973/Letter%20of%20Cesar%20Chavez%20to%20Ernest%20Gallo.pdf.

Ferriss, Susan, and Ricardo Sandoval. 1997. *The Fight in the Fields: Cesar Chavez and the Farmworkers Movement*. New York: Harcourt Brace & Company.

Griswold del Castillo, Richard, and Richard Garcia. 1995. *Cesar Chavez: A Triumph of Spirit*. Norman: University of Oklahoma Press.

Pawel, Miriam. 2009. *The Union of Their Dreams: Power, Hope, and Struggle in Cesar Chavez's Farm Worker Movement*. New York: Bloomsbury Press.

Shaw, Randy. 2008. *Beyond the Fields: Cesar Chavez, the UFW, and the Struggle for Justice in the 21st Century*. Berkeley: University of California Press.

"Game, The"

In the mid-1970s, at a time in which Cesar Chavez could look back at extraordinary progress in establishing a farm workers movement, he and many of his close advisors became embroiled in a devastating internal struggle over the future direction of the UFW. A revealing element of that struggle and its pervasive mistrust and fear was something called "The Game." It was introduced to Chavez by a revolutionary drug and alcohol rehabilitation program called Synanon that had been founded by a charismatic alcoholic named Charles Dederich Sr. in 1958. Dederich and his many followers used "The Game," a kind of psychological warfare scheme in which addicts were subjected to relentless attacks, in order to break down their psyches so they could begin life anew. It pitted small groups of people against others in a raw and ruthless series of personal attacks meant to purge members of bad practices and habits. A form of the encounter group therapies popular in the 1970, it taught participants to gang up verbally and emotionally against other members, ostensibly with the goal of strengthening the group. If Chavez saw in the scheme a means to once again reassert the union's commitment to sacrifice and nonviolent social change, he instead introduced with "The Game" elements of mistrust and alienation that led not to renewal but, in some cases, to disintegration.

Brought up in a strict Catholic environment in Ohio, Dederich briefly attended the University of Notre Dame, went through two broken marriages and a number of jobs, began to drink heavily, and ended up in California. He joined Alcoholics Anonymous and sobered up. With much charm and native intellect, he began to attract a number of followers who saw in his example of overthrowing addiction a road to their own recovery. Starting with a rented storefront in Ocean Park, he founded the Tender Loving Care Club, which he soon renamed Synanon (from the word *symposium*) and within a year had moved to Santa Monica with a newly thriving detoxification program.

Dederich called his encounter detoxification therapy "tough love." As he began to attract wealthy drug and alcohol abusers, his Synanon enterprise began to gain national attention. It became a $30 million nonprofit business owning vast real estate investments. Chapters sprung up in places as far from California as Germany and Malaysia.

But by the late 1960s, Dederich's organization had taken on cultlike qualities. Dederich became more controlling, strongly urging that members divorce themselves from families and life outside Synanon and devote their loyalty and property to him. In 1974, Dederich declared Synanon a religion.

As Chavez became increasingly consumed with thoughts that his leadership was under threat of revolt and even that communist sympathizers might be infiltrating the organization (an ironic change of heart for Chavez, considering the attacks early on in his career that he might be a communist himself), Chavez was convinced that the techniques Dederich used to purify and recommit the members of his organization might be useful for the UFW leadership. After all, Synanon, in its own way, Chavez came to believe, was an alternative community that would offer valuable lessons for a communal organization that the UFW leader had in mind. Always something of an aesthete, he never envisioned the UFW as a traditional labor union but, in his own, somewhat idiosyncratic way, more as a social movement with many things to offer the poor beyond union contracts for higher wages and improved working conditions. He grew interested in the Hutterite communities of North America and the Israeli *kibbutzim* as possible models.

Chavez first introduced "The Game" to UFW colleagues on the 1975 One Thousand Mile March from the Mexican American border to La Paz after encountering on the march members of Delancy Street, a self-help organization founded in 1971 for substance abusers, ex-convicts, and the homeless. Delancy Street members had adopted many of Dederich's techniques. Chavez confidant LeRoy Chatfield remembered that UFW marchers played "The Game" almost daily from the time they reached San Luis Obispo until the march ended.

Chavez visited Dederich and was mightily impressed. Here was an organization that thrived as a community, was disciplined, and was dedicated. Dederich told Chavez that if he really wanted La Paz to be such a thriving community with totally shared goals and interests, he should introduce the Synanon game. Chavez could not have imagined at the time that Dederich's empire would gradually come crashing down amid scandal, corruption, violence, the stockpiling of guns, and even attempted murder.

And so in 1977, Chavez made "The Game" a required and regular exercise for his leadership team. He warned that the UFW might be headed toward a system in which sacrifice was abandoned, in which volunteer involvement out of passion and spirit would be lost. This psychological tool, he emphasized, would help him and others in the union come to realize that the UFW was not a normal trade union and that it had a greater purpose.

Thus "The Game" took hold. This disciplinary practice, in which UFW staff were obliged to stand in the middle of a circle and submit to fierce questioning and criticism, did not spawn a contrite recommitment to original principles as Chavez had hoped, but instead created much disgust and suspicion. Some of Chavez's closest aides went along with the practice; others openly expressed their humiliation and degradation. Chavez persisted in forcing the reluctant to participate. He began to believe that the exercises were beginning to show the true colors of some of his closest advisors, and he did not like what he saw—perhaps traitors in his midst; perhaps others who were plotting to take over the union.

In looking back over the internal turmoil of these years, in which a number of UFW leaders left after humiliating rebukes, general disagreements or, in some cases, actual purges, many felt that "The Game," this pseudo practice of psychotherapy, was, if not a major cause of the fractures within the organization, at least a reflection of them.

Finally, realizing that imposing this exercise, this form of monastic discipline, upon people with whom he had worked so closely was seriously damaging morale, Chavez abandoned the practice. Most of the leadership involved with the UFW, executive board members as well as staffers, believed he should not have introduced "The Game" in the first place.

Further Reading

Bardacke, Frank. 2011. *Trampling Out the Vintage: Cesar Chavez and the Two Souls of the United Farm Workers*. New York: Verso.

Ferriss, Susan, and Ricardo Sandoval. 1997. *The Fight in the Fields: Cesar Chavez and the Farmworkers Movement*. New York: Harcourt Brace & Company.

Morantz, Paul. n.d. "Synanon." http://www.paulmorantz.com/the_synanon_story/.

Pawel, Miriam. 2009. *The Union of Their Dreams: Power, Hope, and Struggle in Cesar Chavez's Farm Worker Movement*. New York: Bloomsbury Press.

Shaw, Randy. 2008. *Beyond the Fields: Cesar Chavez, the UFW, and the Struggle for Justice in the 21st Century.* Berkeley: University of California Press.

Yates, Michael. 2009. *In and Out of the Working Class.* Winnipeg: Arbeiter Ring.

Gandhi, Mohandas Karamchand (Mahatma)

When the iconic independence leader of India, Mahatma Gandhi, was assassinated in Delhi on January 30, 1948, 20-year-old Cesar Chavez, already a Navy veteran, was back in his hometown of Delano, California, working in the harvest fields. He would soon marry Helen Fabela. Young Chavez had heard of Gandhi in the newspapers, and in movie houses he had seen some brief newsreel snippets about the Indian revolutionary leader. A few years later, with the encouragement of Father Donald McDonnell, a Catholic priest from San Francisco who did pastoral work among farm workers, Chavez began to read passionately, studying many books, satisfying a hunger for knowledge that his sporadic times in schools had not satisfied. The life and words of Gandhi began to hold special meaning. Here was a man who through the power of his ideas, his personal commitment, and his willingness to sacrifice in order to right injustice had shaken the British Empire. He had done it not with an army but with the power of nonviolent resistance—through fasts, boycotts, marches, and the strength of character to bring together hundreds of thousands to his side for the cause of social justice. For Chavez, Gandhi's example would have special meaning and direction.

Born in Gujaret, India, on October 2, 1869, into the Hindu family of the chief minister (*diwan*) of the city of Porbanadar, Mohandas Gandhi studied law at the University of Bombay for one year and then moved to London, entering University College. He graduated in 1891 and was admitted to the bar of England. As he began a legal career, he traveled to South Africa on behalf of a client and, while riding in a first-class compartment of a train, was forcibly removed for violating segregation policies. Outraged by that incident and by the social injustice he witnessed in South Africa, he began a civil rights movement that succeeded in changing a few of the laws. While involved in the movement, he developed a philosophy for challenging the social and political order through nonviolence, a concept he called "Soul Force."

Back in India, Gandhi began to challenge his fellow countrymen to confront their own political and social subjugation under the rule of the British Crown and became active in the struggle for Indian independence. He became one of the leaders of the Indian National Congress. In 1918, Gandhi opposed a British tax levied during World War I and was arrested for organizing the civil resistance of tens of thousands of landless farmers and serfs. In jail, Gandhi went on a hunger strike, and thousands of supporters gathered around the jail. His followers began to address him as Mahatma (Great Soul). The mass protest worked. The British suspended the tax.

He began to live an ascetic life of prayer, meditation, and fasting. He no longer wore the clothes of a British lawyer but began to dress in the simple, plain loincloths and robes of an Indian farmer. Even when he traveled back to England representing the Indian National Congress, he wore the plain garments, much to the astonishment of his diplomatic colleagues and the British press. His life and work became symbolic of nonviolent resistance to oppression. He advised Indians to boycott British-made products and to replace them with goods made in their own country. He encouraged them not to enroll in British universities as he had done. He told them to refuse to follow British customs. All of this, he believed—this nonviolent, massive resistance—could eventually persuade the British to leave India to its own rule and future. He was jailed many times during his various protests.

In late 1929, the Indian National Congress adopted a resolution calling for complete independence from the British. In 1930, Gandhi led a march of nearly 250 miles to Dandi on the coast of the Arabian Sea. Often called the Salt Satyagraha, the march was a protest directed against the British taxes on salt. For 24 days, Gandhi, followed by thousands, marched in open defiance of the British. When they arrived in Dandi, Gandhi and his followers made salt by evaporating seawater. The action, calling on all Indians to refuse to pay the tax and manufacture their own salt, was a powerful symbolic gesture of independence. It was also illegal, and Gandhi was once again placed under arrest. He was not the only one. In the course of the civil disobedience campaign, over 100,000 people were incarcerated, filling the jails and foisting on the British authorities a bureaucratic nightmare. This was the essence of nonviolent protest.

Gandhi campaigned to improve the lives of the lowest in the Indian caste system, the people known as the untouchables. Gandhi called them *Harijans* (the children of God) and spoke out in favor of equal rights, including the right to vote.

As World War II broke out, Gandhi declared that India should not be involved on the side of Britain unless it had its independence. He began a campaign called "Quit India" that led to massive numbers of arrests, including his own. He spent two years in jail until his release in May 1944.

India finally did win independence in 1947, but part of the British Parliament's Indian Independence Act included the partition of the country into India and Pakistan. The action brought violent clashes between Hindus, Muslims, and Sikhs. While pleading for peace among the various factions, Gandhi fell victim to an assassin's attack.

As Cesar Chavez began his seemingly impossible quest to unshackle farm workers from their oppressed condition, the work of Gandhi was often on his mind. Chavez once wrote in admirable terms about Gandhi's description of nonviolent tactics as "moral jujitsu"—keeping the oppressor off balance, unsure of how to respond to methods that discouraged outright violent retribution. The fasts, boycotts, civil disobedience, and marches of the farm workers movement had been nonviolent weapons in Gandhi's arsenal.

When Chavez ended his first major fast in Delano in 1968, a number of observers noted that close beside him was a photograph of Gandhi.

Further Reading

Fischer, Louis. 2004. *Life of Mahatma Gandhi*. New York: HarperCollins Publishers.

Gandhi, Mohandas Karamchand (Mahatma). 2011. *Gandhi, An Autobiography: The Story of My Experiments with Truth*. CreateSpace.

Holmes, Robert, and Barry Gan. 2011. *Nonviolence in Theory and Practice*. Long Grove, IL: Waveland Press.

Orosco, Jose-Antonio. 2008. *Cesar Chavez and the Common Sense of Nonviolence*. Albuquerque: University of New Mexico Press.

Sharp, Gene. 1973. *The Politics of Nonviolent Part Two: The Methods of Nonviolent Action*. Boston: Porter Sargent Publishers.

Yinger, Winthrop. 1975. *Cesar Chavez: The Rhetoric of Nonviolence*. Hicksville, NY: Exposition Press.

Ganz, Marshall

For Cesar Chavez, the black civil rights movement was one of the inspirations for his dream to form a union of farm workers. A number of veteran civil rights activists traveled to Delano when the movement was underway to help La Causa. Marshall Ganz was one who made an enormous contribution. His father was a rabbi and his mother a teacher. Born in Bay City, Michigan, in 1943, Ganz spent three of his earliest years in Germany as his father worked with the U.S. Army ministering to the needs of displaced people. A few years later the family moved to California, where he lived for periods of time in Fresno and Bakersfield. Both from his father and his mother, Ganz learned about the horrors of the Holocaust and about the race hatred that plagued the United States. From an early age, he was attracted to people and movements struggling to fight injustice.

In 1960, Ganz traveled across the country to enter Harvard University and began an affiliation that would last for much of his life. Deeply touched by the stories about Martin Luther King Jr. and of young people joining the civil rights movement, he dropped out of school during the Mississippi Freedom Summer campaign in 1964 and headed south. He became a field secretary for the Student Nonviolent Coordinating Committee (SNCC) in McComb, Mississippi.

He later moved back to California, got involved in a number of activist causes, and became both intrigued and inspired by the audacious efforts of the young Chavez to take on California agribusiness and right-wing political forces on behalf of an impoverished and powerless minority.

In October 1965, his friends LeRoy Chatfield, who had left his job as a Catholic high school principal in Bakersfield to join the farm workers movement, and Mike Miller of the SNCC introduced Ganz to Chavez in San Francisco when he was on a fund-raising trip to help the infant union. Ganz agreed to join Chavez in the fall of 1965. Fluent in Spanish, he soon became a chief strategist and organizer.

He later said that when he joined the farm workers movement, he and other activists who had been in the South began to see how the events they had witnessed in the civil rights struggle and the power relations at work in attempting to overcome entrenched interests had given them "Mississippi eyes." He also said that Chavez recognized clearly how both movements involved a strong sense of cultural identity and pride.

In the spring of 1966, during the movement's first major strike of California grape growers, Ganz helped organize the 300-mile peregrination from Delano to Sacramento. He became a major organizer of the DiGiorgio campaign as well as a number of grape and lettuce boycotts. In July 1969, Ganz traveled to Toronto with Jessica Govea and Catholic priest Mark Day to spearhead a boycott office in the city that was the third largest export market for California grapes.

He battled with the United Farm Workers (UFW) union in the Salinas Valley against the Teamsters' attempts in 1970 to attract farm workers. He was also a national executive board member from 1973 to 1981.

Ganz was a powerful influence on the union's strategic organizing philosophy that enabled Chavez and his colleagues to succeed in drawing together groups of farm workers who before had little inclination or experience to work together. He taught the need to motivate, to educate, and to develop skills in negotiating.

But amid the rupture of the union's solidarity in its executive ranks in the late 1970s and early 1980s, Ganz left the UFW. He concluded that Chavez's leadership had become too insular, that the organizing efforts that had been so vigorous in past years had been sacrificed to Chavez's insistence on consolidating his personal control, and that he had cut out from union decision making the foundation on which the union's success had been built—the workers themselves. Ganz decried the lack of direction and lack of planning that began to erode the union's strength. As personal quarrels engulfed some of the major figures in the UFW, Ganz decided to move on.

In the early 1980s, he pursued other avenues of grassroots organizing in California, including work with the state's Democratic Party. His tactics led to increasing voter participation by Mexican Americans in California.

In the early 1990s, Ganz again changed the course of his career, moving back to Massachusetts to continue his studies at Harvard that he had left decades earlier.

Not only did he complete his undergraduate degree, but he went on to earn an MPA in 1993 at the Kennedy School of Government. He joined the faculty at Harvard after completing a Ph.D. in sociology in 2000. From his position at Harvard, Ganz has taught organizing philosophy and tactics to a generation of students interested in social justice.

Ganz also took his skills and philosophy back into the field, organizing for several mayoral, congressional, and senatorial candidates. He was a valuable organizing guru for the campaign of Barack Obama for president. He helped train thousands of Obama campaign volunteers in organizing communities and voters.

In 2009, Oxford University Press published Ganz's book *Why David Sometimes Wins: Leadership, Organization and Strategy in the Unionization of California Agriculture*. He dedicated the book "To the organizers who, with hopeful heart, critical eye, and skillful hand, bring us together to change ourselves, our communities, and our world." The work emphasizes what Ganz calls "strategic capacity," a combination of motivation, creativity, enthusiasm, and patience. It is what inspired and drove the UFW and its leadership, and it was David's slingshot to Goliath's agribusiness power.

Further Reading

Bardacke, Frank. 2011. *Trampling Out the Vintage: Cesar Chavez and the Two Souls of the United Farm Workers*. New York: Verso.

Ferriss, Susan, and Ricardo Sandoval. 1997. *The Fight in the Fields: Cesar Chavez and the Farmworkers Movement*. New York: Harcourt Brace & Company.

Ganz, Marshall. 2009. *Why David Sometimes Wins: Leadership, Organization, and Strategy in the California Farm Worker Movement*. New York: Oxford University Press.

Levy, Jacques. 2007. *Cesar Chavez: Autobiography of La Causa*. Minneapolis: University of Minnesota Press.

Pawel, Miriam. 2009. *The Union of Their Dreams: Power, Hope, and Struggle in Cesar Chavez's Farm Worker Movement*. New York: Bloomsbury.

Giumarra Vineyards

In the early 1900s, a Sicilian immigrant named Giuseppe Giumarra sold fresh produce from a stall in the 7th Street Wholesale Fruit Market in Los Angeles. In 1922, he joined his brothers John and George and his brother-in-law Dominick Corsaro to found Giumarra Brothers Fruit Company, Inc. By the mid-1960s the Giumarra Vineyards, along with another family corporation, was a $25 million business owning more than 12,000 acres in Kern and Tulane Counties, California, and was the major table-grape-producing company in the United States. In the fall

On July 29, 1970, John Giumarra Jr. of Giumarra Vineyards holds aloft the union label of the farm workers union. On one of the momentous days in the history of the United Farm Workers, officials of 17 companies signed contracts with Cesar Chavez. (AP/Wide World Photo)

of 1965, at the beginning of the Delano grape strike, many workers at Giumarra had walked out. They were quickly replaced by scab labor. Although companies such as Schenley Vineyards had finally agreed to contracts with the United Farm Workers Organizing Committee (UFWOC), Giumarra remained relatively unaffected by the union's early successes. In July 1967, the UFWOC decided to take on the giant. Union cofounder Dolores Huerta told a reporter, "if we can crack Giumarra we can crack them all" (Ferriss and Sandoval 1997, 138).

The fight would not be easy. Now led by John Giumarra, known as "The Grape King," the large company could call on its vast financial assets and Republican political connections to fend off the challenge. Its owners were defiant and ready to use force and slander to combat what they regarded as impudent amateurs. The writer John Gregory Dunne later described the Giumarras as "a rough bunch of boys," a network of fathers and brothers and sons and sons-in-law "not especially known for their enlightened views about the labor movement" (Dunne 1971, 183). Upon learning of the UFWOC's plans to aim its strike at the company, one Giumarra official dismissed the union as a "socialist-civil rights movement" comprised of "do-gooder elements, beatniks, and socialistic-type groups" ("Farm Union Pins . . . " 1967).

At a large rally on August 3, 1967, most Giumarra workers voted to strike, and two-thirds of the 5,000 workers walked out of the fields during the harvest. Giumarra responded, as it had done before, with a coordinated effort to bring an influx of Mexican laborers from across the border. Also, Giumarra managed to convince a Kern County Superior Court judge to issue an injunction restricting the distance between individuals on the picket lines and banning the use of bullhorns.

Chavez responded to the counterattack with the tactic he most favored—the boycott. The Giumarras were ready. When the UFWOC sent boycott leaders around the country to begin what would become a prolonged fight to persuade store owners to stop buying the Giumarra label, the company prevailed on other growers to allow them to use their labels in place of the Giumarra label. Store owners and customers would thus be unsure what brands to avoid. Chavez had a simple answer. He decided to boycott every California table-grape grower. The battle was joined; the nationwide boycott would test whether the UFWOC had enough resources, enough volunteers, and the necessary coordination to pull off such a herculean effort. Chavez was determined to show Giumarra and the world that this movement was far from a fanciful lark led by beatniks and socialist types, as characterized by Giumarra, but a forceful drive for social justice.

As the boycott continued, passions and patience were tested. Some union members squared off in a number of violent confrontations, almost always resulting in the arrest or injury of the union members. Expressing a renewed call for nonviolence, Chavez began his historic fast, not only a symbol of penance but a gesture that energized the movement. Through the turbulent year of 1968, with the assassinations of Martin Luther King Jr. and Robert Kennedy, the antiwar protests, and the election of Richard Nixon to the presidency, the boycott endured. As the boycotters across the country stretched their energies and pocketbooks to carry on the struggle, the sales of grapes began to slide dramatically in 1969. Union workers in various cities across the country refused to handle table grapes, and consumers sympathetic to the cause refused to buy them.

Nevertheless, the growers refused to yield. Giumarra launched a $2 million advertising blitz with the public relations firm Whitaker & Baxter. Soon there were newspaper and television ads and articles and bumper stickers encouraging the public to stand up for their "consumer rights" and to eat California grapes.

Unfortunately for Giumarra, the advertising buy did not seem to have any noticeable effect. Indeed, by the spring of 1969, some growers feared that the boycott would, in the end, be ruinous to the industry. Coachella grower Lionel Steinberg, president of David Freedman & Company, admitted that the boycott had "literally closed Boston, New York, Philadelphia, Chicago, Detroit, Montreal, [and] Toronto completely from handling table grapes" (Maika and Maika 1982, 195). Rejecting pleas from a number of fellow growers that he not back down, Steinberg instead became the first table-grape grower to sign a contract with Chavez's union.

Finally, on July 25, UFWOC counsel Jerry Cohen received a call from John Giumarra Jr. asking to meet with him and Cesar Chavez as soon as possible. A few hours later, at 2:30 AM, the young Giumarra met with Chavez and Cohen at the Stardust Motel in Delano. Later, with the momentous meeting firmly in his memory, Cohen even remembered that it was Room 44. The Giumarra company was now willing to discuss terms of an agreement. Realizing they were dealing from a position of strength, Chavez and Cohen insisted there would be no agreement unless Giumarra was also able to bring the other growers in the Delano area to the table.

By the next day, Giumarra had convinced all of them. On July 29, 1970, after meeting for three days, the UFWOC and more than 20 growers signed contracts that brought an end to the long boycott of table grapes. It increased wages and included new safety requirements on the use of pesticides as well as a health plan.

The union celebrated that night in Delano. They sang "Nosotros venceremos," the civil rights song of "We Shall Overcome." They shouted "Viva La Huelga!" Cohen later called it a "stunning victory" (Cohen 2008).

But three years later, when the contracts with Giumarra and the other companies expired, the battles would begin all over again. There would be violence in the fields, clashes with the Teamsters Union, which attempted to oust the farm workers union from power, and even the deaths of two union strikers. Well into the twenty-first century, Giumarra was still the target of small strike attempts and appeals to treat its farm workers with better working conditions and decent pay. But when Jerry Cohen remembers his work with Chavez and the union, he prefers to think of that night in Room 44 of the Stardust Motel in Delano and those feelings of triumph.

Further Reading

Bardacke, Frank. 2011. *Trampling Out the Vintage*. New York: Verso.

Cohen, Jerry. 2008. "Gringo Justice: The United Farm Workers Union, 1967–1981." https://www.amherst.edu/media/view/314670/original/Gringojustice.pdf.

Dunne, John Gregory. 1971. *Delano: The Story of the California Grape Strike*. Berkeley: University of California Press.

"Farm Union Pins Its Hopes on Victory in Coast Grape Strike." 1967. *New York Times*, October 2, 43.

Ferriss, Susan, and Ricardo Sandoval. 1997. *The Fight in the Fields: Cesar Chavez and the Farmworkers Movement*. New York: Harcourt Brace & Company.

Levy, Jacques. 1970. "The Black Eagle Wins." *Time*, August 10, 14.

Levy, Jacques. 2007. *Cesar Chavez: Autobiography of La Causa*. Minneapolis: University of Minnesota Press.

Maika, Linda, and Theo Maika. 1982. *Farm Workers, Agribusiness, and the State*. Philadelphia: Temple University Press.

Matthiessen, Peter. 1969. *Sal Si Puedes (Escape If You Can): Cesar Chavez and the New American Revolution*. Berkeley: University of California Press.

Govea, Jessica

Jessica Govea was in the second grade when she met Cesar Chavez in the backyard of her family's home in Bakersfield, California. Born on January 4, 1947, in Porterville, California, she was the daughter of farm workers and began working in the fields with her parents when she was very young. She spent every summer until she was 15 picking grapes, cotton, and prunes. Her second-grade encounter with Chavez came about because her father, Juan Govea, was an activist, a member of the Community Service Organization (CSO), for which Chavez was an organizer. For a time he worked with the Santa Fe Railroad. No one in the backyard that day could have realized that the second grader, listening to the organizers plan their next action, might a decade later become one of Chavez's most valuable lieutenants.

She was an eager activist from the beginning, distributing flyers and going door-to-door with her father for CSO campaigns, joining the Junior CSO and becoming its president, and leading a petition drive to build a park honoring a neighborhood child who had died in a traffic accident. In 1964, she graduated from Bakersfield High School, where she had excelled on the debate team. She attended a community college for two years with thoughts of later going to law school. At the age of 19, however, Govea dropped her college plans and made a bold move that would mark her life's career. She joined Chavez's farm workers union.

Soon after beginning work at the union headquarter in Delano, Govea met three female farm workers who were complaining about nausea, dizziness, rashes, and double vision. They had been told by the foreman at the ranch that they were likely suffering from heat exhaustion. All three had their doubts, and so did

Govea. She remembered her own experience in the fields where there were often no bathrooms or clean drinking water and recalled having many of the same symptoms. Govea became convinced early on that the use of pesticides by the growers was having severe health effects on the workers. Shortly after meeting the three women, Govea expressed her concerns to Jerry Cohen, the union's lead counsel. So, convinced by Govea that the issue was of paramount concern to the movement, Cohen began to encourage Chavez and other union leaders to examine the issue carefully. It would become a major focus of the United Farm Workers (UFW) for decades to come. "Jessica never took any credit for any of this," Cohen later said. "Almost no one knew she was instrumental in raising the issue in the first place" (Cohen 2008).

Govea's energy, infectious enthusiasm, and drive to make a difference in the lives of farm workers was clearly evident to Chavez and the UFW leadership from the start. In July 1968, she joined organizer Marshall Ganz and Catholic priest Mark Day in launching a grape boycott in Toronto, Canada. A number of Toronto newspaper reporters, impressed not only by her arguments in favor of the boycott but also by her own personal story, ran articles favorable to La Causa. She gave numerous spirited talks to a variety of audiences and helped convince several food chains to support the boycott. The boycott team in Toronto was so successful that the mayor of Toronto proclaimed November 23, 1968, as "Grape Day" in the city.

In January 1969, Govea, now 22, was directed by Chavez to head to Montreal. She was now in charge of the boycott of the entire province of Quebec. The city of Montreal was the fourth largest grape-consuming city in North America. Govea was an organizing dynamo, working with labor officials and gaining the support of religious groups and public officials. Working in a city where about three-fourths of the population spoke French, she recruited bilingual organizers and gathered enough supporters to develop a door-to-door campaign in certain areas of the city near grocery chains that were the largest grape sellers. She set up picket lines and even organized a street-theater group to perform skits for the picketers, much as Luis Valdez's Teatro Campesino had done in California.

It did not take long for the inhabitants of Montreal and those in Quebec province to begin to eat far fewer grapes. The strike and boycott against Delano growers ended in August 1970. The victory was in no small part helped by considerable pressure directed at California growers by Canadian purchasers.

When she returned to California, Govea worked on the union's lettuce boycott, becoming one of the campaign's international coordinators. She later returned to Toronto to run the Gallo boycott from 1973 to 1975. Govea also became a skilled political fighter, especially in forging ambitious voter-registration efforts in both the presidential primary of Robert Kennedy in California in 1968 and the gubernatorial campaign of Jerry Brown in 1974. In 1977, in recognition of her inestimable contributions to the union's successes, she was elected to the UFW's executive board.

During a turbulent period of internal dissension and mistrust within the UFW, Govea left the union in 1981. She continued to work as an advocate for oppressed and disenfranchised people.

She traveled to El Salvador to work with the national leadership of the coffee-processing workers union to help rebuild the union after a war in that country. In New York City, she worked with political candidates from minority populations. She became an assistant director for civil rights in a large textile union.

Later, she began to share her organizing wisdom in the classroom. She became a faculty member in the Labor Studies and Employment Relations Department at Rutgers University.

On January 23, 2005, she passed away from breast cancer at age 58. According to her husband, Kenneth Thorbourne Jr., whom she married in 1987, she believed that the disease had resulted from her years of exposure to pesticides in the fields. At the time of her death, she was a labor educator at Cornell University's School of Industrial and Labor Relations in New York City.

At a memorial gathering in Salinas in her honor that brought together UFW members and former members, nearly every speaker mentioned not only her invaluable work with the UFW and other organizations seeking rights for the oppressed but also her glorious singing voice. They remembered her singing union songs, Mexican ballads, and folk songs such as "Cu cu ru cu cu Paloma" and the civil rights anthem "We Shall Overcome," all of which gave witness to her indomitable spirit in fighting for social justice.

Further Reading

Bardacke, Frank. 2011. *Trampling Out the Vintage: Cesar Chavez and the Two Souls of the United Farm Workers*. New York: Verso.

Cohen, Jerry. 2008. "Gringo Justice: The United Farm Workers Union, 1967–1981."https://www.amherst.edu/media/view/314670/original/Gringojustice.pdf.

Hoose, Philip. 2001. *We Were There, Too!: Young People in U.S.* New York: Farrar, Straus and Giroux.

Pawel, Miriam. 2009. *The Union of Their Dreams: Power, Hope, and Struggle in Cesar Chavez's Farm Worker Movement*. New York: Bloomsbury Press.

Shaw, Randy. 2008. *Beyond the Fields: Cesar Chavez, the UFW, and the Struggle For Justice in the 21st Century*. Berkeley: University of California Press.

Grape Strike, 1965

In September 1965, Cesar Chavez's National Farm Workers Alliance (NFWA) joined a grape strike in Delano, California, begun by the Agricultural Workers Organizing Committee (AWOC), a union of mostly Filipino Americans. It marked the beginning of one of the most remarkable periods in farm labor history—a five-year struggle of farm workers and their allies not only to improve meager wages and wretched working conditions in the harvest fields but also to assert the basic dignity of themselves and their labor and the right to be recognized as a collective bargaining partner with their employers. They faced an entrenched wall of opposition—growers, political officials, law enforcement, and other established groups and organizations willing to use all forms of resistance to stop such a farm workers movement. By the time grape growers sat down with union officials in 1970 to sign the first farm workers contracts in history, it was, for the farm workers, only after a long road of battle—picketing, violence, sacrifice, marches, a historic fast, and tragic losses of friends and supporters. Nevertheless, they persevered and prevailed.

Chavez had not believed his new organization was ready for a strike in 1965 when the AWOC asked him to combine forces. The union had little money or experience. But it had the spirit, he felt, to join with the small Filipino group in a strike against Delano table- and wine-grape growers. He decided that he could not turn down the opportunity. At an NFWA meeting at the Delano Catholic church, his call was answered with thunderous approval. The cry was now "Viva la Huelga!" (Long Live the Strike!). Chavez appealed for nonviolence.

On September 20, 1965, farm workers stayed away from the fields and joined picket lines. Some religious groups, students, and civil rights veterans were pulled into the battle by the strikers. Some people in the community opened their homes to house meetings, joined picket lines in front of grocery stores, leafleted neighborhoods, and joined in prayer vigils and rallies.

To others, the protestors were nuisances at best and leftist fellow travelers at worst. The writer John Gregory Dunne, who visited Delano in the early years of the strike, remembered local newspapers and organizations going to great lengths trying to compare Chavez to the Russian Marxist revolutionary Leon Trotsky. Dunne said that he had never heard the name of Trotsky so often. "One mystery I was never able to clear up," he said, "was how the townspeople had bypassed Marx, Lenin, and Stalin in favor of Trotsky as the black angel of the NFWA" (Dunne 2008, 111).

The union strove in other ways to foster an unbreakable unity in the members. "Huelga Priests" held masses for the workers several times a week. Workers began to speak about their Latino culture, to talk about Mexican history and the relationship of this strike to other battles of the poor and dispossessed. They waved banners of the Virgin of Guadalupe, the patron saint of Mexico, and carried both the Mexican and United States flags. They chose as an anthem a Spanish hymn called "De Colores."

By the fall and winter of 1965, the strike attracted widening support from labor, church, and civil rights groups. United Auto Workers president Walter Reuther traveled to Delano to support the strikers.

Faced with increasing violence on the picket lines by local police and grower security forces, Chavez turned to another weapon in December 1965—the boycott. Across the country, union forces began to establish boycott centers in major cities.

Prominent Americans began to throw their support to Chavez, including Senator Robert F. Kennedy, who visited Delano as part of a U.S. Senate Subcommittee of Migratory Labor hearing during the spring of 1966. Dr. Martin Luther King Jr. sent a message to Chavez likening his nonviolent protest movement for social justice to that of the civil rights campaigns.

In 1966, Chavez led strikers on a 340-mile march from Delano to the state capitol steps in Sacramento. Reminiscent of the marches of the civil rights movement, the so-called *perigrinación* (pilgrimage) energized the movement. At every stop along the route, there were rallies and meals for the marchers. As the march reached new locations, it picked up additional participants: boys and girls on bicycles, elderly men and women who had been in the fields for decades, nuns and priests carrying banners, all of them joining in the chanting and the singing —a kind of festival of protest. It ended on Easter Sunday, drawing approximately 10,000 people and much national attention. It also prompted Schenley Vineyards to negotiate an agreement with NFWA, the first genuine contract between a grower and farm workers union in U.S. history.

By the summer of 1966, the NFWA and the AWOC had merged to form the United Farm Workers Organizing Committee (UFWOC). It would later be renamed the United Farm Workers of America (UFW).

As the national media focused more intently on the farm worker struggle, as the stakes became higher, so did tensions and anger. Growers sprayed insecticide and fertilizer on picketers. Hired thugs taunted the union members; many wielded clubs. Increasingly restive and barely able to continue their nonviolent methods, a number of strikers and boycotters fought back. In a number of cities, fights broke out. In some cases, protestors roughed up a number of individuals suspected of being company spies. Some strikers set fire to packing crates and pelted scabs with marbles hurled with slingshots. In response to the violence, Chavez, on February 15, 1968, began a fast to rededicate his movement to nonviolence. It was a nonviolent practice he had learned from reading about the life of Indian independence leader Mohandas Gandhi. For 25 days he fasted, ending it on March 10, accompanied by Robert F. Kennedy. Both Kennedy and Martin Luther King Jr. would lose their lives soon thereafter to assassination, events tragic both to the nation and to the farm workers movement.

But the long grape strike and the boycott had taken their toll on California's grape industry. On July 29, 1970, grape growers assembled at the union hall at the UFWOC field office at Forty Acres west of Delano to sign their first union contracts. The union's victory extended to 85 percent of the state's table-grape industry. It not only provided for substantial wage increases, health care, and protections against pesticide poisoning but also for union-run hiring halls that gave UFWOC control over the distribution of available work and grievance procedures to rescue the individual worker from the arbitrary authority of the bosses.

More struggles were ahead. But on this day, as they jubilantly sang the songs of La Causa, as they sang the civil rights song of "We Shall Overcome" and as they shouted the slogans of "Viva la Huelga," the farm workers were asserting newly won respect. This was a day for which the union leaders had labored for so long, a day for the *campesinos*, the field workers, many with their backs bent, their hands roughed, and skin weathered like leather. That day in Delano, many of their eyes filled.

Further Reading

Bardacke, Frank. 2011. *Trampling Out the Vintage: Cesar Chavez and the Two Souls of the United Farm Workers*. New York: Verso.

Dunne, John Gregory. 2008. *Delano: The Story of the California Grape Strike*. Berkeley: University of California Press.

Ganz, Marshall. 2009. *Why David Sometimes Wins: Leadership, Organization, and Strategy in the California Farm Worker Movement*. New York: Oxford Press.

Matthiessen, Peter. 1969. *Sal Si Puedes: Cesar Chavez and the New American Revolution*. Berkeley: University of California Press.

Pawel, Miriam. 2009. *The Union of Their Dreams: Power, Hope, and Struggle in Cesar Chavez's Farm Worker Movement*. New York: Bloomsbury.

H

Hartmire, Chris

After growing up in Upper Darby, Pennsylvania, a suburb of Philadelphia, Wayne C. "Chris" Hartmire received a scholarship to Princeton University, where he began study to become a civil engineer. After working for two summers at camps for low-income boys and experiencing joy in helping those in need, he decided on a new road. "Something clicked," he said. He made plans to study for the ministry.

After graduating from Princeton with his civil engineering degree, however, he put his plans to attend a seminary on hold when he married Jane "Pudge" Eichner in 1954. He had known her since he was in the seventh grade. The newlyweds took jobs to get a financial footing—he with the Navy Civil Engineering Corps at the Philadelphia Naval Shipyard and she as a public health nurse in Philadelphia.

In 1957, he entered Union Seminary in New York City. After graduating with a master of divinity degree from Union in 1960, he joined the East Harlem Protestant Parish (EHPP) and began to minister to young people. In 1961, when the Congress of Racial Equality asked the EHPP to send one white minister on an interracial Freedom Ride through the South, it was Hartmire who thus plunged into the civil rights movement on the front lines.

In 1961, Hartmire was asked to replace Doug Still as director of the California Migrant Ministry (CMM), a program ministering to the needs of California's migrant field workers in the San Joaquin and Imperial Valleys. In his early days as director of the CMM, Hartmire recognized clearly the extraordinarily unfair labor practices that had kept migrant agricultural workers mired in poverty and deprivation.

The Bracero Program, enacted at the beginning of U.S. involvement in World War II to provide temporary farm laborers from Mexico to U.S. growers, had kept wages low for everyone in the fields. Hartmire soon became a strong voice lobbying against the continuation of the program long after it was needed. Prompted by protests from labor groups and other religious organizations, the Bracero Program ended in 1963. In the eyes of many of California's growers, Hartmire and other religious figures had crossed the line into local politics.

The ire that Hartmire drew from agribusiness interests would grow. Hartmire soon met Fred Ross of the Community Service Organization (CSO), a group that led voter-registration drives and political outreach to Mexican Americans, and his prize recruit, Cesar Chavez.

In 1965, after Chavez had left the CSO to organize a drive to unionize farm workers under an organization he called the National Farm Workers Association (NFWA), he called Hartmire to enlist the young minister in the cause. Soon, he was working with Chavez in the Delano grape strike.

So enamored was Hartmire with the chance to make a profound difference in the lives of Mexican American farm workers that he virtually turned the CMM into an adjunct of Chavez's La Causa. He was an invaluable ally to Chavez in providing a religious presence in the movement in its earliest days, lending credibility to Chavez in fending off charges that he was engaged in anti-American activities. In all of these efforts, he faced continuous hostility from many of the established church denominations, who felt that Hartmire was bending religious commitment toward political movement. Nevertheless, he fought off the firestorm of controversy and began to raise money from some national denominations for the movement.

Hartmire was in the center of major events in the farm workers struggle. He was with Chavez in the peregrination to Sacramento in 1966. He worked as an organizer in the DiGiorgio campaign. He skillfully wrote, spoke, and disseminated information justifying the grape boycott and enlisting new recruits. He handed the first piece of bread to Chavez as the union leader sat next to Robert Kennedy at the fast in Delano in 1968. A year later, he also fasted—at a parking lot in Los Angeles urging shoppers not to buy grapes. He went to jail with farm workers on many occasions.

He coordinated marches in the lettuce strike in 1971. At the behest of Chavez, he turned the CMM into the National Farm Worker Ministry, an ecumenical organization that consolidated religious communities behind La Causa. In 1972, he organized workers to help defeat Proposition 22, the initiative that sought to outlaw secondary boycotts. In 1973, during the battle between the union and the Teamsters union, he helped convince nearly 100 United Church of Christ ministers to visit Coachella to show their support. In 1975, after California passed the Agricultural Labor Relations Act of 1975 to protect the right of workers to organize and negotiate, he worked with the union through various elections and contract negotiations to help ensure the law's effectiveness.

So dedicated was Hartmire to the movement, even through the years of inner turmoil, mistrust, and firings, that in 1981 he resigned as director of the National Farm Worker Ministry to move to the UFW's headquarters at La Paz and devote himself solely to the union, unattached to other affiliations.

For several years, Hartmire became one of Chavez's closest advisors and in 1988 became secretary-treasurer, the second highest ranking position on the union's executive board. But in January 1989, at the union's board meeting, Hartmire suddenly found himself embroiled in a controversy that reflected the continuing conflict and paranoia infesting the UFW's management. Accused of not firing an accountant who had defrauded the union of funds, the UFW board, led by Chavez himself, made Hartmire the scapegoat for the incident. Such a humiliating and devastating attack against Hartmire, a man whose loyalty to Chavez had never been in question, inflicted deep emotional scars on the minister. He left La Paz after devoting over 27 years to Chavez and La Causa.

Hartmire continued his ardent efforts for those in need. He worked in Sacramento for Loaves and Fishes, an organization dedicated to feeding and housing the homeless. He also founded Clean & Sober, a recovery center for the homeless. He again became a member of the board of National Farm Worker Ministry and worked as a consultant for the Service Employees Industrial Union.

Further Reading

Bardacke, Frank. 2011. *Trampling Out the Vintage: Cesar Chavez and the Two Souls of the United Farm Workers*. New York: Verso.

Griswold del Castillo, Richard, and Richard Garcia. 1995. *Cesar Chavez: A Triumph of the Spirit*. Norman: University of Oklahoma Press.

Hartmire, John. 2000. "At the Heart of a Historic Movement." *Newsweek*, July 24, 12.

Pawel, Miriam. 2010. *The Union of Their Dreams: Power, Hope, and Struggle in Cesar Chavez's Farm Worker Movement*. New York: Bloomsbury Press.

Smith, Sydney D. 1987. *Grapes of Conflict*. Pasadena, CA: Hope Publishing House.

Watt, Alan. 2010. *Farm Workers and the Churches: The Movement in California and Texas*. College Station: Texas A & M University Press.

Wells, Ronald. 2009. "Cesar Chavez's Protestant Allies: The California Migrant Ministry and the Farm Workers." *Journal of Presbyterian History*, Spring/Summer, 5–16. http://www.farmworkermovement.us/essays/essays/cec.pdf.

Higgins, George

A number of prominent Catholic clerics in the United States have been known as "labor priests," men who have been outspoken and have worked relentlessly to fight for the rights of workers, not only from their pulpits but on picket lines, in union halls, and as members of organizations committed to fair wages, decent working conditions, and most of all human dignity. None were more determined and influential than Monsignor George Higgins. For Cesar Chavez and the farm workers movement, Higgins became a powerful influence not only through his writings and vocal support that bridged the Church and the farm labor movement but also in many active mediation roles, bringing together warring sides in labor disputes to bargaining tables and to agreements. Chavez credited Higgins with being one of the most influential forces in the development and success of the United Farm Workers (UFW).

Born on January 21, 1916, into a devout Catholic family in Chicago, Higgins came of age during the Great Depression and saw firsthand the struggles of working people. Many of his close relatives, including his father, a postal worker, were union members—machinists, firefighters, and engineers. He attended Archbishop Quigley Preparatory Seminary and the University of St. Mary of the Lake. Ordained for the Archdiocese of Chicago in 1940, he traveled to Washington, DC, to study at the Catholic University of America, where he received a Ph.D. in labor economics in 1944.

He served on the staff of the National Catholic Welfare Conference, later known as the National Conference of Catholic Bishops/United States Catholic Conference from 1944 to 1980, becoming director of the Department of Social Action in 1954. The department was established as a service department for Catholic lay organizations, Catholic schools, and the Catholic press to promote progressive thought in areas of social action. Under Higgins's direction, the department focused on industrial and interracial relations. It published books and pamphlets, conducted conferences and institutes, and sponsored lectures. For over 50 years, Higgins was a prolific columnist for *The Yardstick*, a press column syndicated by the Catholic News Service. He began writing the column in 1945, producing nearly 3,000 articles over a period of 56 years. He also wrote numerous articles in other journals on social justice issues.

In 1953, he became papal chamberlain with the title of monsignor. In 1959, he was named a domestic prelate.

A strong supporter of the growing civil rights movement, he not only wrote many articles on discrimination and the need for Christians to stand against racism and injustice, but he also, on numerous occasions, walked with protest marchers and heard the taunts and jeers from whites lining the streets and steeled himself against threats of violence.

As early as 1951, Higgins addressed problems of the farm workers. He wrote about the abuses by so-called respectable growers who hired men, women, and children to pick their cotton, grapes, and beets for a pittance in wretched conditions and with poor housing, inadequate health facilities, and racial intolerance that struck at their dignity. As with any criminal or organized crime figure, Higgins declared, much scorn should be directed toward those who would subject "our brothers in Christ" to such treatment.

Through the 1950s into the early 1960s, Higgins continued to rail in his writings against the injustices meted out to migratory workers. They had no protections under federal or state laws. They were hurt by the federal Bracero Program, which allowed growers to bring in temporary contract workers from Mexico at the expense of local laborers. He urged the repeal of the program. He chastised Congress for not enacting legislation to aid U.S. farm workers.

In the late 1960s, Higgins wrote powerful columns in support of the farm workers' national grape boycott and urged Catholic bishops to formally endorse it.

When some of the bishops asserted reservations about such an overt stand on the issue, Higgins and others went along with an alternative plan—a Bishop's Ad Hoc Committee on Farm Labor. It was chaired by Bishop Joseph Donnelly of Hartford, Connecticut, who had extensive knowledge and experience in labor issues. It also included Monsignor Roger Mahoney of California, who had ministered to workers in bracero camps. Higgins was the committee's main consultant.

In January 1970, the bishop's committee gathered in Fresno and was able to coordinate a meeting between Chavez and the major growers against whom the grape strike and boycott had been targeted. It was the beginning of hundreds of sessions of bargaining between Chavez's union and various growers over the next four years. Higgins spent more time in California than he did in this period at his home in Washington, DC. The mediation role of Higgins, who persuaded the bishops that farm workers deserved the right of collective bargaining, proved critical in the negotiations and led to many successful contracts.

Higgins was often in the middle of violent confrontations in the harvest fields. In July 1973 in Coachella, California, as Higgins acted as a mediator between the farm workers union and the Teamsters, strikers faced vicious attacks along picket lines. Teamster goons, armed with pipes, chains, brass knuckles, clubs, and even machetes waded into striking farm workers with a viciousness that shocked Higgins and, for a time, prompted Chavez to pull the protesters from the fields. Nearly 100 strikers, including women, were injured, and many were hospitalized. Higgins accused the Teamsters of "throwing sand in the gears" of reasonable arbitration and, along with Chavez, demanded that the local authorities take action. Finally, the Riverside County sheriff's office dispatched nearly 150 deputies to restore order.

From the beginning of the Teamsters' efforts to destroy Chavez's union, Higgins, both in negotiations and in his writings, sided strongly with the farm workers. He regarded the Teamsters' actions as "obscene." Following the passage of California's Agricultural Labor Relations Act (ALRA) in 1975, legislation that gave the UFW the right to collectively bargain and to have fair elections, the Teamsters, facing an uphill battle, finally ended their effort to displace the farm workers union. Chavez regarded Higgins's efforts on behalf of the farm workers against the Teamsters as crucial. Chavez later said of Higgins, "I think he was proud that we had decided to fight" (Costello 1984, 117).

Higgins later served as an adviser to the Second Vatican Council as a member of the U.S. bishops' press briefing team. He was awarded the Presidential Medal of Freedom by President Bill Clinton in 2000. He died on May 1, 2002.

Further Reading

Bardacke, Frank. 2011. *Trampling Out the Vintage: Cesar Chavez and the Two Souls of the United Farm Workers*. New York: Verso.

Costello, Gerald. 1984. *Without Fear or Favor: George Higgins on the Record*. Mystic, CT: Twenty-Third Publications.

"Court Order Seeks to End Planned Attacks." 1973. *El Malcriado*, July 13. http://farmworkermovement.com/ufwarchives/elmalcriado/1973/No.%2014%20July%2013,%201973.pdf.

Higgins, George. 1993. *Organized Labor and the Church: Reflections of a "Labor Priest."* Mahwah, NJ: Paulist Press.

Levy, Jacques. 2007. *Cesar Chavez: Autobiography of La Causa*. Minneapolis: University of Minnesota Press.

Huerta, Dolores

They were partners for four decades. Dolores Huerta first met Cesar Chavez in the 1950s when they were young organizers under the tutelage of Fred Ross with the Community Service Organization (CSO). In 1962, she joined Chavez in forming a new union of farm workers. From the early strikes in Delano, California, to nationwide boycotts, she was a driving force behind the successes of the union —a fierce negotiator and an inspiring organizer. In a world of labor union fights and political battles, usually dominated by men in these years, she took on the union's agribusiness and right-wing political enemies with fierce determination and great skill. In contract negotiations and in lobbying efforts, she was so forceful that opponents called her "the dragon lady," an appellation she appreciated. In New York and other cities she mobilized boycott operations with proficiency and extraordinary energy. She gained the admiration of young activists, joined with national feminist leaders in pushing for women's rights, and continued to influence national Latino civil rights struggles well into the twenty-first century. The defiant organizing cry of the United Farm Workers (UFW) and of other progressive drives was one she coined in a fight for union rights: Si, Se Puede! (Yes, we can!). It defines her career.

She was born in Dawson, New Mexico, in 1930. Her father was a migrant farm worker and miner who joined a number of labor and political groups protesting the treatment of workers. When her parents divorced in 1936, she moved to Stockton, California, with her mother and two brothers. She completed high school in Stockton and later received a degree and teaching certificate from Stockton College. After a short period in the classroom, she left teaching, discouraged and disillusioned about attempting to help educate children whose lives had been so compromised by poverty and discrimination.

She saw the CSO, with its mission of providing services and fighting racism against Mexican Americans, as a vehicle to make a difference, and she gave her considerable energies to the work, setting up a Stockton chapter. Attractive and gregarious, Huerta became an especially effective representative for CSO in

On May 29, 2012, President Barack Obama presents United Farm Workers cofounder Dolores Huerta with the Presidential Medal of Freedom. (AP Photo/Carolyn Kaster)

face-to-face meetings with local government leaders and with potential donors. She also took on lobbying efforts with members of the California legislature in Sacramento for such issues as the expansion of state disability assistance to agricultural workers. While still active with the CSO, Huerta also helped establish the Agricultural Workers Organizing Committee (AWOC), an infant union that began to push for better working conditions for oppressed farm workers.

Although she valued her efforts with the CSO, the idea of beginning a large farm workers union envisioned by Chavez appealed to her daring and forceful nature, and she, like Chavez, gave up the CSO for this revolutionary, if seemingly quixotic, venture. Her early experience with the AWOC would help Chavez in his quest.

Along with Gilbert Padilla, another CSO organizer, she joined Chavez in Delano, California, in 1962. On September 30, in an abandoned movie theater in Fresno, California, approximately 200 workers gathered to show their solidarity to a new union they called the National Farm Workers Association (NFWA). By 1964, over 1,000 workers had joined the new union.

In 1965, members of the AWOC, mostly led by Filipinos, decided to begin a strike against grape growers in the Delano region. They asked Chavez, Huerta, and the other leaders of the NFWA to join in the strike. Although Chavez, Huerta, and the other leaders of the NFWA had not anticipated taking on the growers at such a stage in their own union's development, the AWOC action left them little choice. On September 16, 1965, NFWA members gathered at a church in Delano and voted unanimously—around 500 of the workers and their leaders—to join the strike. From the church, the cry sounded: *Viva la Huelga!* Long live the strike!

Huerta seemed born for such clashes. Tough-minded and focused, she coordinated the picket lines, entreating those who grew tired to keep up the pressure. She joined workers in jail for violating local ordinances. It would be the first of many arrests over the course of her career, all of which she saw as badges of honor, just as black Americans in the civil rights struggle had gone to jail in the name of freedom. By April 1966, Schenley Industries agreed to sign a contract with the farm workers union, the first time in the history of the U.S. labor movement that a farm labor union had received such recognition. Huerta negotiated the contract, as she would many others that the union would win in the farm workers movement.

In the late 1960s, Huerta worked mostly out of New York as the director of the table-grape boycott for New York City. She mobilized other unions and political activists and enlisted the support of Latino associations, religious groups, peace organizations, and consumers across racial and ethnic lines.

By 1971, the union, which became known as the United Farm Workers of America (UFW), had won pivotal contracts, and Huerta was named vice president. In 1973, as the UFW began a nationwide consumer boycott not only of grapes but also of lettuce and other products, she acted as East Coast director, bringing together community workers, religious groups, women's organizations, and others to the cause.

In September 1988, outside the Sir Francis Drake Hotel on Union Square in San Francisco, Huerta was once again in a picket line, this time demonstrating against the use of pesticides that had been proven to be injurious to the health of field workers. In a scuffle with police, Huerta, now 58 years old, was clubbed by a policeman and suffered severe injuries, including a ruptured spleen that had to be removed. The beating eventually led to a string of lawsuits that forced the San Francisco Police Department to change some its practices regarding crowd control and police discipline.

Huerta became a national figure on two fronts because of her gender. On the one hand, the sight of this Latino woman across the table in contact negotiations made an immediate impression on many savvy veterans of the labor wars. On the other hand, because of the sudden appearance of a woman in a position almost totally dominated by males, she achieved immediate status in the feminist movement. While in New York, she became personal friends with Gloria Steinem, writer and founder of *Ms.* magazine, and with other activists. With an increased consciousness raised by the feminist movement against gender stereotypes and discrimination, she began to speak out on sexual harassment issues, lobbied hard for federal and state legislation favorable to welfare mothers, and pushed for laws prohibiting discrimination against women in the workplace.

After Chavez's death in 1993, Huerta continued the UFW's work in the political arena and at the collective bargaining table. In 1993 Huerta was inducted into the National Women's Hall of Fame. In 1998, Huerta was one of three *Ms.* magazine's "Women of the Year" and the *Ladies' Home Journal*'s "100 Most Important Women of the 20th Century." In 1999, President Bill Clinton presented Huerta with the Eleanor Roosevelt Human Rights Award.

Well into the twenty-first century, Huerta remained an active crusader for the rights of farm workers, feminist causes, and progressive political ideals. She also launched the Dolores Huerta Foundation, whose purpose is described in her life's work: "To inspire and motivate people to organize sustainable communities to attain social justice" (Chicago Foundation for Women 2009).

In May 2012, Huerta received from President Barack Obama the Presidential Medal of Freedom. In presenting the award in the East Room of the White House, President Obama quipped, "Dolores was very gracious when I told her I had stolen her slogan, 'Si, se puede'—Yes, we can. Knowing her, I'm pleased that she let me off easy. Because Dolores does not play" ("Remarks . . . " 2012).

Further Reading

Bardacke, Frank. 2011. *Trampling Out the Vintage*. New York: Verso.

Chicago Foundation for Women. 2009. "2009 Impact Awards: Dolores Huerta, Pioneer Award Recipient." http://www.cfw.org/page.aspx?pid=1022.

Dunne, John Gregory. 1976. *Delano: The Story of the California Grape Strike*. New York: Farrar.

Griswold del Castillo, Richard, and Richard A. Garcia. 1955. *Cesar Chavez: A Triumph of Spirit*. Norman: University of Oklahoma Press.

Jones, Carol Larson Jones. 1997. "Dolores Huerta: Cesar Chavez' Partner in Founding the United Farm Workers Union in California." http://www.csupomona.edu/~jis/1997/Mullikin.pdf.

Perez, Frank. 1996. *Dolores Huerta*. Austin, TX: Raintree Steck-Vaughn.

"Remarks by the President at Presidential Medal of Freedom Ceremony." 2012, May 29. http://www.whitehouse.gov/the-press-office/2012/05/29/remarks-president-presidential -medal-freedom-ceremony.

Southwest Research and Information Center. 2004. "An Interview with Dolores Huerta, October 29, 2003." Voices from the Earth. http://www.sric.org/voices/2004/v5n2/ huerta.php.

International Brotherhood of the Teamsters (IBT)

When Cesar Chavez launched his farm workers movement, he understood well and anticipated the impediments to success that seemed mountainous—the power of agribusiness interests and their political friends, the lack of funds, and the formidable task of organizing workers so far removed from the United States' social mainstream. Yet one adversary that would prove daunting and destructive, one that would frustrate and inflame the ire of Chavez and his fellow organizers, was not from the world of business or politics. It was from another union—the Teamsters. By the mid-1960s, the International Brotherhood of the Teamsters (IBT) was the largest union in the United States. Its members included not only truckers but a wide variety of workers in other industries including agriculture. In California, the Teamsters represented about 50,000 packing-house, cannery, and food-processing workers.

The Teamsters had weathered turbulent battles, leadership scandals, and corruption since its formation in 1903. A number of scandals within the Teamsters in the 1950s led AFL-CIO president George Meany to eject the Teamsters from the organization. Recently, federal investigations had uncovered extensive connections between the union and organized crime. By the time of the Delano grape strike in 1965, former Teamsters president Dave Beck was finishing a prison sentence, and its most recent president, James Hoffa, had been convicted in 1964 of fraud and attempted bribery of a grand juror. He would spend the next three years unsuccessfully appealing the conviction and would enter Lewisburg Federal Penitentiary in March 1967. His replacement, Frank Fitzsimmons, would increase the Teamsters' strong political relationship with the Republican Party, especially after the election of Richard Nixon to the presidency in 1968. One of Fitzsimmons's most aggressive actions upon taking over the reins of the Teamsters would be against Chavez and the farm worker movement.

The first confrontation between Chavez's union and the Teamsters erupted in 1966 after Schenley Industries, battered by the farm workers grape strike and boycott, agreed to recognize the union and sign a contract. It was then that DiGiorgio Fruit Corporation and Perelli-Minetti Vineyards, revolted by the prospect of being forced to deal with Chavez, turned instead to the Teamsters, whose organizing director in the West, William Grami, offered "sweetheart" deals with the growers—contracts that were far less favorable to the workers than the one signed by Schenley Industries. In allying themselves with the Teamsters, the growers believed, they could destroy Chavez's union.

For Chavez this was nothing short of an unholy alliance—business interests working with another union to bust his own union. And to Chavez and his allies, the whole enterprise smacked of something else—a cultural assault by Anglos against a movement comprised largely of Mexican Americans seeking not only labor rights but dignity and respect.

The farm workers union prevailed in the first fight against the Teamsters as Chavez and his organizers intensified the boycott, increased the national visibility of the movement, and gained support from other unions appalled at the action of the Teamsters. The battle was finally resolved through secret-ballot elections of workers in which Chavez's farm workers union, the United Farm Workers Organizing Committee (UFWOC), won resounding victories. Representatives of the UFWOC and the Teamsters then signed an agreement laying out the jurisdictional limits for each union. It recognized the right of the UFWOC to organize farm workers; it recognized the Teamsters as the rightful union for the truck drivers, canneries, packing sheds, and other parts of the agricultural industry.

In the summer of 1970, the war resumed. When the UFWOC, after successful strikes and a national boycott, celebrated new labor contracts with grape growers, the Teamsters, violating the terms of the jurisdictional agreement, once again tried to ruin the celebration. In California's Salinas Valley, lettuce growers, attempting to avoid the same fate that befell the grape growers, began signing union contracts with the Teamsters—agreements far more favorable to the growers than any contracts they could possibly work out with Chavez's farm workers union. Chavez was furious at the blatant violation of the earlier agreement. Although he had not planned to take on the lettuce growers so quickly after the grape boycott, Chavez responded forcefully to the collusion between the Teamsters and the companies.

Some 6,000 UFWOC workers struck the Salinas Valley growers in what was the largest farm worker strike in U.S. history. From Monterey County to Santa Cruz, the strikers marched, waving flags, singing, and handing out pamphlets. Growers quickly hired additional armed guards who were not reluctant to flash guns before the eyes of the picketers. UFWOC counsel Jerry Cohen said, "It looked like a revolution, and some of these right-wing growers thought it was" ("The Black Eagle Wins" 1970).

The fight turned bloody in the fields. In the fall of 1970, Teamster thugs hit strikers with baseball bats and chains. On November 4, a UFWOC regional office was bombed. A few weeks later, federal investigators indicted six Teamster men of violating gun-control laws by bringing in firearms and explosives to use against the UFWOC. They were later sent to San Quentin Prison.

Chavez himself was jailed for ignoring an injunction against picketing, an action that brought to Salinas a number of national celebrities including Ethel

Kennedy, widow of slain U.S. Senator Robert Kennedy. When the series of strikes ended in 1971, the farm workers union had again fought off the Teamster attack. Once again, the Teamsters and UFWOC signed a jurisdictional agreement reaffirming the UFW's right to organize field workers.

Still, the fight with the Teamsters did not end for Chavez. In fact, it grew increasingly political. In 1972, Charles Colson, one of President Nixon's advisors, sent a memo to several federal departments emphasizing the administration's desire that the Teamsters prevail in their struggle with Chavez. And in 1973, led by Teamster president Fitzsimmons, the struggle became even more violent. When many of the 1970 contracts were up for renewal, the Teamsters again reneged on the jurisdictional agreement and began signing up growers, especially in Coachella County. The move triggered more strikes that, in turn, brought new violence in the fields—beatings with billy clubs, attacks by vicious dogs with long leashes, mace, and strike-breaker goons getting in the faces of protestors and yelling racial and ethnic insults. Hundreds of strikers went to jail.

Chavez again turned up the heat with a boycott. But the turning point came in August 1975 with the passage of California's Agricultural Labor Relations Act (ALRA), a legislative triumph for the farm workers union working with newly elected Democratic governor Jerry Brown. Under the provisions of the ALRA, a union was required to prove that it represented a majority of the workers. With the passage of the act, the UFW and the Teamsters would go head to head in elections at various California companies that hired farm workers. With this unprecedented opportunity to demonstrate that the majority of workers in these companies preferred Chavez's union, his lieutenants went to political war with fierce determination. A force of over 200 volunteers fanned across harvest fields throughout agricultural areas all over the state cajoling and persuading workers to sign ballots on behalf of the UFW. When the individual elections at the companies ended, the UFW had prevailed in 214 companies; the Teamsters in 115.

On March 10, 1977, the Teamsters and the farm workers union reached a five-year jurisdictional agreement granting Chavez's union exclusive rights to represent the field workers covered by the ALRA. With the ALRA in place, the Teamsters finally realized that there was little chance of gaining traction with California's farm labor workers. They preferred their own union.

Further Reading

Bardacke, Frank. 2011. *Trampling Out the Vintage: Cesar Chavez and the Two Souls of the United Farm Workers*. New York: Verso.

"The Black Eagle Wins." 1970. *Time*, August 10, 14.

Daniel, Cletus. 1995. "Cesar Chavez and the Unionization of California Farmworkers." In *Working People of California*, edited by Daniel Cornford. Berkeley: University of California Press.

Ferriss, Susan, and Ricardo Sandoval. 1997. *The Fight in the Fields: Cesar Chavez and the Farmworkers Movement*. New York: Harcourt Brace & Company.

Ganz, Marshall. 2009. *Why David Sometimes Wins: Leadership, Organization, and Strategy in the California Farm Worker Movement*. New York: Oxford University Press.

Velie, Lester. 1974. "The Teamsters' Campaign to Smash a Union." *Reader's Digest*, December. http://www.farmworkermovement.com/essays/essays/MillerArchive/055% 20The%20Teamster's%20Campaign.pdf.

Itliong, Larry

When the historic Delano grape strike erupted in 1965, it was not Cesar Chavez's farm workers union that ignited it. Larry Itliong, a dynamic Filipino labor organizer working for the AFL-CIO's recently formed Agricultural Workers Organizing Committee (AWOC), led a walk-out of fellow Filipino vineyard workers in Kern County. Growers refused to negotiate even for a pay raise of 15 cents an hour. Retaliating against what they regarded as an impudent challenge to their authority, some growers sent security forces to beat up strikers or shut off the gas, lights, and water in the labor camps. Many were evicted. It was then that Itliong, a 52-year-old veteran of a number of strike actions over the years in Alaska, Washington state, and California, asked Chavez and his infant National Farm Workers Association (NFWA), formed in 1962, to join in the struggle. Together, their combined forces would make farm labor history.

Born on October 25, 1913, in the Philippines, Itliong, at age 15, came to the United States seeking greater opportunities for himself and his family. Like thousands of young Filipino men and teenagers in the 1920s, he was lured by labor contractors needing field and packing-house workers. With immigration to the United States from the Philippines limited to working men, they arrived to an isolating existence. They were prohibited by antimiscegenation laws from marrying Caucasians, were not allowed to buy land and, like blacks and Mexicans, were met with ugly and fierce racial hostility.

Itliong worked in Alaskan fish canneries and the harvest fields of Washington and California picking a variety of fruits and vegetables. A naturally dynamic leader and self-educated, he was not one to accept meekly the physically and emotionally corrosive system that was inflicted on him and his Filipino brothers. The short, cigar-smoking Itliong rebelled, realizing early on that farm workers could not improve their condition unless they banded together to fight back. He became involved with unions and strikes from his earliest years in the United States and had natural leadership abilities that drew men to his side. Nevertheless, as Chavez had discovered during his own early years working in the fields and seeing aborted strikes in which his father had engaged, Itliong realized the formidable adversaries that were allied against farm worker protests—the growers and their security forces, the local police, the courts, the politicians, and the oppressive discrimination toward minorities.

Yet he pressed on. In 1956, he founded the Filipino Farm Labor Union in California. He became deeply immersed with Filipino community groups and organizations, especially in Stockton, and served as an official with the Council of United Filipino Organizations of Northern and Central California. When the AFL-CIO formed a new farm workers union called AWOC, Itliong became a leading organizer.

In the spring of 1965, Itliong, working with another Filipino leader, Ben Gines, led an AWOC strike in Stockton against asparagus and table-grape growers in the area. The short strike led to a small wage increase but not a formal recognition of the union or a contract.

Increasingly confident with the partial victory in Stockton, Itliong soon launched another strike. On September 8, 1965, Filipino workers of the AWOC, once again led by Itliong and Gines, announced a strike of 10 grape growers near Delano, California, the area where Chavez had headquartered the NFWA and where he had already conducted two small-scale strikes of his own.

Although the NFWA had made substantial progress by 1965, Chavez was not yet planning a major strike. At the time the union had been founded in September 1962, he had figured that it would take at least five years of organizing before it would be ready to take on the large growers. But after several discussions with Itliong, Chavez decided to ask the members of the union to join the strike. It was a unique opportunity too important to resist.

The strike would last several years. On August 22, 1966, Chavez's NFWA and Itliong's AWOC merged to form a more cohesive, coordinated force to take on the growers. They called it the United Farm Workers Organizing Committee (UFWOC). At a ceremony, national AFL-CIO director Bill Kircher presented the large charter to both Chavez and Itliong. Chavez became director of the UFWOC Executive Board; Itliong was the assistant director.

By 1970, the alliance between the Filipinos and Mexican American farm workers brought much success—contracts that recognized the UFWOC and its right to collective bargaining, wage increases, medical plans, better educational facilities, and even the beginnings of the Agbayani Village, a home for retired Filipino workers. Itliong, along with other Filipino leaders such as Philip Vera Cruz and Andy Imutan, worked hard in the strikes and boycotts that brought victories. A powerful speaker and a highly respected leader in the Filipino community, Itliong earned the position of national boycott coordinator for the union.

Nevertheless, the cultural tensions that had long existed between the Filipinos and Mexican Americans weighed on the alliance. Itliong felt uneasy about the direction of UFWOC policy, which was directed, he believed, more as a civil rights movement than a labor organization. He also believed that the input of Filipino members was constrained by the presence of Anglo clergymen, lawyers, and student activists who dominated much of the decision making.

Itliong resigned from the UFWOC on October 15, 1971, and moved on to further efforts to help the Filipino community. He became the president of the Filipino American Political Alliance, a national organization between Filipino professionals and laborers that established chapters in cities across the United States.

He died in February 1977 at the age of 63. Chavez spoke at his funeral, hailing him as a pioneer.

Further Reading

DeWitt, Howard. 1980. *Violence in the Fields: California Filipino Farm Labor Unionization during the Great Depression*. Saratoga: Century Twenty One Publishing.

Ganz, Marshall. 2009. *Why David Sometimes Wins: Leadership, Organization, and Strategy in the California Farm Worker Movement*. New York: Oxford University Press.

Meister, Dick. 2012. "The Farm Workers' Filipino-American Champion." *Truthout*, March 30. http://truth-out.org/opinion/item/8211-the-farm-workers-filipino-american -champion.

Scharlin, Craig, and Lilia Villanueva. 2000. *Philip Vera Cruz: A Personal History of Filipino Immigrants and the Farmworkers Movement*. Seattle: University of Washington Press.

Valledor, Sid. 2006. *The Original Writings of Philip Vera Cruz*. Indianapolis: Dog Ear Publishing.

K

Kennedy, Robert

That a U.S. senator from the state of New York would become a champion of a movement led by poor farm workers from California was improbable. That the individual would be Robert F. Kennedy would be of vital significance to Cesar Chavez in his quest to build a union. Kennedy's life story and work were well known throughout the world—born in 1925 to a family of wealth and power, the brother of a charismatic president, U.S. attorney general, senator, and a candidate for president. Yet to farm workers, his support of their movement, his ability to connect emotionally with their struggles, and his willingness to embrace their cause made him an iconic figure, one whose picture would hang in homes of Mexican American workers long after his tragic death.

Kennedy met Chavez briefly in late 1959 in Los Angeles. Kennedy was working on John F. Kennedy's presidential campaign, and Chavez was helping the Community Service Organization (CSO) conduct a voter-registration drive.

It was not until March 1966 that Senator Kennedy became deeply interested in the farm worker struggles. Kennedy was a member of the U.S. Senate Subcommittee on Migrant Labor that arrived in California to investigate conditions in the farm labor sector. Before leaving on the fact-finding trip, he had been briefed by United Auto Workers president Walter Reuther and labor activists among his staff about the wretched working conditions under which laborers suffered at the hands of California agribusiness interests and about Chavez, his farm workers union, and the strike now underway against grape growers.

The subcommittee toured the union offices in Delano with large numbers of curious farm

Portraits of Robert Kennedy, often alongside those of Cesar Chavez, have hung on the walls of Latino families since the 1960s. A supporter of Chavez and the farm workers movement, Kennedy, as no other Anglo politician, touched the hearts of Latinos with his calls for justice and equality. (Lyndon B. Johnson Presidential Library)

workers trailing the group, with cameras flashing and reporters taking down notes. At the jammed Delano High School auditorium that served as the meeting hall, both supporters and opponents of the strike gathered. Large numbers outside surrounded the building to get first word about the deliberations. At the meeting, Kennedy asked penetrating questions, particularly of the local sheriff, who had been arresting nonviolent picketers without any particular authority. After the hearing, Kennedy went to Delano Hall. Angered by what he heard in the meeting and impressed by Chavez, Kennedy embraced the farm workers movement in clear terms as exuberant union members cheered. He even asked to be taken to a nearby picket line at the DiGiorgio Fruit Corporation. In a pinstripe suit, he moved along the line of picketers in work clothes and shook their hands.

Chavez, who had been the target of FBI investigations on possible links to the Communist Party and had been vilified in the press by the growers for anti-American attitudes, said later that the Kennedy visit and his support had given him and the union invaluable legitimacy. "I think it was a turning point in the vicious campaign on the 'Red-baiting' issue and us," Chavez said. "He turned it completely around, completely destroyed it, tore it apart . . . people just wouldn't believe them anymore" (Bender 2008, 21).

Amid the social upheaval, political division, and war protests of the early months of 1968, Kennedy was considering a run for the presidency. When President Lyndon Johnson, embattled by the intractable problems of the Vietnam War, decided not to run for reelection, Vice President Hubert Humphrey and anti-war candidate Senator Eugene McCarthy were running for the Democratic nomination. Kennedy was under intense pressure to enter the race and was nearing a decision in the early months of 1968.

In mid-February, the strike of Chavez's United Farm Workers Organizing Committee (UFWOC) against Giumarra Vineyards and other growers had turned increasingly violent. Chavez decided to begin a fast to rededicate his movement to nonviolence. Three weeks later, on March 10, a weakened Chavez finally yielded to the entreaties of his family and colleagues who feared for his life and ended the fast. Kennedy was there to lend his presence and to break bread with his friend.

As Kennedy's aides formed a shield around him, people pressed close trying to get a glimpse. Some were able to touch him or shake his hand, and others waved and blessed themselves as he passed. Dolores Huerta later said, "It was the most wild moment in my life. All these farm workers really loved Bobby. They called him brother and saw him as more saint than politician" (Brinkley 2000).

As a crowd of several thousand watched, Chavez sat with his wife and mother and Kennedy. At an open-air Mass, several priests and nuns distributed bread to the crowd. Addressing the 8,000 onlookers, Senator Kennedy heaped praise not only on Chavez but on the workers themselves who had, through nonviolence, achieved profound victories in asserting the rights of Mexican Americans and of farm workers.

On March 16, 1968, less than a week after the end of Chavez's fast, Kennedy announced his candidacy for president. Chavez asked one of the union's most politically astute organizers, Marshall Ganz, to lead a vigorous UFWOC campaign to help Kennedy win the upcoming California primary race.

Ganz and his union team focused intently on Mexican American communities to register new voters and get them to the polls on June 6. Chavez made several public appearances a day encouraging voters to support Kennedy. The vigorous support of the union was critical as Kennedy, indeed, swept the precincts targeted by Ganz. Kennedy won the California primary and his campaign, for a brief moment in history, seemed ready to soar.

The celebration turned to nightmare. On election night in California, after Kennedy finished thanking his supporters at the Ambassador Hotel in Los Angeles, he walked off the stage, headed from the ballroom into the kitchen, and became, like his brother five years earlier and Martin Luther King Jr. just two months earlier, a victim of assassination. For the country and especially for the farm workers community, the killing of Robert Kennedy was a profoundly tragic loss.

Further Reading

Bender, Steven. 2008. *One Night in America: Robert Kennedy, Cesar Chavez, and the Dream of Dignity*. Boulder, CO: Paradigm Publishers.

Brinkley, Douglas. 2000. Presentation at Robert F. Kennedy Conference, November 18, John F. Kennedy Library and Museum. http://www.jfklibrary.org/~/media/assets/Education%20and%20Public%20Programs/Forum%20Transcripts/Robert%20F%20Kennedy%20Conference.pdf.

Chavez, Cesar. 1970. Oral history interview. January 27. Boston, MA: Robert F. Kennedy Oral History Program, John F. Kennedy Library.

Ferriss, Susan, and Ricardo Sandoval. 1997. *The Fight in the Fields: Cesar Chavez and the Farmworkers Movement*. New York: Harcourt Brace & Company.

Levy, Jacques. 2007. *Cesar Chavez: Autobiography of La Causa*. Minneapolis: University of Minnesota Press.

Schlesinger, Arthur Jr. 2002. *Robert Kennedy and His Times*. New York: Mariner Books.

King, Martin Luther, Jr.

In December 1955, a 26-year-old black minister of the Dexter Avenue Baptist Church in Montgomery, Alabama, became the leader of a nonviolent protest against racial segregation that would help launch the civil rights movement. Dr. Martin Luther King Jr., graduate of Boston University and son of a legendary preacher from Atlanta, Georgia, accepted a plea by local black leaders in Montgomery to lead a boycott of the city's transit system to protest city regulations that forced blacks sit at the back of buses. Rosa Parks, a secretary of the local chapter of the National Association for the Advancement of Colored People, had been arrested for violating the demeaning law. Led by the dynamic minister, the boycott succeeded in mobilizing black citizens as never before to demand social justice. The boycott, which would last a year, would eventually lead to a U.S. Supreme Court decision that declared laws requiring segregated buses to be unconstitutional. The Montgomery bus boycott thrust civil rights issues to the forefront of American social and political attention and moved King into the national spotlight as the most prominent leader of the movement.

Ahead would be days of marches and sit-ins, of freedom riders and violence, of school desegregation battles and the March on Washington—where King, in 1963, would deliver one of the most celebrated orations in American history with its refrain "I have a dream." Ahead would be the victory of the Civil Rights Act of 1964 and, for King, the awarding of the Nobel Peace Prize. Ahead would be a Poor People's Campaign and his opposition to the Vietnam War. And ahead would be his tragic assassination in 1968. But, in 1955, the young King, fresh out of graduate school, had already become a national figure.

In 1955, another young man, a Mexican American two years King's senior, was working in California for the Community Service Organization (CSO), helping farm workers understand their constitutional rights, registering them to vote, and getting them involved in various self-help activities. Cesar Chavez later remembered avidly reading about the bus boycott in Montgomery and the ways in which people who for so long had been oppressed responded to this grassroots, nonviolent campaign of resistance. Even in these early years as a CSO organizer, Chavez thought of ways of bringing together seemingly powerless groups of people to forge an effective protest movement. Chavez followed the tense struggle in Birmingham, the personal abuse heaped on King, the bombing of his house, his arrest, and his defiant determination to struggle ahead. When the bus boycott was successful, Chavez said later, he began to believe that such a tactic might work in the drive for farm worker rights.

Through the years of the civil rights struggle, when newspaper and television accounts carried news of the marches, the demonstrations, the jails filling after protests of civil disobedience, the peaceful defiance of protestors against all kinds of virulent hatred and violence, and the national impact that nonviolent protest had made under King's leadership, Chavez watched and learned. He later said that the stories would "jump out" at him.

The two men never met personally. Although they both led social protest movements to better the lives of oppressed minority people, they were from very different backgrounds—King from a middle-class and prominent black family and Chavez from a family of poor, Mexican American farm workers. King's educational credentials were formidable; Chavez received little formal education. Yet both had read the writings of Gandhi, and both saw ways to incorporate his methods of nonviolent protest in their respective movements. They both appealed to religious instincts and symbols of their culture. King recognized early on the direction in which Chavez was taking his farm workers crusade.

In September 1966, after enduring a summer of protests and marches in Chicago in which King's own beliefs in nonviolence were tested by angry and sometimes violent crowds, King sent a telegram to Chavez expressing his admiration for the actions of the farm workers union in its strike of California grape growers. It was a message about the unity of their causes. "As brothers in the fight for equality," King wrote, "I extend the hand of fellowship and good will and wish continuing success to you and your members. The fight for equality must be fought on many fronts—in the urban slums, in the sweat shops of the factories and fields" (Levy 2007, 246). For Chavez, the message was inspirational.

In early March 1968, Chavez, to encourage a cessation of violence in the grape strike, decided to conduct a fast, a method of peaceful protest most exemplified by Gandhi. King was planning a Poor People's Campaign to encourage national action against poverty. It was a vision of a broad mobilization of the poor, strikingly similar, at least in its planning stages, to the direction Chavez had seen for the farm workers.

One of King's closest associates, Andrew Young, had visited Chavez in early February and had been very pleased by Chavez's encouraging words about the effort. On March 5, King sent a telegram to a physically weakened Chavez, now in the third week of the fast. "You and your valiant fellow workers have demonstrated your commitment to righting grievous wrongs forced upon exploited people," King wrote. He talked about Chavez, in his fast, being "a living example of the Gandhian tradition with its great force for social progress and its healing spiritual powers" (Mariscal n.d.). Chavez said later that he was "profoundly moved" by King's words.

A month later, on the evening of April 4, 1968, while standing on the balcony of his motel room in Memphis, Tennessee, where he was to lead a protest march in sympathy with striking garbage workers of that city, King was gunned down by an assassin. A stunned Chavez heard the news while in Sacramento, California, campaigning for Senator Robert F. Kennedy's presidential drive.

Shortly after King's death, the farm workers newspaper, *El Malcriado*, paid tribute. On the cover of its April 15, 1968, issue was a photo of King with the words "I am a Man: Killed Helping Workers to Organize." Chavez said, "It was Dr. Martin Luther King who taught us to value ourselves as individuals. His example proved for us that all farm workers, Mexicans, Filipinos, Negroes, Anglos, could live together and work together to gain the place in society which we merit as men" (*El Malcriado* 1968).

Further Reading

Bogater, Julian. 2009. "King, Chavez Shared Social Justice Spirit on Road to Change." University of Michigan, *The University Record Online*, January 22. http://www.ur.umich.edu/0809/Jan19_09/20.php.

El Malcriado. 1968, April 15. http://farmworkermovement.com/ufwarchives/elmalcriado/1968/April%2015,%201968%20No%204_PDF.pdf.

Griswold del Castillo, Richard. 1955. *Cesar Chavez: A Triumph of Spirit*. Norman: University of Oklahoma Press.

King, Martin Luther, Jr. 1966. Telegram to Cesar Chavez. September 19. Martin Luther King Jr. and the Global Freedom Struggle. http://mlk-kpp01.stanford.edu/index.php/encyclopedia/documentsentry/telegram_to_cesar_chavez/.

Levy, Jacques. 2007. *Cesar Chavez: Autobiography of La Causa*. Minneapolis: University of Minnesota Press.

Mariscal, Jorge. n.d. "Cesar and Martin, March '68," http://farmworkermovement.com/essays/essays/mariscal.pdf.

Kircher, William

At a critical time in the early efforts of Cesar Chavez to organize a farm workers union, he had the good fortune to gain as an ally a long-time veteran of United Automobile Workers (UAW) battles. His name was William Kircher, and he was in 1966 national director of organizing for the AFL-CIO. Although he arrived in California with little knowledge of the history of farm worker struggles to organize, he soon gained great admiration for Chavez and La Causa. Kircher's strategic advice was crucial as Chavez and other farm worker union leaders negotiated the early challenges of forming a cohesive and coordinated drive to establish a movement that could survive the pitfalls and obstacles strewn ahead.

Born March 2, 1915, in Athens, Ohio, Bill Kircher graduated from Ohio University in 1936 with a bachelor's degree in journalism. After working on several newspapers as a reporter and editor, he began work at the Wright Aeronautical Plant near Cincinnati. It was while at the defense plant during the war that Kircher became immersed in labor union issues, helping form a UAW local in the area. Thus he began a career with the union that took him to various locations in the Midwest. By 1965, Kircher was director of organization of the AFL-CIO, a high-ranking figure in U.S. labor circles.

Kircher was dispatched to California by AFL-CIO president George Meany in the spring of 1966, shortly after the combined forces of the Agricultural Workers Organizing Committee (AWOC) and Chavez's infant union, the National Farm Workers Association (NFWA), had joined together in launching the Delano grape strike. It was the AWOC, a mostly Filipino union affiliated with the AFL-CIO, that had convinced Chavez to join forces. In late 1966, Chavez had upped the ante in the grape struggle, calling for a nationwide boycott. The AWOC was invited to join the boycott but declined for legal and strategic reasons. Concerned about the how the working relationship between the two unions would eventually be resolved, Meany sent Kircher to solve the AWOC problem.

Kircher, a genial but tough veteran of union warfare, arrived at the beginning of momentous times in the farm worker struggle. Chavez had planned a long march (*peregrinación*) from Delano to Sacramento and the steps of the state capitol to bring national attention to the strike and to encourage the state government, led by Governor Pat Brown, to enact legislation to protect farm workers.

Days before the beginning of the march to Sacramento, the Senate Subcommittee on Migratory Labor held hearings in Delano on the conditions of farm worker labor and possible national legislation to address problems. Kircher was in the room as members of the subcommittee, including Senator Robert Kennedy (D-MA), directed tough questions to growers and to those sympathetic to the grape strike, including Chavez. Kennedy was soon grilling the Kern County sheriff who had arrested picketers on his failure to understand the U.S. Constitution. Kircher heard Chavez, in his quiet but determined manner, plead the case for the strikers. Kircher later talked about Chavez's charisma and how it was obvious that it was the NFWA and not the AWOC that was leading the grape strike.

Kircher joined the marchers as they headed toward Sacramento. He later said, "I got some old clothes, and I figured the best goddam way to find out what was going on was to avoid the experts and live with the people, so I walked with them and I talked with them" (Ganz 2009, 155–56).

A Catholic, Kircher appreciated the daily Mass given on the march. He saw immediately the cultural and religious nature of the movement, far different from the bare-knuckles union organizing with which he was so familiar. Like Kennedy, Kircher warmed to the movement and to Chavez.

The Sacramento march was a spectacular success. It resulted in a NFWA contract with Schenley, a major grape grower, one in which Kircher signed on as a witness. With this triumph as a backdrop, Kircher in August 1966 helped negotiate a merger between the NFWA and the AWOC. The new organization would now become the United Farm Workers Organizing Committee (UFWOC); it would be affiliated with the AFL-CIO, and it would be run by Chavez. Later it would be called the United Farm Workers (UFW). For Kircher's AFL-CIO, it seemed like a rather strange marriage, but Kircher himself convinced others that Chavez had the potential to pull off a miraculous organization of farm workers. With the nation's preeminent union now behind his farm workers movement, Chavez looked forward with renewed confidence.

Kircher became a stout supporter of Chavez and the new union. The two traveled together to Texas and participated in a march in support of melon workers.

Kircher helped Chavez and his leadership fight off incursions by the Teamsters, who would continue through the years to dislodge the UFW from California's harvest fields. On one occasion, when Teamster thugs began some of their usual rough tactics with UFW picketers, Kircher called the president of the International Seafarers Union, who immediately sent carloads of muscled sailors to march on the picket lines. Relative nonviolence ensued. It was also Kircher who arranged for the union to hire a full-time attorney. Jerry Cohen became the first general counsel for the UFWOC.

Bill Kircher left his AFL-CIO leadership post in 1973 and accepted an appointment with the Hotel and Restaurant Employees and Bartenders International Union. From this position in Washington he lobbied for an increase in minimum-wage legislation covering his union's workers. After four years of service he retired. He passed away in November 1989. Kircher had been a key ally of the UFW in its formative years.

Further Reading

Ferriss, Susan, and Ricardo Sandoval. 1997. *The Fight in the Fields: Cesar Chavez and the Farmworkers Movement*. New York: Harcourt Brace & Company.

Ganz, Marshall. 2009. *Why David Sometimes Wins: Leadership, Organization, and Strategy in the California Farm Worker Movement*. New York: Oxford University Press.

Griswold del Castillo, Richard, and Richard Garcia. 1995. *Cesar Chavez: A Triumph of Spirit*. Norman: University of Oklahoma Press.

Levy, Jacques. 2007. *Cesar Chavez: Autobiography of La Causa*. Minneapolis: University of Minnesota Press.

Matthiessen, Peter. 1969. *Sal Si Puedes: Cesar Chavez and the New American Revolution*. New York: Random House.

L

La Paz

In 1971, Cesar Chavez moved the main headquarters of the farm workers union, at the time called the United Farm Workers Organizing Committee (UFWOC), from Delano, California, to a location southeast of Bakersfield in Keene, California, in the Tehachapi Mountains. Chavez called the new headquarters Nuestra Senora Reina de la Paz or "Our Lady, Queen of Peace," combining religious imagery with the idea of serenity. It became known as La Paz. Once the site of historic Stony Brook Hospital, built in 1929 by Kern County as a tuberculosis sanatorium, the 250-acre facility had been closed for many years and was put up for public auction in 1970. At Chavez's request, Edie Lewis, a Hollywood producer, purchased the facility on behalf of the National Farm Worker Service Center, which made the mortgage payments and ultimately took title to the property. There was much work ahead to transform an aged and unused hospital into the headquarters of the union. Nevertheless, it was here that Chavez would attempt to carry out his visions of what the farm workers movement might become.

The victories in several strikes and boycotts in the late 1960s and the increasing union membership—approaching 70,000—required the UFWOC to fulfill the promises it had made to its new membership. It expanded benefit programs, established medical clinics and retirement communities, and trained farm workers to serve as organizers and representatives to administer contracts. All of this activity, Chavez believed, could not be coordinated in the relatively small Delano compound.

As early as 1968, anticipating the need for a larger facility for the headquarters of the growing union, Chavez turned to one of his closest lieutenants, LeRoy Chatfield, to look around for an ideal location. After exploring a number of possible sites over the next two years, Chatfield advised Chavez of a former public tuberculosis sanatorium a few miles down the mountain from Tehachapi. It had in place a wide range of housing units, hospital rooms, offices, and kitchen and dining facilities and was in a secluded area, a place where union leaders would have a better opportunity, Chavez believed, for reflection, introspection, and a semblance of relief from the daily, ordinary grind of running a functioning union operation. For Chavez, La Paz would become, he believed, not only the headquarters of the union but something of a spiritual haven.

In the Tehachapi Mountains of Kern County, California, Cesar Chavez established a permanent headquarters for the United Farm Workers called La Paz. In 1975, he is shown walking at the site with a group of children. (Cathy Murphy/Getty Images)

For many union staff members, moving to La Paz seemed like entering a religious seminary or monastic setting far removed from the usual, simple society activities to which they were accustomed. The nearest town was over 10 miles away, and it was mostly motels. Going to a movie or to a restaurant suddenly became nearly impossible. A move to La Paz meant for union volunteers a very different lifestyle.

Looking back, many historians and other observers, including several of Chavez's closest colleagues, felt that the move to the relative isolation of La Paz was perhaps the most significant factor in the deteriorating personal relationships among his organizers and a reflection of an increasingly fractured policy structure that affected the union in the coming years. The move to La Paz, many believed, was one of the greatest mistakes of Chavez's remarkable stewardship of the union, one that ultimately led to bitter antagonisms, misunderstandings, and the loss of numerous talented organizers.

At La Paz, Chavez was not only physically removed from much of the action in the fields and around bargaining tables but became more convinced that the union must move beyond the ordinary functions such as organizing. At a time when the union needed to concentrate on the administration of union business and to build on its growing power, Chavez increasingly looked to social experiments to mold the farm workers movement to greater fulfillment. For example, he explored the idea of establishing communal farms. He talked about building a Poor Peoples Union.

It was at La Paz that he became enamored with Synanon, the cultlike organization headed by Charles Diderich. It was at La Paz that he insisted that his organizers and advisors engage in "The Game," a process designed to purify the motives and commitment of those who engaged in it but which, in many cases, led to humiliation and understandable resentment and anger. It was also at La Paz that Chavez, more strongly than ever, began to insist that the farm workers movement should be the province of volunteers, not paid employees. And while at La Paz, Chavez began, many said, to assert greater individual power and became more unwilling to tolerate dissent, fearful that his governing authority was being challenged. All of this divided Chavez from many of those individuals to whom the success of the union had owed so much in its critical development over the first decade.

Yet there were other reflections about La Paz. Governor Jerry Brown remembered the first time he visited Chavez in the mountain headquarters: "The place was totally off the beaten path," Brown remembered, "yet there were hundreds of people around—mostly young and with infectious vitality and enthusiasm. It was clear that the United Farm Workers was a movement" (Brown 1993).

And for that movement, despite the internal conflicts within the union, Chavez continued to work with avid purpose. He brought farm worker leaders to La Paz for planning and training. He used the facilities to operate schools to train negotiation techniques. The union even set up a Montessori school. And, long after Chavez's death, La Paz remains a center of activity devoted to outreach, training, and political influence leading to social change.

In 2012, the National Chavez Center at La Paz, now a complex of buildings and cabins that extends over 187 acres, still serves as the headquarters of the UFW. It now includes a 7,000-square-foot visitor center and a recently opened conference and retreat center. La Paz has also been placed on the National Register of Historic Places. It is also the final resting place of Cesar Chavez.

On October 8, 2012, President Barack Obama dedicated La Paz as a new national memorial—the Cesar E. Chavez National Monument.

Further Reading
Bardacke, Frank. 2011. *Trampling Out the Vintage: Cesar Chavez and the Two Souls of the United Farm Workers*. New York: Verso.

Brown, Edmund G., Jr. 1993. "Chavez Based His Life on Sharing and Frugality." *San Francisco Examiner*, April 25, 2.

Chatfield, LeRoy. n.d. "La Paz Headquarters." http://www.farmworkermovement.org/essays/essays/chatfield2009/10%20LA%20PAZ%20UNITED%20FARM%20WORKER%20HEADQUARTERS.pdf.

Pawel, Miriam. 2009. *The Union of Their Dreams: Power, Hope, and Struggle in Cesar Chavez's Farm Workers Movement*. New York: Bloomsbury Press.

Lettuce Strike, 1979

By 1979, although plagued by disturbing and disrupting internal disputes within its leadership, the United Farm Workers (UFW) had gained strength. The Teamsters no longer battled with the UFW for farm worker contracts. UFW membership rolls and financial resources reached levels that enabled the union to fight for even greater benefits for its workers. In lettuce-growing areas near Salinas, south of San Francisco, and in the Imperial Valley southeast of Los Angeles down to the Mexican border, growers faced new contract negotiations with the UFW. Union leaders sensed an opportunity to press for appreciable wage and benefit gains at a time when the lettuce industry was recording record profits. As the two sides—the growers and the unions—held initial negotiations, however, the bitterness and hostility fed by years of battles proved intractable. Talks broke down. The UFW decided to launch a major lettuce strike. Cesar Chavez confidently declared, "I am spirited and encouraged" (Ferriss and Sandoval 1997, 216).

Led by Marshal Ganz, Jessica Govea, Mario Bustamante, and other organizers, the UFW workers displayed unusually tight-knit and coordinated strike actions. Unlike the earlier days of the union when everyone, from management on down, was inexperienced, lurching ahead with little preparation, the UFW field workers, up and down the valleys, acted with surprising discipline. They went about the business of picketing and fending off grower intimidation with much determination. Two weeks into the strike, 3,000 UFW workers had nearly shut down eight companies that supplied a third of the nation's winter lettuce crop. Lauding the courage and solidarity of the field workers, Ganz said, "It was a coming of age for us as a union" (Ferriss and Sandoval 1997, 216).

The growers hired an advertising firm to run a publicity campaign against Chavez and the union. In local communities, the strike evoked fierce confrontations among whites and Mexican Americans, even among high school students. The lettuce strike of 1979 even brought to the forefront in California an old organization skilled in stoking racial and ethnic divides—the Ku Klux Klan. As the white race had been under assault by an emerging black culture challenging oppression, Klan leaders saw in the events in the lettuce fields a new sign of danger—the white race being challenged by Mexican Americans. Thus, a cross was burned in a lettuce field. Klan members scrambled, with no appreciable success, to find white laborers to act as scabs replace striking workers. Let it be said that the Klan never discriminated: Mexican Americans were just as much an abomination as black people.

On February 10, 1979, the strike turned deadly. News spread quickly that a 28-year-old UFW member named Rufino Contreras had been gunned down in a lettuce field in Calexico while attempting to speak with a crew of scab laborers. The funeral was held in a place the workers called "El Hoyo" (The Hole), a parking lot of the Calexico Employment Development Department where farm workers routinely gathered in hopes of finding work. During the funeral, as family members and UFW workers spoke in memory of Contreras, a crop-duster helicopter buzzed the mourners. Ellen Starbird, a UFW organizer, said later, "To mock a funeral, a sacred religious service, what mortal would be so depraved?" ("Ellen M. Starbird" n.d.). The crop duster belonged to the owner of the field in which Contreras had been killed, Mario Saikhon.

In the days following, the strikers, against the nonviolent character of the farm workers movement, struck back. They slashed tires, broke irrigation ditches, overturned tractors, and threw rocks at security guards and police. Chavez was infuriated that Ganz and others had lost control. Thus, the internal struggles of the union intensified even further. With the outbreak of violence and the death of one of the union members, Chavez was inclined to pull back on the strike and begin a boycott. Nevertheless, the strike continued, carried on by ever-growing determination by thousands of farm workers along the picket lines.

On a brief trip east, Chavez said to a crowd at Harvard University's School of Government, "We asked for a little more money and the employers responded with bullets. The hunting season is on every time we hit the picket line. . . . It is unfortunate that the men, women, and children who plant and harvest the greatest quantity of food ever in this country don't have enough for themselves" (Forst 1979).

In late summer of 1979, Chavez, still angered by the eruptions of violence by union strikers, nevertheless escalated his protests. For 12 days, two separate groups of farm workers near San Francisco began a 12-day march to Salinas. The marchers gained numbers as they sang, chanted slogans, and passed by the summer harvest fields. Many farm workers simply threw down their tools and joined up. By the time the marchers reached Salinas, the group numbered more than 25,000 individuals. Chavez, who fasted for part of the journey, was visibly tired. The end of the march, however, brought a rousing celebration as marchers filled the center of the town.

In late August, many growers, their crops rotting in the fields, gave in to UFW demands and signed contracts. Under the new arrangements, workers would receive a 40 percent increase in wages, an improved medical plan that covered families of farm workers, and protections against pesticide use. The laborers would also begin to benefit from a system in which union representatives, paid by the companies, would administer labor contracts at the company work sites.

The end of the 1979 lettuce strike was an apex of UFW power. The strike itself had demonstrated that the union was now strong enough to exert considerable pressure on growers from strike actions alone and without national boycotts. Although further internal ruptures from inside the UFW and an increasingly hostile political atmosphere in California loomed ahead, these days of victory were heady.

Further Reading

Bardacke, Frank. 2011. *Trampling Out the Vintage: Cesar Chavez and the Two Souls of the United Farm Workers*. New York: Verso.

"Ellen M. Starbird, 1975–1979." n.d. http://farmworkermovement.com/essays/essays/171%20Starbird_Ellen.pdf.

Ferriss, Susan, and Ricardo Sandoval. 1997. *The Fight in the Fields: Cesar Chavez and the Farmworkers Movement*. New York: Harcourt Brace & Company.

Forst, Edward. 1979. "Chavez Speaks on Lettuce Workers Strike; Farm Workers Want Chiquita Banana Boycott." *Harvard Crimson*, April 6. http://www.thecrimson.com/article/1979/4/6/chavez-speaks-on-lettuce-workers-strike/.

Pawel, Miriam. 2009. *The Union of Their Dreams: Power, Hope, and Struggle in Cesar Chavez's Farm Worker Movement*. New York: Bloomsbury.

Shaw, Randy. 2008. *Beyond the Fields: Cesar Chavez, the UFW, and the Struggle for Justice in the 21st Century*. Berkeley: University of California Press.

Levy, Jacques

In 1975, W.W. Norton & Company published *Cesar Chavez: Autobiography of La Causa*, an expansive exploration of the rise and battles of a new social and labor movement of farm workers. Its author was Jacques Levy. A California journalist who was the same age as Chavez, Levy became his unlikely friend and collaborator. Born into a wealthy Jewish family and educated at Harvard University, Levy was a teacher, a writer interested in political and labor issues, a man who did not speak Spanish and had no taste for Mexican food or music, and an atheist. Chavez, born into poverty and with no formal academic credentials, was a devout Catholic, Mexican American farm worker, and grassroots organizer. Yet it was Levy whom Chavez trusted to help tell the story of La Causa, the momentous drive to bring justice and fair treatment to the United States' harvest fields. The two connected personally. For one thing, Levy had an unexpected talent with which Chavez was immediately taken—he was a dog trainer. Levy spent hours with Chavez and his two dogs, Boycott and Huelga. But it was much more than that. Chavez simply sensed that Levy sought to discover and tell the truth about the movement. At one of their first meetings, Chavez said, "Truth is on our side, even more than justice, because truth can't be changed. It has a way of manifesting itself" (Levy 2007, xxiv).

Before his traveled to Delano to undertake his research on the farm workers movement, Levy had worked for a number of newspapers around the country before landing in Santa Rosa, California, where in 1954 he joined the *Press Democrat* as a political reporter and assistant news editor. In 1957, he wrote a five-part series entitled "Target: Poverty" that won an award from the San Francisco Press Club. He also taught a course in journalism for two years at Sonoma State College.

In February 1969, Levy met Chavez and showed him an outline of a proposed book. Before Levy's visit, Chavez had resisted the overtures of others to help write a biography of the union leader. But after a long conversation, Chavez could see that this was something different—a chance to record the advent and growth of the farm workers movement, showing how an oppressed minority could take on an entrenched and massive establishment and assert its own power.

By the time of the meeting, much had already occurred in the life of the movement—the formation of the infant organization in 1962, the beginning of the grape strike in 1965, the celebrated march from Delano to Sacramento in 1966, the first contracts from growers, the fast in 1968 to encourage nonviolence, and then the tragic loss by assassination of Martin Luther King Jr. and Robert Kennedy, both of whom had supported the United Farm Workers (UFW). Impressed by Levy's suggested approach—a series of interviews not only of Chavez but of other participants—Chavez asked the opinion of others in the leadership about the project. Along with Chavez, they were enthusiastic. And so the project was born. Levy estimated it would take a year to complete. By the time he finished the work, he had spent six years.

Chavez made himself available to Levy often for lengthy interviews about his early life, his family, his ethnic heritage, and the steps that led down the road to the UFW. Chavez encouraged others to participate fully in the project, and Levy made many friends among them.

Although not an organizer or formal advisor, Levy was much more than a historian gathering research material. He often drove Chavez to picket lines, rallies, and executive board meetings of the UFW. He often took notes for the union at contract negotiations. Sometimes he acted as a press agent, answering difficult questions from reporters wanting inside information on the union's battle plans. He travelled with other UFW leaders. On a day in the summer of 1970, as the UFW battled the Teamsters for contracts in the Salinas Valley, Levy was following union counsel Jerry Cohen with a camera into a field where workers were staging a sit-in. When Cohen was confronted by muscled Teamster thugs, he told Levy to take a picture. Soon, Cohen was unconscious on the ground after vicious blows to the head. One of the goons smashed Levy in the head and drop-kicked his camera into the bushes. Cohen would be hospitalized for a week. Levy needed a new camera.

In 1971, an informant alerted police that several growers were planning to assassinate Chavez. Aided by contacts he had made over the years as an investigative reporter, Levy went to work trying to unearth credible evidence of a plot and even enlisted the help of a private detective. When Levy later presented material to law enforcement agents, they refused to conduct their own investigation. Levy suspected something of a cover-up—that state government officials had little inclination to go after political friends among the moneyed growers.

As he followed Chavez and other organizers to union meetings, court hearings, and labor negotiations, Levy assiduously recorded field notes in spiral notebooks. He recorded over 300 audiotapes of interviews with Chavez, his family members, colleagues, politicians, and growers. He spoke with them in homes, on the road, on picket lines, in cars, on planes, at meetings—anywhere he had at hand his recorder and a willing subject. Levy even travelled with Chavez to Europe in 1974 and taped meetings with European labor leaders.

Levy continued his research on La Causa and Chavez long after the completion of the book, interviewing UFW members and Chavez family members. He even helped Chavez write his speech nominating Jerry Brown for president at the 1976 Democratic National Convention. He began to work on a full-length biography to complement the 1975 book but never finished it. In 2007, three years after Levy's death, the University of Minnesota Press issued a new edition of *Autobiography* that included a forward by Fred Ross Jr., son of Chavez's mentor Fred Ross, and an afterword authored by Levy's daughter, Jacqueline Levy. She recalled that the word *huelga* was the first Spanish word she ever learned as a child.

Levy's work remains an invaluable source for the study of Chavez and the farm workers movement. His papers, including the recordings, notebooks, correspondence, and other materials, are housed at Yale University. The *Autobiography* remains the best firsthand treatment of the early years of Chavez's life. Presented in the form of reminiscences in the first person as taken from his interviews, Levy left an indelible portrait of a unique reformer. A political liberal, Levy saw in Chavez an extraordinary populist leader who saw social change as coming from genuine shared sacrifice and commitment to a cause. Chavez had shown the way, Levy wrote, "by using militant non-violent tactics and organizing people of various backgrounds, political persuasions and faiths. In an era of great cynicism, La Causa is showing that individuals can make a difference, can help themselves and others and can keep the principles, although the task is hard and is never-ending" (Levy 2007, 535).

Further Reading

Bardacke, Frank. 2011. *Trampling Out the Vintage: Cesar Chavez and the Two Souls of the United Farm Workers*. New York: Verso.

Ferriss, Susan, and Ricardo Sandoval. 1997. *The Fight in the Fields: Cesar Chavez and the Farmworkers Movement*. New York: Harcourt Brace & Company.

Griswold del Castillo, Richard, and Richard Garcia. 1995. *Cesar Chavez: A Triumph of Spirit*. Norman: University of Oklahoma Press.

Levy, Jacques. 2007. *Cesar Chavez: Autobiography of La Causa*. Minneapolis: University of Minnesota Press.

Lyons, Mack

Cesar Chavez began his quest to organize a union of farm workers at a time of great social reverberation in American society, most notably the black civil rights movement. When Chavez held his first organizational meeting in Delano, California, in 1962, the drive for civil rights reform had already shaken the foundations of Jim Crow laws. The names of cities such as Montgomery, Little Rock, and Birmingham and the stories of the Freedom Rides had gained notice across the country. Soon, Martin Luther King Jr. would lead a massive March on Washington that would make clear that there was no turning back on social change. Chavez's farm workers movement would use many of the same tactics so prominent in the civil rights struggle, from marches to boycotts. Although the leadership of the farm workers struggle would be almost entirely comprised of Latinos, Filipinos, and white activists, one prominent black American became a forceful organizer and a highly respected confidant of Chavez. His name was Mack Lyons.

Born on May 20, 1941, in Texas, Lyons was the son of farm workers. He grew up in the fields, picking cotton while not attending school. After graduating from high school, he moved to Las Vegas with a brother and made a living for a brief time shooting pool. By 1965, he was in Bakersfield, California, driving a cotton-picking machine and a tractor. Later he took a job at the grape fields of DiGiorgio Fruit Corporation in Arvin. Lyons was thus not too far from Delano, California, when two farm worker unions, the Agricultural Workers Organizing Committee (AWOC) and Cesar Chavez's National Farm Workers Association (NFWA) combined forces to launch a strike against area grape growers. It was while working at DiGiorgio that Lyons met Marshall Ganz and other NFWA organizers passing out leaflets encouraging workers to strike. The tall and somewhat imposing-looking Lyons, toughened in the fields and in the pool halls, was soon ready for the action.

Lyons helped NFWA organizers petition workers at DiGiorgio. He joined a delegation that met with grower Robert DiGiorgio to plead their case for holding elections at the company, confident that a majority would choose to join Chavez's union. When DiGiorgio made it clear that he had no intention of allowing elections, Lyons and others refused to leave. They were arrested. When released, they returned to the DiGiorgio offices and were arrested again. Thus began the organizing career of Lyons with the farm workers union.

The protests eventually persuaded the company to hold elections. After the workers voted to join the union, Lyons later remembered the faces of the workers, most of them Latinos, with some whites and blacks: "You could see that all of these people had something in common. And that was probably the most inspirational, the most heart-warming, the greatest thing that ever happened to me" (Levy 2007, 252).

Lyons was chosen by the workers to be the ranch committee chairman. He participated in the contract negotiations with the company. Finally, he became the head of the hiring hall in Lamont, California, south of Bakersfield after the contract negotiations were completed. He was now a paid member of the union—five dollars a week and paid rent.

Lyons accompanied Dolores Huerta and other union organizers to help in some of the tough negotiations on union contracts with the growers. For example, he went to San Francisco with Huerta and fellow organizers Marshall Ganz and Jose Luna to finalize a contract with the Almaden Winery, a protracted negotiation that left the usually indefatigable Huerta in such weariness that she fainted and was taken to the hospital.

In 1969, when increasing numbers of letters and telephone calls threatening Chavez's life began to reach Delano, Lyons organized the union leader's security detail and travelled across the country with him on behalf of the international boycott of grapes. In October 1969, he appeared alongside Chavez, union attorney Jerry Cohen, and others at a hearing before a panel of members of the U.S. House of Representatives Education and Labor Committee to report on the state of the farm workers movement. In his testimony, Lyons recounted the victory at DiGiorgio and the two years following the contract when working conditions and wages improved. But he also told members that DiGiorgio had sold the ranch to another grower, who then voided the contract. The union was, therefore, back where it started at that particular ranch. It would again be the target of union action.

Lyons helped organize the grape boycott in New York City. In 1970, he travelled to Cleveland, Ohio, to help organize the lettuce boycott and was able to enlist such strong supporters for the farm workers union as Governor Richard Celeste and U.S. Congressman Dennis Kucinich. Lyons then moved on to Florida to fight for the boycott in that state.

In 1973, Lyons was elected to the United Farm Workers's (UFW's) National Executive Board. In 1976, he moved with other members of the leadership team to La Paz, the UFW's new organizational headquarters in Keene, California, to head up the political arm of the union. Later, he and his family took up temporary residence in Sacramento, where he could lobby state legislators on a number of issues facing the UFW's interests and future, especially efforts led by Republican politicians and other grower interests in weakening California's Agricultural Labor Relations Act (ALRA), the landmark legislation that had given farm workers the right to organize and had institutionalized collective bargaining for those workers.

Caught up in the maelstrom that divided members of the UFW's leadership in the late 1970s over such issues as future organizing efforts and the direction of the union as well as personal antagonisms and Chavez's increasingly controlling power over all aspects of union activity, Lyons resigned in 1978.

For a time, he trained Peace Corps volunteers and later, with his sons, organized a small consulting firm. He passed away on April 28, 2008.

For the UFW and for activists of various backgrounds—Mexican, Puerto Rican, Filipino, Cuban, African American, and Anglo—Lyons was a catalyst in strengthening commitment among various people toward common goals and purpose.

Further Reading

ABC-CLIO. 2011. "A Transcript of, 'A Dialogue with Congress,' October 1, 1969." History in the Headlines. http://www.historyandtheheadlines.abc-clio.com/Content Pages/ContentPage.aspx?entryId=1665638&currentSection=1665275&productid=41.

Levy, Jacques. 2007. *Cesar Chavez: Autobiography of La Causa*. Minneapolis: University of Minnesota Press.

Matthiessen, Peter. 1969. *Sal Si Puedes (Escape If You Can): Cesar Chavez and the New American Revolution*. Berkeley: University of California Press.

M

Mahoney, Roger

In 1991, Roger Mahoney, archbishop of Los Angeles, a cleric whose principal ministry was to poor Mexican Americans, especially farm workers, and who had worked closely with Cesar Chavez and the United Farm Workers (UFW), was named a cardinal in the Catholic Church. Through the turbulent years of the growth of the farm workers movement, Cardinal Mahoney demonstrated, as few powerful religious figures had ever done, a deep-felt commitment to righting the injustices suffered by immigrant workers.

He was born in February 27, 1936, in Hollywood, California. His father ran a poultry farm in the San Fernando Valley, and Mahoney later remembered the wrenching sight of a raid by agents from the Immigration and Naturalization Service as they drove away with a number of illegal Mexican farm workers. It was then, he said, that the plight of poor immigrants and their treatment in the United States became a burning focus in his life. While attending St. John's Seminary in Camarillo, California, in the late 1950s, he often accompanied priests who visited nearby labor camps of agricultural workers.

Roger Mahoney was nine years younger than Chavez. Both, at critical stages of their lives, met the same man who helped transform their worldview. Father Donald McDonnell, the priest who played such a vital role in introducing a relatively uneducated Chavez to the world of books and philosophy, also influenced Mahoney. The young seminarian spent a summer assignment with the priest. "During that summer," Mahoney said later, "my heart and soul were converted to the work of service to our migrant brothers and sisters, and since then, my life and ministry have been focused on them" ("Priest Who Inspired . . ." 2012).

In 1962, he was ordained to the priesthood in the Diocese of Monterey-Fresno. The young, Spanish-speaking cleric began to celebrate Mass with Mexican field workers. He became a strong advocate of Cesar Chavez and the fight of the farm workers movement not only to strive for higher wages and better working conditions but, most of all, to encourage a growing sense of self-respect and dignity and the belief that they could assert their own power.

Mahoney wrote of Chavez:

His integration of faith and action was reflected in the manner in which he led the movement. Rallies began with the celebration of mass; marches were

For his entire life in the Catholic Church, Cardinal Roger Mahoney of the Los Angeles Archdiocese has pursued a ministry that seeks to help Mexican Americans. A staunch supporter of the farm workers movement, Cardinal Mahoney (left) is seen in May 2006 in Los Angeles during a protest in favor of less restrictive immigration laws. (AP Photo/Nick Ut)

conducted under the banner of Our Lady of Guadalupe while the rosary was prayed; and his speeches and writings frequently referred to gospel values as he quoted the church's documents on human rights and justice. Cesar Chavez truly understood his Christian vocation to build up the kingdom of God in this world. ("Champion of Farm Workers Dies" 1993)

In October 1962, Pope John XXIII convened the Second Vatican Council in Rome, a series of meetings dedicated to modernizing the church. The periodic sessions lasted for several years, closing under Pope Paul VI in December 1965. The Catholic Church reaffirmed the right of workers to organize, to bargain collectively, and to strike. The reports from the Second Vatican Council confirmed in the minds of Chavez and other union leaders, and especially in the mind of Roger Mahoney, the commitment of the church to justice and social change.

In late November 1969, a number of Catholic bishops led by Monsignor George Higgins formed a U.S. Bishops Committee on Farm Labor to help mediate disputes and labor negotiations between farm workers and growers. In August 1970, for example, the Bishop's Committee, comprised of Bishop Joseph Donnelly of Hartford, Connecticut, Higgins, and Mahoney, mediated an agreement between the United Farm Workers Organizing Committee and the Teamsters Union. Under the agreement, the Teamsters agreed to withdraw from the fields but not the food processing plants where they had represented workers for some time. A few weeks later, the deal broke down, scuttled by the growers who wanted to keep the favorable Teamster contracts. Through many such frustrating negotiations, Mahoney continued to press on, attempting to bring the two sides to an accommodation that would not stall the positive movement of the farm workers.

In 1975, Mahoney was named by Pope Paul VI the auxiliary bishop for the Diocese of Fresno. That same year, following the enactment of the historic Agricultural Labor Relations Act (ALRA) of 1975, Governor Jerry Brown made the first appointments to the Agricultural Labor Relations Board (ALRB), the body that would oversee the implementation of the law. Brown entrusted the leadership of the five-member board to Mahoney, who was made chairman. Also included on the board were former UFW organizer LeRoy Chatfield and two liberal Democrats. Republican politicians and the growers, stung first by the law itself and now by the composition of the board, immediately began to craft legislative and legal challenges.

As the ALRB began its work, it unexpectedly faced the same kind of treatment from the International Brotherhood of Teamsters that strikers had long suffered in the fields. In the fall of 1975, a group of Teamster thugs stormed into the ALRB offices, accused Chatfield and Mahoney of farm worker bias, punched a hole through an office wall, hit Chatfield with picket signs, and forcibly pinned Teamster buttons on Mahoney. Later, when he walked to his car, Mahoney found that the tires had been slashed.

In early February 1976, Mahoney testified before committees of the California state legislature that the funds allocated for the ALRB had nearly run out because of the volume and demand involved in conducting elections and settling disputes. The success of the UFW in acquiring contracts had ironically overloaded the ability of the ALRB to keep pace. The board had conducted over 300 elections in the fall of 1975, settled a number of disputes, and had dozens of additional ones pending. If more funds were not allocated, Mahoney said, the board would simply be forced to shut down.

Here was an opening that the opponents of the farm workers law could readily exploit. To Republican politicians and growers, shutting down the board would be essentially shutting down implementation of the law. And that is exactly what they did. For Republicans, the strategy was clear. When a Republican held the governor's chair, they would work to starve the ALRB. When a Republican took over the governorship, he would simply pack the board with anti-union members.

In 1980 Mahoney was named bishop of Stockton. Five years later, he became archbishop of Los Angeles. In 1993, Cardinal Mahoney presided over a huge outdoor Mass at the funeral of Chavez. He offered the personal condolences of Pope John Paul II.

Throughout his entire life, Cardinal Mahoney championed the rights of immigrants. After the State of Arizona passed a stringent law in 2010 targeting illegal immigrants, Cardinal Mahoney stood on a truck bed at a demonstration in Los Angeles and chanted "Si se puede!"

Further Reading

"Cardinal Joins Fight for Undocumented Workers Rights." 2006. *Washington Post*, April 6.

"Champion of Farm Workers Dies." 1993. *The Christian Century*, May 12, 513.

Costello, Gerald. 1984. *Without Fear or Favor: George Higgins on the Record*. Mystic, CT: Twenty-Third Publications.

Ferriss, Susan, and Ricardo Sandoval. 1997. *The Fight in the Fields: Cesar Chavez and the Farmworkers Movement*. New York: Harcourt Brace & Company.

Levy, Jacques. 2007. *Cesar Chavez: An Autobiography*. Minneapolis: University of Minnesota Press.

"Priest Who Inspired Cesar Chavez Dies at 88." 2012. *National Catholic Reporter*, March 2. http://ncronline.org/printpdf/news/people/priest-who-inspired-cesar-chavez-dies-age-88.

Prouty, Marco. 2006. *Cesar Chavez, the Catholic Bishops, and the Farmworkers' Struggle for Social Justice*. Tucson: University of Arizona Press.

March (*Peregrinación*) to Sacramento, 1966

On the morning of March 17, 1966, Cesar Chavez and about 100 supporters of the farm workers strike against grape growers gathered in Delano, California, to begin a 300-mile march to the steps of the state capitol in Sacramento. Much like the marches of civil rights protestors led by Dr. Martin Luther King Jr., the march to Sacramento was a strategic move by Chavez not only to energize the movement and solidify the commitment of the strikers but also to bring greater national awareness to La Causa. And for Chavez, the march, or in Spanish the *peregrinación*, had deeply symbolic meaning rooted in centuries-old religious traditions of Spanish culture. It would be, he believed, a pilgrimage for the downtrodden. He talked about the Lenten penitential processions of his Catholic faith in which marchers, often dressed in sackcloth and ashes, traveled to religious shrines.

The striking farm workers—the *huelgistas*—would march to do penance for the ills they might have committed during the strike. The march would help cleanse their feelings, Chavez felt, for any violent actions, either committed or planned. The march, he said, "has strong religious-cultural overtones. But it is also the pilgrimage of a cultural minority who have suffered from a hostile environment, and a minority who mean business." The themes of the march, as Chavez explained, were thus "Peregrinacion—Penitencia—Revolution" (Ferriss and Sandoval 1997, 117).

The march would take the farm workers and their supporters through many of the San Joaquin Valley towns in which they had worked in the fields—places such as Madera, Fresno, Modesto, Stockton, and others. Onto Highway 99 the marchers began, followed by members of the press, several Federal Bureau of Investigation (FBI) agents, and other onlookers. They carried banners, portraits of the Virgin of Guadalupe, and the blazing red union flag with its Aztec eagle emblem. Others carried flags of both the United States and Mexico. Some wore Veterans of Foreign Wars hats. Some carried large wooden crosses adorned with rosary beads.

Luis Valdez, playwright and creator of the farm workers theater Teatro Campesino, carried "Plan of Delano," a statement of the goals of the farm workers movement that would be read at each stop and be signed by local workers. Valdez invariably added to the statement the sentiments felt by all those determined to reach Sacramento. This is a social movement, he said, spreading wherever there are oppressed farm workers. "In order to survive," he said, "we are ready to give up everything, even our lives, in our fight for social justice ... without violence ... for the purpose of ending the poverty, the misery, the injustice with the hope that our children will not be exploited as we have been" ("Plan of Delano" 1966).

As the marchers, led by duly elected march captain Robert Bustos, a 23-year-old grape picker, began to reach small towns, many local workers and their families, yelling and shouting, would run toward them and swell their numbers. They cooked hamburgers, tortillas, and beans and rice to feed those in the protest. Covering about 15 miles a day, some of those who had started the journey in Delano began to suffer blistered feet. By the time they had reached Stockton, the group of marchers had grown to approximately 1,500, many of whom were provided lodging by locals in the towns through which they passed. As the marchers walked through the towns, they lit candles.

As it progressed through the San Joaquin Valley toward Sacramento, the march drew increasing national publicity, with many reporters comparing it to the Selma-to-Montgomery civil rights march a year earlier. This was a pageant not only to lift the spirit and confidence of union members but also to stir the media.

Toward Sacramento they marched, two abreast—Mexican American and Filipino farm workers, students, black civil rights workers, nuns and priests, mothers with children—all uncomfortable but chanting and singing. At the back of the march line, the Rev. David Havens of the California Migrant Ministry pulled a red wagon by a rope attached to his waist. In the wagon were his two daughters, ages three and four. With each passing mile, new marchers fell in line, including, as the march entered its final days, Librado and Juana Chavez, the parents of Cesar.

On April 3, a week before the marchers were due to reach Sacramento, Chavez received a call from a representative of Schenley Vineyards. Already damaged by the publicity garnered by Chavez and hurt economically by the strike and boycott, the company had decided to cut its losses. It decided to enter into negotiations with Chavez for a union contract. Anxious to settle before the marchers reached Sacramento and the inevitable landslide of publicity that the event would produce, the company signed a preliminary agreement. Dolores Huerta was charged with drawing up a full contract that would be finalized within 90 days.

The company agreed to recognize formally the National Farm Workers Association. This was the first time in U.S. history that a grassroots farm labor union had achieved recognition by a corporation. Schenley agreed to a substantial increase of wages and to an improvement of working conditions.

Hopeful that the march would help mobilize religious organizations to join the farm workers struggle, Chavez was cheered by a statement dated April 6 from the Council of Churches in Southern California. Asking its constituent denominations to send delegations to Sacramento on Easter to greet the grape marchers, the Executive Committee of the council called the march a symbolic rebuke of the humiliation inflicted on farm workers over the years and a call to action for people of faith.

On the grounds of Our Lady of Grace School on a hill looking across the Sacramento River on the evening before Easter, Roberto Roman, a farm worker who had carried a wooden cross draped in black cloth for the entire trek from Delano, stayed up most of the night redraping it in white and covering it with flowers. The next morning, Easter 1966, Roman joined Chavez and 50 others—the *originales*—who had walked the entire distance. They marched triumphantly across the bridge, down the mall, and up the capitol steps to thunderous and welcoming cheers.

Further Reading

Dunne, John Gregory. 1976. *Delano: The Story of the California Grape Strike*. New York: Farrar.

Ferriss, Susan, and Ricardo Sandoval. 1997. *The Fight in the Fields: Cesar Chavez and the Farmworkers Movement*. New York: Harcourt Brace.

Jenkins, J. Craig. 1985. *The Politics of Insurgency: The Farm Worker Movement in the 1960s*. New York: Columbia University Press.

"The Plan of Delano." 1966. http://chavez.cde.ca.gov/ModelCurriculum/teachers/Lessons/resources/documents/plan_of_delano.pdf.

McDonnell, Donald

In 1956, a young Catholic priest named Father Donald McDonnell arrived in a barrio in east San Jose, California, that many of the locals called Sal Si Puedes, or "Get Out If You Can." The name was a kind of jocular testament to the poverty and hopelessness of the area, mostly populated by Mexican American farm workers. The young priest, educated at St. Patrick's Seminary in Menlo Park and ordained in 1947, came to help establish a community parish among the farm laborers. Sensitive to social issues and injustices, he asked the San Francisco diocese to be assigned to the poorest parish. It was here in Sal Si Puedes that Father McDonnell met a young farm worker recently out of the Navy whose life and intellect he would help mold. Cesar Chavez credited Father McDonnell with introducing him to a world of learning that was not only invigorating but that would profoundly affect his understanding of religious institutions, social justice, and history.

During his days at St. Patrick's, McDonnell, along with his good friend Thomas McCullough and three other seminarians, formed a group that planned to turn their religious calling into progressive reform efforts. They taught themselves Spanish. They discussed contemporary Catholic movements to help the poor such as the Catholic worker movement in New York. After they left the seminary, the group created what they called the Spanish Mission Band. The clerics would offer mission services to those in need in the harvest fields of California. They set out to apply to farm workers the principles of social justice and what came to be known as Catholic social action that emanated from the great labor encyclicals of Pope Leo XIII's 1891 *Rerum novarum* and Pope Pius XI's 1931 *Quadragesimo anno*. They would also begin to advocate measures such as unionization that would draw the ire of California agribusiness interests. The men traveled to various areas of California to begin their calling.

In Sal Si Puedes, McDonnell began to hold religious services for farm workers that extended beyond the small barrio into migrant labor camps in the valley. He held services in whatever buildings he could gain permission to use and even in homes. He went from camp to camp, setting up altars.

Chavez and other family members began to attend Masses conducted by McDonnell in a garage. The two men, nearly the same age, became close, and Chavez began accompanying McDonnell to the migrant camps and the county jail. McDonnell found an inexpensive, dilapidated building he believed could become a real church. Unfortunately, it was located a distance from Sal Si. Puedes. With the help of Chavez and his brother Richard, some of the worshippers were able to cut the building in half and transport it to a convenient location in the barrio. Thus was born Our Lady of Guadalupe Church.

With McDonnell's encouragement, Chavez began to read many books that the cleric had found illuminating in his own education. They discussed them at length, and Chavez found the interaction enlightening. He read books on Gandhi's independence movement in India that happened only a few years earlier in 1947. In his monumental reform movement, Gandhi used fasts and organized pilgrimages and campaigns of civil disobedience, refusing to obey unjust laws. Chavez was fascinated. He read biographies of labor organizers John L. Lewis and Eugene V. Debs. He read the papal encyclicals and the teachings of St. Francis of Assisi. He read works by Henry David Thoreau and even transcripts of hearings in the United States led by Robert LaFollette (D-WI) on agriculture, strikes, and the tactics of big business in busting those strikes. Chavez intently took it all in, developing his own perceptions of the social order and how to challenge its injustices.

McDonnell saw in Chavez the potential to be a community leader and introduced him to Fred Ross of the Community Service Organization (CSO). After a few months, Ross hired Chavez as a paid staff person for the CSO.

In the fall of 1958, Father McDonald and his close friend, Father McCulloch, set out to form a labor association for farm workers. It was to be called the Agricultural Workers Association (AWA). The two clerics traveled to the East Coast and visited labor leaders Walter Reuther and George Meany in an effort to enlist support for the organization. Although they were not successful in convincing either man to provide funds, McDonnell and McCulloch did convince Dolores Huerta, a young activist of the CSO, to lend her help quietly behind the scenes. When the largely Filipino-led Agricultural Workers Organizing Committee (AWOC) was set up in 1959 under the auspices of the AFL-CIO, McDonald and McCulloch threw their support behind it and dropped their own efforts to build a union.

Controversies surrounding the Mission Band's organizing efforts on behalf of pro–farm labor unionizing led to its downfall in 1961. The California Farm

Bureau and other anti-union forces were able to convince California's Catholic Church leadership that the Band's activist posture would lead to a loss of financial support from some quarters and to escalating protests by clerics and parishioners opposed to political and social activity on behalf of farm workers.

McDonnell would continue his pastoral work. Chavez would stake out his career in community organizing and, in 1962, with the help of Huerta, would found a new labor union for farm workers. And it was the combined forces of the AWOC and Chavez's new labor union that would launch the famous Delano grape boycott in 1965.

Father McDonnell passed away in February 2012. He was 88 years old. McDonnell's association with Chavez "perhaps changed the course of history," said Bishop Gerald Wilkerson, auxiliary bishop in the Los Angeles Archdiocese and president of the California Catholic Conference.

In 2011, the community of Mayfair in San Jose dedicated a historic building. Mayfair was once called Sal Si Puedes; the building was the original mission church for Our Lady of Guadalupe parish. The building is now called McDonnell Hall.

Further Reading

Bardacke, Frank. 2011. *Trampling Out the Vintage: Cesar Chavez and the Two Souls of the United Farm Workers*. New York: Verso.

Ferriss, Susan, and Ricardo Sandoval. 1997. *The Fight in the Fields: Cesar Chavez and the Farmworkers Movement*. New York: Harcourt Brace & Company.

Levy, Jacques. 2007. *Cesar Chavez: Autobiography of La Causa*. Minneapolis: University of Minnesota Press.

London, Joan, and Henry Anderson. 1970. *So Shall Ye Reap*. New York: Thomas Y. Crowell.

McFarland Rose Grafters Strike, 1965

In May 1965, Cesar Chavez's National Farm Workers Association (NFWA) conducted its first strike—a small-scale protest on behalf of approximately 85 rose grafters in McFarland, California. The strike was aimed at Mount Arbor Nurseries, the state's largest grower of roses. The NFWA, now over two years old, had enrolled many families in its drive to gather support from farm workers. Nevertheless, wary of launching a major strike against large, wealthy companies and their agribusiness allies without sufficient experience, Chavez would use this strike as a testing ground for the great showdowns he foresaw down the road. Here, in McFarland, less than 7 miles from Delano in the San Joaquin Valley,

Chavez would attempt to instill some discipline among his organizers and introduce them to basic tactical, nonviolent methods to gain footholds and assert power. Could his new recruits exercise necessary restraint when faced with intimidation and ridicule? Could they keep their forces together when the workers were faced with the loss of jobs and wages? He was about to find out.

The impetus for the strike came from a visit to Delano by a rose grafter named Epifanio Camacho. Knowing of the NFWA's growing reputation as an organization that could perhaps make a difference in fighting the unfair working conditions and miserable wages under which he and his fellow rose grafters labored, he came to seek Chavez's support. He told Chavez that he and some of his friends were ready to do battle.

Rose grafting was skilled labor that took years to learn. It required workers to cut slices in the stems or branches of rose plants and insert parts from other plants to produce hybrids. The process strengthened plants' resistance to disease, enabled better adaptation to different soils and climate conditions, and produced new multiflowered species. This was precision work that called for careful and knowledgeable laborers. It also called for those skilled workers to crawl along the ground in searing heat and to endure endless tiny cuts to the hands from thorns. For this kind of work, the owners of Mount Arbor Nurseries were paying their rose grafters a wage of less than $7 per thousand plants. The growers were, in turn, selling the plants for $350 per thousand.

Chavez asked his former fellow member of the Community Service Organization (CSO) Gilbert Padilla and his cousin Manuel Chavez to hold meetings at Camacho's house to gauge the possibilities of taking on Mount Arbor. At the first meeting, only four workers showed up. Discouraged but not defeated, Camacho made the rounds of other rose grafters and finally, with the help of NFWA members, persuaded nearly all of the workers to show up at a follow-up meeting. They signed cards asking the NFWA to bargain on their behalf. As he would throughout his career, Chavez appealed to religious symbols and impulse. As Dolores Huerta, the cofounder of UFWA, held a crucifix, the rose grafters grasped it and pledged not to break the strike.

On Monday morning, May 3, 1965, Chavez dispatched a number of his organizers to check the workers' homes. None of the rose grafters broke their pledge. With company bosses now aware that a strike was underway and that the NFWA had managed to persuade all workers to stay home, Huerta drove up in her green truck and attempted to speak to the company foreman about the strikers' demands. He called her a communist and told her to get out. The NFWA then enlisted the help of clergyman Chris Hartmire, a man who would become a farm labor champion for the farm workers movement for years to come. He contacted the company headquarters in Shenandoah, Iowa, to encourage a bargaining session. Company officials also turned down that attempt at negotiation.

A few days later, Chavez heard from a couple of his organizers that two or three workers living in a particular house had discussed breaking ranks. Huerta took action. She drove her truck into their driveway pinning their vehicle in place, turned off the motor, hid the keys, and refused to move.

For two days, there was no rose grafting occurring in the fields of Mount Arbor Nurseries. Soon, however, the company attempted retaliation. Labor contractors hired by Mount Arbor were able to recruit migrant workers from Tangancícuaro, a town in the Mexican state of Michoacan. These were not the kind of skilled rose grafters that were on strike, but they would serve an intermediate purpose—to escalate the tension through strike-breaking and to show the McFarland rose grafters that the company was determined not to bend to the pressures of the strike.

Chavez was so incensed at the importation of workers from Tangancícuaro that he sent a letter to the town's mayor asking him to post a list of strike breakers on the downtown bulletin board, branding them as enemies of the farm workers movement. The mayor did as Chavez asked.

The strike lasted only a few days. Realizing that the new workers from Mexico did not have the requisite skills to match the abilities of the strikers, Mount Arbor's owners decided to propose a deal. They offered to raise the wages to more than twice the amount they had formally paid but refused to recognize the NFWA as a union or to sign a contract. The workers agreed and returned to work. The first strike by Chavez's farm labor movement was now history.

Pleased that the NFWA had made some progress, Chavez still felt that the organization was far from ready to take on the large corporate interests. His organizers needed more experience, he believed. They needed additional small strike actions to hone their tactics and gain a greater sense of the possibilities of increasing their power. But circumstance and opportunity alter most plans. Chavez had no way of knowing that only a few months later, the NFWA would be in the midst of what would become known as the Great Delano Grape Strike. It would last five years and would change the face of farm labor organizing.

Further Reading

Dunne, John Gregory. 2008. *Delano: The Story of the California Grape Strike*. Berkeley: University of California Press.

Ganz, Marshall. 2009. *Why David Sometimes Wins: Leadership, Organization, and Strategy in the California Farm Worker Movement*. New York: Oxford University Press.

Levy, Jacques. 2007. *Cesar Chavez: Autobiography of La Causa*. Minneapolis: University of Minnesota Press.

"Smells from the Flower Industry." 1966. *El Malcriado*, May 5. http://farmwork ermovement.com/ufwarchives/elmalcriado/1966/May%205,%201966.pdf.

McWilliams, Carey

Cesar Chavez had a limited formal education. Nevertheless, he became an avid reader of books on philosophy, religion, history, race relations, and many other subjects, all of which are reflected in his writings, his speeches, and his approach to social change. He read about Gandhi. He read about the history of the Catholic Church and the development of the American Southwest. He read labor history. He once said, "In those early years I was hungry for any information on organizing, particularly farm labor" (Richardson 2005, 158). Some of the first books he read included *Factories in the Fields*, *North from Mexico*, and *Brothers under the Skin*. They were three of many books written by Carey McWilliams, a pioneer researcher, writer, editor, lawyer, activist, and advocate for the struggling classes held down by powerful political and social forces.

Born December 13, 1905, in Steamboat Springs, Colorado, of Scots-Irish roots, McWilliams came with his family to California in 1922. After obtaining a law degree in 1927, he began a legal career that immediately introduced him to individuals and cases involving the rights of the powerless, including striking Mexican farm workers. In the 1920s, McWilliams also befriended a number of writers including Mary Austin, Upton Sinclair, and H. L. Mencken. It was Mencken who suggested McWilliams's first book, a biography of writer Ambrose Bierce.

Early in the 1930s, amid the Great Depression, McWilliams began working with a number of left-wing political organizations including the American Civil Liberties Union and the National Lawyers Guild. After making an extended trip through the Central Valley of California and observing the sordid working conditions and exploitation of migrant workers, he began publishing articles in a number of periodicals such as *Pacific Weekly* and *The Nation* that showed how despite farm subsidies and extensive government benefits received by farmers, migratory workers were treated as little more than slaves.

From 1939 to 1942, he headed California's Commission of Immigration and Housing, where he fought to increase inspections of labor camps and other reforms. Soon, McWilliams became the growers' most persistent nemesis. McWilliams became such a high-profile enemy to the growers that they began to call him Agricultural Pest Number One, worse than pear blight or boll weevils.

McWilliams was always in a swirl of reform and progressive activity. In Los Angeles, he helped clear the names of 17 young Mexican American men who had been unjustly sentenced to prison, most of them in San Quentin, for a killing in the famous "Sleepy Lagoon Murder" case. McWilliams chaired a committee to attack their obviously biased conviction. The successful appeal in 1944 has been seen by some historians as the beginning of the Chicano movement.

In 1943, when riots in Los Angeles between U.S. sailors and Latinos gained nationwide attention, McWilliams covered the story for several publications with an eye to the racial prejudice that surrounded the fights. His prominent voice helped convince Governor Earl Warren to call for a gubernatorial commission to investigate the racial divisions in the city. Luis Valdez, friend of Chavez and creator of El Teatro Campesino, the farm workers theater, credited McWilliams's work in inspiring and informing his own work in creating the play *Zoot Suit*.

In 1944 McWilliams published *Prejudice*, a withering assault against the internment of more than 100,000 Japanese Americans during World War II.

McWilliams helped organize groups attempting to help the poor, defending the rights of immigrants, guarding civil liberties, and organizing farm labor. He served as a trial examiner for the newly formed National Labor Relations Board. He worked with Cesar Chavez's mentor, Fred Ross, in establishing the Community Service Organization to help battle employment and housing discrimination and police abuse.

He helped defend Hollywood screenwriters, directors, and producers targeted as communists by the U.S. House Committee on Un-American Activities. When witnesses declined to answer questions and were convicted of contempt of Congress, McWilliams drafted an *amicus* brief for the Supreme Court appeal. McWilliams himself was called before the committee. Although he was not a communist, FBI director J. Edgar Hoover placed him on a list of individuals to be detained in case of a national emergency.

He wrote articles vigorously attacking McCarthyism and its assault against individual liberties. Later, he would become a strong voice on behalf of the civil rights movement and a strident foe of the Vietnam War.

One of the most notable muckraking progressive writers of the twentieth century, McWilliams wrote over 200 articles and nine influential books between 1939 and 1950 alone. And from his work on labor, race, ethnicity, and California politics Cesar Chavez learned much.

Factories in the Fields: The Story of Migratory Farm Labor in California appeared in 1939, the same year John Steinbeck's *Grapes of Wrath* became a bestseller. One of McWilliams's most enduring works, it detailed the lives of California's farm workers as no book had ever done, exposing the abuses of workers and environmental damage brought on by unchecked agribusiness practices.

In *Brothers under the Skin: African-Americans and Other Minorities*, published in 1943, McWilliams examined the cultural barriers faced by minorities in the United States including Latinos, Chinese, Filipinos, and others. The book, published during World War II, even before the U.S. military was desegregated, and before the beginning of the civil rights movement, was a stirring call for affirmative action.

North from Mexico: The Spanish-Speaking People of the United States appeared in 1949. The book became a classic survey of Chicano history and culture that continued to have a major influence in college courses into the twenty-first century.

In 1955, McWilliams became editor of *The Nation*, a position he would hold for two decades. The country's foremost journal of progressive thought dated back to the nineteenth century. In McWilliams's position as editor he helped launch the careers of such writers as Ralph Nader and Hunter S. Thompson.

In 1979 in Los Angeles, many influential writers, reformers, activists, and others joined in an event honoring McWilliams. Chavez extolled McWilliams's writings as invaluable to his own education and efforts in the farm workers movement.

McWilliams died on June 27, 1980. He left a legacy as one of the most notable crusading journalists and writers in American history.

Further Reading

McWilliams, Carey. 1964. *Brothers under the Skin*. New York: Little, Brown & Company.

McWilliams, Carey. 1978. *The Education of Carey McWlliams*. New York: Simon and Schuster.

McWilliams, Carey. 2000. *Factories in the Field: The Story of Migratory Farm Labor in California*. Berkeley, University of California Press.

McWilliams, Carey. 1990. *North from Mexico: The Spanish-Speaking People of the United States*. New York: Praeger Paperback.

Richardson, Peter. 2005. *American Prophet: The Life and Work of Carey McWilliams*. Ann Arbor: University of Michigan Press.

Meany, George

In 1955, at a time when Cesar Chavez was working in California as a young organizer in the Community Service Organization (CSO), the American labor movement witnessed a major development in its history—the merger of the American Federation of Labor (AFL) and the Congress of Industrial Organizations (CIO). A divided labor movement united under the new AFL-CIO. Its first president was George Meany. Now over 70 years old, Meany had been a labor administrator from his earliest years. He had seen the pitched battles waged by labor organizations and labor leaders of all kinds to help workers win their rights. Yet in the early years of the 1960s, when a new farm labor movement arose in California led by Chavez and a group of farm workers, religious leaders, students, and activists, Meany was skeptical. Of all the labor unions he had seen in his long years, this was a strange creation with which he was not familiar.

AFL-CIO president George Meany and Cesar Chavez meet in Washington, D.C., on September 9, 1974. Although Meany did not have high regard for the kind of union organizing practiced by Chavez, the two were united by a common enemy—the Teamsters Union, continuing its fight to take over representation of farm laborers at the expense of the United Farm Workers, now an affiliate of the AFL-CIO. (AP/Wide World Photo)

He was born in 1894 in New York City, the son of a plumber who was president of the Bronx local of the United Association of Plumbers and Pipe Fitters. Meany himself worked as a plumber and joined the union as an apprentice when he was 16. In 1920, he became a member of the local union's executive board and then a full-time business agent. From one executive position to another, Meany's career in labor management progressed, and in 1934 he became president of the New York State Federation of Labor. By the late 1930s, Meany had risen in the ranks of the national AFL, becoming its secretary-treasurer. During World War II, he played an important part in forming the National War Labor Board, made up of political, business, and labor leaders with the responsibility of mediating between parties in industrial disputes. He became president of the AFL in 1952 and, three years later, was instrumental in unifying the AFL with the CIO.

Meany was never a progressive. He had little interest in the civil rights movement just beginning to gain momentum in the late 1950s. A tough-minded business executive, he was not concerned with most social causes. Yet it was

Meany, in 1959, who found himself and the AFL-CIO backing a project to steer the organization toward an organizing effort among farm workers in California. It was an effort that would challenge the political power of agribusiness and would follow the organization's stated goal to "organize the unorganized." The AFL-CIO thus created the Agricultural Workers Organizing Committee (AWOC).

Plagued by weak leadership and a lack of clear organizational direction, the AWOC, headquartered in Stockton, would not be able to launch a successful farm workers union. It would, however, be this union, dominated by Filipino workers, that would in 1965 begin a strike against grape growers and enlist the help in that strike of another farm workers movement led by Cesar Chavez.

In 1965, Bill Kircher, a long-time veteran of the United Automobile Workers (UAW) who had become highly supportive of Chavez, was picked by Meany to head the AFL-CIO Department of Organization. For Chavez, this move would prove to be decisive in the ability of the farm workers movement to gain increasing traction with Meany and in the board rooms where he and his colleagues made financial and tactical decisions about the larger labor movement in the United States.

It was Kircher who pushed for a formal merger of the AWOC and Chavez's infant union, the National Farm Workers Association (NFWA). On August 22, 1966, the United Farm Workers Organizing Committee (UFWOC) was born under the umbrella of the AFL-CIO. Chavez and his union would now receive organizing funds from the national labor organization.

Through the early years of the grape strike and boycott waged by the UFWOC, Meany remained leery about the composition of its leadership, its tactical moves, and its possible future. To Meany, Chavez remained an elusive figure. He was, Meany believed, admirable, untiring, with strong purpose and concern for the workers. At the same time, he was, Meany concluded, an idealistic dreamer who drew to his side other idealistic dreamers, from church workers to students, who had little or no experience in establishing a labor union. Also, Meany worried that a cult of personality was beginning to envelop the farm workers movement that could lead to organizational chaos.

Nevertheless, Meany grew to admire Chavez's tenacious, unbending defiance in the face of agribusiness interests, political opposition, and, especially against the International Brotherhood of the Teamsters (IBT), whose leadership, aligned with Republican Party and grower interests, sought to destroy Chavez's organization. In early 1972, Meany and his AFL-CIO leadership changed Chavez's union from that of an organizing committee to one of a full-fledged affiliate—the United Farm Workers of America (UFW).

In 1974, infuriated at the continued muscling of the UFW by the Teamsters, Meany, the 80-year-old, crusty union leader who never had much use for progressive causes, said this: "The Teamsters are doing more than suppressing a union. They are suppressing a minority—the Mexican-Americans who were just beginning to raise their heads and assert their rights under their own leaders" (Velie 1974). The Teamsters, Meany charged, appeared more interested in maintaining cordial relations with growers than in acting like true trade unionists. The AFL-CIO had given the UFW more than $6 million in recent years, Meany told a reporter, and was determined to help it withstand the most vicious strike-breaking and union-busting tactics he had ever seen in his lifetime. The issue, Meany continued, was not only that of wages and other bread-and-butter matters; it was also a question of morality.

Nevertheless, Meany and Chavez were wary, distant partners. Meany's politics remained conservative. Indeed, the union leader refused to back the left-wing Democratic candidate, George McGovern, in the 1972 election against President Nixon. In return for Meany's continued financial assistance to the UFW, Chavez was forced into uncomfortable concessions. He agreed, for example, to host meetings at UFW headquarters for various Latin American labor leaders who were being courted through a foreign operation of the AFL-CIO that was aiding the Central Intelligence Agency.

After years of struggle against the Teamsters, the most potent weapon for the UFW turned out to be a legislative victory. In August 1975, led by new Democratic Governor Jerry Brown and UFW lobbyists, California enacted the Agricultural Labor Relations Act. The passage of the act enabled the UFW to go head to head against the Teamsters in elections to demonstrate the true preference of the workers for union representation. In the ensuing elections, the UFW prevailed in most. The Teamsters finally decided to back down in their efforts to sign farm workers and to strike down the UFW.

In 1979, Chavez would no longer have to continue his uneasy relationship with George Meany. The AFL-CIO leader stepped down as the president. He died in 1980.

Further Reading

Bardacke, Frank. 2011. *Trampling Out the Vintage: Cesar Chavez and the Two Souls of the United Farm Workers*. New York: Verso.

Daniel, Cletus. 1995. "Cesar Chavez and the Unionization of California Farmworkers." In *Working People of California*, ed. Daniel Cornford. Berkeley: University of California Press.

Levy, Jacques. 2007. *Cesar Chavez: Autobiography of La Causa*. Minneapolis: University of Minnesota Press.

Robinson, Archie. 1982. *George Meany and His Times: A Biography*. New York: Simon & Schuster.

Velie, Lester. 1974. "The Teamsters' Campaign to Smash a Union." *Reader's Digest*, December. http://www.farmworkermovement.com/essays/essays/MillerArchive/055% 20The%20Teamster's%20Campaign.pdf.

Medina, Eliseo

In 1965, a 19-year-old grape picker named Eliseo Medina joined the historic Delano grape strike and became one of Cesar Chavez's most influential lieutenants. A year after he first joined the union, Medina appeared on the cover of its newspaper, *El Malcriado*, and was called one of the farm workers union's "Young Tigers." Filled with a fighting spirit, bright, and energetic, Medina would rise in the union as a trusted organizer, leading boycott activities, directing field offices, and gaining election as the union's second vice president. When he left the United Farm Workers (UFW), his career as a fighter for social justice continued well into the twenty-first century as he became a high-ranking official of one of the largest labor unions in the United States, the Service Employees International Union (SEIU). Looking back on those early days of the grape strike, Medina would say later that if it had not been for the farm workers union, he might have stayed in Delano and might still be picking grapes. Those who have worked with Medina, however, would give that assertion little credence. He was, indeed, a young tiger in those days and in the years that followed, and his drive for reform and to take on the establishment never abated.

Eliseo Vasquez Medina was born on January 24, 1946, in Huanusco, a town located in the Mexican state of Zacatecas. The son of a laborer who worked in the California fields under the Bracero Program, Medina moved to Delano, California, with his family at the age of 10 after spending almost two years in Tijuana waiting for permission to cross the border because his mother insisted on obtaining legal entry. In the mid-1950s, Medina's parents, along with his two older sisters, worked in the fields picking grapes, peas, peaches, and other crops. After Eliseo finished the eighth grade, he joined the family in the fields at the age of 15 making, he remembered later, about 90 cents an hour.

When the grape strike broke out in Delano in 1965, an excited Medina was in the hall when the decision was made by Chavez and his fellow union members. He remembered his astonishment at Chavez's small stature but was soon taken aback by the moral force of Chavez's bearing, his words, and how he interacted with the workers. Medina had saved up about $15 and immediately turned most of it over to the union for three months' worth of dues. He had watched stories of the civil rights movement on the family's small television set and thought, "God, if they can do it, we can to."

He was soon on the picket lines, energized by the feelings of power that he felt had been unleashed in himself, challenging authority, attempting to take on the establishment for elemental rights. When his family had first worked in the fields after immigrating to the United States, he had felt a sense of hopelessness—that there was no way in which their lives could improve under the labor situation as it existed. Now he saw a chance.

In 1967, Chavez asked the charismatic Medina to head the union's grape boycotting efforts in Chicago. When Medina arrived in Chicago he was, as he said many times, "one scared kid." Carrying with him $100 and a bag of UFW buttons, his mission was to persuade supermarkets to stop selling grapes. Wide-eyed at the traffic and the big-city atmosphere, relatively unschooled in labor union tactics, the youngster from California's Central Valley shook off the fears and plunged into the work with raw enthusiasm for the cause. He organized rallies and fund-raisers. He led sit-ins and pray-ins. He enlisted civic groups, labor organizations, churches, and student and women's groups. He and his small team made speeches, printed out literature to be handed out on street corners and in front of grocery stores, and managed to get media attention. He raised thousands of dollars to support the UFW boycott, and he gained confidence in his ability to make a difference.

For 13 years, Medina participated in most of the major organizing battles fought by the union. In Florida, he successfully organized a lobbying effort that helped persuade the state legislature to defeat an agribusiness bill that would have banned union hiring halls, a measure that threatened the already limited powers of the UFW. In 1973, he was elected to the UFW Board of Directors. He worked tirelessly in organizing activities in California, preparing for farm worker elections, and devising new tactics to combat grower stalling maneuvers in complying with the procedures of the California Agricultural Labor Relations Act (ALRA) that guaranteed the right of the farm workers union to bargain collectively.

In 1977, Medina was elected second vice president of the UFW. Many in the union, including Dolores Huerta, believed that Medina might eventually succeed Chavez as president of the UFW. Nevertheless, in the summer of 1978, Medina left the UFW over disputes about the direction in which the union was headed. He felt that Chavez, instead of consolidating union gains and attempting to build a solid organizing team, was more interested in turning the UFW into something akin to a poor people's campaign and social movement. Chavez, he felt, had relegated organizing and attaining new contracts to a lower level of commitment than generating various social and political activities. With tensions escalating, Medina, with his resignation, shocked those in the union who saw him as the future leader.

Medina's work on behalf of exploited workers did not end with his departure from the UFW. After organizing workers in California and public employees in Texas, he joined the SEIU in 1986 and, within five years, had rebuilt a declining SEIU local in San Diego.

In 1996, Medina was elected to serve as international executive vice president of SEIU. He led SEIU campaigns on behalf of janitors and for home health care workers.

In 2010, Medina was unanimously elected to serve as international secretary-treasurer of the SEIU, now a 2.1-million-member union. He led the union's efforts to achieve comprehensive immigration reform to secure equal labor and civil rights protections for workers and to provide a path to citizenship.

Studs Terkel, the famed chronicler of oral history, interviewed Medina for his book *Hope Dies Last*. Medina said, "Thirty-something years ago, when I was first here as a young farmworker, I heard a labor song, and it talked about how freedom is a hard-won thing, and it said that every generation has to win it again" (Terkel 2003, 127). Medina has, indeed, done his part.

Further Reading

Aubry, Erin. 1996. "Conversation with Labor Ground-Breaker Eliseo Medina." *The Los Angeles Times*, May 4.

Bardacke, Frank. 2011. *Trampling Out the Vintage: Cesar Chavez and the Two Souls of the United Farm Workers*. New York: Verso.

Ganz, Marshall. 2010. *Why David Sometimes Wins: Leadership, Organization, and Strategy in the California Farm Workers Movement*. New York: Oxford University.

Pawel, Miriam. 2009. *The Union of Their Dreams: Power, Hope, and Struggle in Cesar Chavez's Farm Worker Movement*. New York: Bloomsbury.

Terkel, Studs. 2003. *Hope Dies Last*. New York: The New Press.

Modesto March, 1975

On February 28, 1975, the CBS *Evening News* with Walter Cronkite featured a story about a march of thousands of United Farm Workers (UFW) strikers heading from San Francisco toward the town of Modesto, California, the home of the Gallo Wine Company, at the edge of the San Joaquin Valley. Cesar Chavez's union had, once again, through a nonviolent protest demonstration, made national news from the harvest fields of California in its movement to improve working conditions of grape pickers and other farm laborers. The Modesto March came shortly after the *New York Times* ran a story entitled "Is Chavez Beaten?" The article explained how Chavez had started something of a revolution of farm workers but that another union was invading his turf. The rival union was the International Brotherhood of the Teamsters (IBT), an organization that was battling to destroy the UFW and take over all farm worker contracts in California and across the country. But the 1975 march would not only prove that the UFW was, indeed, not dead but very much alive. So effective was the boycott of Gallo grape products and the culminating protest march that within six months of the march, the Teamsters would leave the harvest fields and the California legislature and Governor Jerry Brown would work with the UFW in crafting the first state legislation recognizing farm workers' right to organize in unions and engage in collective bargaining.

By early February 1975, the UFW had been boycotting Gallo, the nation's largest winery, since 1973. Gallo had been one of the union's most persistent foes, signing a sweetheart deal with the Teamsters in 1973 and refusing to allow elections among the workers to determine whether they supported the UFW. In 1966, the union had made dramatic progress with its celebrated *peregrinación* or march from Delano to San Francisco that attracted international attention. UFW leaders decided to use the tactic again. They set out not only to prove that the UFW's critics were wrong that the union was beaten but rather that its political influence had increased to the point that its fight for a state farm workers law was anything but quixotic.

A few hundred supporters gathered on February 22 in San Francisco's Union Square, site of many progressive reform meetings that had occurred there over the years. Representative Philip Burton (D-CA), long-time friend of the union and a stanch advocate of the boycott, spoke as did other supporters. Inside the Hyatt Hotel, Teamsters leaders had earlier held a press conference denouncing the march as a cheap publicity stunt being launched by a declining and desperate union. At the nearby St. Francis Hotel, Gallo officials had erected a large banner to mock the beginning of the march, which said, among other things "Marching Wrong Way, Cesar." Considering the Teamsters press conference and the Gallo banner, UFW leaders sensed that the march had, indeed, struck fear into their corporate and rival union foes.

At the same time the march began in San Francisco, other contingents of UFW supporters awaited to set out from other locations such as Fresno and Stockton. There would be rallies along the route in such towns and cities as Oakland, Hayward, Pleasanton, Tracy, and Livermore. The marchers would thus converge on the winemaker in Modesto—a kind of siege of Gallo.

With marchers spending nights at the homes and businesses of supporters along the routes, the marchers moved toward Modesto, picking up hundreds of additional recruits. The main contingent, the San Francisco marchers, made its way through the Sacramento River Delta country. Luis Valdez and his Teatro Campesino (the Farm Workers Theater) made appearances along the route as they had done in the Delano to San Francisco march. A number of unions including the Longshoremen's and Warehousemen's Union showed their solidarity.

On March 1, more than 10,000 supporters carrying the UFW's red flag with the black Aztec eagle converged on the dusty streets of Modesto, singing "Chavez, *si*; Teamsters no!" Fred Ross, Chavez's mentor of over a decade, was exuberant, declaring that the *New York Times* had been premature to say that Chavez was beaten. Ross's son, Fred Ross Jr., following in his father's footsteps as an organizer, had been instrumental in convincing Chavez to undertake the strike. He had also helped the massive coordination effort and had predicted a large turnout. On this day, however, the numbers exceeded his wildest hopes. Folk singer Joan Baez was at the main city park to welcome Chavez, as was the union leader's mother.

Although Ernesto Gallo, chairman of the company, went out of his way to maintain that the boycott had been a failure, that the reported number of stores not selling Gallo wines had been exaggerated, and that the company had little use for Chavez and his cohorts, there was a sign in Modesto hanging from Gallo's headquarters that sent a different message. The sign read "73 more miles to go. Gallo asks UFW to support NLRA-type laws in Sacramento to guarantee farm-worker rights" (Ferriss and Sandoval 1997, 195).

The banner was, to most of the marchers, puzzling. UFW counsel Jerry Cohen was astonished. In a sense, it was a type of capitulation, encouraging Democratic Governor Jerry Brown and the state legislature in Sacramento to work with the UFW in crafting legislation legitimizing the farm workers union and their right to collective bargaining. On the other hand, the Gallo sign made reference to the National Labor Relations Act (NLRA), the major federal legislation that covered labor-management issues for all industries except those involving farm workers. Ironically, the UFW, because it had not been part of the NLRA, was not required to adhere to its legal strictures. One of those restrictions was secondary boycotts, the same kind of protest action that the UFW was using against Gallo. Other growers had admitted to reporters that the boycott was severely damaging their industry.

The UFW would do exactly what the Gallo sign in Modesto said that day. It would work with Brown and the legislation to frame the Agricultural Labor Relations Act (ALRA) of 1975. Marc Grossman, one of Chavez's lieutenants, would say later, "Gallo tastes a lot sweeter today" (Berenstein 2012).

Further Reading

Berenstein, Erica. 2012. "Si Se Puede: "Cesar Chavez and His Contribution to the American Wine Industry." *Wine-Searcher*, April 23.

Ferriss, Susan, and Ricardo Sandoval. 1997. *The Fight in the Fields: Cesar Chavez and the Farmworkers Movement*. New York: Harcourt Brace & Company.

Levy, Jacques. 2007. *Cesar Chavez: Autobiography of La Causa*. Minneapolis: University of Minnesota Press.

Shaw, Randy. 2008. *Beyond the Fields: Cesar Chavez, the UFW, and the Struggle for Justice in the 21st Century*. Berkeley, University of California Press.

Tyson, Samuel. n.d. "Farm Workers." *Roots and Fruits* (Stanislaus Peace-Life Center), http://www.stanislausconnections.org/r&f/0205The%20Fa.htm.

N

Nathan, Sandy

Cesar Chavez and his farm workers movement benefitted enormously from a skillful legal team. It steered the United Farm Workers (UFW) through murky case law, fought admirably against well-heeled counsel representing growers and state and local government, and devised strategies that enabled Chavez and his organization to secure victories in the courts as they carried on their nonviolent fight in the fields. Prominent on the legal team was Sanford "Sandy" Nathan. A young attorney fresh out of Columbia Law School, Nathan was drawn to the movement after learning of the oppressive and unjust labor system that preyed on migrant laborers with little regard for their lives or livelihoods. When asked why he joined the movement, Nathan said, "You go where your heart is" (Kilbourn 2010). Through seven challenging and exciting years, with the future of the UFW in the balance, Nathan successfully represented the union in a number of important areas. Yet his time with the UFW would represent only the beginning of his professional career. The internal administrative turmoil within the UFW—the personal and professional fractures splitting apart its very structure—left Nathan with little choice but to leave. Even with the knowledge that he had done wonderful service to La Causa, he carried with him a great measure of disappointment and regret.

Even though he had grown up in a small steel town in western Pennsylvania where his father was in a union, labor law had not been Nathan's focus in law school. He was more interested in the civil rights and antiwar movements and politics. He traveled to California, passed his bar exam, and worked for a poverty project at the University of California—Los Angeles. In 1973, he met with Jerry Cohen, the UFW's lead counsel, and joined the legal team.

He certainly was not in it for the money. The annual salary of a UFW staff attorney was about the same as some legal offices charged for two weeks of a lawyer's representation. But he saw the farm workers movement as an opportunity to use his legal training on behalf of an extraordinary effort toward social justice.

Now in his late twenties, tall, with long hair and a prominent beard, he was easily spotted among UFW supporters. He helped defend the UFW against all kinds of judicial assaults resulting from strikes and boycotts.

The legal team played a prominent role leading up to the 1975 passage of the landmark Agricultural Labor Relations Act (ALRA), legislation that for the first time allowed farm workers to unionize and enjoy the rights of collective bargaining. The team now concentrated on the most effective ways to make the legislation work best for the UFW. Nathan became the lead attorney to work on ALRA matters. He probed the intricacies of the legislation and built strategies for the benefit of the farm workers. He worked with members of the Agricultural Labor Relations Board (ALRB), the body created by the law to implement its terms, and with other state officials.

He spent some time in jail. In 1975, he was arrested for demanding access to a group of farm workers detained for protesting at a Salinas ranch. In 1977, the police nabbed Nathan again, this time during a strike by tomato pickers. He was thrown into a cell with 25 workers and one UFW organizer. On the police report regarding Nathan's arrest, under the box entitled "Weapon," the arresting officer wrote, "hand, feet and mouth" (Pawel 2011, 237).

In the late 1970s, personal disagreements became increasingly tense between Chavez and others of his lieutenants. Always with an aesthetic bent, Chavez suddenly became infatuated with a strange drug-rehabilitation organization called Synanon and its leader, Charles Dederich, and demanded that his lieutenants engage in some of the practices of the cultlike group in order to receive purification. One of the practices was called "The Game," a form of so-called attack therapy, involving highly confrontational, verbal humiliation directed at members of a group. Chavez had demanded that the entire leadership of the UFW participate in the exercise. All of the legal staff resisted, considering the practice nonsensical as well as cruel. Nevertheless, Chavez insisted that the legal team participate.

On six separate days in April and May 1978, Nathan and the others reluctantly went through the motions. On one day, the legal team showed up dressed in short-sleeved white shirts with ties, looking very much like young Mormon missionaries, and marched in formation, all the while singing and chanting. The mockery was not amusing to Chavez.

The relationship between the UFW leader and his legal team had become combustible. In the spring of 1978, the UFW's executive board, following the lead of Chavez, narrowly voted to stop paying salaries to the legal team and to have the entire organization work as an all-volunteer staff. For Chavez, all those in the movement, he believed, should follow his own example of sacrifice.

For Sandy Nathan, who had for over five years managed to scrape by financially with the help of his parents, such a dictum from UFW's leadership was a hammer blow. He was 33 years old and had already sacrificed for the union by accepting a salary far lower than he could have received outside the UFW. Now, Chavez and the UFW were demanding even more. This would be the end of Nathan's work with the UFW. It would be the end of the powerful legal team that had guided the movement so skillfully through the shoals of grower and government legal opposition. It would be a hammer blow to the UFW itself. Soon, the legal team would have five inexperienced lawyers and a few paralegals to pit against their formidable adversaries.

After he left the UFW in 1979, Nathan worked at a number of influential labor organizations in San Francisco, including the Amalgamated Transit Union and the International Brotherhood of Electrical Workers. He also opened a law practice in Kansas dedicated to mediation and conflict resolution.

Looking back on the glory days of the UFW, the days of victories over impossible odds, the days of playing David against the Goliaths, and the days when volunteers gave their hearts and energies into helping others, Nathan said, "We were working for a cause, a passion. It was not a job at all" (Kilbourn 2010).

Further Reading

Bardacke, Frank. 2011. *Trampling Out the Vintage: Cesar Chavez and the Two Souls of the United Farm Workers*. New York: Verso.

Gordon, Jennifer. 2005. "Law, Lawyers, and Labor: The United Farm Workers' Legal Strategy in the 1960's and 1970's and the Role of Law in Union Organizing Today," *U. Pa. Journal of Labor and Employment Law*. http://www.law.upenn.edu/journals/jbl/articles/volume8/issue1/Gordon8U.Pa.J.Lab.&Emp.L.1(2005).pdf.

Kilbourn, Clara. 2010. "Book Recounts Attorney's Activism: McPherson Lawyer One of Eight Featured in Work on Chavez's Labor Fight." *The Hutchinson News*, January 24. http://www.hutchnews.com/Localregional/bookrecounts.

Pawel, Miriam. 2009. *The Union of Their Dreams: Power, Hope, and Struggle in Cesar Chavez's Farm Worker Movement*. New York: Bloomsbury Press.

Nonviolent Protest

"Nonviolence is not cowardice," Cesar Chavez once said. (Hammerback and Jensen 2003, 37) On the contrary, nonviolent protest is militant resistance and active coercion on behalf of a just cause. The term *nonviolent protest* encompasses a range of methods to promote social change that avoid using, in all situations, physical violence, even in retaliation for violence used against the protest. The goal is to persuade others who have power to join the struggle for reform.

For Chavez, the farm workers movement would attempt through a variety of these methods to gain the attention and the support of the public, law makers, church organizations, and others who could affect actual change in the lives and working conditions of those working in the harvest fields. In the campaign of the United Farm Workers (UFW), Chavez employed a number of nonviolent tactics and strategies—strikes, boycotts, fasts, marches, and civil disobedience. If a local judge filed an injunction against picketing that violated their rights of free speech, Chavez and his supporters would be willing to be arrested and to go to jail as an expression of their dedication to the cause.

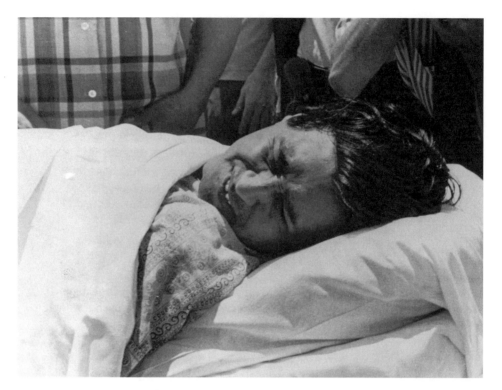

On May 31, 1972, Cesar Chavez, suffering from the effects of a water-only protest fast of nearly a month, is wheeled from the Santa Rita Center in Phoenix, Arizona, to be moved to a hospital. Chavez was leading a protest against an Arizona law that prohibited farm workers from unionizing or engaging in boycotts. (AP/Wide World Photo)

Nonviolent protest can be a creative and often effective means of persuasion, garnering exposure to make the case that the reforms sought are just and deserved. It is active, not passive, demonstrating a willingness to sacrifice and to suffer. Chavez often explained to members of the UFW that nonviolence was not only morally and ethically sound but also provided the farm workers movement the best chance to achieve success. He argued that violence, on the other hand, played into the hands of those who resisted social change, giving evidence that the protest movement was out to cause chaos and destruction. In violent confrontation, the reason for the social protest gets lost in the quest for victory or vengeance. The movement of the farm workers for social justice proved to be a powerful example of nonviolent protest achieving nearly unimaginable gains in the face of overwhelming odds.

The most celebrated advocate of nonviolent protest in the twentieth century was unquestionably Mahatma Gandhi, the leader of the national liberation struggle of India against British imperialism. In the early 1950s, Chavez, under the tutelage of Father Donald McDonnell, began to find much joy and enlightenment in reading.

One of the books that most interested Chavez was a biography of Gandhi. It was Gandhi, highly educated in Britain, who took on the might of British authority while dressed in the clothes of the poorest of the Indians. Living an ascetic existence, he led resistance through noncooperation. He fasted, led a long march, encouraged a boycott, and went to jail—all to resist oppression. From the life of Gandhi, Chavez learned much.

While working in the Community Service Organization (CSO) in the 1950s and, later, as he began to organize what became the UFW in the early 1960s, Chavez also saw the maturation of the civil rights movement and the emergence of the leadership of Martin Luther King Jr., who was himself a student of Gandhi. So much admiration did King have for Gandhi that he carried a Gandhi quote in his wallet. Under the leadership of King and others, black Americans carried on an unprecedented nonviolent crusade for justice. Civil rights protestors marched through hostile crowds, conducted sit-ins and rallies, faced fire hoses, and suffered beatings and all manner of humiliations. And they filled jail cells. Some died. But against the threats, taunts, ridicule, and the physical assaults, the movement remained nonviolent. And it brought change. From the work of King, Chavez also learned much.

Chavez also brought to his nonviolent campaign the traditions inherent in Latin American fights for social justice that went back hundreds of years. Others had fasted, had engaged in pilgrimages, and had used the Catholic mass as ways of mobilizing communities and of stirring change. Chavez had learned from them also.

Throughout the drive to establish the UFW and in all of its struggles thereafter, Chavez used every opportunity to emphasize the nonviolent nature of the movement. Such frequent proclamations encouraged religious individuals and organizations to rally to the cause. It encouraged volunteers who might have otherwise been fearful of reprisals. It framed the contest between the rich and the poor and the powerful and the powerless. In such a David-versus-Goliath battle, especially in the international table grape boycott, the public rallied to the side of the farm workers. Nonviolence, in spurring public opinion through newspaper, television, and radio coverage, thus became a public relations and communications weapon.

On March 5, 1968, during Chavez's fast in Delano, King sent a telegram that said, "I am deeply moved by your courage in fasting as your personal sacrifice for justice through nonviolence." He spoke of the fast as being "in the Gandhian tradition with its great force for social progress and its healing spiritual powers" (Mariscal n.d.). After King was assassinated in Memphis, Tennessee, just a few weeks later, Chavez wrote to King's widow, Coretta Scott King, "his nonviolence was that of action—not that of one contemplating action. Because of that, he will always be to us more than a philosopher of nonviolence. Rather, he will be remembered by us as a man of peace" (Mariscal n.d.).

Chavez saw in nonviolence both the philosophical and theological foundation of his commitment to social change. He spoke often about Gandhi's assertion that the tactics of nonviolence were a kind of moral jujitsu, keeping the opponent off balance with unexpected moves. In using nonviolent protest as a powerful force against discrimination, inequality, and injustice, Chavez himself became a master.

Further Reading

Hammerback, John, and Richard Jensen. 2003. *The Rhetorical Career of Cesar Chavez.* College Station: Texas A & M University Press.

Holmes, Robert, and Barry Gan. 2011. *Nonviolence in Theory and Practice.* Long Grove, IL: Waveland Press.

Levy, Jacques. 2007. *Cesar Chavez: Autobiography of La Causa.* Minneapolis: University of Minnesota Press.

Mariscal, Jorge. n.d. "Cesar and Martin, March '68." http://farmworkermovement.com/essays/essays/mariscal.pdf.

Orosco, Jose-Antonio. 2008. *Cesar Chavez and the Common Sense of Nonviolence.* Albuquerque: University of New Mexico Press.

Sharp, Gene. 1973. *The Politics of Nonviolent Part Two: The Methods of Nonviolent Action.* Boston: Porter Sargent Publishers.

Yinger, Winthrop. *Cesar Chavez: The Rhetoric of Nonviolence.* Hicksville, NY: Exposition Press, 1975.

One Thousand Mile March, 1975

On July 1, 1975, Cesar Chavez embarked on what would be his longest march—1,000 miles from San Ysidro at the Mexican border across from Tijuana, Mexico, then along the coast to Salinas, on to Sacramento, and then south down the Central Valley to the headquarters of the United Farm Workers (UFW), known as La Paz, in Keene, California, southeast of Bakersfield. The march was both a celebration and a call for action. The celebration was for the recently passed California Agricultural Labor Relations Act (ALRA), the first legislation on behalf of farm workers that ensured their rights to unionize and participate in collective bargaining. The call for action was in anticipation of the upcoming votes across the agricultural regions of California under ALRA for elections at the various vineyards, ranches, and other agricultural sites that would determine whether farm workers at those individual locations would choose to have themselves represented by the UFW, the Teamsters Union, or no union at all.

After extensive lobbying efforts by the UFW and tense negotiations with both houses of the California legislature in passing the ALRA bill, Governor Jerry Brown signed the legislation into law on June 4, 1975. It established a five-member Agricultural Labor Relations Board (ALRB) to administer the provisions of the law. It also defined procedures for holding secret-ballot elections. The law was set to go into effect on August 28, 1975, with ALRB establishing rules and regulations involving the elections at the farms, orchards, and ranches in the harvest areas of California. ALRB rules would give organizers the right access to the fields beginning on August 29 to try to convince workers to sign on with the union. Chavez was determined that the workers would be ready and eager to participate in the newly won legislative process.

Less than a month after Governor Brown signed the legislation, Chavez organized the latest *peregrinación*. The tactic had been enormously successful in the early grape strike and, most recently, in a march to Modesto, California, in support of the pending legislation. This long-range trek, Chavez believed, would rally the troops of the UFW, inform workers along the extensive route about their rights under the law and the upcoming elections, and, through press coverage, signal that the union was on the march toward unparalleled success in its commitment to organize farm workers.

With 60 supporters, Chavez led the marchers north after touching a fence at the U.S.-Mexico border. The grape harvest was just beginning, and the group would stop daily after about 20 to 25 miles to hold rallies encouraging workers to join the UFW. At the end of each day, Chavez would take a stick and mark an "X" in the ground, and it was at that point that the march would begin the next day. The gesture struck some fellow marchers as a mite obsessive.

Each night at the rallies held for the farm workers in the various towns, the march organizers would show the film *Fighting for Our Lives*, a documentary nominated for an Oscar showing clips of the 1973 grape strike in which workers walked off the job from Coachella to Fresno and withstood assaults by police and antistrike thugs. The movie, Chavez believed, was a moving testament to the nonviolent bravery that the farm workers movement represented and to which it continued to aspire.

Sticking to a strictly vegetarian diet, often eating watermelon while others in the group ate tacos or carne asada, Chavez seemed, as the days wore on, more ebullient, confident, and even physically energized. Now middle-aged, he strutted in the front at a pace that left some of the other younger walkers somewhat winded.

A photojournalist named Cathy Murphy, who had first photographed Chavez when she was a student at Brooks Institute of Photography in Santa Barbara, joined the march at the beginning. "Cesar was walking the highways and going into communities all along the way," she said,

> telling workers in the field they finally had their right to organize and to vote for union representation. . . . Walking in front of Chavez were his two large German Shepard dogs, Boycott and Huelga. Behind and beside him were security guards. I jumped into the line, behind the dogs and directly in front of Chavez. I raised my camera and Chavez' dark, piercing eyes looked directly into the lens. (Young 2009)

The march ended 58 days after Chavez had touched the fence at the Mexican border. Shortly afterward, on September 5, 1975, the first election under ALRA was held at the small artichoke farm near Delano called the Molera Agricultural Group. It had been working under a Teamster contract. When many of the workers cast their ballots in a tractor shed set up as the election site, most emerged shouting "Viva Chavez." The UFW had 17 votes to 5 for the Teamsters.

When the first round of voting across the state ended in February 1976, 47,000 workers had cast ballots in 425 elections. The UFW won 214 elections with approximately 23,000 votes; the Teamsters, 115 with around 11,500 votes; and "no union" prevailed in only 33 elections with around 7,500 votes. Considering the fact that Teamster leaders had been confident that the elections were going to go decidedly in their direction, the success of the UFW gave the union renewed strength in the fields. Although the election results were, not surprisingly, contested, with much contention between the UFW and the Teamsters and the growers, the union was now in a better strategic position than before the law had been passed. Within less than two years, UFW membership would rise to 30,000, nearly back to its peak in 1971.

Although no one can be certain of the effect that the One Thousand Mile March had in convincing workers to vote for the UFW, Chavez was serene in the belief that it had served the union's purpose.

Further Reading

Bardacke, Frank. 2011. *Trampling Out the Vintage: Cesar Chavez and the Two Souls of the United Farm Workers*. New York: Verso.

Ferriss, Susan, and Ricardo Sandoval. 1997. *The Fight in the Fields: Cesar Chavez and the Farmworkers Movement*. Harcourt Brace & Company.

Young, Anna. 2009. "Marching through History with Cesar Chavez." April 29. http://sixties-l.blogspot.com/2009/04/marching-through-history-with-cesar.html.

Oxnard Organizing Campaign, 1958

In August 1958, Cesar Chavez arrived in Oxnard, California, to establish an office of the Community Service Organization (CSO). The lush agricultural fields around Oxnard, northwest of Los Angeles, were familiar to Chavez. As a young boy with his family members who had lost their farm in Arizona, he had moved in the late 1930s to La Colonia, the barrio in Oxnard. He had joined his family in the nearby fields picking peas and beans, and for a time they lived in a tent. And now, two decades later, he returned to Ventura County to help farm workers assert their rights as citizens and enable them more effectively to move into the mainstream of American society. He would set up citizenship classes, voter registration drives, and other campaigns. He would use the techniques of organizing taught to him by Fred Ross and other CSO leaders to encourage farm workers to battle discrimination, to band together to fight for better wages and working conditions and better schools, and to join in political efforts to improve their lives. For Chavez, the experience in Oxnard would be a vital training ground, helping provide a vision and direction for his life's work.

The project in Oxnard was a joint effort of the CSO and the United Packinghouse Workers of America, whose leaders sought to expand its union base of laborers who worked in the lemon-packing sheds. If Chavez, through a new CSO chapter, could embolden the workers and show them the possibilities of improving their lives through organizing, the Packinghouse union would stand a much better chance of increasing its own strength and numbers.

Chavez said later that the idea of mobilizing workers in Oxnard had a special appeal. Remembering the treatment meted out to his family by growers in the region years before, Chavez said, "When we were migrants, Oxnard was an extremely bad place for us. In the back of my mind, I thought that going back would be a little revenge. I just wanted to go back and fight" (Levy 2007, 126).

Chavez began the drive in Oxnard as he had launched other organizing efforts. He held house meetings. He held citizenship classes in Bonitas School, which would later be named Cesar Chavez School. He began a vigorous voter registration drive, convincing Mexican American citizens that they had enormous untapped political power. People responded. Voter rolls began to include hundreds of Spanish surnames as never before. But as he went from house to house, Chavez realized that the overwhelming issue over which the local workers were most concerned was the way in which growers had rigged the Bracero Program to avoid hiring available labor in the community.

The Bracero Program had been designed to ameliorate labor shortages during World War II by admitting Mexican laborers for short-term employment. Now, long after the labor shortage ended, the program had continued. Oxnard's Buena Vista bracero camp, created by the local Ventura County Farm Labor Association, was one of the largest of its kind in the nation. Growers were supposed to use braceros only when no local workers were available. Instead, growers ignored the applications from local workers and continued to use braceros, who would cost them less money. The federal government was thus subsidizing labor for growers at the same time the program was displacing domestic workers.

Chavez decided on a plan to prove to state employment officials and federal labor investigators that the growers were perpetrating fraud against the resident *campesinos*. For over a month, he carefully documented the names of individuals who had filled out job applications properly and had been refused work or had been fired for no reason and then replaced with bracero labor. After accumulating a large stack of documentation, Chavez then hit on a scheme that would bring the unscrupulous practices of the growers to attention. He alerted newspapers, local and state television stations, and government officials that there would be a demonstration that they would not want to miss.

Cesar Chavez was about to embark on a lifetime's work of nonviolent protest. A caravan of cars filled with workers and their families converged on a tomato farm. They sang Mexican songs, including one about Pancho Villa. They carried pictures of the Virgin of Guadalupe, the patron saint of Mexico. They built a bonfire near the farm. By now, the press and cameras and local labor officials were fully attentive, wondering what would ensue. The workers then pulled out of their pockets piles of legitimate job referral cards that had been rejected by growers and tossed them into the fire.

In succeeding weeks and months, Chavez organized other nonviolent protest actions. He set up pickets at various work sites. He held sit-ins. He helped workers deluge the state labor offices with hundreds of written complaints. And, most of all, he led marches. On one evening, hundreds of workers and supporters marched through the streets of Oxnard at night carrying lighted candles, singing, and calling out for jobs. Chavez said later that the several marches he conducted in Oxnard convinced him of their power, reminding Mexican Americans of religious pilgrimages of their Catholic faith. He would use the tactic of the march again and again.

For over a year, Chavez and his growing number of supporters kept up the pressure. Finally, the state government administration fired the head of the Farm Placement Service and forced growers to give local workers first consideration at jobs. The CSO was even able to drive up the wages of farm workers.

In the end, the victory in Oxnard for the farm workers lasted only as long as Chavez remained in town. In 1959, the CSO asked him to move to Los Angeles to work in the organization's headquarters. Within six months, various machinations by growers and their political supporters brought braceros back into the fields and local farm workers back to their previous oppression.

The effort in Oxnard, however, convinced Chavez that he could mobilize enough Mexican American and farm worker support to build a union. His one-year campaign of 1958 would be prelude to a historic campaign that would follow.

Further Reading

Altman, Linda. 1994. *Migrant Farm Workers: The Temporary People*. New York: Franklin Watts.

Barajas, Frank. 2012. *Curious Unions: Mexican American Workers and Resistance in Oxnard, California, 1898–1961*. Lincoln: University of Nebraska Press.

Bardacke, Frank. 2011. *Trampling Out the Vintage: Cesar Chavez and the Two Souls of the United Farm Workers*. New York: Verso.

Levy, Jacques. 2007. *Cesar Chavez: Autobiography of La Causa*. Minneapolis: University of Minnesota Press.

Ross, Fred. 1989. *Conquering Goliath: Cesar Chavez at the Beginning*. Keene, CA: El Taller Grafico Press.

P

Padilla, Gilbert

Along with Cesar Chavez and Dolores Huerta, Gilbert Padilla was there at the beginning of the movement that led to the creation of the United Farm Workers (UFW). From his early days with the Community Service Organization (CSO), where he first met Chavez in the mid-1950s, to the heady days of the formation of the union, the victories in the early strikes, the battles with the Teamsters Union, and the marches and boycotts in California, Texas, Pennsylvania, and other states, Padilla was a close lieutenant and advisor of Chavez. One of most resourceful and dedicated leaders of La Causa, Padilla envisioned a life's work battling with the UFW—organizing new contracts and fighting new battles on behalf of the farm workers. Regrettably, he, as did a number of other union leaders, found themselves in the whirl of internal strife and disagreement that drove many away from the UFW in the late 1970s and 1980s. While he was secretary-treasurer, Padilla left the union in 1980, bitter about the direction in which Chavez was leading the union and hurt by the personal gulf that had inexplicably resulted between the two. Nevertheless, he had been a prominent leader in the birth and development of La Causa and firmly committed to securing rights and social justice for those people for whom the movement was directed—the nation's farm workers.

He was born in 1927 in a labor camp near Los Banos, California, a child of migrant farm workers from Zacatecas, Mexico. Padilla traveled with his family throughout California, where they picked cotton and fruit. From his earliest years, he recoiled against the institutionalized racism that his family faced in the harvest fields. He remembered a public swimming pool in Azusa, California, where white children could swim every day and where Mexicans and African Americans were allowed only on Friday nights. The pool was cleaned early Saturday morning before the white kids took their next swim.

Following military service in the U.S. Army, in which he earned a number of commendations, Padilla returned to the cotton fields once again to face the same deprivations and insults as before. He looked for a way to fight back, and in 1955, he found an answer. Padilla met Chavez, who convinced him to join the CSO. Padilla saw the organization as a way to challenge the inequalities and injustices he personally saw and felt in the harvest fields. "Gilbert was my discovery," Chavez later told an interviewer.

For the next eight years, Chavez and Padilla worked in the CSO, conducting citizenship classes and voter-registration drives, battling police brutality and discrimination, and fighting for many issues: pensions for noncitizens, immigrants' rights, and disability insurance for farm workers. When Chavez quit as director of CSO in 1962 and began to organize farm workers, Padilla, along with Huerta, joined him.

"Everyone who came into the organization didn't do it for power or for glory," Padilla said, "but to change a population of people in this country that was completely disenfranchised" (Moreno 2011). His wife, Esther, also from a family of farm workers, joined him in the movement.

In September 1962, at an abandoned movie theater in Fresno, California, the National Farm Workers Association (NFWA), one of the precursors of the UFW, held its first convention. Padilla became an area director and, over the next few years, worked not only on organizing drives but also in registering farm workers to vote.

Padilla took on major responsibilities in organizing the boycotts of both Schenley Industries and the DiGiorgio Fruit Corporation. In January 1967, he was dispatched to Texas. In the summer of 1966, at the time when the NFWA was conducting strikes and boycotts against California growers, union farm workers in the Rio Grande Valley went on strike at Las Casitas Farm, led by organizer Eugene Nelson. The strike even featured a 400-mile march, or *peregrinación*, modeled after Chavez's march from Delano to Sacramento earlier in the year. Accompanied by Rev. James Drake, Padilla tried to come to the assistance of strikers who had been beaten by Texas Rangers. As Padilla and Drake approached the courthouse in Rio Grande City, they were ordered off the steps for using "abusive language." Instead of leaving, they knelt down to pray. They were arrested, Padilla later joked, for praying.

Padilla kept up the pressure. There were more arrests but no convictions. Years later, aided by a civil rights group in Texas and by an investigation conducted by the U.S. Senate Subcommittee on Migratory Labor, the UFW sued the Texas Rangers and won the case.

Padilla worked on the grape boycott in Philadelphia in 1970 and in Wisconsin in 1972. In 1973, he traveled to Washington, DC, and not only led picketing campaigns but also testified before U.S. Senate subcommittees on behalf of the UFW. In September 1973, at the UFW constitutional convention, Padilla was elected secretary-treasurer.

In October 1975, Padilla moved to the UFW's new headquarters at La Paz, where, in addition to his duties as secretary-treasurer, he was also in charge of field office administration and contract negotiations. But it was at La Paz that Padilla and others realized that Chavez was determined to take the union into other areas of development that meant less organizing in the field and less leadership in administering the union's obligations to its members. It was at La Paz that Padilla felt Chavez lost control over the union's principle mission. And it was there that the personal hostilities and anger increasingly flared and long-time supporters left or were forced to leave. After a particularly humiliating exchange at a meeting in which he was accused of sabotaging UFW goals, Padilla tendered his resignation to Chavez over the phone. The two never spoke again.

For Padilla, the memories of the movement were conflicted, especially about Chavez. "He was the best man in my daughter's wedding and he was a close friend," said Padilla, "but he changed" (Moreno 2011). Padilla would have preferred to have stayed, would have given his all to continue and to have helped the union's march to greater power and success. But Chavez's leadership and the personal recriminations not only against Padilla but also to others that he saw threatening the direction of the union had finally made it impossible to continue. But Padilla understood fully the enormous contribution to Latino self-identity that the movement represented. When the March 31, 2011, annual Cesar Chavez Birthday Celebration, hosted by the Cesar Chavez Service Club, was held in San Diego, Gilbert Padilla was there having his picture taken, surrounded by young Latino children.

Further Reading

Bardacke, Frank. 2011. *Trampling Out the Vintage: Cesar Chavez and the Two Souls of the United Farm Workers*. New York: Verso.

Hubner, John. n.d. "Cesar Chavez: Is Anyone Following the Leader?" http://farm workermovement.com/essays/essays/CESAR%20CHAVEZ-%20IS%20ANYONE %20FOLLOWING%20THE%20LEADER.doc.pdf.

Moreno, Cynthia. 2011. "We Marched with Cesar." *Vida en el Valle*, March 20. http:// www.vidaenelvalle.com/2011/03/30/867394/we-marched-with-cesar.html.

Padilla, Gilbert. n.d. "Gilbert Padilla 1962–1980." Farmworker Movement Documenta-tion Project. http://farmworkermovement.com/essays/essays/005%20Padilla_Gilbert. pdf.

Pawel, Miriam. 2009. *The Union of Their Dreams: Power, Hope, and Struggle in Cesar Chavez's Farm Worker Movement*. New York: Bloomsbury.

Perelli-Minetti Strike and Boycott, 1966

In September 1966, the Perelli-Minetti California Winery, in order to avoid nego-tiating with Cesar Chavez's farm workers union, the United Farm Workers Organ-izing Committee (UFWOC), signed with the Teamsters Union a so-called sweetheart deal—a contract that involved far fewer concessions to the workers than any contract that the company could have negotiated with the UFWOC.

Perelli-Minetti's action, taken shortly after the farm workers union had achieved major success with its strikes and boycotts of both Schenley Vineyards and DiGiorgio Corporation, marked an escalation in the growing fight between the UFWOC and the Teamsters. It was a fight that Chavez was determined to win. Soon, he concentrated his strike and boycott forces against Perelli-Minetti.

First established in 1912, the Perelli-Minetti vineyard was a family business started by an Italian immigrant and passed down to his sons. The company, with headquarters in McFarland, California, produced bulk wine, vermouth, and brandy and marketed products under such brand names as Tribuno Vermouth and Eleven Cellars wine. Not one of the largest wineries in California, Perelli-Minetti nevertheless took on the UFWOC at a time when the union could not afford to back down. If the UFWOC lost this battle, Chavez believed, it would not only stall the momentum and enthusiasm of the Schenley and DiGiorgio victories but would also help solidify an alliance between the Teamsters and the growers that could conceivably threaten the survival of the farm workers union.

On September 9, 1966, workers at Perelli-Minetti walked out, demanding a wage increase and union representation. Following a meeting between UFWOC leaders and company officials that left union officials believing they might be able to work out a contract, Perelli-Minetti pulled a surprise attack. It suddenly brought in three busloads of scab workers and announced on September 16 that it had signed a union contract with the Teamsters. Soon, Teamster thugs, armed with pistols and chains, began intimidating picketers at the company's work sites. On September 13, the UFWOC announced a boycott of the company.

It was at the beginning of the Perelli-Minetti boycott that Chavez hired a young lawyer who had worked briefly with California Rural Legal Assistance to become the lead counsel. Jerry Cohen and his legal team would become a powerful force for Chavez and the union in the coming years, and Cohen became an immediately valuable asset in the current struggle between the union and its adversaries in the Perelli-Minetti boycott.

First, the union boycotted the major cities in California, pressuring distributors and retail outlets to refuse handling Perelli-Minetti products. In Los Angeles, union organizers set up "sip-ins" in the Brookside wine-tasting rooms. In San Francisco, almost all of the members of the Glass Bottle Blowers Union, employed by Owens Illinois Glass Company, the manufacturers of the boycotted bottles, refused to cross the union picket line. The Bartenders Union and the Retail Clerks Union offered support.

Within months, the boycott became national as union organizers traveled to large cities across the country. Eliseo Medina, age 20, a Mexican-born farm worker who joined Chavez in the early days of the union and who showed much promise as an organizer, took over boycott operations in Chicago. He had no experience with such an operation but learned quickly—fund-raisers, rallies, sit-ins—all of it he and his allies tackled on the spot. He borrowed ideas from the civil rights movement, he said, and improvised. He visited union leaders, colleges, and churches.

With young leaders such as Medina making news across the country, Perelli-Minetti products began disappearing from the shelves of retail outlets. In attempting to obtain an injunction against the union, company officials told a judge that the strike and boycott were costing Perelli-Minetti $10,000 a day.

By the summer of 1967, the company and the Teamsters had endured enough bad publicity and, for the company, damaging financial losses. When the parties agreed to a showdown meeting in Burlingame in July, Perelli-Minetti lawyers and company officials had such animus toward Chavez that would not even speak to him directly. Jerry Cohen recalled, "Fred Perelli-Minetti would not talk directly to Cesar, he would talk to his attorney, a guy named Dick White, who would then talk to me and then I'd talk to Cesar. That's how strained relations were. . . ." Chavez later said that the nonsense became something of a game between him and Cohen: "Now, Cesar, Mr. Perelli-Minetti tells his attorney to tell me to tell you that they want to know from you through me through the attorney back to them . . . " ("Jerry Cohen, Tape 72").

The winery finally agreed to hold representational elections to determine which union should have the contract. When the UFWOC prevailed, the Teamsters turned over the existing contract to the farm workers union. Although the UFWOC would have to wait two years to renegotiate a contract with more favorable rights for the workers, at least Chavez and his union had forced both the company and Teamsters into an agreement embarrassing to both.

In addition, under pressure from a committee of clergymen, Chavez and the Teamsters agreed to a jurisdictional pact to prevent such turmoil in the future. The Teamsters would organize works in food processing, trucking, and other activities involved in the industry; the UFWOC would organize the farm workers. The jurisdictional pact, as Chavez and others might have suspected, would not be honored in the future by the Teamsters. They would not go quietly from this battle. Nevertheless, the victory in the Perelli-Minetti struggle was yet another sign that Chavez's union was marching forward.

Looking back, the union's master organizer Fred Ross said that the Perelli-Minetti victory inspired union leaders to take on their biggest target yet— Giumarra Corporation, the largest table grape ranch of them all.

Further Reading

Ganz, Marshall. 2009. *Why David Sometimes Wins: Leadership, Organization, and Strategy in the California Farm Worker Movement*. New York: Oxford University Press.

Griswold del Castillo, Richard, and Richard Garcia. 1995. *Cesar Chavez: A Triumph of Spirit*. Norman: University of Oklahoma Press.

"Jerry Cohen, Tape 72." Farmworker Documentation Project. http://www.farmwork
ermovement.org/media/oral_history/ParadigmTranscripts/CohenJerry.pdf.

Levy, Jacques. 2007. *Cesar Chavez: Autobiography of La Causa*. Minneapolis: University
of Minnesota Press.

Ross, Fred. 1974. "History of the Farm Worker Movement as told by Fred Ross, Sr., Day-
ton, Ohio, October, 1974." http://clnet.ucla.edu/research/chavez/themes/ufw/history2.
html.

"Plan of Delano"

"Plan of Delano" was a manifesto of the newly formed National Farm Workers
Association (NFWA) that issued a revolutionary call to action for the rights of
oppressed Mexican American farm workers.

In the spring of 1966, in the midst of the first major grape strike undertaken by his
infant farm workers union, Cesar Chavez organized a march or *peregrinación* from
the union's headquarters in Delano, California, through the San Joaquin Valley to
the state capitol in Sacramento. It was on this march, at evening rallies along the
route, that workers and others gathering each night would hear read aloud "Plan of
Delano," a statement of purpose explaining the goals and ideals behind the farm
workers movement. The statement began: "PLAN for the liberation of the Farm
Workers associated with the Delano Grape Strike in the State of California, seeking
social justice in farm labor with those reforms that they believe necessary for their
well-being as workers in the United States" ("The Plan of Delano" 1966).

For Chavez, organizing the farm workers was not merely the creation of a union
but also a demand for social justice, a claim for all to be accorded their "God-
given rights as human beings." Chavez entrusted the writing of the document to
Luis Valdez, the creative playwright who had joined forces with the new farm
workers movement to form El Teatro Campesino, a dramatic theater company that
began to give performances at strike sites.

Both Chavez and Valdez saw the movement as steeped in the history of the fight
against the oppression of lowly workers and peasants. They also saw in it a
revolutionary fervor that could be traced to certain aspects of the Mexican Revolution over half a century earlier.

With Chavez's encouragement, Valdez modeled "Plan of Delano" after the
so-called "Plan de Ayala," authored by Mexican revolutionary martyr Emiliano
Zapata. Born into peasantry in 1879 in the state of Morelos, Zapata worked as a
tenant farmer on a sugar plantation. Nevertheless, he did not suffer the same fate
as that of many in his class whose families lost their lands to a system of peonage
in which, under the rule of Porfirio Diaz, great hacienda landowners unscrupu-
lously confiscated small farms. Zapata married into a middle-class family but carried with him a burning resentment against the treachery carried out by wealthy

Cesar Chavez and Luis Valdez in New York City, April 11, 1979. In the early years of the farm worker movement, the playwright Valdez formed El Teatro Campesino, an acting group that performed at union rallies and on picket lines and later became an influential force in Chicano theater. Valdez also authored "Plan of Delano," the forceful statement about the plight of farm workers and the fight for their rights. (AP Photo/Daniel Goodrich)

landowners against the poor such as those he had known from his childhood. He once led a group of peasants in forcibly reclaiming land recently taken from them. He briefly spent time in jail. After becoming a bullfighter and a horseman for a time, he turned to politics and, in 1909, was elected mayor of a tiny village. Within two years, he had become deeply involved in a revolution that in 1911 swept Diaz from power.

Early in the revolution, Zapata issued the "Plan de Ayala," his call for justice and action. It demanded that all lands stolen under the Diaz regime be returned to the people. Large plantations owned by a single person or family would have one-third of their land nationalized and given to poor farmers. If they refused, all of their lands would be seized.

For eight years, through the rise and fall of several leaders, brief alliances and betrayals, and battles and short-lived ascensions to power, Mexico reeled with political uncertainty. In 1919, any hope of Zapata gaining power and implementing his plan to redistribute the land to peasants died with his assassination. Nevertheless, the revolution in Mexico did eventually result in some agrarian reforms.

And for Zapata, his life and the "Plan of Ayala" became the stuff of legend, a rallying cry of the Mexican poor and dispossessed and a call for revolution. His picture, along with that of Gandhi, hung on the office wall of Chavez. His name was on a fence at the union's headquarters in Delano. At the parish hall in Delano, when the grape pickers voted to strike the grape growers in 1965, many of the workers that night carried posters with an image of Zapata.

On March 17, 1966, at the start of the march to Sacramento, the "Plan of Delano" was first read to those assembled. It spoke of the pilgrimage they were about to undertake that sought an end to the suffering of farm workers, of their determination to be heard, and of their resolve to follow their God. It talked about the injustices over many decades inflicted on farm workers—starvation wages, intolerable working conditions, fraudulent contractors, lack of medical care, sub-human living conditions—all of it leaving the workers without power or representation and subject to the caprice of their rancher bosses.

This was a social revolution in which they were engaged, it said. It promised unity and inclusion of workers of all faiths and races; it vowed to conduct strikes and to pursue a nonviolent revolution of the poor, a revolution for "bread and justice."

And so, throughout the *peregrinación* to Sacramento, Valdez carried with him "Plan of Delano." He read it aloud at each stop and asked local workers to sign it. "WE SHALL OVERCOME," it concluded:

Across the San Joaquin Valley, across California, across the entire Southwest of the United States, wherever there are Mexican people, wherever there are farm workers, our movement is spreading like flames across ad dry plain. Our PILGRIMAGE is the MATCH that will light our cause for all farm workers to see what is happening here, so that they may do as we have done. The time has come for the liberation of the poor farm worker. History is on our side. MAY THE STRIKE GO ON! VIVA LA CAUSA. ("The Plan of Delano" 1966)

Further Reading

Bardacke, Frank. 2011. *Trampling Out the Vintage: Cesar Chavez and the Two Souls of the United Farm Workers*. New York: Verso.

Brunk, Samuel. 2008. *The Posthumous Career of Emiliano Zapata*. Austin: University of Texas Press.

Ferriss, Susan, and Ricardo Sandoval. 1997. *The Fight in the Fields: Cesar Chavez and the Farmworkers Movement*. New York: Harcourt Brace & Company.

Levy, Jacques. 2007. *Cesar Chavez: Autobiography of La Causa*. Minneapolis: University of Minnesota Press.

McLynn, Frank. 2000. *Villa and Zapata: A History of the Mexican Revolution*. New York: Carroll and Graf.

"The Plan of Delano." 1966. http://chavez.cde.ca.gov/ModelCurriculum/teachers/Lessons/resources/documents/plan_of_delano.pdf.

Proposition 14, 1976

The Agricultural Labor Relations Act (ALRA), passed in 1975, was landmark legislation that for the first time allowed farm workers the right to unionize. A short year later, the law's power had suddenly been weakened. The board empowered to carry out the law's enforcement, the Agricultural Labor Relations Board (ALRB), had not been provided with sufficient funds to operate. It had run out of money, and in February 1976, for lack of funds, the new state agency was forced to close its doors and lay off its employees. Republican opponents of Cesar Chavez's United Farm Workers (UFW) in the state legislature refused to take action to put it back in business. Furious, Chavez fought back. He promoted a bold initiative to place on the November 1976 election ballot in California. It became known as Proposition 14. This was a farm labor initiative aimed at preventing interference by political enemies in the state legislature in implementing the ALRA. "Prop 14" would make the ALRA, the ALRB, its funding, and other provisions of the law permanent and unalterable only by another such state initiative. Chavez declared, "We're going to teach the growers a lesson they'll never forget once and for all" (Shaw 2008, 157). Through the ballot initiative, Chavez would ask the voters of California to provide a constitutional shield of protection for the farm workers law.

Chavez's decision to attempt a ballot initiative put massive pressure on the UFW organization. First, the union would have to gather enough signatures throughout California just to get the initiative on the ballot. Then, if the union succeeded in obtaining the necessary number of valid signatures, it would face the daunting challenge in the general election of overcoming the political forces arrayed against it—the Republican political machine and the formidable war chest of money that the growers would certainly use to saturate television and radio stations with advertising blasting the UFW's positions on the issues. Although Chavez and his lieutenants realized that the growers would demonize the initiative and spread misleading and malicious lies about its provisions, Chavez remained confident that the UFW could prevail through a vote of the people.

Chavez asked Marshal Ganz, a superb organizer and strategist with canny political instincts, to run the campaign. As news of the UFW's operation spread, scores of volunteers, many of whom had worked on strikes and boycotts, made their way from across the country to California to be dispatched to various parts of the state. In a remarkable display of coordination and grassroots support, the volunteers were able to mount an efficient and effective statewide campaign, securing over 700,000 signatures in just 29 days. Prop 14 would be on the ballot in November.

As the election campaign of 1976 got underway, the electorate of California was closely divided. Republican President Gerald Ford faced off against Democratic challenger Jimmy Carter, governor of Georgia. Polls indicated a very close race between the two in California. For the UFW, the fate of Prop 14 did not seem to rest on the national race. Indeed, the state had a Democratic governor, Jerry Brown, who threw his support behind the initiative, declaring, "I will vote yes on 14 because it is right. Because it saves taxpayers money and it will bring peace and the rule of law to the fields of California" ("Preserve Secret Ballot . . . " 2011).

The UFW, as it had done in gathering the signatures to get the initiative on the ballot, worked feverishly to persuade voters that the election was about the continued exploitation of farm workers and the Republican Party's allegiance to the interests of growers. One of the fliers prepared by the union spoke about the farm worker legislation that had been passed a year before to ensure secret elections and an honest system to allow workers to choose to join a union. "But the big corporate growers didn't like the results of the elections," the flier declared, "so they put pressure on a small group of state legislators and cut off funds for the Board. The result: no more elections. No more law and justice in the fields. An invitation to the growers to go back to child labor, spraying pesticides on workers, beating up farm worker organizers" (Roberts 2012).

But, unfortunately for the UFW, the main issue in the campaign, driven by a high-priced advertising blitz against the measure, framed the issue in a far different light. Instead of challenging the right of farm workers to organize and join a union, the growers and their Republican supporters honed in on one of the provisions of the initiative. Part of Prop 14 involved the issue of access by union organizers to the farm workers who lived and worked in grower-owned camps. In effect, the initiative would have, in many ways, exempted union members from the usual restrictions of private property rights. For example, "No Trespassing" signs, in many cases, might not apply to union organizers attempting to enter private fields or camps to speak to laborers.

It was this provision that Prop 14's opponents attacked with much zeal and to great effect. Prop 14, their ads proclaimed, was an assault against an individual's right to determine who may or may not enter his or her private land. Television commercials featured a farmer expressing fear for his daughter's safety if union organizers had unrestricted access to his property and even his home. Another ad asked the simple question: "Would you want someone coming on your property without permission?" Thus, the election, to the union's dismay, soon became not one centered on the rights of farm workers but on the property rights of private citizens.

Despite an aggressive voter-registration drive by UFW organizers and intensive door-to-door canvassing, the fate of the initiative was inextricably tied to the farmer fearing for the safety of his daughter and his right to defend his property. California narrowly voted for Ford in the presidential election carried nationally by Carter. Prop 14 was defeated by 14 percent. It was a devastating political defeat for Chavez and the UFW.

Further Reading

Bardacke, Frank. 2011. *Trampling Out the Vintage: Cesar Chavez and the Two Souls of the United Farm Workers*. New York: Verso.

Chatfield, LeRoy. 2010. "A Turning Point." Cesar Chavez Service Clubs. http://chavezclubs.org/wp-content/uploads/2012/01/A-Turning-Point.pdf.

Pawel, Miriam. 2009. *The Union of Their Dreams: Power, Hope, and Struggle in Cesar Chavez's Farm Worker Movement*. New York: Bloomsbury Press.

"Preserve Secret Ballot for State Farm Workers." 2011. *San Francisco Examiner*, May 22. http://www.sfexaminer.com/opinion/editorials/2011/05/preserve-secret-ballot-state-farm-workers.

Roberts, Dave. 2012. "Cesar Chavez Backed Secret Union Votes."2012. *CalWatchdog*, April 4. http://www.calwatchdog.com/2011/05/23/chavez-must-be-spinning-in-his-grave/.

Shaw, Randy. 2008. *Beyond the Fields: Cesar Chavez, the UFW, and the Struggle for Justice in the 21st Century*. Berkeley: University of California Press.

Proposition 22, 1972

In 1972, California's agribusiness interests, led by the 60,000-member California Farm Bureau, attacked the United Farm Workers (UFW) with yet another weapon—a statewide ballot initiative, Proposition 22, designed to strike down the power of the union. The initiative sought to prohibit secondary boycotts (those at stores and other retailers selling wines and grapes and other agricultural products targeted by the union). It proposed to delay harvest strikes for 60 days. It also tried to bar the union from bargaining on work rules. In other words, the legislation, crafted by Republican legislators and their friends in the agricultural industry, aimed to render the UFW harmless. This was a life-and-death issue for Chavez and the UFW. If this statewide ballot initiative passed, the UFW, despite the remarkable success it had made in one decade, would be without weapons to take on the business establishment. But the verdict would not come from the legislators or the growers; it would come from a vote by the people in the November election. Chavez mobilized every force he had available to convince those voters to reject Proposition 22.

The election in the fall of 1972 did not promise to be a propitious time for the UFW to defend itself against the Republican establishment. President Richard Nixon, a California native, was most certainly going to carry the state against Democratic candidate George McGovern. Nixon, who had no use for the UFW, openly preened before cameras eating grapes in defiance of the union's boycott. The state Republican establishment, led by Governor Ronald Reagan—who, like Nixon, enjoyed publicly popping a grape in his mouth before the press—was anxious to rid itself of Chavez and his annoying influence on its agribusiness and political interests. The Republicans and the growers' organizations planned an ambitious advertising blitz encouraging voters to support the initiative to protect the state's agricultural industry. If the UFW had any hope of winning this contest at the ballot box, it would have to convince many voters who planned to vote for Nixon to also support the union.

Although all of the union leaders would take part in this crucial election, Chavez chose LeRoy Chatfield to direct the campaign. A former high school teacher who had training in a monastic religious order, Chatfield was a savvy organizer with shrewd instincts for political combat. He would later become a campaign director in Jerry Brown's successful run for the governorship.

Chatfield set up 40 campaign teams around the state. Hundreds of UFW workers now on the lettuce boycott in cities across the country headed back to California and joined other volunteers in fanning across the state. Chavez began a barnstorming trip to various towns and cities, calling on voters to reject this assault on working men and women. UFW members vigorously appealed to Latinos to register and vote. UFW leaders raised small amounts of money to print flyers and bumper stickers saying "Justice for Farmworkers, No on 22." A number of 60-second radio spots featuring Hollywood celebrities Jack Nicholson and Warren Beatty added to the campaign. A 30-second TV commercial featuring Chavez even appeared during segments of the immensely popular show *All in the Family.*

For a grassroots campaign, the political operation was sophisticated, carefully keeping tabulations of voters registered, following the progress of leafleting and declarations of support signed by voters who were canvassed in a massive door-to-door operation, and keeping up the spirits of the volunteers. Ellen Eggers, a recent graduate from Ball State University who enthusiastically joined the campaign, later remembered that the organizers showed the volunteers that "our little piece of the puzzle was important" (Shaw 2008, 152).

Meanwhile, in addition to pouring thousands of dollars into ads on radio and television, the anti-UFW, progrower forces began a large-scale campaign of misinformation. Billboards across the state suddenly featured the message "For Farm Workers Rights, Yes on 22!"

The union soon fought back with its so-called human billboard response. In shopping centers and on the sides of roads and highways, drivers now saw volunteers carrying large, 2-foot by 3-foot signs with such messages as "LA Times Says No on 22," "AFL-CIO Says No on 22," "Council of Churches Says No on 22," and, simply, "No on 22!" The UFW team carefully plotted the traffic patterns in various cities and strategically located its workers. For example, in Los Angeles, squads deployed at streets feeding into the major freeway entrances in San Fernando Valley, Santa Monica, and other locations. Those volunteers, standing about 10 yards apart, greeted commuters going in one direction in the morning and then in the opposite direction at the end of the workday. Traffic helicopters picked up the campaign; many drivers honked their approval. It was free advertising on the evening news. At a reunion many years later, one of the volunteers recalled with much pride how she had breathed car fumes for entire days at a ramp of a Los Angeles freeway—all for La Causa.

Approximately two months before the election, Chatfield's team found what it believed could be a "smoking gun" to use against the growers. Led by Chatfield's wife, Bonnie, UFW researchers discovered that many of the petitions that had been submitted to get Proposition 22 on the ballot in the first place had been fraudulent. Hundreds of certified petitions bearing the names and addresses of individuals had been filled out with the same handwriting. It was clear that many paid workers hired by the agribusiness group had simply filled in the petitions using voter registration rolls. The documents had not actually been signed by voters themselves.

The campaign decided to gather statements from voters whose names were on the certified petitions but who had not actually signed the petitions. As LeRoy Chatfield recalled, "We would ask them to sign a statement, under penalty of perjury, that they had not signed the petition, and furthermore, they petitioned the secretary of state to remove their names from the petitions." (Chatfield n.d.)

Hundreds of volunteers marched into Los Angeles precincts and, in just three or four days, the team had more than 500 statements. Encouraged by the progress, Chatfield guided volunteers to precincts in other cities. Armed with several hundred other declarations, UFW officials then approached Secretary of State Jerry

Brown, the only Democratic Party official in a high office in California's state government. They convinced Brown to call a press conference announcing that declarations alleging voter fraud had been brought to his attention and that he was turning the evidence over to the Los Angeles District Attorney for possible prosecution. The news jarred support away from Proposition 22.

The final tally was decisive and remarkable. As Richard Nixon cruised to victory in the presidential election, the UFW and their supporters and their grassroots campaign defied the odds and the money directed against the union and won a resounding 58 percent to 42 percent victory. It had been a masterful political organizing effort that would act as a model for UFW and other underdog political campaigns in the future.

Further Reading

Bardacke, Frank. 2011. *Trampling Out the Vintage: Cesar Chavez and the Two Souls of the United Farm Workers*. New York, Verso.

Chatfield, LeRoy. n.d. "Proposition 22." http://www.farmworkermovement.org/essays/essays/PROP22ESSAY.pdf.

Meister, Dick. 1977. *A Long Time Coming: The Struggle to Unionize America's Farm Workers*. New York: Macmillan.

Shaw, Randy. 2008. *Beyond the Fields: Cesar Chavez, the UFW, and the Struggle for Justice in the 21st Century*. Berkeley: University of California Press.

R

Ranch Committees

As the United Farm Workers (UFW) won victories and gained contracts, Cesar Chavez emphasized the importance of field workers at the local level and the need for democratization of the union. Because the farm workers were spread out among different field locations, each farm or ranch would have its own service center, he promised, run by a ranch committee elected by its own members, much like union stewards in other labor organizations. "The only way that there can be democracy in the Union now and tomorrow and thereafter" he said, "is to have those ranches, those ranch committees, retain as much power to run their affairs as possible" (Pawel 2009, 176). In the day-to-day dealings with employers with whom the UFW had signed contracts, it was the ranch committee and its manager that would enable the union to carry on its normal functions without close, first-hand micromanagement from the top. Together, the workers and their leaders would build the union brick by brick, making it impenetrable from attack and responsible to its membership. Ironically, however, it was the ranch committees in the 1970s that would clash with Chavez over union strategy, help plunge the union into conflict, and test Chavez's true commitment to a union with strong democratic roots.

At the UFW's First Constitutional Convention in 1973, Chavez spoke about how valuable he would consider the views from those in the fields, on the sites where the interaction between the farm workers and their employers was most immediate and challenging. The ranch committees, Chavez said, could provide the insights and inner workings taking place from the fields that could help provide an effective, democratic administrative leadership. One of the union's most effective organizers was Eliseo Medina, a young UFW rising-star organizer whom Chavez sent to Chicago to establish a boycott operation from scratch. Medina had excelled. And now he was working hard in the early 1970s setting up the structures of the ranch committees, carefully planning how each could be subdivided to take over the various responsibilities in administering the contractual conditions to which union workers were now subject.

By the mid-1970s, Medina and others realized that Chavez's embrace of the ranch committee concept seemed to be weakening. Medina said, "We need to set up a program for the ranch committees and staff on how to have meetings, file grievances, generally how to administer the contracts" (Pawel 2009, 184). Indeed,

Eliseo Medina, one of the United Farm Workers' (UFW) "Young Tigers," leads a protest at the Talisman Sugar Cane Company near Clewiston, Florida, October 30, 1972. Medina helped form ranch committees that provided a structure for democratic involvement in UFW operations. Later disagreements over union direction with Chavez led Medina to leave the UFW. (AP Photo/Steve Starr)

debate on the ranch committee structure and the training for those involved in it was nearly ignored in leadership meetings. It was, as Medina complained, a low priority. But the need for and the value of ranch committees had been Chavez's oft-stated position; it was his explanation how the UFW would be a democratic organization, involving the farm workers themselves in generating ideas and plans. What had happened?

As Chavez looked down the road, he began to see in the ranch committees a danger to his own leadership. He explained his wariness in a number of ways. As newer members gained more power, he mused, they would begin to challenge more informed decisions made by those who had created the union and saw the vision of the movement and what it represented beyond a simple labor union of the traditional sort. He also told confidants that the ranch committee heads were likely to begin to demand salaries beyond the subsistence wages now paid to union representatives, who were essentially volunteers. He told others that if farm workers themselves took over the major leadership of the union, it could result in chaos. And so the democratic ideal envisioned by Chavez as the UFW gained greater power gave way to his fear of losing control, of losing the ideal of sacrifice that had given the union its identity. In time, he would begin to see the actions of some of the ranch committee heads as a power grab that he would never tolerate.

In 1979, despite growing internal disputes within the leadership of the UFW over a number of troubling issues such as the ranch committees, the union won a number of strikes against lettuce growers in the Salinas Valley. Chavez himself had doubted whether the strike could succeed without a boycott. But during the intense days of the strike, led by organizers Marshal Ganz, Jessica Govea, and Mario Bustamante, the UFW teams in the field demonstrated well-orchestrated coordination and discipline. The field worker strike actions prevailed without a boycott.

The new agreements, negotiated by counsel Jerry Cohen, provided for company ranch union representatives that would be paid by the companies. For the union, the lettuce contracts, with the "paid-reps" provisions, were significant in asserting the mutual responsibilities of the growers and the union to make the collective bargaining agreements successful working arrangements. Chavez, nevertheless, could see the dangers behind the agreements. Although he praised the workers who had fought as a tightly knit team to win the contracts, he worried that some of the ranch committee heads would attempt to assert their own power at the expense of his own control over union affairs.

In 1981, one of those ranch committee leaders brought the issue to a dramatic showdown. Mario Bustamante, a young, charismatic firebrand with an athlete's physique, had been a *lechugero*, a lettuce picker, since his boyhood days. A Mexican immigrant, he had joined the UFW in 1969. In 1978, the Green Valley company workers elected him as president of their ranch committee. At the 1981 UFW convention, Bustamante did what Chavez had feared—he challenged the union to back up its protestations of democracy.

At the convention, the union prepared to vote for three vacant positions on the UFW board. Chavez and his team at UFW headquarters in La Paz supported three candidates, individuals fiercely loyal to Chavez. But, just as Chavez had long expected, those candidates now had an opposition slate whose most vocal spokesman was Bustamante. Chavez spread the word among the 350 delegates at the convention that Bustamante and others who challenged the loyalists were part of a conspiracy to destroy the union.

After a fractious and bitter confrontation that led to a vote that essentially ruled the opposition slate invalid, Bustamante, along with about 50 supporters, fumed. Indignant at the treatment he had received, the fiery Bustamante took a UFW flag, broke its stick, and flung it to the floor. The challenge of the ranch committee heads to the leadership was lost in an explosion of boos as Bustamante and his supporters walked out.

Further Reading

Bardacke, Frank. 2011. *Trampling Out the Vintage: Cesar Chavez and the Two Souls of the United Farm Workers*. New York: Verso.

Ganz, Marshall. 2009. *Why David Sometimes Wins: Leadership, Organization, and Strategy in the California Farm Worker Movement*. New York: Oxford University Press.

Pawel, Miriam. 2009. *The Union of Their Dreams: Power, Hope, and Struggle in Cesar Chavez's Farm Worker Movement*. New York: Bloomsbury Press.

Reuther, Walter

In 1965 and the early days of the Delano grape strike, Cesar Chavez needed allies in his quest to form a union of farm workers. He could neither have hoped for nor expected to see arrive in Delano a better friend of the movement than Walter Reuther, long-time president of the United Automobile Workers (UAW). Reuther was one of the most celebrated labor leaders in U.S. history. Born in 1907, the son of a brewery-wagon driver and union leader in Wheeling, West Virginia, Reuther and his two brothers, Roy and Victor, moved to Detroit, Michigan, to find jobs in the auto industry. By age 29, he was president of a UAW local and in a little over a decade had become the union president in 1946. Under the auspices of the Committee on Industrial Organization (CIO), the UAW, headed by Reuther, grew to more than 1.5 million members and was in the forefront of establishing safety provisions, pensions, and health benefits for its members.

In 1952, Reuther, while still president of the UAW, also became president of the CIO. He soon joined with George Meany, president of the American Federation of Labor (AFL), in merging the two organizations into the AFL-CIO.

In the late 1950s, Reuther promoted a policy within the AFL-CIO to "organize the unorganized," especially farm workers. In 1959, AFL-CIO president Meany acceded to pressures from a number of religious and activist groups, as well as from Reuther and others in the organization, to establish a farm worker organizing project. The result would ultimately be the founding of the Agricultural Workers Organizing Committee (AWOC).

Although AWOC would seek the improvement of wages and working conditions for farm workers, mostly in lobbying efforts, it never became an effective farm workers union that incorporated experienced union organizers who could mobilize a largely Mexican American workforce. Nevertheless, it was the AWOC that in 1965, directed mostly by Filipino leaders, decided to launch a strike of grape growers in Delano. And it was the AWOC that convinced Cesar Chavez to join his own infant farm workers union, the National Farm Workers Association (NFWA), in the strike.

On December 16, 1965, Reuther visited Delano to pledge his support for the strike and a recently announced nationwide boycott that had been planned by the NFWA. Nearly 1,000 farm workers and others joined in a spirited rally. For Reuther to have made this visit to Delano was an enormous boost to Chavez at this critical time in the strike, giving powerful national visibility and endorsement to the movement.

Carrying an NFWA picket sign that read "HUELGA," he joined a march from the airport. He told the assembled farm workers, "There is no power in the world like the power of free men working together in a just cause" (Ferriss and Sandoval 1997, 114). Although local police had warned that protestors would be arrested if they marched because they had no permit, the arrival of Reuther and along with him dozens of writers from major newspapers soon resolved the issue. The police would not enforce the ban. As the marchers walked through the streets of Delano, groups of farm workers or *campesinos* shouted, "Viva Reuther! Viva Reuther!"

He met with the Delano mayor and other city officials. He then interviewed a few of the local growers willing to talk. After the meetings, Reuther said of the farm workers, "Sooner or later these guys are going to win" (Lichtenstein 1997, 410).

Later, Reuther took the stage at the union's hall, along with Chavez and Larry Itliong of the AWOC. Reuther spoke out in favor of the grape strike and the boycott. When growers refuse to sit down at the negotiating table in an honest effort at collective bargaining, he said, unions must act decisively. He promised to help attempt to mobilize union support across the country on behalf of the boycott. "This is not your strike," he declared, "this is *our* strike" (Ferriss and Sandoval 1997, 114). An enormous cheer engulfed the room. Reuther then ratcheted up the enthusiasm to even greater heights. He pledged on behalf of the UAW to provide $5,000 a month each to the NFWA and the AWOC for "as long as it takes to win this strike."

The AWOC was already receiving $10,000 a month from the AFL-CIO in support of the strike and some contributions from other unions such as the clothing workers, seafarers, and packinghouse workers. Although the financial pledge by Reuther was especially welcome, especially because it would be a monthly payment, it did not solve the financial hardship involved in conducting a serious strike. Already, the strike was costing an estimated $40,000 a month, even considering that most of the work was being done by volunteers with little compensation. Nevertheless, the Reuther visit and pledge of support was a vital contribution in giving the NFWA, the AWOC, and the strike and boycott a national stamp of legitimacy. This effort launched in the small town of Delano would now be a continuing national story that would affect millions of people across the country.

"It was a very significant day," Chavez recalled later. "The press played up the visit, and the strike took on national importance. The following day we had three times the number of people willing to come and join the picket line" (Levy 2007, 204).

It was not unusual for Reuther to demonstrate a personal commitment to social justice issues. He had marched with civil rights activists in Mississippi and hospital workers in South Carolina. Reuther was one of the few non–African American speakers at the 1963 March on Washington and the scene of Martin Luther King Jr.'s "I Have a Dream" speech. He continued to support the work of Chavez and the farm workers union.

In May 1966, as Chavez's union carried on its nationwide boycott, Reuther welcomed a delegation of strikers led by Chavez to a UAW convention in Los Angeles. There, the delegates committed the organization to provide assistance to boycotters in their local areas.

When Chavez engaged in his celebrated fast in 1968 during the strike against Giumarra Vineyards to demonstrate his commitment to nonviolence, his action drew a number of national figures to Delano to offer their help. One of those was Reuther, who brought more than just good wishes. He donated $50,000 to help pay for the construction of a new building at the union headquarters at Forty Acres.

In 1968, Reuther, his wife, May, and two others were killed in a tragic private plane crash. Upon his death, *El Malcriado*, the farm workers newspaper, published on May 15, 1970, a tribute that declared,

> He was a man who thirsted for justice and freedom—who wanted to see the good things of the earth shared by all, including the least of his brethren. But to us in Delano, Walter was a friend. He came and helped us when we needed help so desperately. He encouraged our leadership. With him we felt more powerful, and more capable of continuing our struggle. ("There Is No Greater Calling . . . " 1970)

Further Reading

Barnard, John. 2005. *American Vanguard: The United Auto Workers during the Reuther Years, 1935–1970*. Detroit: Wayne State University Press.

Ganz, Marshal. 2009. *Why David Sometimes Wins: Leadership, Organization, and Strategy in the California Farm Worker Movement*. New York: Verso.

Levy, Jacques. 2007. *Cesar Chavez: Autobiography of La Causa*. Minneapolis: University of Minnesota Press.

Lichtenstein, Nelson. 1997. *Walter Reuther: The Most Dangerous Man in Detroit*. Champaign: University of Illinois Press.

Ferriss, Susan, and Ricardo Sandoval. 1997. *The Fight in the Fields: Cesar Chavez and the Farmworkers Movement*. New York: Harcourt Brace & Company.

"There Is No Greater Calling Than to Serve Your Brothers: Walter P. Reuther, 1907–1970." 1970. *El Malcriado*, May 15. http://www.farmworkermovement.org/ufwarchives/elmalcriado/1970/May%2015,%201970%20%20No%2025_PDF.pdf.

Rodriguez, Arturo

When Cesar Chavez died in 1993, Arturo Rodriguez became the second president of the United Farm Workers (UFW). Born in San Antonio, Texas, on June 23, 1949, the son of a sheet-metal worker and a teacher, he earned a bachelor of arts degree in sociology from St. Mary's University in San Antonio in 1971 and a master's degree in social work from the University of Michigan in 1973. He first learned about the organizing work of Chavez and the emergence of the farm workers union from a parish priest and became active with a union grape boycott in Michigan. Following graduation, he decided to head to California to meet Chavez.

After seeing firsthand the energy and passion of the union workers fighting to make a difference for farm workers, Rodriguez decided to join the UFW full-time in 1973. He married Linda Chavez, one of Cesar's daughters, at La Paz, the UFW's headquarters. The two worked together on the boycott in Detroit in 1975.

Rodriguez helped organize union representation elections in the Salinas Valley and later in the Imperial Valley vegetable fields and Ventura County orchards. In 1978, he was chief instructor for a training school for union organizers at La Paz. In 1980, he established a service center in Ventura County to help farm workers resolve grievances involving issues such as housing, education, and government services. He also worked on political campaigns for Jerry Brown and Edward Kennedy. He was elected to the UFW National Executive Board in 1981.

When he assumed leadership of the UFW after Chavez's death, its membership rolls had severely declined. Rodriquez launched an effort to reinvigorate its organizing efforts and attempt to move the union back to the basic goal of recruiting farm workers to the union and winning new contracts.

He first targeted the California strawberry industry, vowing to organize the 20,000 to 25,000 pickers employed for six months or more picking berries at about 5 cents a pint. Cofounder of the union Dolores Huerta, who continued to work with the union, charged that strawberry workers made an average of $8,000 a year with no health insurance or other benefits. Such conditions amounted to something close to slave labor. The slogan became "five cents for fairness," a campaign promising workers it would seek to double their wages and, at the same time, assuring the public that the cost of strawberries would rise only a nickel in the supermarket.

In late March, 1996, the UFW organized marches in New York City, San Antonio, San Francisco, Los Angeles, and Chicago to demand rights for California strawberry workers. In the front line of the marchers in New York and San Francisco were familiar faces from the early days of the farm worker movement, such as Jerry Brown and Richard Chavez, brother of Cesar.

When the UFW took on the largest employer of strawberry pickers, a subsidiary of Monsanto, the company responded to the challenge by selling its strawberry farms to investors, who renamed them Coastal Berry. Even though AFL-CIO president John Sweeney hailed the UFW's strawberry campaign, it took several years before the union won the right to represent 1,500 Coastal Berry workers. Nevertheless, the vast strawberry industry remained largely nonunion.

The UFW did manage to win other important victories, including contract signings by growers in a variety of crops in California, Washington, and Florida. Since 1999, the UFW helped win a number of new laws and regulations aiding farm workers, including seat belts in farm labor vehicles, fresh protections for workers cheated by farm labor contractors, a historic binding mediation law, and new pesticide protections. In 2007, the UFW signed its first contract with Salinas-based D'Arrigo Brothers, California's third largest vegetable company, one that the UFW had sparred with for decades.

But the UFW of the early years of the twenty-first century was not the powerful organizing force it had been in its heyday. Much had happened since the massive marches and the nationwide boycotts and battles with the politicians, the Teamsters, and the growers in which this unlikely fight in the fields, spearheaded by Chavez, had seemed to herald a new day for farm workers. Although the UFW had fought for and won the most far-reaching state legislation granting the right of farm workers to unionize, most workers now in the harvests of California were not members of the union. Working conditions were still, in many cases, wretched.

For Rodriguez and the leadership of the union, it was now essential that they find ways to continue to make a difference. The union fought public advocacy campaigns, supported educational training programs, worked with social help organizations, and lobbied hard for legislation protecting the rights of farm workers. For example, under Rodriguez's direction, the UFW was influential in persuading California Governor Arnold Schwarzenegger to issue the first state regulation to help prevent farm and other outdoor workers from dying or becoming ill because of extreme heat. The union made increased use of Radio Campesina, a chain of stations based in California geared toward news of interest to Mexican Americans. It also pushed national legislation that would allow undocumented farm workers and their family members to earn legal status by working in agriculture.

In 2012, Rodriguez declared, "And we're going to continue to push . . . for the types of laws that would really give farm workers the same opportunities as other workers in this country; to have a better life, to be able to have a decent wage, a living wage, be able to have a medical plan for their families, and to take care of their basic needs" (Bernstein 2012).

Further Reading

Bernstein, Dennis. 2012. "At 50, Cesar Chavez's UFW Legacy." *Consortiumnews*, April 12. http://consortiumnews.com/2012/04/01/at-50-cesar-chavezs-ufw-legacy/.

Ferriss, Susan, and Ricardo Sandoval. 1997. *The Fight in the Fields: Cesar Chavez and the Farmworkers Movement*. New York: Harcourt Brace & Company.

Ganz, Marshall. 2009. *Why David Sometimes Wins: Leadership, Organization, and Strategy in the California Farm Worker Movement*. New York: Oxford University Press.

United Farm Workers. "Biography of Arturo S. Rodriguez, President, United Farm Workers of America." 2002. http://www.ufw.org/_page.php?menu=research&inc=history/06.html.

Ross, Fred

Look up the word *mentor* in various dictionaries and a number of modern usages are found. Most use the word *advisor*. Others refer to *role model*, *counselor*, *nurturer*, *friend*, and *sponsor*. To Cesar Chavez, Fred Ross was all of those things. He was an invaluable mentor. Ross taught Chavez how to be a community organizer. Chavez, in turn, became one of the greatest community organizers in American history.

Born on August 23, 1910, in San Francisco, California, Ross graduated from the University of Southern California with a teaching credential. Unable to find a teaching job, he became a case worker for the state relief administration. Later, he took a position with the U.S. Farm Security Administration, one of most notable New Deal programs launched during the Great Depression.

In 1939, Ross became the director of a farm labor camp near Bakersfield, California, that was mired in labor unrest among striking cotton pickers protesting against miserable working conditions and extraordinarily low wages. He soon became deeply involved with the challenges facing farm workers and other migrants and began to seek ways to encourage those workers to fight for their rights by grassroots organizing.

During World War II, Ross left the migrant camp to work with Japanese Americans on the West Coast who were herded into internment camps during World War II. Assisting the American Friends Service Committee, he helped internees win release by finding them jobs in the steel plants and other industries that produced vital war materials.

After the war, he returned to southern California and worked with the renowned community organizer Saul Alinsky and the Industrial Areas Foundation to help African Americans and Mexican Americans fight against unfair housing ordinances, school segregation, and police brutality. In 1946, he became an adviser to a

Long-time warriors of the United Farm Worker (UFW) movement, Cesar Chavez and Fred Ross march together in 1988.
More than any other individual, it was Ross who taught Chavez
and other UFW leaders the dynamics of community organizing.
(Walter P. Reuther Library, Wayne State University)

group of Mexican Americans who sued the Orange County city of Westminster
challenging racial segregation in public schools. The decision in federal court
for the plaintiffs in *Mendez et al. v. Westminster School District* was a landmark
civil rights victory prohibiting separate Mexican schools.

In 1947, with the help of Edward Roybal, later an influential congressman
from California, Ross created the Community Service Organization (CSO), a

group that sought to organize Latino communities through educational outreach, voter-registration drives, legislative campaigns, lawsuits, and other efforts to challenge a political and economic system that kept them mired in underclass poverty and powerlessness. Ross taught various organizing techniques including so-called house meetings. From such simple concepts, organizers were able not only to gain the confidence of workers wary of joining an organization but also to engender a sense of community and camaraderie that drew them together.

After registering thousands of voters in East Los Angeles, the tall and lean Ross moved on to San Jose in 1953 to organize another CSO chapter. It was there that he met a young apricot picker named Chavez. He recognized immediately from the fire in Chavez's personality that he was a man who could make a difference. Chavez later said that Ross did such a good job of explaining how poor people could gain power that he could taste it. Chavez joined the CSO and began to establish a chapter in Oxnard, California. Chavez would later say that Ross became to him something of a hero.

Ross also recruited Dolores Huerta, a young schoolteacher from Stockton, California, who set up CSO operations in her home town, and Gilbert Padilla, a farm worker and Army veteran who joined Chavez in Oxnard.

By the end of 1959, Chavez had established in Oxnard a so-called hiring hall from which many of the growers agreed to find workers. He had essentially turned the local CSO into a union hall. It was here that he began to see clearly in his mind the exciting potential of organizing the farm workers of California into a union. He proposed to the board members of CSO that they found such a union.

Although Ross and others at CSO shared the belief that some kind of activism was necessary to improve the lot of the field workers, they did not agree to take the CSO in a direction that might adversely affect the work they were already undertaking, principally as a social service organization aimed at urban communities. Chavez's plans, CSO directors believed, would have moved the organization toward rural activism.

At a convention of the CSO, Chavez presented a proposal to form a union and lost the vote. He resigned. In 1962 Chavez, armed with little more than a dream, headed to Delano, California, to form a union. Huerta and Padilla joined him.

Shortly after Chavez, Huerta, and Padilla left the CSO, Ross also moved in other directions, first working for the National Presbyterian Church organizing Yaqui Indians in Guadalupe, Arizona, near Phoenix. For a brief period, from 1965 to 1966, Ross taught a course on community organizing at Syracuse University.

By the time Chavez's farm workers movement became a reality, Ross was drawn to the work and returned to California. He became an integral part of many of the boycott and election campaigns and a close adviser and confidant of Chavez, Huerta, and other UFW leaders. He trained hundreds of organizers for the union and helped organize many of the UFW's strikes and boycotts including the Giumarra strike of 1967, the grape boycott of 1968, the lettuce strikes of 1970 and 1973, and the Gallo wine boycott of 1973.

When the UFW faced its first union election vote in 1967, Chavez turned to Ross to run the campaign. His meticulous approach to winning the election in the fields became the model for the UFW's electoral outreach approach.

Remaining close to the work of the UFW for the rest of his life, Ross also lent his formidable skills to other organizing campaigns. He worked for antinuclear and peace groups and helped the campaigns of several liberal politicians including Jerry Brown's campaign for governor of California in 1978.

With his son Fred Jr., who followed in his father's footsteps to become a skilled and dedicated community organizer, he helped found in 1986 Neighbor to Neighbor, first organized to recruit and train organizers to put political pressure on Congress to stop U.S. military aid to right-wing forces in Central America. The group continues its work in the twenty-first century training political activists.

After the death of Ross on September 27, 1992, former UFW general counsel Jerry Cohen said that Ross had fought more fights for the oppressed, trained more organizers, and planted more seeds of protest against injustice than any individual we are ever likely to see again.

Further Reading

Bardacke, Frank. 2011. *Trampling Out the Vintage: Cesar Chavez and the Two Souls of the United Farm Workers*. New York: Verso.

Ganz, Marshall. 2009. *Why David Sometimes Wins: Leadership, Organization, and Strategy in the California Farm Worker Movement*. New York: Oxford University Press.

Levy, Jacques. 2007. *Cesar Chavez: Autobiography of La Causa*. Minneapolis: University of Minnesota Press.

Ross, Fred. 1989. *Conquering Goliath: Cesar Chavez at the Beginning*. Keene, CA: El Taller Grafico Press.

Shaw, Randy. 2008. *Beyond the Fields: Cesar Chavez, the UFW, and the Struggle for Justice in the 21st Century*. Berkeley: University of California Press.

S

Salad Bowl Strike, 1970

South of San Francisco, a few miles inland from Monterey Bay, is Salinas Valley, a narrow strip of the most verdant growing land in the world. More than 80 percent of the salad greens consumed in the United States each year are grown in the Salinas Valley. Known not only for its iceberg lettuce and other varieties such as romaine, endive, and red leaf but also for numerous other vegetables from spinach and broccoli to onions and beans, Salinas Valley, known as the "nation's salad bowl," has not only rich crops but also a rich history—from its generations of growers and producers to its workers in the fields. For Cesar Chavez's United Farm Workers Organizing Committee (UFWOC), Salinas Valley and its people played a vital role. In 1970, Salinas became the center of a raging labor clash between the farm workers union and the International Brotherhood of the Teamsters (IBT) over union contracts. It would severely test the power of the farm workers union to extend its remarkable success after the long grape strike and boycott that began in Delano in 1965.

As the end of the grape strike finally brought victory to the UFWOC with the signing of many contracts, Chavez and his organization immediately confronted a new, daunting challenge. Many lettuce growers, determined to avoid dealing with the now successful UFWOC, decided to sign backdoor sweetheart contracts with the Teamsters. There had been no elections among farm workers, and they were told that they had to agree to the terms of the contracts in 10 days or risk being fired. Those Teamsters contracts provided far less benefits and protections for workers than the ones negotiated between the farm workers union and grape growers.

Realizing that his union had to fight back forcefully, Chavez, wearing a straw Filipino hat, held a rally at a teen center in a Mexican American neighborhood of Salinas. Soon, he set up a temporary headquarters inside the Salinas Office of the Mexican American Political Association.

On Sunday, August 2, over 3,000 farm workers marched through Salinas streets, carrying union flags and chanting "Huelga," and entered Hartnell College's athletic field. Speaking alternatively in English and Spanish, Chavez blasted the growers and Teamsters officials: "It's tragic that these men have not yet come to understand that we are in a new age, a new era, that no longer can a couple of white men sit together and write the destinies of all of the Chicanos and Filipino workers in this valley" (Levy 2007, 330). *Time* magazine reported on the new farm labor clash in the harvest fields of California with the headline "From Fruit Bowl to Salad Bowl."

In late August 1970, Chavez and his leadership called for a strike. By August 24, 1970, just a day into the strike, the Salinas *Californian* reported that agriculture in the area was "virtually shut down." Amid violent clashes with Teamster heavies carrying baseball bats and chains, thousands of farm workers walked out of the fields and joined the UFWOC struggle. From Monterey County to Santa Cruz, the strikers waved flags, sang, and handed out literature. Growers quickly hired additional armed guards who were not reluctant to flash guns before the eyes of the picketers. Jerry Cohen, general counsel for the UFWOC, said of the scene, "It looked like a revolution, and some of these right-wing growers thought it was" (Ferriss and Sandoval 1997, 170).

A few lettuce companies, including InterHarvest and Purex Fresh Pict, rescinded their contracts with the Teamsters and signed on with the UFWOC. However, in September 1970, a Republican judge in Salinas issued an injunction outlawing all farm worker union strikes. Nevertheless, more workers walked off the job in the succeeding weeks, and shipments of fresh lettuce nationwide almost ceased, causing the price of lettuce to double almost overnight.

With lettuce growers suffering grievous financial losses, a state district court enjoined Chavez and his union from picketing. The union refused to obey the court order. Instead, in late September 1970, the union asked consumers nationwide to boycott all lettuce that had not been picked by members of the UFWOC.

On September 5, 1970, gunfire broke out near the pickets as goons wielding baseball bats smashed cars, flattened tires, and broke windshields. A rancher threatened to blow the guts out of the protestors as he shot a rifle in the air. A ranch foreman smashed into a number of cars owned by strikers with his bulldozer. Volleys of rocks pelted the strikers. On November 4, a UFWOC regional office in Watsonville in the northern part of Salinas Valley was bombed with dynamite. A few weeks later, federal investigators indicted six Teamster men of violating gun-control laws by bringing in firearms and explosives to use against the UFWOC.

Union leaders worried about Chavez's safety. U.S. Treasury agents notified the UFWOC that they had learned of a so-called bounty of $25,000 that had been placed on the head of Chavez. Sketchy details identified the suspected trigger man as a hired gun, sporting a "Born to Lose" tattoo on his right leg, wanted in another homicide.

A delegation of religious leaders from around the country arrived, including the recently retired bishop of Los Angeles, Roger Mahoney. They would attempt to mediate a peace between the Teamsters and the UFWOC.

On December 4, 1970, federal marshals arrested and jailed Chavez for violating the court injunctions against the strike and boycott. But the jailing of Chavez gave additional spirit to his union and additional nationwide publicity to La Causa, especially as notable national figures including Ethel Kennedy and Coretta Scott King arrived at the Salinas jail to meet with Chavez. National television had brought the bitter strike activities into American homes.

Chavez was released on December 23 pending an appeal that was eventually successful. He continued the strike. The pressure worked. The "Salad Bowl Strike" ended on March 26, 1971, as the Teamsters and UFWOC signed a jurisdictional agreement reaffirming the farm workers union's right to organize. Against formidable odds, Chavez's union had rebuffed the Teamsters and taken over most of the contested contracts in the Salinas Valley.

Nevertheless, as Chavez and other union leaders suspected, the battle victory would not end the war. As Chavez had long realized, the treachery of the Teamsters seemed boundless. The fight in Salinas Valley was not over.

Further Reading

Day, Mark. 1971. *Forty Acres: Cesar Chavez and the Farm Workers*. New York: Praeger Publishers.

Ferriss, Susan, and Ricardo Sandoval. 1997. *The Fight in the Fields: Cesar Chavez and the Farmworkers Movement*. New York: Harcourt Brace & Company.

Kyriakou, Niko. 2011. "40 Years Later: Salinas Valley Labor Clashes Still Resonate." *The Salinas Californian*, March 26. http://farmworkersforum.wordpress.com/2011/03/26/40-years-later-salinas-valley-labor-clashes-still-resonate/.

Levy, Jacques. 2007. *Cesar Chavez: Autobiography of La Causa*. Minneapolis: University of Minnesota Press.

Salandini, Victor

No other Catholic priest fought with as much passion for Cesar Chavez's farm worker movement and with such profound consequences to his own career as did Fr. Victor P. Salandini. When his own personal crusade to better the lives of Mexican American migrant workers in San Diego, California, melded into a close association with Chavez, Salandini fought with and defied the church hierarchy on issues of social justice and suffered parish transfers and suspensions. At the same time, he led marches, picketed, acted as an emissary and lobbyist in Washington, DC, for Chavez's union, tended to his pastoral duties among the farm worker population, wrote articles and gave speeches in major cities both in the United States and Canada, and even was at the side of Chavez at a time of one of the union leader's most harrowing confrontations with and ill treatment by law enforcement officials. "To thousands of farm worker, especially Mexican farm workers who still slave in the hot sun of California agricultural fields," Chavez once said, "he is a prophet" (Chavez 1992).

The son of immigrant parents from Italy, Salandini was born August 12, 1927, in the state of Washington. He was a little over four months younger than Cesar Chavez. His father, who worked in a lumber mill, moved the family to Escondido, California, in 1936, where he bought a small, 40-acre grape ranch. During the summers, Victor picked fruit in the local vineyards and got to know well many Mexican farm workers.

In 1945, he enrolled at St. Francis Seminary near San Diego After his ordination as a Roman Catholic priest in 1952, he became assistant pastor at the Immaculate Conception Church, a parish in the Old Town section of the city that ministered largely to Mexican American families. For the next decade, he served in several Southern California parishes with mostly Latino congregants, many of whom were farm laborers.

During this time, he became involved with a newly formed labor union for farm workers, many of whom were Filipinos, called the Agricultural Workers Organizing Committee (AWOC). When the infant union decided to strike lettuce growers in the Imperial Valley, Salandini was outspoken in his support. His church superiors, determined to remain neutral in such labor disputes, took action against Salandini, who, despite their protestations, refused to back down. For the first of several times in his ministry, Salandini was silenced by the diocese. He was transferred to high-school teaching duties in San Diego.

While in San Diego, he completed his B.A. degree at San Diego City College in 1962 and then spent time in the Midwest, where he received an M.A. degree from St. Louis University in 1965. When he returned to California, the diocese allowed Salandini once again to resume work with a Mexican American parish, this time at Our Lady of Mount Carmel in the border town of San Ysidro, California.

In March 1965, the AWOC made a fateful decision to begin a strike of California grape growers. It was this launch by the AWOC of its strike that prompted Chavez to ally his own union, the National Farm Workers Association (NFWA), in the struggle. Thus began the famous Delano grape strike. When Salandini joined the campaign by making the church hall available for organizational meetings, the diocese again released the defiant Salandini from his position as parish priest. He decided to renew his education and to travel to Washington, DC, to study labor economics at Catholic University, where he would later receive a Ph.D.

In August 1965, Salandini met Chavez for the first time. Chavez spoke about the NFWA as more than a union. It was, he said, a social movement dedicated to helping farm workers get higher wages, better working conditions, suitable housing, and other necessities, and it was also grounded in the idea that entire families should be represented and active. It was the kind of message that Salandini had long envisioned. He eagerly offered his services to Chavez's union.

While studying in Washington, he lobbied members of Congress on behalf of the union and started what he called the Washington D.C. Huelga Committee to spread the word of the union's grape strike and boycott. He even led a march to the U.S. capitol.

While on a trip back to the San Diego area in June 1966, Salandini found himself, along with the Rev. Wayne C. Hartmire of the California Migrant Ministry (CMM), in the middle of a bitter and divisive power struggle between Chavez's union, the Teamsters union, and workers at the DiGiorgio Corporation. On June 27, 10 striking grape workers who had been fired by DiGiorgio tried to return to the heavily protected labor fields to gather their belongings. Chavez, Hartmire, and Salandini decided to accompany them.

"As soon as we set foot on DiGiorgio turf," Salandini later recalled, "the thirteen of us were accosted by four goons armed with pistols and rifles and accompanied by two police dogs. We were placed in a closed truck and kept there for three hours" (Salandini 1992). After the time in the sweltering truck, the men were shackled and chained and driven to the county jail in San Diego. There, they were strip-searched, fingerprinted, given prisoners' garb, and jailed until the next morning. Later, when Chavez introduced Salandini on different occasions, he would say that he and the priest had been busted together.

After receiving his Ph.D. in 1969, Salandini returned to California from Washington to rejoin La Causa. He became the union's research director, a position he would hold for two years. He traveled to various cities in the United States and Canada, speaking about the work of the farm workers movement and generating much interest and support.

In July 1971, Salandini, who by this time had almost entirely devoted his priesthood duties and activities to the farm workers and Chavez's union, faced a climactic showdown with diocesan officials. He was suspended for wearing a burlap serape emblazoned with the union's Aztec eagle emblem and for giving communion using corn tortillas. He also conducted a Mass, using an ironing board, in front of the home of a local grower being picketed by the union. UFW cofounder Dolores Huerta once said that no other priest had lost his power within the church for helping farm workers.

Although church officials later reinstated Salandini, he returned to an academic career, becoming an associate professor of labor economics at Fresno State College. Nevertheless, for the rest of his life, he participated in strikes and boycotts and other activities on behalf of the union.

Salandini passed away in Escondido in early August 1994. Chavez, who died a year earlier, said of Salandini,

On more than one occasion in the past when I have spoken to farm workers, I have compared Father Victor to Father Hidalgo who, in 1810, led the Mexican people in revolution against an oppressive Spanish regime. Father

Victor, like Father Hidalgo, was abandoned by his church and bishops. Father Victor follows in Father Hidalgo's footsteps in leading the farm workers to dignity and justice. It is unfortunate that more priests have failed to heed the prophetic voice of Father Victor. (Chavez 1992)

Further Reading

Chavez, Cesar. 1992. Foreword to Victor Salandini, *Confessions of the Tortilla Priest.* http://www.farmworkermovement.org/essays/essays/CESAR%20CHAVEZ% 20CONFESSIONS%20FOREWARD.pdf.

Ferriss, Susan, and Ricardo Sandoval. 1997. *The Fight in the Fields: Cesar Chavez and the Farmworkers Movement.* New York: Harcourt Brace & Company.

Levy, Jacques. 2007. *Cesar Chavez: Autobiography of La Causa:* Minneapolis: University of Minnesota Press.

Online Archives of California. 1992. "Guide to the Victor P. Salandini Papers." Stanford University. http://www.oac.cdlib.org/findaid/ark:/13030/tf3f59n673/.

"Religion: Tortilla Flat." 1971. *Time,* July 26. http://www.time.com/time/magazine/article/0,9171,877038,00.html.

Salandini, Victor. 1992. *The Confessions of the Tortilla Priest.* San Diego: San Diego Review. http://farmworkermovement.com/essays/essays/VICTOR%20SALANDINI% 20CONFESSIONS.pdf.

Salinas Jail, 1970

On December 4, 1970, Cesar Chavez, head of the United Farm Workers Organizing Committee (UFWOC), entered the old brick Monterey County Jail in Salinas, California, a site mentioned by author John Steinbeck, a native of Salinas, in several of his most notable works including *Tortilla Flat* and *Cannery Row.* Chavez had refused to obey a court order to end a nationwide boycott of lettuce that had been launched in a struggle between the farm workers union and the International Brotherhood of the Teamsters (IBT) over contracts in the Salinas Valley. After the Teamsters had signed sweetheart deals with the growers without a vote from workers in the fields, Chavez had called a strike and then a boycott. Some began to call it the "Salad Bowl Strike"—this battle between the union on one side and the growers and the Teamsters on the other in this lush agricultural haven of Salinas Valley. When a local court filed injunctions against both the strike and boycott, Chavez decided to press ahead. Ignoring the court orders, Chavez invited arrest, especially when he admitted that the boycott against Bud Antle Company, one of the major growers, would continue. Chavez not only did not deny that the boycott would proceed, he later remembered saying in a deposition, "We're boycotting the hell out of them" (Levy 2007, 426). By going to jail, Chavez knew, he could again make the farm workers struggle a national news story.

Ethel Kennedy, widow of Robert Kennedy, whose support of the farm workers movement had made him an iconic figure among many in the Latino community, joins a march in Salinas, California, in 1970 protesting the jailing of Cesar Chavez. (AP/Wide World Photo)

Approximately 2,000 UFWOC members and other supporters, by some counts, marched to the courthouse for Chavez's noontime appearance before Superior Court Judge Gordon Campbell. Carrying union flags and candles, sometimes kneeling to pray, supporters filled the inside halls of the courtroom and spilled out onto the grounds in front. Inside, during a 3-1/2 hour hearing, an angry Campbell declared, among other things, that he would not stand for the disobedience of the court's order and sentenced Chavez to two consecutive five-day jail terms for violating the antiboycott injunctions. Judge Gordon added that Chavez would remain in jail until he and his union cohorts called off the boycott. Everyone in the court that day and those gathered outside knew that Chavez had no intention of doing any such thing.

Teamster officials correctly sensed that Chavez, by going to jail, would bring enormous national publicity to the side of the workers, and they encouraged the company not to press for a court hearing. Nevertheless, Judge Campbell, angered that court injunctions had been rebuffed, continued with the proceedings. Chavez went to jail.

As the Teamsters feared, the scene in Salinas was now in the living rooms on television sets across the United States. The Teamsters, along with the growers and the judicial system, were not garnering positive reviews.

In a parking lot across the street from the jail, farm workers and their supporters erected a makeshift shrine on the back of a pickup truck, complete with the Virgin of Guadalupe, flowers, candles, and an altar draped in black cloth and decorated with flags of the United States and Mexico. The veterans of the grape strike had often set up such shrines on picket lines. One of the farm workers decided to fast until Chavez was released. The strikers held mass often at the shrine, sang, and talked with passersby about the goals of the union, and they were careful not to clutter the area or incite confrontations with the police or Teamster hecklers.

It got worse for Chavez's foes. Two days later, Ethel Kennedy, wife of slain Robert Kennedy, arrived to show her support for Chavez and the farm workers. Locking arms with Olympic decathlon champion Rafer Johnson, a long-time friend of the Kennedys, she walked through a cordon of police while Teamster members and right-wing political demonstrators hissed and jeered on one side and union supporters cheered on the other. Some of the protestors yelled obscenities and carried signs such as "Ethel Go Home" and "Kennedys Are Jailbirds." When one of the grower goons reached toward Ethel Kennedy, a deputy felled him with a karate chop. When she reached inside the visitors' section of the jail to meet briefly with Chavez, she broke the tension by quipping, "... you throw some weird parties!" (Levy 2007, 431).

Letters to Chavez began arriving at the jail from towns and cities across the country. Many said that the scenes on television had persuaded them to join the boycott against lettuce. At the parking lot, UFWOC members read letters from bishops and other religious figures. They read aloud an editorial from the *New York Times* that expressed its support for the boycott. Cheers erupted from the crowd.

In mid-December, another famous visitor arrived in Salinas, another widow by an assassin's bullet. Mrs. Coretta Scott King, wife of Dr. Martin Luther King Jr., also met with Chavez and threw her full support to the UFWOC and its movement. All of these events, given exposure in the national media, played fully into

Chavez's canny tactic of civil disobedience—of going to jail for a principle—that King himself had used so effectively in the civil rights movement.

Chavez remained in the Salinas jail for 20 days, all of which prompted candlelight vigils, singing, praying, and a string of other visitors. Finally, on Christmas Eve, 1970, Chavez was released pending the outcome of an appeal. As he walked out the jail, print and television reporters surrounded Chavez. He seemed unfazed by the attention, carefully answering questions with a quiet but clearly determined demeanor.

Supporters celebrated that Christmas Eve with a mass at the parking-lot shrine. "Jails were made for men who fight for their rights," Chavez declared. "My spirit was never in jail. They can jail us, but they can never jail the Cause" (Levy 2007, 433).

Four months later, the California Supreme Court ruled that the injunction had been unconstitutional. The fight in the lettuce fields and the boycott continued.

Further Reading

Day, Mark. 1971. *Forty Acres: Cesar Chavez and the Farm Workers*. New York: Praeger Publishers.

Ferriss, Susan, and Ricardo Sandoval. 1997. *The Fight in the Fields: Cesar Chavez and the Farmworkers Movement*. New York: Harcourt Brace & Company.

Kyriakou, Niko. 2011. "40 Years Later: Salinas Valley Labor Clashes Still Resonate." *The Salinas Californian*, March 26. http://farmworkersforum.wordpress.com/2011/03/26/40-years-later-salinas-valley-labor-clashes-still-resonate/.

Levy, Jacques. 2007. *Cesar Chavez: Autobiography of La Causa*. Minneapolis: University of Minnesota Press.

Schenley Boycott, 1965

Schenley Industries, a vast corporation best known for distributing such brands as Cutty Sark whiskey, Ancient Age bourbon, and Roma wines, traced its history back to the nineteenth century. It was, however, in the 1920s, at the beginning of the nation's great experiment of Prohibition, that a wily investor and whiskey broker named Lewis Solon Rosenstiel, head and chief stockholder of Schenley, outmaneuvered others in the business of spirituous liquors and turned the company into a giant. As distillers fled from the liquor business, he invested in it, betting on its eventual repeal. He bought up whiskey. He started a corporation to sell medicinal bulk whiskey. He bought various distilleries and hundreds of thousands of cases of rye and other liquors at bargain prices and waited. When Prohibition ended in the early 1930s, as Rosenstiel had bet that it would, Schenley thrived. In 1965, Delano, California, became the center of Cesar Chavez's seemingly quixotic quest to form a union of farm workers, the National Farm Workers Association (NFWA). It would strive to lead farm workers to higher wages, better working conditions, and, most of all, a sense of dignity. Schenley owned a 4,500-acre vineyard near Delano. It became one of Chavez's main targets.

Although Chavez was pleased with the activity on the picket lines in the early weeks of the Delano grape strike that included the Schenley vineyards, he realized that it would be extraordinarily difficult to defeat the wealthy growers, who were aided by the political establishment and local law enforcement, with strike action alone. His reading of the writings and work of Mohandas Gandhi and suggestions by one of his closest lieutenants, Jim Drake of the California Migrant Ministry (CMM), led Chavez to a fateful decision in December 1965. That decision would turn this local agricultural labor unrest in California into a national cause. He decided on a boycott.

Chavez said that he learned from reading about Gandhi that the boycott is the "most nearly perfect instrument of nonviolent change." It allowed masses of people to actively engage in a cause. "Even if people cannot picket with us or contribute money or food," he said, "they can take part in our struggle by not buying certain products. It is such a simple sacrifice to make" (Hammerback and Jensen 2003, 97).

With Drake leading the early coordination of the boycott, Chavez and his fellow leaders quickly moved to raise money, find union volunteers willing to move temporarily to various parts of the United States with little pay, develop tactics for achieving maximum media attention, and anticipate countermeasures. Volunteers drove or hitchhiked to New York, Chicago, St. Louis, and other major cities.

They carried with them strict directives from the NFWA"

Picket lines should be at customer entrances only. Slogans should indicate that you are not picketing the store. For example, "Don't Buy Schenley Liquors" or "Don't Buy Delano Grapes" or "Support striking farm workers in California—Don't buy Delano Grapes." Your purpose is to inform consumers so that they may decide to support you. ("National Boycott . . . " 1966)

Recruiting additional volunteers from churches, community organizations, labor organizations, universities, and civil rights organizations, the boycott leaders began to set up centers. Soon, picketers were carrying signs imploring people not to purchase products produced by Schenley. "Boycott, Baby, Boycott" became a rallying chant among many of the youthful activists. In Boston, for example, boycotters led a protest it called the Boston Grape Party. The farm workers' cause had thus moved from the isolated fields of California to urban areas. It also began to attract additional attention.

Boycott leaders appeared on local television stations explaining the union's goals to listeners. Newspapers ran stories about these unlikely but committed workers and their cause. Boycott stories hit the major metropolitan papers and national media outlets.

In mid-March 1966, Chavez and other NFWA leaders began a 300-mile march or *peregrinación* from Delano to the state capitol of Sacramento in order to mobilize support for the strike and boycott. It was on April 6, 1966, near the end of the march, that Chavez received word that Schenley had decided to sign a contract with the farm workers union.

It was a milestone. The NFWA had won the first field contract in the history of farm labor organizing in California. Wages rose. All workers employed by Schenley in the field would be members of the union. Schenley no longer would hire workers through labor contractors but through the union.

Schenley had decided to negotiate not because it had been hurt financially but because of the sudden besmirching of its national liquor brands. For Schenley, the Delano vineyards were but a tiny part of its international business empire. But the boycott had penetrated the national consciousness in a way that could prove devastating to its reputation. Gandhi's philosophy had been right; Jim Drake had been right. The boycott, taking La Causa from the lonely California harvest fields to the centers of retail trade, had convinced Schenley directors that they needed to end this public relations disaster as quickly as possible.

It was west of Lodi, California, that marchers in the *peregrinación* first learned of the news. A few gathered in the "radio-telephone car" to hear, as best they could, the message from Chavez, who was calling from Los Angeles. Suddenly, Terry Gannon, the press secretary for the march, climbed atop the car and made the announcement while Roberto Bustos, the march leader, translated Gannon's English into Spanish. Schenley, he said, had agreed to sign a contract. Loud cheers erupted. There were some tears. *The Movement*, the newspaper of the Student Nonviolent Coordinating Committee, reported a few days later with a peculiar but perhaps apt declaration. The shock of the Schenley agreement, it said, "had begun to knock a whole lot of apples out of the trees" ("Schenley Signs!" 1966).

Further Reading

Bardacke, Frank. 2011. *Trampling Out the Vintage: Cesar Chavez and the Two Souls of the United Farm Workers*. New York: Verso.

Ganz, Marshall. 2009. *Why David Sometimes Wins: Leadership, Organization, and Strategy in the California Farm Worker Movement*. New York: Oxford University Press.

Hammerback, John, and Richard Jensen. 2003. *The Rhetorical Career of Cesar Chavez*. College Station: Texas A & M University Press.

Levy, Jacques. 2007. *Cesar Chavez: Autobiography of La Causa*. Minneapolis: University of Minnesota Press.

Meister, Dick, and Anne Loftis. 1977. *A Long Time Coming: The Struggle to Unionize America's Farm Workers*. New York: Macmillan.

"National Boycott Schenley Liquors and Delano Grapes." 1966, March. http://www.farmworkermovement.com/essays/essays/MillerArchive/013A%20Boycott%20Developments%201.pdf.

"Schenley Signs!" 1966. *The Movement*, April. http://www.farmworkermovement.org/ufwarchives/sncc/12-April%201966.pdf.

Shaw, Randy. 2008. *Beyond the Fields: Cesar Chavez, the UFW, and the Struggle for Justice in the 21st Century*. Berkeley: University of California Press.

Short-Handled Hoe

The farm workers called it "El Cortito" ("The Short One") and "El brazo del diablo" (the devil's arm). It was a simple tool with a 12-inch handle, only slightly longer than a hand trowel, that farm workers were forced to use in the harvest fields. Growers insisted that the short-handled hoe was more efficient and effective in thinning and weeding and getting crops picked more quickly. Farm workers knew better. To them it was a dreaded enemy, a tool whose use meant hour after hour of stooping and bending that, in turn, led to crippling back injuries and, for most workers, lifelong pain.

As a young man toiling as a farm worker, Cesar Chavez had used the short-handled hoe, especially in the lettuce and sugar-beet fields. Hunched over at the waist, day after day, working his way down mile-long rows without touching his knees to the ground, pounding the tool into the soil with little relief (after all, standing up meant to the field bosses that you were not working), Chavez lived with back pain, often excruciating, for his entire life. He said later that the stooped labor was one principal reason that many farm workers died before they were 50. He also said that growers looked at farm workers themselves as implements, not people, and that inflicting torture seemed to be of little concern.

Farm worker Jesus Serrano, who began working in the fields when he was 13 years old, later talked later about his own experiences in using El Cortito. As a young man he became disabled and could no longer bend over. His friends used to make fun of him, he said, because he walked forward like a gorilla.

Despite such testimony from hundreds of farm workers gathered by various relief organizations and Chavez's union, the owners refused to back down in their insistence that the tool must be used. Using long hoes, they claimed with no

Farm workers using the hated short-handled hoe ("El Cortito"). Forced by growers to use the tool, especially in lettuce and sugar-beet fields, workers suffered debilitating back injuries, often permanent, from the contorted position in which they labored. After intense lobbying by the United Farm Workers, the tool was outlawed in 1975. (Walter P. Reuther Library, Wayne State University)

evidence whatsoever, would lead to less production and possible bankruptcy. They would not listen to the pleas of their workers or the evidence assembled by physicians that the use of the tool produced everything from ruptured spinal disks to arthritis. They would have to be forced through the courts or by political action to relent on the issue.

In 1968, Maurice "Mo" Jourdane, a lawyer for California Rural Legal Assistance, Inc. (CRLA), a nonprofit legal services program founded in 1966, met a group of farm workers in a pool hall in Soledad, California. If CRLA wanted to assist farm workers, they told Jourdane, the organization should work to ban El Cortito. Watching the limping gait of the workers, Jourdane realized this might be a cause that needed aggressive support.

He asked the workers to take him to the fields so he could try the work himself. It did not take long to realize the oppressive conditions to which the workers were subjected. After about an hour using the short-handled hoe, he said, it became torture.

Within a few weeks of experimenting with the short-handled hoe, Jourdane had convinced the CRLA to battle for its extinction in California's harvest fields. Jourdane took depositions from farm workers. He interviewed physicians, including the doctor who had treated Chavez. In 1972, he submitted a formal complaint to the California Division of Industrial Safety. The lead plaintiff was a 46-year-old farm worker named Sebastian Carmona who had moved to California from Texas. He testified that from the very first day he had used the short-handled hoe, he began having searing pain in his back. As the days and months wore on, Carmona's condition worsened.

In *Carmona v. Division of Industrial Safety*, Jourdane and the CRLA argued that the short-handled hoe was an "unsafe hand tool" which was prohibited by law. In a series of hearings, 11 doctors testified that the use of the tool would cause degeneration of the spine, resulting in irreparable back injury and, in many cases, permanent disability. Despite such testimony, the division decided against Jourdane and the CRLA, declaring that the harm caused by the short-handled hoe arose only from the manner in which the tool was used and not from any inherent defect in the tool itself. The CRLA appealed the decision to the California Supreme Court.

Meanwhile, the issue had become a cause taken up by Chavez's union and others who saw the case as an issue of oppression directed at a class of people and a fight for empowerment against that oppression. In the spring of 1973, a group of farm workers in Salinas Valley gathered beside the buses that were preparing to take them to their shacks. They kept in hand the short-handled hoes, laid them in a pile, doused the pile with gasoline, and tossed in a burning match. Shouts of protest rung out as the hated tools burst into flame.

In 1975, the California Supreme Court overturned the decision by the Division of Industrial Safety. Although the action cheered Jourdane, he and other supporters of banning the use of the short-handled hoe pointed out that state regulators had not approved written rules forbidding its use. Working with Chavez and the UFW, Jourdane pressured Democratic governor Jerry Brown to take action. He did. Thus, the state of California in 1975 formally banned the use of El Cortito. Mo Jourdane said of the victory that never again would future generations of farm workers be subjected to such a symbol of oppression.

At Cesar Chavez's funeral in 1993, someone laid on top of the plain, pine coffin built by his brother Richard a short-handled hoe. It was gesture of triumph, and it seemed fitting.

Further Reading

Carmona v. Division of Industrial Safety, 13 Cal. 3d 303. 1975, January 13. http://scocal .stanford.edu/opinion/carmona-v-division-industrial-safety-30281.

Ferriss, Susan, and Ricardo Sandoval. 1997. *The Fight in the Fields: Cesar Chavez and the Farmworkers Movement*. New York: Harcourt Brace & Company.

Jourdane, Maurice. 2005. *Struggle for the Health and Legal Protection of Farm Workers: El Cortito*. Houston, TX: Arte Publico Press.

Murray, Douglas. 1982. "The Abolition of El Cortito, the Short-Handled Hoe: A Case Study in Social Conflict and State Policy in California Agriculture." *Social Problems*, October, 26–39.

Steinberg, Lionel

In April 1970, Lionel Steinberg became the first table grape grower to sign a contract with Cesar Chavez's infant farm workers union in response to the union's boycott. Steinberg was an unusual fit in the agribusiness community in California's Coachella Valley—a Jewish liberal Democrat in a world of Christian conservative Republicans. Steinberg's relationship with Chavez and the union would be tenuous and strained; nevertheless, his move to accept unionization, one that angered his fellow growers, signaled much progress by the union in its drive to force change in the harvest fields of California.

Born in 1919 in Fresno, California, Steinberg was a lifelong Democrat who served as a local party chair, served twice as a delegate to the Democratic National Convention, and was a member of the Urban League. In his youth he was president of the California Federation of Young Democratic Clubs, and he became over the years a major supporter of state and national Democratic candidates.

The owner of three large vineyards in Coachella Valley, he was the longtime president of David Freedman & Co., based in Thermal. He had the unusual distinction of being a Democratic appointee to the State Board of Agriculture under both Governor Edmund G. "Pat" Brown Sr. and his son, Governor Edmund G. "Jerry" Brown Jr. Steinberg was named board president in 1975.

Steinberg was not generally opposed to unions; indeed, he made overtures to a number of labor officials in the 1950s about the feasibility of farm worker unionization. For Steinberg, however, a man who had great respect for such labor leaders as George Meany, Cesar Chavez's farm worker movement was not at all what he had in mind. This was not the birth of a labor union, Steinberg believed, but instead a social movement run by amateurs, young left-wing activists, students, and farm workers who had no chance of building a successful organization. Yet here he was in 1970, faced with the fact that Chavez had accomplished something Steinberg thought would be impossible for this young, ragtag group—he had forged a coalition of volunteers, church leaders, and others who had waged a nationwide boycott against table-grape producers and had made those growers see their financial balance sheets tumble.

In the summer of 1969, Steinberg resigned from the California Grape and Tree Fruit League when he claimed that the group had falsified information in an attempt to deny the damage that had been done by the boycott. He fumed that the group was trying to sweep the problem under the rug while Coachella Valley wine growers were facing a disaster.

The national boycott, he knew, had severely disrupted sales of table grapes at the major distribution centers in the United States as well as Canada—New York, Chicago, Detroit, Boston, Philadelphia, Montreal, and Toronto. In an attempt to limit the damage, 10 growers from Coachella had agreed to talk with union negotiators. When the talks floundered, a committee from the National Conference of Catholic Bishops convinced some of the growers to resume discussions in the spring of 1970. Steinberg was the most receptive of the growers.

In April 1970, much to the consternation of other growers who preferred to keep fighting the union, Steinberg decided to sign with Chavez. The signing of the contract made the front pages of newspapers across the country. "The immediate response from the other growers was dismay," he said later (Ferriss and Sandoval 1997, 155). To his pleasant surprise, however, news of his agreement soon reached distributors, and major chain stores began to request his grapes with the union label.

Although Steinberg continued to resent the pressures under which he had been forced to negotiate and complained about the arrogance of some of the union representatives with whom he had to deal, workers at his Coachella vineyards began to see major changes. In addition to easier access to water and portable bathrooms, Steinberg's fields now made it possible for women workers to get higher paying jobs such as stacking boxes.

The 1970 agreement signed by Steinberg quickly led to contracts with virtually all of his fellow growers, who realized, along with Steinberg, that the effects of the boycott had cost them around 20 percent of their market. The capstone signing occurred just three months later when John Giumarra Sr., head of the giant Giumarra Vineyards, and other growers travelled to Delano and, following the lead of Steinberg, signed contracts with the farm workers union. Thus, in July 1970, there was exhilaration among the union organizers. They had taken on the powerful agribusiness interests and, for the moment, had prevailed.

But, as Chavez and his organizers realized, tough and challenging battles were on the horizon. A number of those very grape growers that agreed to sign on with the union in the summer of 1970 would, in the future, again be adversaries. Yet in 1973, when most growers refused to renew their contracts with Chavez's union, Steinberg again signed.

Steinberg passed away in 1999 in Palm Springs, California, six years after Chavez died. Looking back on the career of Chavez, Steinberg remained consistent in his belief that the union leader should have, with the help of more established union organizers, moved his organization in the direction of a professional trade union rather than the social and political reform movement that it ultimately became. As he had predicted from the beginning, Steinberg said, Chavez, with his insistent use of volunteers and his lack of focus on maintaining and consolidating organizing power, had lost a chance to make the UFW a great union. Steinberg did say, however, that Chavez's work had led to the improvement of working conditions for farm workers and had, most of all, "brought dignity to the individual farmworker. . . . I had a high regard for Cesar," Steinberg said, "He was an honest man" (Oliver 1999, 15).

Further Reading

Bardacke, Frank. 2011. *Trampling Out the Vintage: Cesar Chavez and the Two Souls of the United Farm Workers*. New York: Verso.

Ferriss, Susan, and Ricardo Sandoval. 1997. *The Fight in the Fields: Cesar Chavez and the Farmworkers Movement*. New York: Harcourt Brace & Company.

Levy, Jacques. 2007. *Cesar Chavez: Autobiography of La Causa*. Minneapolis: University of Minnesota Press.

Meister, Dick. 2011. "The Grower Who Made It Happen." *Syndic Literary Journal* 5 (December). http://syndicjournal.us/syndic-no-5/.

Oliver, Myrna. 1999. "Lionel Steinberg; Grower Signed 1st Pact with Chavez's Union." *Los Angeles Times*, March 10, 15.

Steinberg, Lionel. Transcript of Oral History Interview. Farmworkers Documentation Project. http://farmworkermovement.org/media/oral_history/ParadigmTranscripts/SteinbergLionel.pdf.

Student Nonviolent Coordinating Committee (SNCC)

In the spring of 1960, led by civil rights leader Ella Baker, students on the campus of Shaw University in Raleigh, North Carolina, founded the Student Nonviolent Coordinating Committee (SNCC). The creation of SNCC followed a historic day in February 1960 when several African American students sat down at a segregated Woolworth's lunch counter, thus sparking a wave of sit-ins across the South and launching another front in the drive for equal rights. Led by such individuals as John Lewis, Julian Bond, and later Stokely Carmichael, SNCC would coordinate the sit-ins and provide organizational support for various kinds of student activity on behalf of the civil rights movement, including voter registration. More than any other civil rights organization, SNCC leaders recognized early on that Cesar Chavez's efforts on behalf of Mexican American farm workers were strikingly similar to those efforts of Martin Luther King Jr. and others to combat racial and ethnic prejudice and to improve the lives of oppressed people. Their support of Mexican Americans during the farm workers movement thus set them apart from other civil rights organizations that were focused almost entirely on African American rights and causes.

Mike Miller, head of the San Francisco SNCC office, had been a student activist while at the University of California at Berkeley and had, through his friend Saul Alinsky, often met with Fred Ross. He thus became familiar not only with the work of the Community Service Organization (CSO) but also with the advent of the farm workers union pioneered by Cesar Chavez and Dolores Huerta. Shortly before the Delano grape strike in 1965, Miller arranged for a meeting between Huerta and some of the SNCC leaders including Bob Moses and Carmichael.

When the grape strike began, the SNCC became a valuable ally for the farm workers movement. In areas such as direct action confrontation, the need to organize

Ella Baker, one of the leaders of the Student Nonviolent Coordinating Committee (SNCC), seen here in 1968. SNCC leaders saw in the farm workers movement much common cause and gave it valuable support. (AP Photo/Jack Harris)

minority groups from within, and the appeal to religious symbols and messages, SNCC leaders readily saw the connection between the African American cause and the farm workers struggle. When Chavez and Huerta asked officials of SNCC to send some representatives to help the strikers overcome the natural instincts to lash back at the repressive tactics of local police and goons hired by companies to incite violence, the organization quickly responded. They sent veteran workers who had been thoroughly trained and tested in nonviolent protest to California and helped mobilize student volunteers.

One of the first SNCC representatives to arrive was Marshall Ganz from the San Francisco office. Born in Bakersfield, California, the son of a rabbi, Ganz had been a Harvard student who participated in the Mississippi Freedom Summer civil rights campaign in 1964. When word of the new unionizing activities in the fields of California reached Ganz, he eagerly joined the struggle, recognizing the same injustices suffered by blacks and by field workers—racial discrimination, intolerable working conditions, lack of political power, and the excesses of capitalist greed and disregard for the rights of working people. Fluent in Spanish, he joined Chavez in 1965 and became a chief strategist and organizer. A number of others who had worked in the Mississippi Freedom Summer campaign also traveled to California to join the farm workers movement. Dickie Flowers, a staff member of SNCC from Greenwood, Mississippi, would later be especially effective in organizing farm workers in Bakersfield, an area where there was a concentration of African American workers.

One of SNCC's first contributions to the NFWA strikers was a supply of two-way radios. As the area of the strike expanded over hundreds of miles, the radios became effective in alerting leaders along the strike route of any new influx of scab labor or harassment and violence perpetrated against the workers.

Student support for the farm workers movement became exceptionally valuable for Chavez in the early days of the strikes and boycotts. The young people were willing to travel to various parts of the United States and Canada, were willing to live on subsistence wages, and brought infectious enthusiasm to picket lines and marches.

The San Francisco Bay Area branch of SNCC was particularly fired up for La Causa. Field Secretary Terry Cannon, who had done much work with the SNCC newspaper *The Movement*, did press work for Chavez. *The Movement* itself launched a series of stories about the farm workers struggle in December 1965 with a special "Boycott Supplement," and the paper began carrying rich stories, with many photographs, of the grape strike and the march to Sacramento.

So influential did SNCC members become in the early fights of the union that Mike Miller was asked to work alongside Rev. Jim Drake to coordinate the boycott. SNCC field offices soon became hubs of boycott activity in several cities across the country, with hundreds of student volunteers manning picket lines.

In March 1966, when Chavez launched the momentous *peregrinación* to Sacramento that gained national attention for the farm workers movement and led to the union's first major contract with Schenley, Ganz was the chief organizer and planner for the logistical support, and Terry Cannon served as the press coordinator.

As SNCC in the later years of the 1960s became increasingly identified with the Black Power struggle and its image began to reflect a more menacing, potentially violent bent, Chavez reluctantly backed away from an open partnership with the group, fearful that the nonviolent commitment of the farm workers movement could be compromised. Nevertheless, many SNCC members and former members continued their active participation in the activities of the union. Ganz, for example, became one of Chavez's most trusted advisors and one of the union's best organizers.

The SNCC embrace of the farm workers movement and the idealism and concern for social justice championed by the students was a vital element to the success of Chavez in the early years of the union. Chavez later said, "It's beautiful to work with other groups, other ideas, and other customs. It's like the wood is laminated" (Griswold del Castillo and Garcia 1995, 48).

Further Reading

Behnken, Brian. 2012 *The Struggle in Black and Brown: African American and Mexican American Relations during the Civil Rights Era*. Lincoln: University of Nebraska Press.

Ferriss, Susan, and Ricardo Sandoval. 1997. *The Fight in the Fields: Cesar Chavez and the Farmworkers Movement*. New York: Harcourt Brace & Company.

Griswold del Castillo, Richard, and Richard Garcia. 1995. *Cesar Chavez: A Triumph of Spirit*. Norman: University of Oklahoma Press.

Miller, Mike. "The Farmworkers and Their Allies in the Early to Mid-1960s." http://www.farmworkermovement.org/essays/essays/REVISED%20FINAL%20MIKE%20MILLER.pdf.

"The Movement Boycott Supplement." 1965. *The Movement*, December. http://farmworkermovement.com/ufwarchives/sncc/09-December%201965.pdf.

Shaw, Randy. 2008. *Beyond the Fields: Cesar Chavez, the UFW, and the Struggle for Justice in the 21st Century*. Berkeley: University of California Press.

T

Texas Melon Strike, 1966

In the spring of 1966, shortly after Cesar Chavez's infant farm workers union, the United Farm Workers (UFW), had signed its first contract with a California winery, a new battle for workers' rights broke out in an unexpected place—Starr County, Texas, on the lower Rio Grande. Melon growers in south Texas, just beginning to harvest a bountiful, multimillion dollar crop, were paying wages to melon pickers as low as 40 cents an hour. News about Chavez's success in California spurred a few activists in Texas to consider forming their own union to encourage workers to demand higher wages and improved working conditions. The response from growers had not been helpful, one of them remarking that he would rather see the crops rot than deal with a union. Into the tinderbox situation arrived Eugene Nelson, a veteran of the early days of the California grape battles. He was not one who would be intimidated by Texas agribusiness interests. He would, instead, spark the great Texas melon strike of 1966.

A native of Stockton, California, Nelson, who would later become a writer, worked for a time with Mexican immigrants thinning sugar beets. He learned to speak Spanish and gained firsthand understanding not only of the plight of oppressed farm workers but also of the racial hatred that undergirded the farm labor system. When the grape strike erupted in California, he eagerly joined Chavez as a picket captain. And now in Texas, Nelson began to organize workers. He kicked off the drive with a rally in Rio Grande City in late May 1966 and within a week had 700 members of an organization they named the Independent Workers' Association (IWA). Soon, the small union decided to launch a strike against eight major growers in Starr County.

They had no money, no experienced organizers, and no base of volunteers they could count on for the various kinds of support necessary to conduct a successful strike. Not surprisingly, they had little success against the local growers, who were aided by their security forces, local police, the courts, and even the Texas Rangers. Strikers ended up in jail, faced with excessively high bonds. County employees sprayed union members with insecticide. Judges issued injunctions prohibiting strike activity. A number of picketers were beaten.

The embattled new union's next step came from Nelson's fond remembrance of his involvement in Chavez's brilliant strategy just months earlier in California of conducting a march or *peregrinación* (pilgrimage) from Delano to Sacramento that had drawn much national news and many volunteers. Nelson worked on plans for a similar march in Texas.

On the Fourth of July, 1966, hundreds of marchers set out on a 400-mile trek from south Texas to the state capitol grounds in Austin. As the marchers made their way north, Texans became aware of the farm workers movement and La Causa. Winding through south Texas towns such as Grulla and Edinburgh, the march picked up endorsements from mayors, added more marchers, and gained increasing coverage in the media. In San Juan, Bishop Humberto Medeiros held a special mass for the marchers. Along the way, a number of religious leaders arrived from various parts of the state to express their support. On Labor Day, 1966, over 15,000 people held a rally in Austin, including officials of the AFL-CIO, leaders of Mexican American groups, farm workers and their families, and Cesar Chavez.

For Chavez and other union leaders in California, the Texas strike was a distraction from the main activity around Delano. Nevertheless, Chavez sent a number of his most trusted organizers to help Nelson, including Gilbert Padilla, Eliseo Medina, and others. Padilla would eventually take over the operation. The workers of IWA would later vote to join Chavez's union.

In October 1966, strikers placed a picket line at the international bridge at Roma in an attempt to keep Mexican national strike breakers from entering the United States. When they briefly forced the closure of the bridge, a number of union leaders were arrested, including Eugene Nelson.

By the spring of 1967, strikers faced a new harvest season with greater numbers and many lessons learned. Nevertheless, the determination of agribusiness interests had also hardened. Picketers again entered jails and suffered injuries at the hands of law enforcement and the Texas Rangers.

Accompanying union officials from California to Texas in 1967 was a 21-year-old aspiring poet and teacher named Ed Frankel. It was in Starr County, he wrote later, that his run-ins with the Texas Rangers, with their white Stetsons proudly atop their heads and shotguns at the ready, made him think he was in a time warp or in a movie set with John Wayne. At a railroad crossing in Harlingen, Texas, Frankel wrote later, the union had set up a picket line. When a train carrying fruit from nearby ranches arrived at the crossing one day, the box cars were full of Rangers, said Frankel. "It looked like a scene out of Black Jack Pershing's Expeditionary Force going into Mexico to chase Pancho Villa. Very military. Maybe the Rangers thought the ghost of Pancho Villa was going to ambush the train and steal the cantaloupes . . . " (Frankel n.d.).

Rangers chased union organizers around the county. They closed down a Texas version of the UFW paper *El Malcriado* and jailed its editor, Douglas Adair. Eliseo Medina ended up in jail along with other organizers. One black volunteer from the Congress of Racial Equality who was visiting Texas at the time of the strike said that the scene reminded him of the bad civil rights days in Mississippi.

In 1967, Texas officials got another dose of nonviolent protest tactics. When Gilbert Padilla, who had just returned to Texas from a brief visit to California, and Rev. Jim Drake visited the Rio Grande courthouse to talk with strikers who had been jailed for using abusive language, they were ordered off the steps by sheriff's deputies. Instead, they dropped to their knees in prayer. "I was in jail the second day I was in Texas for praying," Padilla remembered (Ferriss and Sandoval 1977, 136).

The prayer tactic worked to perfection later in the strike. After demonstrators continued to endure more beatings from Texas Rangers, Chavez orchestrated a retaliatory action, one in which he secretly invited every member of the media to attend. Many Rangers spent late afternoons in the Catfish Inn to drink beer. One day after normal swilling ended, they walked out of the bar and were face to face with a group of kneeling women dressed in black praying for their souls. Within 24 hours of press treatment of the event, which was embarrassing for the men with the Stetsons, Governor John Connally asked the Rangers to leave the town.

The Texas Melon Strike ended quietly after the second harvest season. The union did not win contracts against overwhelming opposition. But the strike had repercussions. It drew to Starr County members of the U.S. Senate Subcommittee on Migratory Labor who held hearings on farm labor conditions. It spurred a number of lawsuits that eventually resulted in decisions favoring strikers, including a 1974 Supreme Court decision limiting the jurisdiction of Texas Rangers in labor disputes. It laid the groundwork for future farm labor organizing in the state. And it inspired numerous Chicano activists to fight for progressive causes. Years later, looking back on the strike, Gilbert Padilla remembered that several strike supporters who were tutored by union organizers in the Texas Melon Strike had become members of the Texas legislature.

Further Reading

Altman, Linda Jacobs. 1994. *Migrant Workers: The Temporary People*. New York: Franklin Watts.

Arispe, Rudy. 2010. "Voices Unheard: Documentary Sheds Light on the United Farm Workers Movement in Texas." *Ovations*. Fall. http:// http://utsa.edu/ovations/vol4/story/voices-unheard.html.

"Farmworkers Ask Help against 'Terror Campaign.' " n.d. http://chavez.cde.ca.gov/ResearchCenter/DocumentDisplayRC.aspx?rpg=/chdocuments/documentdisplay.jsp&doc=56d6ce%3Aeae63c6e4f%3A-7e83&searchhit=yes.

Ferriss, Susan, and Ricardo Sandoval. 1977. *The Fight in the Fields: Cesar Chavez and the Farmworkers Movement*. New York: Harcourt Brace & Company.

Frankel, Ed. n.d. "In the Lap of the Angel of History." http://edfrankel.com/essays/Frankel_Ed.pdf.

Samora, Julian, Joe Berna, and Albert Pena. 1979. *Gunpowder Justice: A Reassessment of the Texas Rangers*. Notre Dame, Indiana: University of Notre Dame Press.

U

Unionization Attempts on Behalf of Farm Workers

When Cesar Chavez set out in 1962 to form a farm workers organization, he was aware of the struggles of other groups in the past to challenge the oppressive farm labor system that kept harvest-field workers mired in impoverishment and degradation. He had seen his own father join unions and engage in strikes only to watch the powers of agribusiness and their political and law enforcement allies join forces to form an impenetrable opposition. The history of attempts by various organizations to force agricultural growers to grant their farm laborers fair wages, decent working conditions, and other basic needs goes back far beyond the experience of the Chavez family in the United States. Indeed, that history can traced to the early days of the agricultural industry's large fruit and vegetable farms, especially in California—those "factories in the field," as historian and activist Carey McWilliams called them. The history of those efforts to supply labor to those farms had been one of frustration and powerlessness in the face of seemingly intractable forces.

In the late nineteenth century, much of the harvest labor in California was performed by Chinese workers. A rising tide of xenophobia would begin to restrict, through national legislation, further importation of Chinese individuals. In 1884, however, some Chinese hop pickers in Kern County waged a short strike asking for $1.50 a day. The strike was quickly snuffed out as well as any hopes for a union.

The next wave of immigrant farm workers, the Japanese, met with the same kind of racial barriers and harsh treatment. When a few enterprising Japanese workers began a labor union and instigated a sugar-beet strike in Oxnard, California, in 1903, they met the same fate as the Chinese strikers in Kern County a decade earlier.

With the passage of exclusion laws prohibiting all but a few immigrants from China or Japan, California growers persuaded Congress to exempt Western Hemisphere nations from immigration quotas. Soon, Mexican-born workers became the dominant group in the harvest fields of California.

In 1913, in Wheatland, California, the agricultural industry in the state faced its first serious opposition—the Industrial Workers of the World (IWW), also known as the Wobblies. Founded in 1905, the IWW was aimed at organizing workers regardless of industry and skill. The preamble to its constitution declared a state of war between workers and capitalists, and its leaders and propaganda held out a vision of a new society in which "wage slaves" would rise to strike down their class oppressors. The symbol of the militant organization was the black cat, and the call was for a grasping of power by those held down by rampant capitalism. The left-wing Wobblies struck fear into government leaders, businessmen, and any vested interest that saw itself a potential target. In its early years, it made inroads among low-paid factory workers of the industrial eastern United States and, later, began to mobilize migrants. At their protest rallies the Wobblies sang new labor songs printed in their *Little Red Songbook*, gave impassioned speeches, and marched, gaining converts among lumberjacks, miners, and some harvest workers. In early August 1913, they attempted to strike the massive Durst Ranch and its workforce of 2,000 hop pickers.

At a rally, with Wobbly Richard (Blackie) Ford addressing the workers, a sheriff's posse rushed the platform, which collapsed in the assault. In the ensuing chaos, shotgun and handgun blasts rang out, people were clubbed, and four died, including a worker who had seized a gun from one of the deputies. Also dead were the district attorney and a deputy sheriff. What became known as the Wheatland Riot resulted in the arrest of hundreds of Wobblies throughout the West, including Blackie Ford. It would not be the IWW that would successfully organize farm workers.

Nevertheless, through newspaper accounts and government probes, the plight of farm workers became nationally exposed. More than three dozen states passed some forms of legislation to improve the conditions of workers. Unfortunately, those reforms lasted only temporarily. Within a few years, farm workers still faced miserable working conditions, low pay, and few legal protections.

In 1931, the American Communist Party organized the Cannery, Agricultural, and Industrial Workers Union (CAIWU). Led by organizers Pat Chambers and Caroline Decker, the CAIWU drew to its cause nearly 90,000 workers and engaged in over 60 strikes in the early 1930s, many of them in California. In October 1933, the CAIWU struck the cotton fields near the small town of Pixley, California. Strikers lined the roads with over 18,000 workers during the height of the harvest season.

Growers organized so-called protective associations—vigilante groups—to discourage such activity, and the scene quickly turned violent. Three strikers lost their lives. Many were jailed. Despite the intimidation, the Pixley strike did lead to a temporary pay raise for cotton laborers. Nevertheless, the long-term viability of the CAIWU could not be sustained. Its ties to the Communist Party and the increasing determination of growers to form various growers associations to fight off labor incursions proved lethal to the union. When other unions formed in the 1930s, some of them with backing of organized labor, they met the same fate as CAIWU.

In all of these efforts to empower harvest workers, organizers faced daunting obstacles. Much of the labor force was migratory, moving from one ranch or farm to another with the seasons. Organizers, many of whom spoke only English, faced a tough language problem dealing with Mexican or Filipino workers. The various groups that challenged agribusiness efforts also faced entrenched, united opposition from politicians, business groups, law enforcement, and other vested interests as well as the ease with which growers could ward off strike efforts by bringing in scab replacements from Mexico.

Despite the challenges, others took up the fight. In 1946, the American Federation of Labor (AFL) for the first time chartered a farm workers union—the National Farm Labor Union (NFLU). In 1947, the union's leaders decided to take on an agricultural giant—DiGiorgio Fruit Corporation. The company was not just big—the largest distributor of citrus in the nation, with a 12,000-acre ranch in Arvin, California—it was also symbolic. When writer John Steinbeck chronicled the plight of migratory workers in his novel *Grapes of Wrath*, he barely disguised DiGiorgio as the book's greatest antagonist, representative of other corporate agricultural interests. Steinbeck called the company "DiGregorio."

Although NFLU's strike efforts gained national attention and support, including that of many religious leaders and officials of other unions, it could not cope with the influx of scab labor and the vicious strike-breaking force of thugs employed by DiGiorgio, who busted heads and even destroyed the union's headquarters. In the growing Cold War climate of the late 1940s, DiGiorgio also cleverly gained ground in the conflict by linking strike leaders to left-wing groups. Thus, the attack on DiGiorgio ultimately failed, as did the future of the NFLU.

But the DiGiorgio Fruit Corporation had not seen the last of unionization battles with farm worker organizers. In 1947, the same year as the strike, organizer Fred Ross and others launched the Community Service Organization (CSO) to teach grassroots organizing techniques to help Latinos advance political and social programs. One of the CSO's prize recruits was a young farm worker who had returned from service in the military. It would be Cesar Chavez who would finally learn from the spirited but ultimately unsuccessful efforts of the past half-century to mobilize farm workers. It would be Chavez who would devise the necessary strategies and organizing techniques to give DiGiorgio and the others a fierce fight.

Further Reading

Daniel, Cletus. 1982. *Bitter Harvest: A History of California Farmworkers, 1870–1941*. Berkeley: University of California Press.

Day, Mark. 1971. *Forty Acres: Cesar Chavez and the Farm Workers*. New York: Praeger Publishers.

Dunne, John Gregory. 1971. *Delano: The Story of the California Grape Strike*. Berkeley: University of California Press.

Ganz, Marshall. 2009. *Why David Sometimes Wins: Leadership, Organization, and Strategy in the California Farm Worker Movement.* New York: Oxford University Press.

McWilliams, Carey. 2000. *Factories in the Field: The Story of Migratory Farm Labor in California.* Berkeley: University of California Press.

United Farm Workers (UFW)

The United Farm Workers (UFW) is a labor union begun in Delano, California, in 1962 by former migratory worker Cesar Chavez. From its inception, the organization, dedicated to improving the lives and working conditions of agricultural laborers, has been unlike a typical trade union. Chavez and his cofounder Dolores Huerta had both worked in the fields and had learned organizing techniques while members of the Community Service Organization (CSO). They saw their new organization as more than an effort to improve wages and to fight for other labor demands but also as a major drive to empower a group of people, the *campesinos* (farm workers), who had been long oppressed by agribusiness interests and denied basic legal and human rights. They referred to their organization as a farm workers movement or *La Causa* (The Cause).

On September 30, 1962, at an abandoned movie theater in Fresno, California, the new organization—first called the National Farm Workers Association (NFWA)—held a founding convention. Chavez became president. The union unveiled its new flag featuring a black Aztec eagle on a white circle in a red field, emblematic of pride and dignity.

For over two years, Chavez and a small group of organizers traveled up and down California's agricultural valleys, holding house meetings, helping workers with their problems, and inviting farm workers to join their new organization. By 1964, after two years of determined organizing, Chavez and a growing number of volunteers had signed up over 1,000 dues-paying members and established 50 locals. The union launched a newspaper called *El Malcriado*.

In 1965, an organization called the Agricultural Workers Organizing Committee (AWOC), sponsored by the AFL-CIO and led mostly by Filipino workers, began a strike against Delano-area grape growers and asked Chavez and the NFWA to join the picket lines. Chavez and other NFWA leaders agreed, and thus began the historic five-year grape strike that would shake the foundation of California's farm labor industry.

The strike attracted widening support from labor, church, and civil rights groups. In December 1965, Chavez launched a boycott of grape producer Schenley Industries. The boycott would become the union's most potent weapon and, in coming years, would gain much national support.

Dolores Huerta stands next to a mural of the late Cesar Chavez at the dedication of a Chavez monument on the campus of San Jose State University, September 4, 2008. Huerta, still a dedicated activist for social causes, and Chavez were cofounders of the United Farm Workers. (AP Photo/Paul Sakuma)

In March 1966, Chavez led a 340-mile march or *peregrinación* from Delano to the steps of the California state capitol in Sacramento. The march, along with the effects of the strike and boycott, prompted Schenley to negotiate an agreement with the NFWA, the first genuine contract between a grower and a farm workers union in U.S. history.

On August 22, 1966, the NFWA and the AWOC merged to form the United Farm Workers Organizing Committee (UFWOC). Early the following year, the new organization began new strikes and a boycott of Giumarra Vineyards

Corporation, California's largest table-grape grower. For three years, hundreds of union volunteers fanned out across the United States and Canada to organize an international grape boycott.

In early 1968, as violence on the picket lines increased, Chavez, inspired by his study of Mohandas Gandhi's writings and actions on behalf of the Indian independence movement, began a fast to encourage nonviolence. After 25 days, Chavez ended the fast, joined at his side by Senator Robert Kennedy (D-NY), who would soon announce his candidacy for president of the United States. The union would work feverishly to help Kennedy win the California primary race and was deeply shaken by his assassination on June 5, 1968.

In the spring of 1969, the UFWOC announced plans for a worldwide boycott of California grapes. By the summer, the boycott had gained such momentum that California's major grape growers, on July 29, 1970, signed UFWOC contracts.

Following the victory in the grape strike, the UFWOC was met with another major challenge—the decision by the International Brotherhood of the Teamsters (IBT) to challenge the UFWOC for contracts with California's vegetable growers. When most vegetable growers signed sweetheart deals with the Teamsters, the UFWOC responded with a strike and lettuce boycott.

In 1972, the UFWOC was officially chartered as an independent affiliate by the AFL-CIO and became the United Farm Workers of America (UFW). On September 21, 1973, amid growing violence in the strike fields of California's Coachella and San Joaquin Valleys, approximately 350 delegates gathered in Fresno, California, officially to adopt a constitution.

In the spring and summer of 1973, when the UFW's grape contracts with a number of California wineries came up for renewal, many growers, including the E&J Gallo Company, following the lead of vegetable growers, signed deals with the Teamsters. The UFW responded with another nationwide grape boycott.

In June 1975, Democrat Jerry Brown, a supporter of Chavez, became governor of California. Through negotiations between members of the state legislature, Governor Brown, and UFW officials, California passed the Agricultural Labor Relations Act (ALRA). The legislation for the first time guaranteed California farm workers the right to organize, vote in state-supervised secret-ballot elections, and bargain with their employees. The passage of the ALRA and resulting elections favoring the UFW convinced officials of the Teamsters to give up their assault against the farm workers union.

Yet in the late 1970s and early 1980s, faced with increased political attacks by Republicans who regained power in Sacramento and growing turmoil and disaffection within the leadership of the UFW, the union drove away many skilled organizers and, within few years, lost most of its contracts. Although Chavez and his remaining allies would press ahead with campaigns against the use of pesticides by growers and other issues vital to farm workers, the UFW had lost the clout in the fields it once had.

On April 23, 1993, Cesar Chavez died near his birthplace in Yuma, Arizona, while defending the UFW against a lawsuit brought by a vegetable grower. He was succeeded as UFW president by veteran organizer Arturo Rodriguez.

Under Rodriguez's leadership, the UFW in the twenty-first century continues through various solicitation and political efforts its struggle on behalf of the United States' farm workers. Although the UFW never ultimately succeeded in becoming an effective trade union, its influence, as the first major organization of farm workers, was significant.

Chavez, Huerta, and other early UFW leaders attracted to La Causa were extraordinary individuals willing to sacrifice and dedicate themselves to the movement. With few resources, they carried on strikes and national boycotts, won contracts with growers, and battled relentlessly against the Teamsters union and others who resented their audacity and then their success. They influenced legislation, registered people to vote, and changed political dynamics. And, as many of the older farm workers testified, there were the emotional and psychological triumphs of challenging an established order with little more weapons to use than determination and commitment. These were triumphs of spirit and endurance difficult to measure but impossible to underestimate. One of the most enduring legacies from the farm worker battles of the 1960s and 1970s is the abiding influence that Chavez and other UFW leaders had on a successive generation of progressive organizers.

Further Readings

Bardacke, Frank. 2011. *Trampling Out the Vintage: Cesar Chavez and the Two Souls of the United Farm Workers*. New York: Verso.

Dunne, John Gregory. 1971. *Delano: The Story of the California Grape Strike*. Berkeley: University of California Press.

Ferriss, Susan, and Ricardo Sandoval. 1997. *The Fight in the Fields: Cesar Chavez and the Farmworkers Movement*. New York: Harcourt Brace & Company.

Levy, Jacques. 2007. *Cesar Chavez: Autobiography of La Causa*. Minneapolis: University of Minnesota Press.

Matthiessen, Peter. 1969. *Sal Si Puedes (Escape If You Can): Cesar Chavez and the New American Revolution*. Berkeley: University of California Press.

Pawel, Miriam. 2009. *The Union of Their Dreams: Power, Hope, and Struggle in Cesar Chavez's Farm Worker Movement*. New York: Bloomsbury Press.

U.S. Senate Subcommittee on Migratory Labor Hearings, 1966

In mid-March 1966, the U.S. Senate Subcommittee on Migratory Labor, chaired by Democratic Senator Harrison Williams Jr. of New Jersey, held hearings in three California agricultural areas, including Delano, the headquarters of Cesar Chavez's union. The purpose of the hearings was to investigate the condition of migratory labor and to consider possible federal legislation that would protect the rights and labor conditions of farm workers. Coming at a time in the early history of the union, the hearings provided a platform for Chavez and others concerned with the plight of the labor force in the harvest fields and gave the movement national exposure that it desperately needed as it conducted its first grape strike. The hearings also brought to Delano Senator Robert Kennedy of Massachusetts. Kennedy's stalwart support would prove to be vital to the early success of the union.

Cesar Chavez testifies before a U.S. Senate Migrant Labor Subcommittee hearing in Sacramento, California, March 14, 1966. It was during these hearings, including one in Delano, California, a few days later, that Robert Kennedy (D-NY), a member of the subcommittee, became highly supportive of the farm worker movement. (AP/Wide World Photo)

Williams had for several years been a strong advocate for protecting the rights of migratory workers. In 1959, he introduced legislation seeking to clean up a system that allowed unscrupulous labor contractors to exploit workers. Although the bills he introduced had not garnered enough support in Congress, Williams continued to press the issue. With news of the strike actions in California, Williams decided to take the committee on the road to gather firsthand, on-site testimony. The committee hearings began in Sacramento on March 14, moved to Visalia the following day, and then, on March 16, to Delano and ground zero for the union's dramatic grape strike.

Chavez testified at the first hearing in Sacramento. He briefly recounted the history of the farm labor camps in California, the federal investigations headed by Senator Robert LaFollette three decades earlier that had exposed extensive abuses, and the fact that many of the labor camps that were still being used in the 1960s were the same ones exposed during those hearings and continued the same unconscionable treatment of farm workers—the same child labor, the same notion that somehow farm workers were a different breed of people more able to withstand physical hardship and remain happy, and the same kind of justifications used by slaveholders generations before.

Rev. Wayne Hartmire of the California Migrant Ministry and Bishop Hugh Donohoe, representing the Catholic Bishops of California, added a religious perspective to the farm workers struggles. Hartmire referred to the farm workers movement as a righteous struggle. "As Christians," he said, "we cannot assume a position of non-involvement or neutrality in the presence of social injustice which reduces the dignity and well-being of any of God's children" ("Statement of the California Church Council" 1966).

Bishop Donohoe referred to the "Pastoral Constitution on the Church in the Modern World" that had been adopted a few months earlier at the Second Vatican Council. One section of the document, he said, dealt specifically with a principle of social ethics that included the right to organize unions for working people. He appealed for collective-bargaining rights and a minimum wage for farm workers.

Union leaders such as Al Green of the Agricultural Workers Organizing Committee (AWOC) and William Kircher, director of organization of the AFL-CIO, also testified, along with close Chavez confidants Dolores Huerta and Larry Itliong. Even entertainer Steve Allen, an outspoken supporter of liberal causes, was asked to give testimony.

But the drama that would live long after the hearings ended came in Delano, the third stop for the committee in California. Shortly before Senator Kennedy arrived, over 20 picketers had been hauled off to jail by Kern County Sheriff Roy Galyen, a long-time law enforcement official who had no use for the protestors disrupting the peace and tranquility of the local farmlands. He was a perfect foil for Kennedy, the former attorney general of the United States.

Kennedy asked Sheriff Galyen why the protestors had been arrested when there had been no apparent violation of the law. Gaylen explained that there had been reason to believe that they were going to cause a riot, that there had been talk by men in the fields that if the picketers did not leave, "we're going to cut their hearts out. . . . So rather than let them get cut, we removed the cause" (Dunne 1971, 29).

Kennedy called the sheriff's action a "most interesting concept." Somebody reports that there might be a crime and then the sheriff arrests people who had not done anything wrong. As the lunch break arrived, Kennedy cuttingly remarked, "Can I suggest in the interim period of time . . . that the sheriff and the district attorney review their procedures and start by reading the Constitution of the United States!" (Dunne 1971, 29).

From farm supporters in the room there were howls of laughter; from farm owners, local politicians, and law enforcement officials there were glum, angry snickers. Senator George Murphy of California, a member of the committee and staunch spokesman for agribusiness, growled that if the governor of California had acted in the manner that Sheriff Galyen had, the Watts riots might have been prevented. Hisses from the farm workers supporters greeted his words.

According to many individuals close to the farm workers movement, Senator Kennedy's takedown of the local sheriff's law-and-order tactics became a kind of legend, the details being passed on from harvest field to harvest field and to following generations. Kennedy left Delano fully in support of La Causa. Kennedy had, through the hearings, gained a new constituency who would rally to his cause when he decided to run for president. For Chavez, Kennedy's support meant increased legitimacy and access to Democratic Party power brokers in Washington and more nationwide publicity.

Following the hearings, Kennedy accompanied Chavez to a picket line at the vineyards of the nearby DiGiorgio Fruit Corporation. Peter Edelman, a legislative assistant to Kennedy who had accompanied him to California, later said, "Time stopped. The chemistry was instant" (Thomas 2002, 320).

Further Reading

Bardacke, Frank. 2011. *Trampling Out the Vintage: Cesar Chavez and the Two Souls of the United Farm Workers*. New York: Verso.

Dunne, John Gregory. 1971. *Delano: The Story of the California Grape Strike*. Berkeley: University of California Press.

Ferriss, Susan, and Ricardo Sandoval. 1997. *The Fight in the Fields: Cesar Chavez and the Farmworkers Movement*. New York: Harcourt Brace & Company.

Ganz, Marshall. 2009. *Why David Sometimes Wins: Leadership, Organization, and Strategy in the California Farm Worker Movement*. New York: Oxford University Press.

Krebs, A. V. 2007. "Bulldogs and Lapdogs." *The Progressive Populist*, June 15. http://www.populist.com/07.11.krebs.html.

Matthiessen, Peter. 1969. *Sal Si Puedes (Escape If You Can): Cesar Chavez and the New American Revolution*. Berkeley: University of California Press.

"Statement of the California Church Council on the Delano Grape Strike." 1966, March 17. http://farmworkermovement.com/essays/essays/CA%20Church%20Council%20Delano%20Statement.pdf.

Thomas, Evan. 2002. *Robert Kennedy: His Life*. New York: Simon & Schuster.

V

Valdez, Luis

The farm workers movement drew to its side men and women from many backgrounds and with various talents. One was the son of farm workers from Delano, California, who, after working in the fields with his family, had been able to acquire an excellent education, get a start in his profession, and then return to Delano to join Cesar Chavez's cause. He was Luis Valdez, and he was a playwright.

He was born on June 26, 1940, in Delano. When Valdez was a young boy, a schoolteacher in San Jose showed him the art of puppetry. While in high school he appeared on local television showing off his talent. After graduating from high school in San Jose, Valdez earned a scholarship to attend San Jose State College, where he earned a B.A. in English, studied theater, and, through the school's drama department, produced his first full-length play, "The Shrunken Head of Pancho Villa."

In 1964, he joined the San Francisco Mime Troupe, a company that performed open-air, free theater on political and social issues. It was there that he learned the techniques of agitprop (agitation and propaganda) theater. When he heard of the farm workers strike back in his home town where his parents still lived, he realized that he might be able to make a unique contribution.

Valdez remembered as a young boy in Delano seeing the older Chavez, who was then in his late teens dressing in *pachuco* clothes. And now Chavez was leading an infant movement on behalf of the *campesinos*, with whom Valdez closely identified. Chavez listened with much enthusiasm to the ideas of Valdez on how he could, through use of a traveling theater, add additional richness and cultural pride to the efforts of the striking farm workers. Chavez embraced Valdez and his ideas as an integral part of the protest movement in its early years.

The creation was El Teatro Campesino (The Farmworker Theater). Valdez later said that, along with others in the 1960s, he was fighting for civil rights. It seemed sensible, he said, to use biting humor and satire as one of the strategies for inspiring the protestors, for helping to make those long days on the picket lines less demanding, and for making the cause more understandable in terms with which the campesinos could relate.

The young union, of course, did not have actors, stages, equipment, or any experienced stage hands. Valdez, along with several volunteers, made it happen from scratch. Workers briefly became actors, truck beds became stages, and hand-stitched costumes and hand-crafted props and placards became the stuff of surprisingly witty and entertaining presentations in the evenings at strike sites and during marches. At the hands of the talented Valdez, the makeshift theater, harkening back to Mexican folk traditions and mime that he had so recently explored in San Francisco, served up a raucous fare on the foibles and excesses of the bosses and on the outrageous systemic abuse in the migrant labor system in the fields in which he had worked as a boy.

The Teatro's performances were brief—10- to 15-minute morality plays spoken mostly in Spanish with occasional English phrases inserted. The usual characters included a scab laborer, a striker, and a grower. Often the characters would wear signs and armbands further giving their identity.

The actors were given much free reign, and members of the cast often took on multiple roles. Audience reaction was usually loud, boisterous, and encouraged. Valdez called the short presentations "actos." He saw the theater as a vehicle not only to provoke social change but to provide greater perspective and cultural appreciation in the lives of the Chicano people through music, ritual, comedy, and a sense of belonging.

During the early days of the Delano grape strike, the fledgling theater company toured towns to raise money for the strikers. The group performed along the picket lines, starting at dawn, driving from location to location, pulling up at the sides of the roads, and quickly going into action. El Teatro also gave presentations at Chavez's headquarters in Delano. At a time when the future success of the movement was unlikely, Valdez and his theater group revved up the troops, providing entertainment, confidence, and cathartic relief to weary strikers.

In early 1966, Chavez decided to use a tactic that had been successful in the black civil rights movement—a long march. Covering a route from Delano to the state capitol of Sacramento, the march (or *peregrinación*) would attempt to infuse the strikers and the workers along the route with historical purpose and meaning. Valdez thus wrote the so-called "Plan of Delano" to be read in each town through which they marched. It was a statement that followed in the tradition of the leader of the Mexican Revolution, Emiliano Zapata, who had written his "Plan de Alaya," a rallying statement for the underclasses against powerful landowning interests. For the marching farm workers, the "Plan of Delano" became a rallying cry and the march a kind of pilgrimage to seek an end to the suffering of farm workers. "The time has come for the liberation of the poor farm worker," the plan declared. "History is on our side. MAY THE STRIKE GO ON! VIVA LA CAUSA!" ("The Plan of Delano" 1966).

In 1967, Chavez began to question whether some of the material Valdez was beginning to use was appropriate for the union, especially skits relating to the war in Vietnam. The alliance between the two men began to fracture. Although the disagreements remained publicly in the background, Valdez was made aware that El Teatro Campesino would no longer be part of the strike activity. Valdez moved on.

He organized a cultural center and led a more organized El Teatro Campesino to increasing international acclaim. He authored and directed many plays such as *La Virgen de Tepeyac* (1971), *La Carpa de los Rasquachis* (1974), *El Fin del Mundo* (1976), *Tibercio Vasquez* (1980), *Corridos: Tales of Passion and Revolution* (1983) *I Don't Have to Show You No Stinking Badges* (1986), and *The Mummified Deer* (2000). He also directed several films including *Zoot Suit* (1981), based on his earlier play that explored the actual clash of American servicemen and Mexican American youth in Los Angeles in the 1940s, and *La Bamba* (1987), based on the life of the Mexican American rock star Ritchie Valens. Nevertheless, it is his work with El Teatro Campesino where Valdez made a unique contribution, one that has earned him oft-used praise as "The Father of Chicano Theater."

El Teatro Campesino continued into the new century, touring and producing films. And Valdez's towering legacy continued to grow. Beginning with his early days along the picket lines around Delano, Valdez inaugurated a grassroots Chicano artistic movement; created new theater forms; brought to life the history, music, and folklore of his cultural past; and set the stage for the further development of Chicano theater.

Further Reading

Bardacke, Frank. 2011. *Trampling Out the Vintage: Cesar Chavez and the Two Souls of the United Farm Workers*. New York: Verso.

El Teatro Campesino. 2010. "About Us." http://www.elteatrocampesino.com/About/missionhistory.html.

Ferriss, Susan, and Ricardo Sandoval. 1997. *The Fight in the Fields: Cesar Chavez and the Farmworkers Movement*. New York: Harcourt Brace & Company.

"The Plan of Delano." 1966. http://chavez.cde.ca.gov/ModelCurriculum/teachers/Lessons/resources/documents/plan_of_delano.pdf.

Valdez, Luis. 1990. *Early Works: Actos, Bernabe and Pensamiento Serpentino*. Houston: Arte Publico Press, 1990.

Vera Cruz, Philip

Philip Vera Cruz—a Filipino American farm worker and labor leader—played a pivotal role in the growth and early success of the farm workers movement led by Cesar Chavez. That the two men ended up in Delano, California, united in an effort to take on a seemingly mismatched confrontation with California agribusiness interests, was highly improbable. That their alliance would lead to major successes was astonishing. It was the Agricultural Workers Organizing Committee

(AWOC), composed mostly of Filipino workers, that began a strike against grape growers in 1965 and convinced Chavez and his newly formed National Farm Workers Association (NFWA) to join forces that led to the unprecedented victories by farm workers for union contracts. Vera Cruz joined the AWOC at the time of the strike. He would work with Chavez for a dozen years.

Born on December 25, 1904, in Ilocos Sur, the Philippines, Vera Cruz came to the United States in 1926 and began an odyssey of work on farms, in canneries, and in restaurants from Minnesota to Washington state and California. As many Filipino young men in the early part of the twentieth century, Vera Cruz left his homeland with little money but with dreams of finding jobs in the United States that could enable him to send money back to his family in the Philippines.

Outside Seattle in a town called Cosmopolis, Vera Cruz began work in a box factory where he made 25 cents an hour. It was then that he witnessed the first strike action he had ever seen—a walkout by Filipino workers for better pay. The strike failed. Vera Cruz traveled to Spokane, Washington, where he got a job as a busboy working at the Royce Cafeteria.

In 1928, with the onset of the Great Depression and the difficulties of finding work, he heard of a possibility in North Dakota where a company would pay for transportation to work thinning sugar beets. After living for a time in a mosquito-infested shack with no bathroom or wash facilities and able to get water only from a contaminated well, he soon left North Dakota and the sugar beets and traveled to Minneapolis, where he managed to go to high school for a time while working at the Dykeman Hotel.

And then it was back to Spokane, where he worked at the Davenport Hotel and the Spokane Country Club. He managed to get his high school degree and, for a time, attended Gonzaga University. In 1934, he was headed to the Midwest again, this time to Chicago, where he had heard of good work possibilities. The atmosphere of the mammoth city was as different from the small village in which he grew up in the Philippines as he could possibly have imagined. He managed to get busboy jobs in restaurants and began to participate in a number of civic activities in Chicago's Filipino community. Through his early migrations from job to job and town to town he managed to send $25 dollars a month back to his family.

Through these years he experienced firsthand the dismissive racial attitudes of the whites he served—the slurs and sneers, the jokes, and the outright hatred. The so-called equality that existed in the United States that he had learned from teachers in the Philippines turned out, he said, to be "a fake." He began to identify with other Asian minorities such as the Chinese and Japanese. He wrote, "It was as if many of us Filipinos were living behind hidden identities for fear of associating with the realities of our lives, our real names, and therefore, our real identities. . . . My life here was always an emergency" (Sharlin 2000, 17).

In 1942, Vera Cruz entered the U.S. Army and was stationed at San Luis Obispo, California, for basic training. Although assigned to the Second Philippine Infantry, which was sent to Camp Cook, the men over 38 years old were discharged and assigned to defense-related jobs. Vera Cruz ended up in the San Joaquin Valley as a farm worker. It was here in Delano and its surroundings that he would spend most of the rest of his life. It was also here that he would build a career as a union organizer.

In 1965, Vera Cruz was convinced by a friend to pay $2 to join the AWOC. He later said it was the most important $2 of his life. Working together, the AWOC and Chavez's NFWA began to forge a formidable group of striking farm workers. The two organizations soon merged under the auspices of the AFL-CIO to form the United Farm Workers Organizing Committee (UFWOC), and Vera Cruz became one its leaders, elected in 1971 as second vice president. He was now over 60 years old.

He became chairman of a committee to build and establish at Forty Acres, the union's compound, a retirement community for retired Filipino workers. It was called Agbayani Village, named after a Filipino named Paolo Agbayani who died while on the picket line during the grape strike in Delano in 1967.

As a Filipino officer in the union, Vera Cruz played an important role in communicating union business with its Filipino members, most of whom felt isolated in an organization that became by the 1970s largely comprised of Mexican Americans. He also became a valuable instructor to new volunteers who arrived in Delano, explaining to them the history and goals of the farm workers movement.

In 1977, Vera Cruz resigned from the union because of growing differences with Chavez over a number of issues. The main disagreement arose after Chavez, despite the pleas of Vera Cruz and others, accepted an invitation to visit Ferdinand Marcos, the leader of the Philippines, whom some Filipinos in the UFW detested as a brutal dictator. Vera Cruz said later, "One thing the union would never allow was for people to criticize Cesar. If a union leader is built up as a symbol and he talks like he was God, then there is no way you can have true democracy in the union because the members are just generally deprived of their right to reason for themselves" (Scharlin 2000, 115–16).

Despite his resignation from the union, Vera Cruz remained supportive of the UFW and the farm workers movement. He continued to be active in other social justice campaigns, especially the Asian American civil rights movement. In 1988, he visited Manila, where President Corazon Aquino gave him an award for long service to Filipinos in the United States. In 1992, the Asia Pacific American Labor Committee of the AFL-CIO honored Vera Cruz. He passed away two years later, at the age of 88, in Bakersfield, California.

Further Reading

Day, Mark. 1971. *Forty Acres: Cesar Chavez and the Farm Workers*. New York: Praeger Publishers.

Scharlin, Craig, and Lilia Villanueva. 2000. *Philip Vera Cruz: A Personal History of Filipino Immigrants and the Farmworkers Movement*. Seattle: University of Washington Press.

Shaw, Randy. 2008. *Beyond the Fields: Cesar Chavez, The UFW, and the Struggle for Justice in the 21st Century*. Berkeley: University of California.

Valledor, Sid. 2006. *The Original Writings of Philip Vera Cruz*. Indianapolis: Dog Ear Publishing.

Virgin of Guadalupe

In the farm workers struggle, the image of the Virgin of Guadalupe was omnipresent—on flags at rallies, in marches, along picket lines, on the walls the houses and offices of farm workers and union leaders, and at every location where Cesar Chavez and his union members carried on the struggle for social justice. It was not surprising. For over 500 years, throughout centuries of Mexican history from the Aztecs to the Spanish, the image of the Virgin of Guadalupe has been an icon and symbol for various cultural forces—Mexican independence and nationalism, the rights of oppressed people, and the power of religious belief. Essentially, the image of the Virgin of Guadalupe is a Mexican depiction of the Virgin Mary. The Virgin's face is dark; her dress Judeo-Christian. She was a *mestizo*, the first Mexican. She was seen as reflecting both a European deity and native culture.

According to legend, on the top of a hill in the Tepeyac desert near Mexico City, the Virgin Mary in 1531 appeared in the form of a young mestizo woman to an Aztec Indian peasant named Cuauhtlatohuac, who had been baptized by Spanish Catholic missionaries and given the name Juan Diego. The apparition, on more than one occasion, asked Juan Diego to build a church on the spot where they were standing.

When Juan Diego told church authorities of the appearance and asked that the church be built, he was asked to provide proof of his encounters. He was to gather roses from a nearby hillside, a place where roses never grew, and to return them in his *tilma* (cloak) to the church bishop. Juan Diego did find roses, placed them in his tilma, and returned. When he scattered the roses from the tilma, the legend continues, the Virgin's image was imprinted on the garment. Realizing that a miracle had taken place, the bishop placed the image in the cathedral. For nearly five centuries Juan Diego's cloak became a religious shrine, and today it remains on display in Mexico City's Basilica of Our Lady of Guadalupe, one of the most visited Catholic shrines in the world. It was in the basilica that Pope John Paul II,

Statue of the Virgin of Guadalupe, icon and patron saint of Mexico, at Tepeyac Hill, Mexico City, Mexico. Images of the Virgin of Guadalupe were powerful inspirational symbols at marches and meetings of members of the United Farm Workers. (Glow Images)

on July 31, 2002, canonized Juan Diego. The Virgin of Guadalupe is Mexico's most revered religious and cultural image, carrying such titles as "Empress of the Americas" and "Queen of Mexico."

Throughout the centuries, the image of the Virgin became an object of veneration and Tepeyac a destination for religious pilgrimages for both native Aztec cultures and the emerging Catholic faith brought by Spaniards. Tepeyac had been the site of a destroyed Aztec temple of Tonantzin. Thus, the appearance of the Virgin on that very spot helped restore to native peoples a sense of dignity. Her arrival has been described through the centuries to mark the birth of a new land and a new people, neither European nor native.

After a devastating plague in 1737 claimed thousands of lives in and around Mexico City, for example, the surviving citizens claimed the Virgin of Guadalupe as their patron saint. Throughout Mexican society in succeeding centuries, the icon became associated with Mexican identity.

In the twentieth century, the image and tradition became tied to the rights of native peoples and disenfranchised populations. Both Pancho Villa and Emiliano Zapata used the symbol of Guadalupe during their revolutionary struggles. Peasant followers of Zapata, for example, carried banners of the Virgin of Guadalupe into Mexico City after the defeat of General Victoriano Huerta in 1914 during the Mexican revolution. Those followers also made pilgrimages to Tepeyac, the site of the miracle, paying homage to the Virgin as a protector of the lands of oppressed people and the glory of the struggle to bring justice to the persecuted. Thus, the image became an empowering symbol of liberation and action.

Cesar Chavez employed the image of the Virgin of Guadalupe in rallying farm workers from the beginning of the movement. He said consistently that La Causa was not merely the creation of a labor union but a larger quest for social justice, a revolution for the rights of oppressed workers, and a call for moral commitment. The Guadalupe icon harkened back to cultural values and historical memories. Its religious character called out to Christians who might have otherwise been resistant to political change. If a revered hero such as Zapata had carried a flag bearing the image into battle, so must the leader of a movement to right the injustices so long suffered by workers.

In the early days of the movement in Delano, when union workers needed food, a letter asking for assistance read, "For our hope for a better life, and for the love of the Virgin of Guadalupe, please help us." In the pages of *El Malcriado*, the union newspaper, there were constant appeals to the religious tradition exemplified by the Guadalupe icon. Chavez spoke often about shrines to the Virgin in the homes of many farm workers and how the union's battle against the abuses of growers and entrenched interests was in the tradition of others who had marched under her banner.

Cofounder of the union Dolores Huerta said, "She is a symbol of faith, hope and leadership. . . . She has been incorporated into everything we do." Huerta, who stood with Chavez from the beginning and weathered decades of challenging confrontations, including a life-threatening beating, said, "I don't think I could have survived without her" (Yellow Hat Productions 2010).

Luis Valdez, the playwright and founder of El Teatro Campesino, the farm workers theater, accompanied Chavez along the picket lines in the Delano grape strike and walked in the great march or *peregrinación* to Sacramento directing his small theater group's performances for the farm workers. He said later that the presence of the Virgin of Guadalupe was the first hint to workers in the fields and along the march route that La Causa implied social revolution. Valdez talked about Zapata's use of the symbol during the Mexican Revolution and how the standard of the Virgin symbolized the poor and humble of Mexico. She was their protector. "Beautifully dark and Indian in feature," Valdez wrote,

> she was the New World version of the Mother of Christ . . . she is a Catholic saint of Indian creations—Mexican. The people's response was immediate and reverent. They joined the march by the thousands, falling in line behind her standard. To the Catholic hypocrites against the pilgrimage and strike the Virgin said Huelga (Strike)! (Valdez 1966, 42)

Further Reading

Anderson, Carl, and Eduardo Chavez. 2009. *Our Lady of Guadalupe: Mother of the Civilization of Love*. New York: Doubleday.

King, Judy. 2006. "La Virgen de Guadalupe—Mother of All Mexico." MexConnect. http://www.mexconnect.com/articles/1404-la-virgen-de-guadalupe-mother-of-all-mexico.

Poole, Stafford. 1995. *Our Lady of Guadalupe: The Origins and Sources of a Mexican National Symbol, 1531–1797*. Tucson: University of Arizona Press.

Rodriquez, Jeanette. 1994. *Our Lady of Guadalupe: Faith and Empowerment among Mexican-American Women*. Austin: University of Texas Press.

Valdez, Luis. 1966."The Tale of La Raza." *Ramparts Magazine*, July, 40–42. http://farmworkermovement.org/ufwarchives/DalzellArchive/RampartsMagazine/Luis%20Valdez_001.pdf.

Yellow Hat Productions. 2010. "La Virgen de Guadalupe—Reina de la Gente—Mother of the People." 2011. http://beforewesaygoodbyethemovie.com/virgin.html.

Wrath of Grapes Campaign, 1986

In early 1986, Cesar Chavez announced that the new theme in the continuing nationwide grape boycott of the United Farm Workers (UFW) would focus on the tragedy of pesticide poisoning of farm workers and the dangers of pesticide residue for consumers across the country purchasing grapes and other agricultural products. During the 1930s, novelist John Steinbeck vividly portrayed the tribulations of California's migrant workers in his novel *The Grapes of Wrath*. In his attempt to focus the UFW's boycott on the plight of men, women, and children who had suffered disease and death from toxic chemicals recklessly used by growers, Chavez entitled the campaign "The Wrath of Grapes."

The pesticides, Chavez claimed, which were mostly applied on crops from airplanes, often drifted far afield, landing on living areas of farm workers and their families. Even when the poisons accurately hit their targets, the workers had to labor amid the chemicals on and around the plants they picked. Chavez and the union began to show studies suggesting that children were especially vulnerable to the pesticides, with illnesses as varied as cancer and liver disease.

One farm worker later remembered often being sprayed by airplanes. "You came out of there looking like Santa Claus," he said, "you were so full of white powder" (Rodriguez 2010). The white powder was dichlorodiphenyltrichloroethane (DDT).

For Chavez, the fight against pesticides was not new. Chavez and his mentor Fred Ross walked the streets of farm worker communities trying to identify epicenters of disease. Childhood cancer clusters had appeared in farm worker communities such as McFarland in Kern County and Earlimart in Tulare County. The first UFW table-grape contracts, signed in 1970, had provisions addressing the issue. The first ban on the use of DDT was in a union contract three years before the statewide ban of DDT went into effect in California. Such poisons as aldrin, endrin, and dieldrin were banned in some union contracts before the U.S. Environmental Protection Agency (EPA) restricted their use.

In the new Wrath of Grapes campaign, Chavez and the UFW focused on five pesticides that had been listed as possibly hazardous by the EPA. The UFW emphasized in its new information campaign that thousands of acres of California soil had been irrevocably contaminated by the prodigious use of the chemicals. Continuous use of the pesticides in such quantities, the UFW charged, was producing not only a calamitous health disaster for farm workers and their families but also was fast becoming a profound ecological and environmental threat.

As the charges and countercharges over the pesticide issue mounted, both sides armed themselves with studies and scientists, producing a flurry of conflicting evidence. Chavez himself began to arrange speaking engagements around the country to press the issue. The UFW produced a short documentary film claiming evidence of birth defects and high cancer rates of farm workers caused by the use of pesticides in the southern San Joaquin Valley.

Chavez passionately indicted the growers and their Republican political friends for their indifference to human suffering. "Statistics and new articles do not relate the real cost, the human anguish that originates from poisons on our food. They do not tell the tragedies I personally learn of daily," he declared.

> How can I explain these chemicals to 3 year old Amalia Larios who will never walk, born with a spinal defect due to pesticide exposure of her mother. What statistics are important to Adrian Espinoza, 7 years old and dying of cancer with 8 other children—whose only source of water was polluted with pesticides. What headlines can justify the loss of irrigator Manuel Anaya's right hand, amputated due to recurrent infection from powerful herbicides added to the water he worked with in the fields. (Hammerback and Jensen 2002, 134)

His list went on—stillborn babies, deadly lung diseases, teenage children suffering from symptoms and illnesses for which doctors had no explanation other than the poisons to which they had been exposed.

In the summer of 1988, as part of the campaign, Chavez, then 61 years old, conducted a fast to highlight the health dangers pesticides posed to farm workers and their children. In a number of cities across the country, demonstrators formed picket lines, handed out literature, and carried signs that read "Don't Buy Poison Grapes." Many joined Chavez in refusing to eat for periods of time. Considering Chavez's age, his fast lasted an extraordinary amount of time—over a month. As in other fasts, well-known individuals appeared in support—comedian Dick Gregory, Kathleen Kennedy Townsend and other Kennedy family members, and celebrities such as Martin Sheen, Edward James Olmos, and Lou Diamond Phillips. This would be Chavez's last fast. He continued to campaign against pesticides for the rest of his life.

Lupe Martinez, who became a volunteer organizer for the UFW in the late 1960s, was dispatched to Canada during the Wrath of Grapes campaign to spread the word about the dangers of pesticides. Martinez spent a long career with the UFW, becoming a national vice president and head of the organizing department. In 2006, he retired from the union and began work in Delano with a branch of the

Center on Race, Poverty, and the Environment, an organization dedicated to providing legal and organizing assistance to grassroots groups in low-income communities fighting for protection against environmental hazards. When Martinez looked back on his days with the union and its commitment to fight harmful pesticide use, he said of Cesar Chavez, "He was one of the biggest environmentalists—we just didn't realize that is what you called them" (Plevin 2012).

The fight goes on. In 2012, faced with lawsuits and pressure brought by various environmental groups and the UFW, the manufacturer of the toxic pesticide methyl iodide, used heavily in strawberry fields, withdrew the product from the market.

Further Reading

"Cesar Chavez's Wrath of Grapes Speech (1986)." 1986. Milestone Documents. http://www.milestonedocuments.com/documents/full-text/cesar-chavezs-wrath-of-grapes-speech.

Gordon, Robert. 1999. "Poisons in the Fields: The United Farm Workers, Pesticides, and Environmental Politics." *The Pacific Historical Review* (February): 51–77.

Hammerback, John, and Richard Jensen. 2002. *The Words of Cesar Chavez*. College Station: Texas A & M University Press.

Moses, Marion. 1992. *Harvest of Sorrow: Farm Workers and Pesticides*. San Francisco: Pesticide Education Center.

Plevin, Rebecca. 2012. "Latinos Protecting La Tierra: His Cause Is Well-grounded." *Vida en el Valle*, April 3. http://www.vidaenelvalle.com/2012/04/03/1178528/his-cause-is-well-grounded.html.

Rodriguez, Joe. 2010. "Exhibit in San Jose Triggers Memories of Farm Labor for Old Braceros." *Oakland Tribune*, April 2. http://www.highbeam.com/doc/1P2-21492269.html.

"The Wrath of Grapes." 1986. *Food and Justice* (March). http://farmworkermovement.com/ufwarchives/foodjustice/08_FebMar86_001.pdf.

Primary Documents

Farm Labor Organizing—Cesar Chavez Speaks of the Early Years

By 1964, Cesar Chavez's union, established two years earlier, was still in its early organizing efforts—recruiting members, developing strategies, and preparing to take on the forces of agribusiness on behalf of farm workers. Wendy Goepel, who had worked briefly both for the California Department of Health and for the federal antipoverty VISTA program, joined Chavez in these years and became a trusted union worker. She interviewed Chavez about the challenges ahead.

When you mention union in California, most people think of AWOC, the Teamsters, or perhaps the ILWU. Here, there are nationwide superstructures; and it is assumed that one of these will eventually "reach down" and pick up the farm worker.

Some say it will be the Teamsters because they control the necessary transportation link from field to cannery or retail store; others speculate that it will be AWOC because of its activity in the valley during the past five years.

But some other observers feel that a little-known organization called the Farm Workers Association (FWA) is building a union in the real sense. FWA, with headquarters in Delano (Kern County), was begun by Cesar Chavez. Some people may be more familiar with his name than with the organization.

Cesar Chavez was one of the first staff members of the Community Service Organization (CSO), a political and social action movement among Mexican Americans in various California communities. He became a skilled community organizer under the tutelage of Fred Ross of the Industrial Areas Foundation. He worked for CSO in San Jose, Oxnard, Stockton, and elsewhere.

As an organizer, he had to learn what unity and conflict meant, and how they came about. He was forced to figure out why people joined an organization or supported an organization.

It is difficult, he has found, to remain a leader of your own people, rather than to use your people as a vehicle for improving your personal position—for gaining a new social identity for yourself. Many minority group organizations have gained strength in their early days, have earned the awareness of majority groups, and have then sold out the original purpose of the organization for some immediate awareness and appeasement offered to them: either the group has been absorbed or its leaders have been lured off into positions within the "mainstream" of social life. Chavez himself has turned down positions with the Peace Corps and others, to continue what he believes he must try to do and might be able to do.

The Farm Workers Association is almost two years old now. Chavez says, "If you look back, we've come a long way; if you look ahead, we have a long way to go." He says that there is nothing unusual about what he is trying to do now: "I'm just trying to do what everyone else has, and making a few changes where I know we've made mistakes before." But the secret of his success—if there is to be success—will lie in certain unique techniques of worker organization upon which the Farm Workers Association is built.

Cesar begins by saying, "Some farm workers are bums just like some growers are. It's a big mistake to begin by idealizing the workers because they're the 'down and outers.' Most farm workers are just human; they live, like all of us, from day to day; they want happiness and they want to avoid confusion and pain."

Then he continues by asking questions: "The spirit of our Revolution: what has happened to it? Why do people belong to anything or get excited about anything? What do they want? What keeps them going?" "When I was 19," he recalls, "I was picking cotton in Corcoran. A car with loud-speakers came around. The speakers were saying: 'Stop working. You're not making a living. Come downtown to a rally instead.' My brother and I left, with many others. Seven thousand cotton pickers gathered in a little park in the center of Corcoran. There was a platform, and a union leader got up and started talking to all the workers about 'the cause.' I would have died right then if someone had told me how and why to die for our cause. But no one did. There was a crisis, and a mob, but there was no organization, and nothing came of it all. A week later everyone was back picking cotton in the same field at the same low wages. It was dramatic. People came together. Then it was over. That won't organize farm workers."

"A couple of years ago," he continues, "I was driving home from Los Angeles. I passed a Pentecostal church at night and it was full of people and I thought to myself, Why do all the people come there so much? It must be because they like to praise God—and to sing." A union is a group of people who have feeling for one another and a devotion to a common cause. During the first year, 1962,

Chavez spent months just talking with people in various towns—in their homes, in places where they gathered at night, in the fields as they left their places at the end of a day. In the beginning, he says, it is important to let people know exactly what you are trying to do and what role they have in it. It is fairly easy to get people interested, but it is important to find out which people are committed and are willing to work, and which are not really serious. Sometimes it is very hard to know this at first. In the beginning, he recalls, it was easy to get everybody excited. They were ready to join quickly, but they had unrealistic goals and ideas about what they would get. The biggest problem of all is to build a group spirit and to keep people involved and concerned—prepared to make demands, prepared to show their strength and their unity over a long period of time. You have to just begin this by finding the committed people in every little community; this takes time. You begin by talking to people; then you call back on people. You spend evenings having "house meetings"—talking to three or four people who want to spend an evening talking about problems and discussing what they see that has to be done. You build a core of people who keep coming back to talk. You find certain people who are respected as leaders in every community; and you find that some of these leaders are committed to the task ahead. A union, then, is not simply getting enough workers to stage a strike. A union is building a group with a spirit and an existence all its own.

A union must be built around the idea that people must do things by themselves, in order to help themselves. Too many people, Cesar feels, have the idea that the farm worker is capable only of being helped by others. People want to give things to him. So, in time, some workers come to expect help from the outside. They change their idea of themselves. They become unaccustomed to the idea that they can do anything by themselves for themselves. They have accepted the idea that they are "too small" to do anything, too weak to make themselves heard, powerless to change their own destinies. The leader, of course, gives himself selflessly to the members, but he must expect and demand that they give themselves to the organization at the same time. He exists only to help make the people strong.

A union must have members who pay dues regularly. The only people whom the Farm Workers Association counts as members are those who pay their $3.50 a month, every month. Chavez says that farm workers who are committed can afford to pay $3.50 a month in dues, even though they have low incomes. He feels that the members commit themselves to the organization by paying dues regularly. He feels that because they pay so much, they feel they are the important part of the organization, that they have a right to be served. They don't hesitate to write, to call, to ask for things—and to reaffirm their position in the association. Members enjoy certain concrete benefits, and are offered assistance with social, economic, and legal problems that they might have. These benefits can be, and are, used continually by the members. To many, the breadth of services and programs available to association members is new and is most welcome. And the idea that the members are, alone, paying the salary of a man who is responsible to them is very important, both to members and to Cesar Chavez. "Of course," he says, "it is very hard to limit assistance and service to members; many people come to your door because they know that you might be able to help them out with some problem. But helping everyone who came would take up all my time—and more. Then I would have none left to work with the other members. People must come to see assistance to one another as the purpose of the organization, as its very reason for being." Cesar has also learned that you do not build a strong, ongoing organization by simply performing services for any person who has a crisis and needs help. People must come to realize that they join and are associated with a group that they will help, and that will help them, if they ever need it. The people together are not too small. The people together must learn to show their strength. One way that Cesar feels is very important is through concern with legislation. Part of the "training process" that the membership goes through is to learn how legislation is passed, and why certain kinds are often not passed. One of the requirements of membership is to pledge to work on legislation. This is done through letter writing campaigns, for example. Delegations to Sacramento are also part of the program; about forty of the members went to the governor's hearings on farm labor, and those who had never been to Sacramento before went on a tour of the capital. "Legislation will not solve the problems," Chavez says, "but it can certainly make the road smoother."

In the Farm Workers Association, a single membership covers a whole family. Membership fluctuates some, with the fewest members during the time when there is the most work available. During this time, people are too busy to remember to pay dues, and they just aren't as concerned with their problems as they are during slack season. In spite of seasonal fluctuations, the organization has continued to grow every month since it began. Today, the Farm Workers Association is no longer Cesar Chavez. There are local leaders, Farm Workers Association representatives, who work together with one another and with Cesar. Local leaders are responsible for the members in their own town—for helping them with the problems they may encounter, for keeping the local group together, for encouraging people to understand and to use the services available to them as members, for collecting dues, and for recruiting new members in the community. At the present time, there are local leaders and local groups in sixty-seven different areas in eight valley counties. The greatest number of local groups is in Kings County, followed by Kern, San Joaquin, Tulare, and Fresno Counties.

In every community, there are certain types of farm workers who are not potential members of the association. That group of workers who has recently arrived from Mexico is, for example, very hard to organize. They tend to think they are better off here than they really are. For one thing, it is difficult to explain

American-style unionism to the "emigrado." Mexicans tend to assume that the United States Constitution forbids workers to cross a picket line, and that it should therefore be fairly simple to organize a strike and a union. "The Mexican revolutionary constitution is," Chavez says, "kinder to the working man than our own."

The workers who are hired year-round on one farm have a loyalty to the grower and are not willing to lose their security for any improvements in their conditions; they feel they would jeopardize their jobs by joining the association. Another group that usually won't join consists of the "old hands" among the local, temporary workers. These are the workers who have been in one area about twenty years—long enough to know where all the seasonal jobs in a three-or-four county area are. These workers have a fairly regular circuit of jobs, in and out of agriculture. When there is no work available, during certain periods, these workers can draw unemployment insurance from the cannery and other "covered" jobs that they have had. But it is not uncommon for them to collect unemployment insurance and do temporary farm work at the same time to supplement their income. These workers have something to gain, then, by keeping the "system" as it is, and something to lose by joining an association that would change the system.

Thus, there are different kinds of farm workers in any small community, and there is a certain amount of friction, overt or covert, between groups of workers. It is the seasonal farm workers who have been in the United States for some time, but who have not been able to find a full year's employment, who are most likely to be interested in joining the association and in seeing an eventual union of farm workers. Chavez notes that there will probably be real conflict in many little communities before the problems are finally resolved, because of the vested interests that certain workers think they have in the status quo.

The agricultural workers who are FWA members may, then, be characterized as local families who depend on seasonal farm work. Most of them live year-round in the southern San Joaquin. Almost all are family men. They are a stable group to work with, and they are capable members of an ongoing organization.

The biggest problem is keeping the local groups, all the people, united and ready to engage in "direct action" when the time comes. There are not many general meetings of the Farm Workers Association.

Chavez observes that people do not like to go to meetings endlessly. If nothing important happens when they do go, they may become discouraged about the organization and the movement on the basis of the meeting. Too many meetings also give the appearance that nothing important is happening, that there is no progress. When a group must be built to work for a goal which is several years away, it is the most difficult to build and keep a group together. If a group has not grown to the point where some direct action can be taken against some outside person or some problem, then there is a dangerous tendency for the group to weaken or splinter and for in-group factions or group disorganization to take place. So, it is very important during the growth period of a group to tackle small problems which individual members have and which the members can work out with the help of local leaders of the organization. The task of confronting some person or some problem which the group feels is important, and the success obtained when the people work together gives individual members a sense of control over their own lives. It teaches them more about the complexities of modern society, and it gives them an opportunity to work constructively in small, functional units. It gives the group a continual reason for being.

The few large meetings that are held to show and feel the size and the unity of the association are carefully planned. There is appeal to pageantry and a display of the "signs and symbols" that are part of the association. There is a Farm Workers Association song, written by Mrs. Rosa Gloria, a member from Madera, which is sung at meetings. There is a symbol, which Chavez admits is a bit "flashy:" a thunderbird on a red and black field. And there is a slogan: "Viva la Causa," which is the unity to which workers pledge themselves. These "artifacts" are used in the meetings, in greeting one another, and on the association's letterhead stationery. But these large meetings have a limited function. The hard work is done daily in the communities by the leaders and the members.

Of course, the biggest temptation is to "do something dramatic." This would be easier and quicker than working day to day on small problems and keeping people together. "I figure, though," says Chavez, "that even if we had a 50-50 chance of carrying off a successful strike, the gamble would still be too great. You stand always to lose more than you gain by drama when you are working with people. Thirty men may lose their jobs as a result of a strike. You lose thirty members, and you gain thirty 'disorganizers.' So we must work on immediate goals—helping the members get a little better living through using the facilities of the association, through getting what they are entitled to, through learning how to participate more fully in social life. And the hard work of gaining official recognition, including strikes if necessary, will come."

Chavez says that he is not concerned that his organization be the core of a union for farm workers. He says that his membership is ready to unite with any other union, if any other succeeds. He, personally, doesn't want to be the one at the bargaining table. Chavez conceives his real job to be education of the people. "You cannot organize a strike or build a union until the members who must do the real work understand what all this means, what kind of activities are involved. They must, first, be able to articulate their own hopes and goals." He would like very much to hold some short-term schools where the leader-members could discuss and study union organization together. Whatever the outcome of the Farm Workers Association, it is certain that the individuals who have learned and have profited from being members will be a lasting asset to their communities and to the society at large.

Cesar says, finally, "Even if our work succeeds, I don't want to hang on forever. What I would really like is to be alone somewhere—in Mexico or in the mountains —and have time to read all the classics that there are in English and Spanish."

Source: Cesar E. Chavez. "Viva La Causa." Interview by Wendy Goepel. *Farm Labor* 1, no. 5 (April 1964): 23–28. Used by permission of Wendy Goepel Brooks.

"The Plan of Delano" (1965)

In the spring of 1966, as a tactic in the United Farm Workers Association's first major strike, Cesar Chavez led a peregrinación *or pilgrimage from union headquarters in Delano, California, to the California state capital of Sacramento. Chavez asked his friend playwright Luis Valdez, who had joined the union movement, to draft a statement that would declare the reasons for the strike and the goals of the farm workers, one that could be read at each stop during the march. Valdez modeled the statement after the historic "Plan of Ayala," a document written half a century earlier by Emiliano Zapata and his supporters during the Mexican Revolution, a proclamation that called for reform and freedom for the poor. Just as the "Plan of Ayala" was a rallying cry for the Zapatismo movement, "The Plan of Delano" became a stirring call for action for the farm workers.*

PLAN for the liberation of the Farm Workers associated with the Delano Grape Strike in the State of California, seeking social justice in farm labor with those reforms that they believe necessary for their well-being as workers in the United States.

We, the undersigned, gathered in Pilgrimage to the capital of the State in Sacramento in penance for all the failings of Farm Workers as free and sovereign men, do solemnly declare before the civilized world which judges our actions, and before the nation to which we belong, the propositions we have formulated to end the injustice that oppresses us.

We are conscious of the historical significance of our Pilgrimage. It is clearly evident that our path travels through a valley well known to all Mexican farm workers. We know all of these towns of Delano, Madera, Fresno, Modesto, Stockton, and Sacramento, because along this very same road, in this very same valley, the Mexican race has sacrificed itself for the last hundred years. Our sweat and our blood have fallen on this land to make other men rich. The pilgrimage is a witness to the suffering we have seen for generations.

The penance we accept symbolizes the suffering we shall have in order to bring justice to these same towns, to this same valley. The pilgrimage we make symbolizes the long historical road we have traveled in this valley alone, and the long road we have yet to travel, with much penance, in order to bring about the revolution we need, and for which we present the propositions in the following PLAN:

This is the beginning of a social movement in fact and not in pronouncements. We seek our basic, God-given rights as human beings. Because we have suffered—and are not afraid to suffer—in order to survive, we are ready to give up everything, even our lives, in our fight for social justice. We shall do it without violence because that is our destiny. To the ranchers, and to all those who [oppose us], we say, in the words of Benito Juarez, "EL RESPETO AL DE-RECHO AJENO ES LA PAZ."

We seek the support of all political groups and protection of the government, which is also our government, in our struggle. For too many years we have been treated like the lowest of the low. Our wages and working conditions have been determined from above, because irresponsible legislators who could have helped us, have supported the rancher's argument that the plight of the Farm Worker was a "special case." They saw the obvious effects of an unjust system, starvation wages, contractors, day hauls, forced migration, sickness, illiteracy, camps and sub-human living conditions, and acted as if they were irremediable causes. The farm worker has been abandoned to his own fate—without representation, without power—subject to mercy and caprice of the rancher. We are tired of words, of betrayals, of indifference. To the politicians we say that the years are gone when the farm worker said nothing and did nothing to help himself. From this movement shall spring leaders who shall understand us, lead us, be faithful to us, and we shall elect them to represent us. WE SHALL BE HEARD.

We seek, and have, the support of the Church in what we do. At the head of the pilgrimage we carry LA VIRGEN DE LA GUADALUPE because she is ours, all ours, Patroness of the Mexican people. We also carry the Sacred Cross and the Star of David because we are not sectarians, and because we ask the help and prayers of all religions. All men are brothers, sons of the same God; that is why we say to all of good will, in the words of Pope Leo XIII, "Everyone's first duty is protect the workers from the greed of speculators who use human beings as instruments to provide themselves with money. It is neither just nor human to oppress men with excessive work to the point where their minds become enfeebled and their bodies worn out." GOD SHALL NOT ABANDON US.

We are suffering. We have suffered, and we are not afraid to suffer in order to win our cause. We have suffered unnumbered ills and crimes in the name of the Law of the Land. Our men, women, and children have suffered not only the basic brutality of stoop labor, and the most obvious injustices of the system; they have also suffered the desperation of knowing that the system caters to the greed of callous men and not to our needs. Now we will suffer for the purpose of ending the poverty, the misery, and the injustice, with the hope that our children will not be exploited as we have been. They have imposed hunger on us, and now we hunger for justice. We draw our strength from the very despair in which we have been forced to live. WE SHALL ENDURE.

We shall unite. We have learned the meaning of UNITY. We know why these are just that—united. The strength of the poor is also in union. We know that the poverty of the Mexican or Filipino worker in California is the same as that of all farm workers across the country, the Negroes and poor whites, the Puerto Ricans, Japanese, and Arabians; in short, all of the races that comprise the oppressed minorities of the United States. The majority of the people on our Pilgrimage are of Mexican descent, but the triumph of our race depends on a national association of all farm workers. The ranchers want to keep us divided in order to keep us weak. Many of us have signed individual "work contracts" with the ranchers or contractors, contracts in which they had all power. These contracts were farces, one more cynical joke at our impotence. That is why we must get together and bargain collectively. We must use the only strength that we have, the force of our numbers. The ranchers are few; we are many. UNITED WE SHALL STAND.

We shall Strike. We shall pursue the REVOLUTION we have proposed. We are sons of the Mexican Revolution, a revolution of the poor seeking, bread and justice. Our revolution will not be armed, but we want the existing social order to dissolve, we want a new social order. We are poor, we are humble, and our only [choice] is to Strike in those [ranches] where we are not treated with the respect we deserve as working men, where our rights as free and sovereign men are not recognized. We do not want the paternalism of the rancher; we do not want the contractor; we do not want charity at the price of our dignity. We want to be equal with all the working men in the nation; we want just wages, better working conditions, a decent future for our children. To those who oppose us, be they ranchers, police, politicians, or speculators, we say that we are going to continue fighting until we die, or we win. WE SHALL OVERCOME.

Across the San Joaquin Valley, across California, across the entire Southwest of the United States, wherever there are Mexican people, wherever there are farm workers, our movement is spreading like flames across a dry plain. Our PILGRIMAGE is the MATCH that will light our cause for all farm workers to see what is happening here, so that they may do as we have done. The time has come for the liberation of the poor farm worker.

History is on our side.

MAY THE STRIKE GO ON! VIVA LA CAUSA!

Interview with Barrera Family Members on the 1966 *Peregrinación*

Originally from Texas, the Barrera family members all worked in the harvest fields picking grapes, tomatoes, apricots, and other crops after to moving to Porterfield, California. Yolanda Barrera, for example, labored in the fields when she was 10 years old. Remarkably, she later became a lawyer. In this interview, conducted by the Farmworker Movement Documentation Project, a rich and extraordinarily valuable program to gather and make available original source material on the movement, Rico, Jose Marin, and Yolanda Barrera all tell of their various roles in the farm workers' union, especially in the peregrinación to Sacramento from Delano in the early days of the grape strike—Rico and Jose Marin playing music and Yolanda, who was fluent in English at an early age, acting as a translator.

Jose Marin Barrera: We found out that the march was going to come. The one who organized us there in the march was Mr. Manuel Chavez (a relative of Cesar Chavez). Manuel Chavez is the one who went on ahead scouting for people in the towns with whom they (marchers) would stay so they would know where they were going to sleep the following day. When this happened in Ducor, we came to bring them coffee, pastries; but they were few people. We got there a little late, and the people had already left. But from the ones that were there outside sleeping at a house, we realized that they weren't that many.

When they arrived in Porterville, we were already organized in the way in which we were going to do it. So then we came a little late because Mr. (Cesar) Chavez was already there lying in the shade because it was real hot. But just the same, we arrived with these apparatus (accordion and guitar) that we have here in our hands to bring joy to the march that was making its way along; and was suffering, and that would suffer still even more because, in truth, Sacramento was very far. We gave no thought on how it was going to be done, but it was done in a way that every person who met there at the park took a person or two people to their home to sleep; and in the morning we had to make lunch or two lunches, depending, in order to keep moving forward.

We left Porterville for Lindsay and Lindsay was already organized, too, as to where the people would stay; and it gave us so much joy in doing this because in those days, well, we didn't know about marches. We didn't know about organizations. We didn't know anything. But we found out that united we could work so much better than what we had been. It was something that gave us joy; and we even kept on doing it and kept on doing it and kept on doing it. We would go to work and at noon or in the afternoons we would go to meet up with them over there to give them strength, encouragement; and in spite of being extremely tired some young men would even dance there in the hot sun because we had no shade only the sun in those days that we left for Sacramento.

Our experience, I believe, could be used or it could be viewed that we, the organizers that are already in our golden years, the last one third of our lives, have . . . we will leave a great memory to the youth. Well, right now I feel proud with the two daughters that we still have here in the home. They came to visit us; and we told them if they wanted to come to this meeting, and they wholeheartedly came because they suffered the way we suffered in the marches because they, too, participated in walking in picket lines in the town where we live there in Porterville. We did (picket) various stores and they, too, helped us advance our cause. So, I feel proud that they are here with us; and I want a wholeheartedly applause for my daughters—both who are here with us. She (Yolanda Barrera) was the interpreter, in case you don't know. She was the interpreter of some of the meetings of the union. Mr. Cesar Chavez would say, "Come up here, Yolanda." She was fourteen, fifteen years old, she, I think, during that time. (Yolanda speaks in the background giving her exact age at the time.) Thirteen and she would help hold the meetings in Spanish or English. If they spoke English, she would translate for them in Spanish.

When Mr. Cesar Chavez put me as organizer and (union) representative of (because there in my house they made it into an office) the people came to look for work with me . . . to me . . . with me. Schenley was the only one (union contract) we had won during that time.

Then people would come. They would tell me, "How can I join? How can I work for Schenley?" Then I would give them a pass or a paper to present there at the ranch and they would begin to work. At the end of the week they would go and pay. Two dollars and fifty cents was paid in those days to organize or, in other words, to work. So it was an honor for me to have done that for Mr. Chavez whom we so greatly admired.

And the things that he would tell us I can't comprehend. Just now as we were traveling down the road we were remembering that when he would say, "we will do this", he would do it with such confidence that everything was going to turn out well; and it did turn out well for us. Therefore, it is an extremely important thing to me that he is the one who organized us. We did it with the intention that we believed in our mind, we thought that bringing the people together, the more we brought them together the better. In all the towns they had tremendous organization in those days in that if something would happen just like this (the present filming) everyone would turn out from all the towns to the meetings. We in those days beli . . . all along we had believed that the people had to be organized, and what a large number got organized! But all of us did it. We would go to work, we would come (home) at two in the afternoon, we would bathe, and then we would go to the march or in other words, to catch up with the march.

At the time for us it wasn't a hardship. For the ones that it was a hardship was for the actual people who were marching every day with those blisters those things that would break out on their feet; it was a terrible sight. Then, the more we enjoyed . . . or the more effort we put into organizing the people so that we could bring ourselves out from our present condition and from where we did lift ourselves. It may not appear so but a lot has been accomplished. A lot has improved. You who are aware of all the programs; many, many people have benefited from the sacrifices that we made in those days.

(Answering another question) Okay, to start we would need . . . first of all, the one who organized us in Porterville was Jim Drake. (Migrant Ministry). Jim Drake was involved; he too, was from the union. He helped the union a lot during that time. He organized us to buy homes or to put down payments on houses; but at the end it was not possible because many of us had homes in Texas or many did not have the right permits-in other words, that they were United States citizens.

So then he told us, "Wouldn't you like to join Cesar Chavez' union?" "Who is this Cesar Chavez?"

"He is a person in Delano," he said, "that has . . . who has his group, and I would like for you to become organized."

We were organized in the sense that we had an office in Porterville. We sold gas to the members. We sold tires to the members. The one young lady there, Yolanda, uh, she is the one who worked during that time, one hour, to . . . to run that office by regulations, right; because she is a person who truly helped us a lot to organize, also. They (Yolanda and her sister) would go out to pump gas. They would come and pay her.

Then, when they told us about Cesar—"Well then, let's see him, let's meet him."

Then he came to our office and he explained that he . . . his objective and the plans he had in mind and we liked it. Then, all the members that we had there all of us came here to this area (Delano); not to these houses (Casa Hernandez) because these houses weren't (here). And here we had a meeting, and we got organized with him.

Yolanda Barrera interprets for Bill Hatton:	Besides El Teatro (Campesino) if there were any persons who played music? (Inaudible)
Jesus Marin Barrera:	In some towns like Modesto or Sacramento; no, not Sacramento, Fresno. When they were arriving (into towns) mariachis would come out; some people, some mariachis to meet them.
Yolanda Barrera:	But for the march?
Jesus Marin Barrera:	For the march just us-me and my brother and uh . . .

Yolanda Barrera (interprets for Bill Hatton): . . . that I ask you that if by any chance it would have been possible to have reached Sacramento without you. (Yolanda and the audience break into laughter at the question).

Jesus Marin Barrera: That is one of the beautiful things that we leave, right, that we plan to leave—a memory. And that memory—this is the memory (Bill Hutton's film) for our families and for people who come after us of what we did and what we are willing to do as long as we have life. Like this meeting that was convened here, uh, it is very important to see those people who struggled together with all of us. It pleases me to have been here. . . .

Rico Barrera: Well, at the beginning we really were afraid because during that time it was very difficult to organize, well, for the organizers to organize the people. It was very difficult to . . . a lot of people were afraid. One would say to them, "Come over here; join in the march. It is important, you know, because Cesar Chavez is here"—as well all those who were coming marching along, too. Then, well, we would get scared in those days. But with time we started getting more . . . we began losing a bit more of our fear. We were getting rid of our fear, and from then on out we went with confidence every afternoon. We would leave work, we would get dressed; and we would meet up with the march. Every day, every day, we would go meet up with them until they arrived at Sacramento. So then, for us it is an extremely great experience and very important to share with the present generation of this day. It is important that they learn what happened in that time which was the year 1966,-the great and important march of Cesar Chavez. . . .

Rico Barrera: Walking, playing and at times singing with people that came up to us there. We would march singing De Colores, and things like that. Various songs that the people liked; and we, well, we would continue playing. Me and my brother playing—him with the accordion and me with the guitar. And it was, like I say, it was a very important experience for both of us.

Jesus Marin Barrera: With the, with the . . . the accordion is a curious thing that . . . I am not a musician, but in my way of thinking, I believe that we did the best that was possible because we had a strong desire to play; and to reach the people that were marching along. And the accordion is heavy when one is walking. Now sometimes I think to myself, "How did we do it to go every day? To go walking, playing being that I am not a musician? If I was a musician it would be fine, but I am not a musician. . . . One time when we were conducting a march from Woodville to Porterville; well, they told us, "If you are going to pass through Main with that march we are going to arrest everyone." So then, many people were afraid.

But other people would say, "Well, let them arrest us at least there are a lot of us—we are going to pass anyway."

And we were going to pass. With the youngster, my son; there was a car wanting to pass the march because the people had formed a line, right, (around two hundred, three hundred people) and the car wanted to get by. And my son got in front (of the car) with tremendous risk of danger that he would get hit, right? But they (the children), all the time, were involved with us.

When they were going to take us to jail there at Smith, a store, my wife told them, "Why are you taking him?"

"Because he is the leader." "Well, I lead, too."

"Well, then, you go to the can (jail), too"— although, they didn't take us to the can. (Laughter)

But you do feel something strong. Yes, to repeat, the family that is united is so much stronger.

Yolanda Barrera: Tell them about people who bought grapes in the stores and what they did. How they came out of the stores eating grapes.

Jesus Marin Barrera: When they came out with grapes they would eat them, just like the one who was president, Reagan, at that time. He would place the grapes (the bunch near his mouth) and he would pretend he was eating grapes. . . . Okay, when the march that reached Sacramento ended, uh, some people from San Jose came to talk with us asking for us to go play music at a dance; and I said to myself, "Well, how am I going to go play at a dance if I don't know how to play?" (Laughter)

"Well, no, he said, "over there the ones from San Jose," he said, "said that you are helping the union a lot," he said, "and they want to see you and that for you to come play at a dance."

"Hey, well then, let's go over there, too."

And so it was there where, he with his guitar, and me with my accordion and my brother-in-law, (I have a brother-in-law who plays drums and we took him along, too,) we left in two vans to . . . to, San Jose.

No, and then they break out with "these are the men? Wow! They gave us a round of applause." (Laughter)

"Are they the ones??" (Laughter)

They would touch us because some would ask, "These are the ones?" "Yes, yes, these are the ones." (Laughter)

But a lot of them said, most likely said; and we, also, in our own way of perceiving things said, "Since they don't even know how to play; how come they came to play here (dance)?" (Laughter)

But that is the, that is . . . that is why . . . (Continuous laughter). Well, anyway, he (his brother) felt encouraged in that he already knew how to play a little and me, too. But just there at home or for a small fiesta there with our own; but nor for the public. (Laughter)

Well, and here we are still.

Rico Barrera: No, well, like my brother said, we were not professional musicians except that, well, I played a little guitar because I am . . . I am a drummer. I played with the Carlos Casa group that was called The Vagabonds. Well, like I say, I played the guitar; but I didn't play it very well because I only know the keys—straight keys of the guitar. Then, well, I accompanied my brother, you know, on guitar; and I liked it just the same. Only I wanted him to play a little better still, you see; but, well, it wasn't possible (laughter) because we didn't have much experience and he wasn't a musician either. I am a musician. Well, I was a musician because I played the drums; and like I say, well, it gave me great satisfaction in those days to play like that. When the march happened, it was with even greater satisfaction. It was there that we began to pick up a little more . . . me the guitar. I started playing it a little, and like I say, I still play a little; still the same with my brother. Well, I get in there with him and play at a lower register. We sometimes get together by chance there at his house or what have you; and we practice. Just to play like that just a little because, like I say, he knows how to play the accordion a little. But it gives us great pleasure to have played during that time (march).

Jesus Marin Barrera:	The one who, the one who . . . the accordion is a good thing. The one who knows how to play can play it, right? (Laughter)
Rico Barrera:	(Laughing) I agree, yes.
Jesus Marin Barrera:	But, I don't know how to play. I just do it as though I know how to play.
Rico Barrera:	The accordion is a good thing but what it lacks is fingers (of someone who can play.)
Rico Barrera:	(Answers a question from the audience): Yes, my brother-in-law.
Jesus Marin Barrera:	The same song. . . . It's been about forty-three years playing the same one.
From someone in the audience:	Knock yourself out and play one!
Jesus Marin Barrera:	Well, just one. It's the one and only one. (Peals of laughter) It's the only one!

Jesus Marin Barrera:	But we told you that we need to be standing because sitting just won't be . . .
	(Jesus to Rico: Tell them to move the camera a little.)
	(Jesus and Rico Barrera stand adjusting their instruments to prepare to play a song.)
Jesus Marin Barrera:	This is "La Adelita" although it is not precise the way we play it; but just the same.
Yolanda Barrera:	(Introduces song in English.) It's a revolutionary song called La Adelita that they're going to play. That's the one they used to play, he says, although they never really played it all the way through because they didn't know how.
	The Barrera Brothers play "La Adelita" (Clapping and laughter)
	Someone shouts out: Another, another; play another of the same one. (Laughter)
	Jesus Marin Barrera (expressing appreciation to all): We are here with you!!!

Source: "Transcript of an Interview with the Barrera Brothers." http://www .farmworkermovement.us/media/video/Barrera_transcript.pdf. Courtesy of the Farmworker Movement Documentation Project.

Informant Interview to FBI on Cesar Chavez, September 23, 1966

When Cesar Chavez joined the Community Service Organization (CSO) in the early 1950s and then began to enlist supporters in an effort to form a labor union of farm workers, he made enemies, especially among local growers and agribusiness interests and Republican politicians, uncertain about the possible political effects that his infant movement might spark. Zealous right-wing opponents smeared him with charges that he was a communist or a socialist or an anti-American agitator. The Federal Bureau of Investigation (FBI), under Director J. Edgar Hoover, wasted no time in an effort to uncover any such subversive connections. The bureau sent agents to California to infiltrate marches and protests, and interviewed hundreds of individuals who had contact with Chavez. His file at FBI headquarters grew large. They turned up nothing to tie Chavez to left-wing conspiracies. Most of what they turned up is reflected in the following informant interview.

Interview, September 23, 1966

[DELETED] advised . . . that he had known CESAR ESTRADA CHAVEZ since 1952. He said he first met [DELETED] said that CHAVEZ began with the CSO in 1952 as a volunteer organizer and that he became a paid employee with the CSO in the same capacity in 1953. [DELETED] said that almost immediately CHAVEZ became the leader of the San Jose Chapter of the CSO and that inasmuch as the IAF founded and sponsored CSO chapters, it would be proper for him to state that CHAVEZ was an organizer for IAF from 1953 to 1958. He said that from September 1958 until 1961, CHAVEZ was National Director of CSO and accordingly, was paid by CSO. [DELETED] said that since 1961 or early 1962, CHAVEZ has been Director of the National Farm Workers Association (NFWA), now the UFWOC-AFL-CIO. [DELETED] said that CHAVEZ in working for CSO and IAF performed his services in various areas of California.

[DELETED] considers CHAVEZ to be a very close associate [DELETED]. He related that when he first met CAHVEZ he realized that CHAVEZ was "a man among men, thoroughly loyal and dedicated to the goal of bettering the lot of the Mexican people." [DELETED] said CHAVEZ is extremely intelligent and a very hard worker. He said CHAVEZ is a "self-starter" and that he required very little supervision. [DELETED] said that CHAVEZ developed into the best organizer that he has ever known and that it became apparent during their association that this would be CHAVEZ'S destiny. [DELETED] characterized CHAVEZ as "the greatest Mexican leader today and he is one of the greatest leaders in America today. [DELETED] said CHAVEZ is a man of profound judgment, that his decisions are almost always correct, and that he is not the type to make snap judgments. He said that CHAVEZ is extremely well read and is able to draw on a wealth of past experience, even though he has had little formal education. He said that CHAVEZ is self-taught, that he has the uncanny ability to work well with people, and that he is trusted, admired, and well liked by almost everyone with whom he comes in contact. He said that CHAVEZ'S personal life is impeccable and that he has absolutely no question of the loyalty of CHAVEZ to the United States. . . .

Source: Federal Bureau of Investigation. "Cesar Chavez and United Farm Workers." Part 6b, pp. 32–34. http://vault.fbi.gov/Cesar%20Chavez.

Statement of Senator Robert F. Kennedy, Delano, California, March 10, 1968

It had been almost exactly two years since Senator Robert Kennedy had come to Delano as part of a subcommittee investigating migrant labor. Profoundly moved by the stories of the men, women, and children who worked the fields, Kennedy had pledged his support for La Causa. Now, in March 1968, he flew to California to be at the side of Chavez as the union leader broke his fast for nonviolence. According to Peter Edelman, a Kennedy aide, it was on that flight that Kennedy revealed to him that he had decided to run for the presidency and would announce it the following week. Kennedy's remarks at the end of the fast reflect the deep respect he felt for Chavez and his movement. Kennedy did run for the presidency. Chavez and his union fought vigorously for his victory in the California primary. But in the early morning of June 5, 1968, his assassination shattered the dreams of millions, none more so than the thousands of field workers who revered him.

This is a historic occasion. We have come here out of respect or one of the heroic figures of our time—Cesar Chavez. But I come here to congratulate all of you, you who are locked with Cesar in the struggle for justice for the farm worker, and the struggle for justice for the Spanish-Speaking American. I was here two years ago, almost to the day. Two years ago your union had not yet won a major victory. Now, elections have been held on ranch after ranch and the workers have spoken. They have spoken, and they have said, "We want a union."

You are the first—not the first farm workers to organize—but the first to fight and triumph over all the odds without proper protection from Federal law.

You have won historic victories.

Others, inspired by your example, have come to offer help—and they have helped. But the victories are yours and yours alone. You have won them with your courage and perseverance. You stood for the right—and would not be moved.

And you will not be moved again.

The world must know, from this time forward, that the migrant farm worker, the Mexican-American, is coming into his own rights. You are winning a special kind of citizenship: no one is doing it for you—you are winning it yourselves—and therefore no one can ever take it away.

And when your children and grandchildren take their place in America—going to high school, and college, and taking good jobs at good pay—when you look at them, you will say, "I did this. I was there, and the point of difficulty and danger." And though you may be old and bent from many years of labor, no man will stand taller than you when you say, "I marched with Cesar."

But the struggle is far from over. And now, as you are at midpoint in your most difficult organizing effort, there are suddenly those who question the principles that underlies everything you have done so far—the principle of non-violence. There are those who think violence is some shortcut to victory.

Let me say that violence is no answer. And those who organized the steel plants and the auto plants and the coal mines a generation ago learned from bitter experience that that was so. For where there is violence and death and confusion and injury, the only ones who benefit are those who oppose your right to organize. Where there is violence, our nation loses. Violence destroys far more than t can ever create. It tears at the fabric of our society. And let no one say that violence is the courageous route. It takes far greater commitment, far more courage to say, "we will do what must be done through an organization of the people, through patient, careful building of a democratic organization." That road requires far greater militancy. But along that road lies success. Along that road lies the building of institutions and cooperative businesses, of clinics, and schools and homes. So we come here, you and I, in a great pilgrimage to demonstrate our commitment to non-violence, to democracy itself. Just a few miles from here is the tower of the Voice of America—broadcasting across vast oceans and whole continents, the greatness of America. And we say together, we will build, we will organize, we will make America fulfill its promises and we will make our voices heard. We will make America a better place for all Americans.

But if you come here today from such great distances and at such great sacrifice to demonstrate your commitment to nonviolence, we in Government must match your commitment. That is our responsibility.

We must have a Federal law which give farm workers the right to engage in collective bargaining—and have it this year.

We must have more adequate regulation of green-card workers, to prevent their use as strikebreakers—and we must have that this year.

We must have equal protection of the laws. Those are the words of the Fourteenth Amendment to the Constitution of the United States. The California Labor Code, the Federal Immigration Laws, the Federal Labor Department Regulations—these are laws which are supposed to protect you. They must be enforced. From now on.

So I come here today to honor a great man, Cesar Chavez. I come there today to honor you for the long and patient commitment you have made to this great struggle for justice. And I come here to say that we will fight together to achieve for you the aspirations of every American—decent wages, decent housing, decent schooling, a chance for yourselves and your children. You stand for justice and I am proud to stand with you.

Viva La Causa.

Source: "Robert F. Kennedy Statement on Cesar Chavez, March 10, 1968." Robert F. Kennedy Papers, Senate Papers, Speeches and Press Releases, 03/01/1968–03/10/1968. National Archives and Records Administration. http://research.archives.gov/description/194027.

Cesar Chavez's "Letter from Delano," 1969

When E. L. Barr Jr., president of the California Grape and Tree Fruit League, an organization fiercely opposed to the UFW, accused Cesar Chavez and his union members of resorting to violence in the grape boycott, the charge struck at the heart of the union's leader beliefs, everything for which Chavez had stood in his social movement and labor organizing—a nonviolent campaign based on the principles of Mohandas Gandhi and those demonstrated by Martin Luther King Jr. in his struggle in the black civil rights movement. In some instances, especially involving his cousin Manuel Chavez, there had been reported physical assaults by union members in resisting the importation of scab labor from Mexico to break up strikes. But the incidents were few compared to the incessant violent tactics used against members by goon squads hired by growers. Chavez responded with an open letter. Much like Martin Luther King's "Letter from Birmingham Jail" in March 1963, Chavez's "Letter from Delano" in 1969 represented a signal statement of the purposes and tactics of nonviolence and social change.

By Cesar Chavez
Good Friday 1969
E.L. Barr, Jr., President
California Grape and Tree Fruit League
717 Market St., San Francisco, California

Dear Mr. Barr:

I am sad to hear about your accusations in the press that our union movement and table grape boycott have been successful because we have used violence and terror tactics. If what you say is true, I have been a failure and should withdraw from the struggle; but you are left with the awesome moral responsibility, before God and man, to come forward with whatever information you have so that corrective action can begin at once. If for any reason you fail to come forth to substantiate your charges, then you must be held responsible for committing violence against us, albeit violence of the tongue. I am convinced that you as a human being did not mean what you said but rather acted hastily under pressure from the public relations firm that has been hired to try to counteract the tremendous moral force of our movement. How many times we ourselves have felt the need to lash out in anger and bitterness.

Today on Good Friday 1969 we remember the life and the sacrifice of Martin Luther King, Jr., who gave himself totally to the nonviolent struggle for peace and justice. In his "Letter from Birmingham Jail" Dr. King describes better than I could our hopes for the strike and boycott: "Injustice must be exposed, with all the tensions its exposure creates, to the light of human conscience and the air of national opinion before it can be cured." For our part I admit that we have seized upon every tactic and strategy consistent with the morality of our cause to expose that injustice and thus to heighten the sensitivity of the American conscience so that farm workers will have without bloodshed their own union and the dignity of bargaining with their agribusiness employers. By lying about the nature of our movement, Mr. Barr, you are working against nonviolent social change. Unwittingly perhaps, you may unleash that other force which our union by discipline and deed, censure and education has sought to avoid, that panacea shortcut, that senseless violence which honors no color, class or neighborhood.

You must understand—I must make you understand—that our membership and the hopes and aspirations of the hundreds of thousands of the poor and dispossessed that have been raised on our account are, above all, human beings, no better and no worse than any other cross-section of human society; we are not saints because we are poor, but by the same measure neither are we immoral. We are men and women who have suffered and endured much, and not only because of our abject poverty but because we have been kept poor. The colors of our skins, the languages of our cultural and native origins, the lack of formal education, the exclusion from the democratic process, the numbers of our men slain in recent wars—all these burdens generation after generation have sought to demoralize us, to break our human spirit. But God knows that we are not beasts of burden, agricultural implements, or rented slaves; we are men. And mark this well, Mr. Barr, we are men locked in a death struggle against man's inhumanity to man in the industry that you represent. And this struggle itself gives meaning to our life and ennobles our dying.

As your industry has experienced, our strikers here in Delano and those who represent us throughout the world are well trained for this struggle. They have been under the gun, they have been kicked and beaten and herded by dogs, they have been cursed and ridiculed, they have been stripped and chained and jailed, they have been sprayed with the poisons used in the vineyards; but they have been taught not to lie down and die nor to flee in shame, but to resist with every ounce of human endurance and spirit. To resist not with retaliation in kind but to overcome with love and compassion, with ingenuity and creativity, with hard work and longer hours, with stamina and patient tenacity, with truth and public appeal, with friends and allies, with nobility and discipline, with politics and law, and with prayer and fasting. They were not trained in a month or even a year; after all, this new harvest season will mark our fourth full year of strike and even now we continue to plan and prepare for the years to come. Time accomplishes for the poor what money does for the rich.

This is not to pretend that we have everywhere been successful enough or that we have not made mistakes. And while we do not belittle or underestimate our adversaries—for they are the rich and the powerful and they possess the land—we are not afraid nor do we cringe from the confrontation. We welcome it! We have planned for it! We know that our cause is just, that history is a story of social revolution, and that the poor shall inherit the land.

Once again, I appeal to you as the representative of your industry and as a man. I ask you to recognize and bargain with our union before the economic pressure of the boycott and strike takes an irrevocable toll; but if not, I ask you to at least sit down with us to discuss the safeguards necessary to keep our historical struggle free of violence. I make this appeal because as one of the leaders of our nonviolent movement, I know and accept my responsibility for preventing, if possible, the destruction of human life and property. For these reasons, and knowing of Gandhi's admonition that fasting is the last resort in place of the sword, during a most critical time in our movement last February 1968 I undertook a 25-day fast. I repeat to you the principle enunciated to the membership at the start of the fast: if to build our union required the deliberate taking of life, either the life of a grower or his child, or the life of a farm worker or his child, then I choose not to see the union built.

Mr. Barr, let me be painfully honest with you. You must understand these things. We advocate militant nonviolence as our means for social revolution and to achieve justice for our people, but we are not blind or deaf to the desperate and moody winds of human frustration, impatience and rage that blow among us. Gandhi himself admitted that if his only choice were cowardice or violence, he would choose violence. Men are not angels, and time and tide wait for no man. Precisely because of these powerful human emotions, we have tried to involve masses of people in their own struggle. Participation and self-determination remain the best experience of freedom, and free men instinctively prefer democratic change and even protect the rights guaranteed to seek it. Only the enslaved in despair have need of violent overthrow.

This letter does not express all that is in my heart, Mr. Barr. But if it says nothing else it says that we do not hate you or rejoice to see your industry destroyed; we hate the agribusiness system that seeks to keep us enslaved, and we shall overcome and change it not by retaliation or bloodshed but by a determined nonviolent struggle carried on by those masses of farm workers who intend to be free and human.

Sincerely yours,
Cesar E. Chavez
United Farm Workers Organizing Committee, A.F.L.-C.I.O.
Delano, CA

Source: "Cesar Chavez, Letter from Delano." TM/© 2012 Cesar Chavez Foundation http://www.chavezfoundation.org. Used by permission.

Statement of Dolores Huerta before Senate Subcommittee on Migratory Labor, July 15, 1969

In the summer of 1969, the U.S. Senate Subcommittee on Migratory Labor, chaired by Senator Walter Mondale (D-MN), examined major issues surrounding migratory workers, their exploitation by agribusiness, and their powerlessness to improve conditions of their employment. From a stream of witnesses, committee members heard testimony that revealed how such workers were deprived of political and economic power, deprived of cultural identity and pride, and denied the rights that most Americans casually took for granted. Mondale and others on the subcommittee later remarked about the power of the testimony they heard, about the unschooled eloquence of men and women who had spent years of grinding work in the fields or who had worked as community organizers trying to help those who had so little. Dolores Huerta, cofounder of the UFW with Cesar Chavez, issued a powerful indictment of the Department of Defense and the federal government, whose continued purchase of grapes acted against the interests of farm worker organizing and protest movements.

Mrs. Huerta. Mr. Chairman, and members of the committee, we are again glad to be here and present our long, sad story of trying to organize the farmworkers.

We have had tremendous difficulties in trying to organize farmworkers. I don't think, first of all, that we have to belabor the reason why farmworkers need a union. The horrible state in which farmworkers find themselves, faced with such extreme poverty and discrimination, has taught us that the only way we can change our situation is by organization of a union.

I don't believe that it can be done any other way. Certainly, we can't depend on Government to do it, nor can we expect them to take the responsibility. On the other hand, our problem is the government's responsibility, I think, when they try to keep the farmworkers from being organized or actually take action that makes it difficult for farmworkers to organize . . .

As you know, UFWOC has undertaken an international boycott of all California-Arizona table grapes in order to gain union recognition for striking farmworkers. We did not take up the burden of the boycott willingly. It is expensive. It is a hardship on the farmworkers' families who have left the small valley towns to travel across the country to boycott grapes.

But, because of the table grape growers' refusal to bargain with their workers, the boycott is our major weapon and I might say a nonviolent weapon, and our last line of defense against the growers who use foreign labor to break our strikes.

It is only through the pressure of the boycott that UFWOC has won contracts with major California wine grape growers. At this point, the major obstacles to our efforts to organize farmworkers are obstacles to our boycott.

Our boycott has been met with well-organized and well-financed opposition by the growers and their sympathizers. Most recently, several major California grape growers joined with other agribusiness interests and members of the John Birch Society to form an employer-dominated "union," the Agricultural Workers Freedom To Work Association (AWFWA), for the sole purpose of destroying UFWOC. AWFWA's activities have been described in a sworn statement to the U.S. Government, which I would like permission to place in the record at the close of my remarks.

In spite of this type of antiunion activity, our boycott of California-Arizona table grapes has been successful. It is being successful for the simple reason that millions of Americans are supporting the grape workers strike by not buying table grapes.

After 6 weeks of the 1969–70 table grape harvest, California table grape shipments to 36 major cities are down 20 percent from last year, according to U.S. Department of Agriculture reports. The price per lug for Thompson seedless grapes is at least $1 less than it was at this time of last year's harvest. And I might add that that has dropped even more since this statement was written.

It is because of the successful boycott that, on Friday, June 13, 1969, 10 major California growers offered to meet with ITFWOC under the auspices of the Federal Mediation Service. UFWOC representatives and ranch committee members met with the growers for 2 weeks. Progress is being made in these negotiations, which are presently recessed over the issue of pesticides.

However, the U.S. Department of Defense table grape purchases have been very detrimental to our effort.

Now that the boycott has brought us so close to a negotiated settlement of this 3-year-old dispute, we learn that the U.S. Department of Defense (DOD) has doubled its purchases of table grapes. We appear to be witnessing an all-out effort by the military to bail out the growers and break our boycott. Let me review the facts behind this imposing Federal obstacle to farmworker organizing . . .

The DOD argues in its fact sheet that "The total Defense Supply Agency purchases of table grapes represent less than 1 percent of U.S. table grape production." Data from the California Co-op and Livestock Reporting Service indicate, however, that "table" grapes may be utilized in three different ways: fresh for table use; crushed for wine; or dried as raisins. I refer to table I that is attached to this statement. Looking at table II, it is clear that DOD purchases of table grapes for fresh use represents nearly 2.5 percent of all U.S. fresh table grape production.

Table grape prices, like those of other fruits and vegetables, are extremely susceptible to minor fluctuations in supply. DOD purchases of some table grapes are probably shoring up the price of all table grapes and, at a critical point in the UFWOC boycott, are permitting many growers to stand firm in their refusal to negotiate with their workers.

It is obvious that the DOD is taking sides with the growers in this dispute. The DOD fact sheet states that "The basic policy of the DOD with regard to awarding defense contracts to contractors involved in labor disputes is to refrain from taking a position on the merits of any labor dispute. This policy is based on the premise that it is essential to DOD procurement need to maintain a sound working relationship with both labor and management." Nevertheless, many unions in the United States are decrying this fantastic increase in DOD table grape purchases. . . .

DOD table grape purchases are a national outrage. The history of our struggle against agribusiness is punctuated by the continued violations of health and safety codes by growers, including many table grape growers. Much of this documentation has already been submitted to the Senate Subcommittee on Migratory Labor. Such violations are so well documented that Superior Judge Irving Perluss, of California, recently ruled that a jobless worker was within his rights when he refused to accept farm labor work offered him through the California Department of Employment on grounds that most of such jobs are in violation of State health and sanitation codes . . .

If the Federal Government and the DOD is not concerned about the welfare of farmworkers, they must be concerned with protecting our servicemen from contamination and disease carried by grapes picked in fields without toilets or washstands.

Recent laboratory tests have found DDT residues on California grapes. Economic poisons have killed and injured farmworkers. Will they also prove dangerous to U.S. military personnel?

Focusing on other forms of crime in the fields, we would finally ask if the DOD buys table grapes from the numerous growers who daily violate State and Federal minimum wage and child labor laws, who employ illegal foreign labor, and who do not deduct social security payments from farmworkers' wages? . . .

[I]it is clear that DOD is buying adulterated food. For instance, one of the growers the Department of Defense lists as their No. 1 customer is the Giumarra Corp. The Giumarra Corp. was convicted of several counts of violation of law in Kern County. The violations were for not having toilets in the field, and working minors without due regard to the law.

What was the sentence when the Giumarra Corp. was guilty of violating these laws? For 23 counts of violations, they were fined $1,150, but this fine was suspended.

Of course, the Government subsidy that they later on received in that year, $274,000, not only paid for the fine, but offset any losses they may have suffered from the boycott.

The same grower, the Giumarra Corp., used DDT, Parathion, and so forth. All of these are known to have bad effects on the workers, and in accumulation, on the consumer that eats the grapes.

The same grower, the Giumarra Corp., which had 32 occupational injuries reported in 1 year, the majority of which were caused by pesticides in its fields.

Jack Pandol, another grower whom the Department of Defense purchases from, reported seven occupational injuries from pesticides. Another had even more. He had 48 injuries in 1967.

Let me add one other thing as long as we are talking about health. The health care of farmworkers is almost nonexistent, and the rate of tuberculosis is 200 percent above the national average. When you consider that many of the people now picking the grapes are being brought in from Mexico, that they are people without any type of legal residence papers, and therefore, have not been processed through the health regulations that usually apply to immigrants coming into this country, you can imagine what the contamination possibilities are, when the people are coming from a country with lower health standards than the United States.

There is one other thing I want to point out. When people pick table grapes, one of the things they are ordered to do is to be careful not to take off any of the "bloom." The bloom is all the dust, and filth on the grapes. If you wipe it off so the grapes are shiny then the grape will rot much faster. For the same reason, grapes are not washed by the picker or packer, and any of those pesticides or other things that may be on the grapes come straight to the consumer, and grapes are also very difficult to wash. Those grapes are picked and packed right in the field; they don't go through any other kind of processing. They are taken off the vines, put in a box, lidded, taken into the cold storage, and shipped to the customers, and that is the way they come directly to the customers.

The Department of Defense increasing purchases of table grapes is nothing short of a national outrage. It is an outrage to the millions of American taxpayers who are supporting the farmworkers' struggle for justice by boycotting table grapes. How can any American believe that the U.S. Government is sincere in its efforts to eradicate poverty when the military uses its immense purchasing power to subvert the farmworkers' nonviolent struggle for a decent, living wage and a better future?

Many farmworkers are members of minority groups. They are Filipino and Mexican and black Americans. These same minority people are on the frontlines of battle in Vietnam. It is a cruel and ironic slap in the face to these men who have left the fields to fulfill their military obligation to find increasing amounts of boycotted grapes in their mess kits. . . .

The people in the union have to take a tremendous amount of harassment, such as the materials of State Senator Hugh Burns' Committee on Un-American Activities in California. The man who made up that committee report was sitting in his home in Three Rivers. He never once went to Delano. Yet, he wrote a report which has been used all over the country in which he tried to redbait the members of the union.

Among other mistruths, he says 3 years of Cesar Chavez' life are missing, and suggests he was getting some kind of subversive training. Those are the 3 years he spent in the U.S. Navy. That should be put in the record.

Gunmen have gone to our offices, taken canceled checks, membership files, and some of these membership files have been used in blacklisting for jobs.

Our insurance has been canceled for our cars and we would like to have the committee investigate this. We would like to have the committee investigate the Aetna Insurance Co. and ask them why it is they canceled our insurance. Our record has been good.

At one point, the Texaco Co. refused to sell gas to our gas station. There are many types of harassment which can be used against an organization. Our telephone lines are tapped. Many times, when we are in an extremely important conversation, you don't complete the call, because something interferes with the wires. This happens all the time....

Source: "Hearings before the Subcommittee on Migratory Labor of the Committee on Labor and Public Welfare, Part 3-A, Migrant and Seasonal Farmworker Powerlessness." U.S. Senate, 91st Congress, 1st Session, July 15, 1969, pp. 551–62. http://www.archive.org/details/migrantseasonalf03unit.

Delano Grape Workers' Boycott Day Proclamation, May 10, 1969

To Cesar Chavez, a boycott represented the ultimate weapon against agribusiness. Convince the public not to purchase grapes or lettuce produced by companies that exploited human labor, and a union could inflict serious economic danger and force concessions. So enamored was Chavez with the tactic that he named one his dogs "Boycott." By May 1969, Chavez's union had achieved much progress through a combination of strike actions and boycotts. Through the years, the union had escalated the boycott activity not only in location but in scope. Enlisting a cadre of supporters across the country and in some foreign countries, the union had made such an impact that growers began to suffer serious financial reverses. The union declared May 10, 1969, International Boycott Day. Over 25,000 consumers demonstrated against Safeway Stores, a chain that had been hostile to the union. The union issued a proclamation.

We, the striking grape workers of California, join on this International Boycott Day with the consumers across the continent in planning the steps that lie ahead on the road to our liberation. As we plan, we recall the footsteps that brought us to this day and the events of this day. The historic road of our pilgrimmage to Sacramento later branched out, spreading like the unpruned vines in struck fields, until it led us to willing exile in cities across this land. There, far from the earth we tilled for generations, we have cultivated the strange soil of public understanding, sowing the seed of our truth and our cause in the minds and hearts of men.

We have been farm workers for hundreds of years and pioneers for seven. Mexicans, Filipinos, Africans and others, our ancestors were among those who founded this land and tamed its natural wilderness. But we are still pilgrims on this land, and we are pioneers who blaze a trail out of the wilderness of hunger and deprivation that we have suffered even as our ancestors did. We are conscious today of the significance of our present quest. If this road we chart leads to the rights and reforms we demand, if it leads to just wages, humane working conditions, protection from the misuse of pesticides, and to the fundamental right of collective bargaining, if it changes the social order that relegates us to the bottom reaches of society, then in our wake will follow thousands of American farm workers. Our example will make them free. But if our road does not bring us to victory and social change, it will not be because our direction is mistaken or our resolve too weak, but only because our bodies are mortal and our journey hard. For we are in the midst of a great social movement, and we will not stop struggling 'til we die, or win!

We have been farm workers for hundreds of years and strikers for four. It was four years ago that we threw down our plowshares and pruning hooks. These Biblical symbols of peace and tranquility to us represent too many lifetimes of unprotesting submission to a degrading social system that allows us no dignity, no comfort, no peace. We mean to have our peace, and to win it without violence, for it is violence we would overcome—the subtle spiritual and mental violence of oppression, the violence subhuman toil does to the human body. So we went and stood tall outside the vineyards where we had stooped for years. But the tailors of national labor legislation had left us naked. Thus exposed, our picket lines were crippled by injunctions and harrassed by growers; our strike was broken by imported scabs; our overtures to our employers were ignored. Yet we knew the day must come when they would talk to us, *as equals*.

We have been farm workers for hundreds of years and boycotters for two. We did not choose the grape boycott, but we *had* chosen to leave our peonage, poverty and despair behind. Though our first bid for freedom, the strike, was weakened, we would not turn back. The boycott was the only way forward the growers left to us. We called upon our fellow men and were answered by consumers who said—as all men of conscience must—that they would no longer allow their tables to be subsidized by our sweat and our sorrow: They shunned the grapes, fruit of our affliction.

We marched alone at the beginning, but today we count men of all creeds, nationalities, and occupations in our number. Between us and the justice we seek now stand the large and powerful grocers who, in continuing to buy table grapes, betray the boycott their own customers have built. These stores treat their patrons' demands to remove the grapes the same way the growers treat our demands for union recognition—by ignoring them. The consumers who rally behind our cause are responding as we do to such treatment—with a boycott! They pledge to withhold their patronage from stores that handle grapes during the boycott, just as we withhold our labor from the growers until our dispute is resolved.

Grapes must remain an unenjoyed luxury for all as long as the barest human needs and basic human rights are still luxuries for farm workers. The grapes grow sweet and heavy on the vines, but they will have to wait while we reach out first for our freedom. The time is ripe for our liberation.

Source: U.S. Congress. *Congressional Record, Proceedings and Debates of the 91st Congress, First Session.* May 12, 1969.

Testimony of Cesar Chavez and Other Farm Worker Leaders at a Public Hearing before Members of Congress, October 1, 1969

In October 1969, Chavez and several of his UFWOC colleagues had the opportunity to address a public hearing before the U.S. House of Representatives Education and Labor Committee, chaired by Representative James O'Hara (D-MI). Joining Chavez on behalf of the union were vice president Andy Imutan, UFWOC organizer Mack Lyons, and UFWOC attorney Jerry Cohen. The hearing gave the union the chance to discuss a number of perplexing issues standing in the way of farm worker organization that directly involved the federal government, including the dangers of pesticides, the purchase of grapes by the government during the national boycott, and the importation by growers of illegal workers from Mexico to act as scab labor during strikes. Although sincerely sympathetic to the plight of Mexicans who crossed the border seeking work, he knew that their exploitation by growers had a deleterious effect on his hopes of creating a successful union of farm workers. Union members often picketed the offices of the Immigration and Naturalization Service demanding that the U.S. government do more to stem the tide of border crossings.

CONGRESSMAN JAMES G. O'HARA, PRESIDING:

It is a rare occasion when a Member of Congress has the opportunity to introduce a public figure who has made a major contribution to the events of our times, and about whom there swirls no controversy. It is a rare event indeed when a man who has changed the face of his era is without enemies.

This is not such an occasion. Today we are host to a great American, a great labor leader, a truly good and gentle man—but a man who is as controversial as any figure to blaze across our skies in decades.

He has made bitter enemies, and some of us love him for the enemies he has made. He has made devoted friends and some of us are honored to be among those friends. One type of person is very rare around our guest today. There are very few neutrals where Cesar Chavez is concerned.

Cesar Chavez has given us all a profound challenge. To those of us who support his cause, he presents the challenge of rising to the level of leadership and sacrifice he has demonstrated in pursuing that cause.

To those who oppose it, he presents the challenge of demonstrating how the current system under which farm workers are employed can be made consistent with our society's claim to serve freedom and justice and equality.

This is not, I must emphasize, a hearing of any committee of the House. This is a public meeting to which a number of Members of the House have been invited because they share an interest in legislation dealing with the campesino and the harsh world in which he lives so poorly, works so hard, and dies so young.

This group cannot make decisions about legislation. It can serve as a forum in which these grave issues can be discussed and from which the members in attendance can go away with their individual commitments strengthened, or weakened or unchanged, but at least better informed.

STATEMENT OF CESAR ESTRADA CHAVEZ, DIRECTOR, UFWOC, AFL-CIO

MR. CHAVEZ: Thank you very much Congressman O'Hara. I want to thank you and the other Congressmen present for being here this morning to hear a report on the struggles of workers to organize farm workers.

With me this morning are three other people working in the Union—Jerry Cohen, to my right, who is the Legal Counsel, to my immediate left, Mack Lyon, an organizer for the Union, and Mr. Imutan, a Filipino-American who is a Vice President of the Union.

If we do nothing else today, we would like to make it very clear that in rural America today, when farm workers declare a strike, it is not only a strike that happens, but it is a whole revolution in that community. It becomes a civil liberties issue, it becomes a race issue, and it becomes a desperate struggle just to keep the movement going against such tremendous odds.

We have experienced things that we never dreamed we would be confronted with when we began the strike. These small communities are so well knit and the grower influence is so predominant that when we struck in Delano, we not only had the growers against us, but we had the other public bodies like the city council, the board of supervisors, the high school and elementary school districts, passing resolutions and propaganda against the strike and against the union. There was no voice whatsoever from the other side wanting to mediate or offering their services or their influence to find a solution to the problem. The community wanted to destroy us as soon as possible.

We want you to know that in America today, a vast majority of farm workers are poor, and the vast majority are from minority groups. We are brown and black. Also it is good to understand that a lot of the work force are recent immigrants, not only from Mexico, but from Asia, from Portugal, from Arabia, from other parts of the world where people are constantly being brought into work in agriculture. We also want you to know that the employers have used—and I should say very well—the tactic of setting one racial group against the other. This has been a long-standing trick of theirs to break the unions.

Even today in negotiations we find that it takes a lot of time to get the employers to understand that the people should live together and that there should be no separation of workers in camps by racial groups. Today the employers that we're striking have a Filipino Camp, a Mexican Camp, a Negro Camp, and an Arab Camp in some cases.

We want you to know how hard it is for us to get justice because of the concentration of power in the hands of employers. The local authorities come into play immediately to try to destroy the efforts of organizing. At the beginning of the strike, there were mass arrests by the Delano Police Department and by the County Sheriff's Department. We found that the best counteraction was to let the public know what was happening in the valley.

We see the indifference of the local courts. We see how employers can come in and can get injunctions at will, and we see how the injunctions break our strikes. We have some very sad memories of these experiences.

We see that bringing the employers to court when they have broken the law is almost impossible.

The indifference of the federal agencies in regard to enforcement of those few regulations that apply to farm workers is also very bad. We have cases witch the Federal Food and Drug Administration going back two years. The celebrated case of the label switching is an example. We were boycotting the Giumarra Company and Giumarra was able to use over 100 different labels from other employers for his grapes. We had the proof in several cities. We could not get the FDA to take any actions against the growers for lying to the public about the source of their products.

As to the pesticides and their hazard to the workers, we can't do anything with the FDA. Instead of trying to intervene and to do something about the outrageous problem which has become a literal "walking death" for farm workers, the FDA is trying to hide it.

We have had for the last four years a most difficult problem with the Justice Department. A year ago we assigned many of our organizers to do nothing but to check on the law violaters coming from Mexico to break our strikes. We gave the Immigration and Naturalization Services and the Border Patrol stacks and stacks of information. They did not pull workers out of struck fields. Today there are thousands of workers being imported in the strike scene. In fact, I would say the green carders and illegal entries make up ninety percent of the work force at the struck ranches. This is why we are forced to boycott: We have had no enforcement by the Border Patrol. We have been told that it is impossible, there are too many violaters, they do not have enough personnel.

I would like to remind the Congressmen present that in the last week and a half we have seen how effective the Border Patrol can be when they want to stop marijuana from being imported into the country. It seems to me it would be a lot less difficult to stop human beings coming across than to stop the weed coming across. It can be done.

We have a case of some of the biggest employers working together personally, Using their money, their offices, their duplicating equipment, meeting with other people, and setting up a company union, well staffed, well financed. Information discovered by an investigation by the Department of Labor, plus signed statements from two of the officers of the Agricultural Workers Freedom to Work Association prove what the growers were doing. Almost a year has passed since these facts were uncovered and the law-breaking phony union has not been brought to court. I might add here that there were four or five different attempts to establish company unions in the past. We spent a good part of our time trying to beat those attempts. One of them was called "Mothers Against Chavez."

We are subject to disclosure of all our income in the labor reports of the Landrum-Griffin law, and we will do this gladly. The sources of money, when we get the money, is public information. But we don't know where the employers are getting their outside money and we would very much like to know that. We don't know where they are getting $1 million to pay Whitaker and Baxter to set up the so-called Consumer Rights Committee here in Washington to propagandize against our strike and our boycott. We don't know where they are getting the money they are paying to the J. Walter Thompson firm, plus other huge sums of money that are being spent. I think it would be very interesting if we could get those figures.

We have a problem with the U.S. Public Health Service that is coming to be of great concern to a lot of people. In Delano we have the problem of nitrates in the water. This is a cause of concern to some of the experts. Because of large amounts of fertilizers being put in the grape fields, the nitrates find their way into the water table. As a consequence the city water in Delano is heavily polluted with nitrates. The Federal Department of Public Health established a maximum of 45 parts per million as a tolerance. The California Department of Public Health established the same figure.

Just recently, because of investigations, some suits were developing against the city of Delano because of the water. The city council sent out a mailer to all of the water users cautioning them not to use the water for babies under a year old. Then the California Department of Public Health just recently raised the nitrates tolerance to ninety parts per million, double the federal tolerance. The Federals took no action. It is very difficult for us to understand that.

The point we are trying to make here is that the federal agency I and the state agency are almost impossible to deal with. We cannot look to them for any real support and any real help. We don't expect them to take our side, but they ought to carry out the law.

There are other pressures that develop against farm workers isolated in those vast valleys. The Texaco Company locally refused to sell us gas for a couple of days for our picket line cars. We had an arrangement with them, but pressure from the employers forced them not to sell us gas. It was not until we were able to call Washington and New York and other places to try and develop concern that they were able to give us gas. The Aetna Insurance Company cancelled our car insurance. We had to go to the public assigned risk where we paid more money. It was not because we had a bad record. They just did not give us a reason but we were cancelled.

Then of course, we have trouble with the Defense Department, which think is the biggest reason why the growers broke off the negotiations in late June and early July, and why I think that although our boycott is very effective in most of the areas in the country, still we were not able to get the growers to negotiate with us. The Defense Department has increased the shipments of grapes in the last year or so to Vietnam by about 350 per cent. South Vietnam ranked 27th in the importation of grapes. Today South Vietnam is number 3 in importation. Canada is number 1, Venezuela 2, and little Vietnam is now rated the third largest importer of table grapes.

We have a report that some grapes were found in the Saigon black market selling for $42 a box. That is where the grapes are going.

Because of the pressure of the boycott and the strikes we were able to get 12 growers to negotiate with us. We negotiated for about three weeks. It was a difficult negotiation. We said we should be very careful not to permit the negotiations to develop into a name-calling contest. The first day of negotiations they took advantage of my not being present to unload everything that they had on their chests. Right from the beginning, they set an ultimatum. It seemed that every time we came to an issue they would say "either it is this way or we break off negotiations." It became apparent to us that they did not want to negotiate but they had accomplished what they wanted to, and that was that. They hurt the boycott immensely because people throughout the country began to think these were good faith negotiations, and that therefore the strike was about over.

I have no doubt that one or two men of those 12 wanted to negotiate. I think they wanted to negotiate. But as for the rest, they could not prove to us by their actions that they were sincere.

So at the very end it became very apparent they were not going to do anything about wages. We had a wage demand of $2 an hour minimum, plus 25 cents a box during the harvest time, and $2 minimum during the off season. We had what we considered to be a very important health and safety clause in the contract. That is what we need to deal effectively with the whole question of pesticide poisoning for workers. When the negotiations broke off, we understood that the two main points that were in conflict, and could not be resolved, were wages and health and safety. The negotiations broke off on the 3rd of July. Almost two weeks ago I called on the Federal Mediation Service, the agency that brought us together the first time. I told them to relay to the employers the desire on the part of the union to re-open negotiations and to tell them specifically that we were willing to reconsider the wage demand that we had made, but that in all good faith, we could not possibly give in on the whole question of pesticide poisoning of workers. It is almost two weeks and we have not heard from them.

There has been a lot said about the union not representing the workers—that we in fact do not represent the workers, but are just a group of outside agitators with radical ideas. We have had 8 union representation elections. We have won every single election that we have had, and some had to be fought and won at a great disadvantage to our union. Some were won with something like 98 per cent for the union. There is no question in my mind that the workers want a union. They know that the union is the best way out of their condition. But the same employers who claim that we don't represent the workers have steadfastly, since the beginning of the strike, refused to give us elections.

Since we are not covered by the National Labor Relations Act and there is no machinery for elections, the union and employers have to agree to set up some kind of procedure for the election. On eight different occasions we have been able to negotiate the procedure and have the election. Then we win and go into negotiations. The grape growers, the fresh grape growers, have been unwilling to do that.

We say that we are able to prove to them that the whole question of our representing the workers is not in issue. But the 12 growers who agreed to negotiate with us raised the issue. So we gave the Federal Mediation Service cards signed by ninety per cent of the strike-breakers working for the growers at that time. The card said "we support the union."

So the question of whether we represent the workers or not is a phony issue. But the real issue is that we don't think that the workers are going to quit trying to get a union. We are sure of this because not only of what they have done in the four years, but because it is the history of the working man in America.

The real question is "How is it going to be accomplished?" Are the workers, the farm workers, going to be suppressed and forced to go "underground"? Or are the farm workers going to be able to walk out of their poverty and be counted and accepted as true men by their employers? That is a real question, how is it going to be done? That fact that it is going to be done is accepted by all of us who are in the struggle.

I want to have Brother Imutan, who is a Filipino-American, tell you a little bit about the history of the Filipino worker.

Perhaps some of you may not know that the Filipino workers have been subjected to things that even the black Americans have not been subjected to in America. There is very little known about them. But it is a fact that they have been mistreated considerably. I want Brother Imutan to tell you about that.

STATEMENT OF MR. ANDY IMUTAN, VICE PRESIDENT, UFWOC

MR. IMUTAN: When the Delano strike began, September 8, 1965, the Filipino workers in the different camps in Delano walked out from the fields that they were working in, and those that were living in the camps decided to stay in the camps.

The grower-owners of those different camps warned our workers that they would do something to make us either work or not stay in those camps. Although they were told that, the workers thought that the only way probably that they could solve their problems was to stick it out with the rest of the workers.

And what happened was that the light and the water were cut off so that the workers could not cook their food. And when they cooked outside, the security guards of the growers kicked their food to the ground. And when it became time to eat, the guards came back and threw the workers' belongings to the ground and padlocked their rooms.

Because of that the workers were forced to stay in their cars. As the strike went on, a lot of them were staying in the cars and some of them were sleeping in the Filipino Hall and some of them were staying with their friends.

The growers claim that they are paying so much, but the people that are staying in the camps, although they are supposed to have camps housing accommodations free, actually it is not so. Those that are staying in the camps are receiving ten cents less per hour than those that are not living in the camps.

Think about life in the camps. There are no health examinations or anything of that sort. You would see camps during the peak of harvest crowded with people who are side by side. You will see the tubercular worker side by side with the healthy one.

It is not a well known fact to a lot of people that the Filipino workers who were recruited and encouraged to come to this country were deprived of family life. For several decades they were not allowed by the immigration laws to bring in their wives, or women from the Philippines for marriage. Nor were they allowed by the state laws in the West to marry white women. This was done so we would live in the camps and do whatever we were told.

There is a whole race of workers here that 35 years ago were brought here to work, that had no generation after them. Since the war some young people have come. I would say that 85 per cent of the Filipino farm workers are bachelors living in the camps. If the intent of the growers then was to wipe out the workers forever, I think they have succeeded in that.

There is a great concern to the Filipino communities in California: What will happen to Filipinos who are now old and are only receiving $40 from Social Security? Mules and horses are well provided for when they are no longer able to work. For human beings in the farm areas there is no such thing. What is going to happen?

Because of the lack of coverage under the National Labor Relations Act, the farm workers were not able to form a union like other workers in other industries. As you know, in other industries provisions for retirement and other fringe benefits have been provided for to these workers through the unions that have represented them.

MR. CHAVEZ: We have next Mr. Mack Lyons, who came out of the DiGiorgio-Arvin farm, one of the biggest farms in the country. He became the ranch committee chairman. He would like to tell you about the experience that will clearly reflect to you that whether we represent the workers or not has no meaning to the employers.

STATEMENT OF MR. MACK LYONS, ORGANIZER

MR. LYONS: Through the strike and the boycott against DiGiorgio about three years ago, we gained the right to have an election at this particular ranch. We gave up the boycott for an election. All we had was the right to have the election. If we lost, we did not have anything. If we won, well, then we would go on to negotiate a contract. After we won the election we had no power for the negotiations. The negotiations lasted for weeks and weeks because we had no power left, since we had to call off the strike and the boycott against this particular place. The majority of the contract went to arbitration.

From the arbitrator we did not get everything that we wanted. One of the main things we wanted was a "successor clause." He did not give us that. A successor clause means that if the ranch is sold, the labor contract obligates the buyer. But what we got out of the arbitrator, we were happy with and we accepted it, and we made it work, and everybody worked together.

We eliminated a lot of the problems that we had before the contract. Then the problems started again when the DiGiorgio man told us he sold his ranch to S.A. Camp, another one of the growers in that county.

As soon as he bought the ranch, this grower laid off all the workers that were working there. He fired all of the people that were active members of the union, and all the stewards, all of the people that he knew had fought for the union, that spoke out for the union.

The new owner started the same practices that had been used before. He separated people by race and by favorites and all of the rights that we had under the contract, that we had negotiated for, and that we had gotten out of arbitration, were completely discarded. Because we did not get a successor clause, we were right back where we started. Right now we are on strike again. Some of us are working on the boycott.

The contract lasted for two years and in those two years, people really saw a change in their daily lives. The workers were starting to have a little hope. But when the ranch was sold we saw that we really did not have anything. Because of the lack of concern by the laws, and the arbitrators that have power to give you what they think you should have and some of the things that you need they don't give you, we found ourselves back where we started, in the same boat as the people who had been on strike for four years trying to gain something that we had had. What makes it worse is that we had a contract. Now we don't have anything. We had experienced what the union really stands for, what the union is trying to get for all of the farm workers, but the company sold all of our rights. These are the kind of problems we are having right now because of the lack of power, and organization, and law.

STATEMENT OF MR. JEROME COHEN, ATTORNEY FOR THE UNITED FARM WORKERS ORGANIZING COMMITTEE

MR. COHEN: I would just give you one example of the caliber of justice we get in the Kern County Superior Court. Last August 22nd I went to the Kern County Agricultural Commissioner, who keeps records of commercial pesticide applicators, the accounts of poisons that they use and when they use them. I went to the Commissioner to see these reports. He told me to come back the next day. Two hours after I left the office, the Kern County Superior Court issued an injunction forbidding me to see the records. We have been engaged in a battle for over a year to see those records.

We are concerned about the issue of health and safety of farm workers. A recent survey in Tulare County shows that about eighty per cent of the workers are suffering from various symptoms of organic phosphate and other pesticide poisoning. The state of California has some of these statistics but they have decided that they are going to study them for five years. We think the problem is right now.

It is hard for us to understand how the administration could have an Occupational Health and Safety Bill that exempts farm workers, especially in light of the fact that in the state of California agriculture has the highest occupational disease rate, three times higher than the next industry there.

In the battle for the pesticides records, we presented an extensive hearing in January. In the course of that hearing it became apparent that the Judge was weighing the profits that the agricultural industry makes against the health of farm workers, and he continued the injunction. As it stands today, we still can't see the records.

Source: "Transcript of Public /hearing with Cesar Chavez, Director United Farm Workers Organizing Committee, AFL-CIO and Members of His Staff Held by Members of the U.S. House of Representatives in the Hearing Room of the Education and Labor Committee, October 1, 1969." Courtesy of the Farmworker Movement Documentation Project.

Statement by Cesar Chavez at the End of His 24-Day Fast for Justice, Phoenix, Arizona, June 4, 1972

In 1972, the Republican-dominated legislature of the state of Arizona, a major lettuce-producing state, passed an extraordinarily repressive farm labor bill that sought to destroy the right of farm workers to unionize. Worried that the legislation could become a model for other states determined to fight collective-bargaining rights of farm workers, Cesar Chavez traveled to Arizona to lead a vigorous challenge to the law. Governor Jack Williams contemptuously dismissed petitions and letters protesting the law and even refused to meet with union leaders. As part of the protest, Chavez began a so-called Fast for Justice in late May. It was during this campaign that union members began a massive voter-registration drive and collected thousands of signatures on petitions to recall the governor. Although the state attorney general blocked a recall election, the union had changed the political dynamics of the state. In four months over 100,000 individuals sympathetic to the union cause had registered to vote. The new voters paved the way in succeeding elections for Mexican Americans and Native Americans to win several seats in the state legislature and, in 1974, to elect the first Mexican American governor of the state. At the end of his fast, Chavez addressed his supporters.

I want to thank you for coming today. Some of you have been to the Santa Rita Center many times. Some have made beautiful offerings at the Mass. I have received letters and telegrams and lettuce boycott pledges from all over the world. All of these expressions of your love and your support for the farm workers' struggle have strengthened my spirits and I am grateful. I want especially to honor the farm workers who have risked so much to go on strike for their rights. Your sacrifices will not be in vain! I am weak in my body but I feel very strong in my spirit. I am happy to end the Fast because it is not an easy thing. But it is also not easy for my family and for many of you who have worried and worked and sacrificed.

The Fast was meant as a call to sacrifice for justice and a reminder of how much suffering there is among farm workers. In fact, what is a few days without food in comparison to the daily pain of our brothers and sisters who do backbreaking work in the fields under inhumane conditions and without hope of ever breaking their cycle of poverty and misery. What a terrible irony it is that the very people who harvest the food we eat do not have enough food for their own children. It is possible to become discouraged about the injustice we see everywhere. But God did not promise us that the world would be humane and just. He gives us the gift of life and allows us to choose the way we will use our limited time on this earth. It is an awesome opportunity. We should be thankful for the life we have been given, thankful for the opportunity to do something about the suffering of our fellow man. We *can choose* to use our lives for others to bring about a better and more just world for our children. People who make that choice will know hardship and sacrifice. But if you give yourself totally to the non-violent struggle for peace and justice, you also find that people will give you their hearts and you will never go hungry and never be alone. And in giving of yourself you will discover a whole new life full of meaning and love.

Nan Freeman and Sal Santos have given their lives for our movement this past year. They were very young. It hurt us to lose them and it still hurts us. But the greatest tragedy is not to live and die, as we all must. The greatest tragedy is for a person to live and die without knowing the satisfaction of giving life for others. The greatest tragedy is to be born but not to live for fear of losing a little security or because we are afraid of loving and giving ourselves to other people.

Our opponents in the agricultural industry are very powerful and farm workers are still weak in money and influence. But we have another kind of power that comes from the justice of our cause. So long as we are willing to sacrifice for that cause, so long as we persist in non-violence and work to spread the message of our struggle, then millions of people around the world will respond from their hearts, will support our efforts . . . and in the end we will overcome. It can be done. We know it can be done. God give us the strength and patience to do it without bitterness so that we can win both our friends and opponents to the cause of justice.

Source: "Statement by Cesar Chavez at the End of His 24-Day Fast for Justice." 1972. http://chavez.cde.ca.gov/ModelCurriculum/teachers/Lessons/resources/documents/EXR1_Cesar_E_Chavez_Statements_on_Fasts.pdf. TM/© 2012 Cesar Chavez Foundation. http://www.chavezfoundation.org. Used by permission.

Cesar Chavez Speech at Commonwealth Club, San Francisco, November 9, 1984

On November 9, 1984, Chavez delivered the most celebrated prepared speech of his career. Before the prestigious public speaking forum of the Commonwealth Club of San Francisco, his address ranged over a host of social, moral, and political issues including nonviolent protest, cultural prejudice and discrimination, worker health, and labor organizing and tactical strategies. Delivered at a time of Republican intransigence in enforcing labor laws and in the midst of a renewed grape boycott, the Commonwealth Club speech has achieved ranking as a major piece of political and social oratory.

. . . Twenty-one years ago, this last September, on a lonely stretch of railroad track paralleling U.S. Highway 101 near Salinas, 32 Bracero farm workers lost their lives in a tragic accident. The Braceros had been imported from Mexico to work on California farms. They died when their bus, which was converted from a flatbed truck, drove in front of a freight train. Conversion of the bus had not been approved by any government agency. The driver had tunnel vision. Most of the bodies laid unidentified for days. No one, including the grower who employed the workers, even knew their names. Today, thousands of farm workers live under savage conditions, beneath trees and amid garbage and human excrement near tomato fields in San Diego County; tomato fields, which use the most modern farm technology. Vicious rats gnaw at them as they sleep. They walk miles to buy food at inflated prices and they carry in water from irrigation ditches.

Child labor is still common in many farm areas. As much as 30 percent of Northern California's garlic harvesters are underaged children. Kids as young as six years old have voted in states, conducted union elections, since they qualified as workers. Some 800,000 underaged children work with their families harvesting crops across America. Babies born to migrant workers suffer 25 percent higher infant mortality rates than the rest of the population. Malnutrition among migrant workers' children is ten times higher than the national rate. Farm workers' average life expectancy is still 49 years, compared to 73 years for the average American. All my life, I have been driven by one dream, one goal, one vision: to overthrow a farm labor system in this nation that treats farm workers as if they were not important human beings. Farm workers are not agricultural implements; they are not beasts of burden to be used and discarded. That dream was born in my youth, it was nurtured in my early days of organizing. It has flourished. It has been attacked.

I'm not very different from anyone else who has ever tried to accomplish something with his life. My motivation comes from my personal life, from watching what my mother and father went through when I was growing up, from what we experienced as migrant workers in California. That dream, that vision grew from my own experience with racism, with hope, with a desire to be treated fairly, and to see my people treated as human beings and not as chattel. It grew from anger and rage, emotions I felt 40 years ago when people of my color were denied the right to see a movie or eat at a restaurant in many parts of California. It grew from the frustration and humiliation I felt as a boy who couldn't understand how the growers could abuse and exploit farm workers when there were so many of us and so few of them. Later in the 50s, I experienced a different kind of exploitation. In San Jose, in Los Angeles and in other urban communities, we, the Mexican-American people, were dominated by a majority that was Anglo. I began to realize what other minority people had discovered; that the only answer, the only hope was in organizing. More of us had to become citizens, we had to register to vote, and people like me had to develop the skills it would take to organize, to educate, to help empower the Chicano people.

I spent many years before we founded the union learning how to work with people. We experienced some successes in voter registration, in politics, in battling racial discrimination. Successes in an era where Black Americans were just beginning to assert their civil rights and when political awareness among Hispanics was almost non-existent. But deep in my heart, I knew I could never be happy unless I tried organizing the farm workers. I didn't know if I would succeed, but I had to try. All Hispanics, urban and rural, young and old, are connected to the farm workers' experience. We had all lived through the fields, or our parents had. We shared that common humiliation. How could we progress as a people even if we lived in the cities, while the farm workers, men and women of our color, were condemned to a life without pride? How could we progress as a people while the farm workers, who symbolized our history in this land, were denied self-respect? How could our people believe that their children could become lawyers and doctors and judges and business people while this shame, this injustice, was permitted to continue?

Those who attack our union often say it's not really a union. It's something else, a social movement, a civil rights movement, it's something dangerous. They're half right. The United Farm Workers is first and foremost a union, a union like any other, a union that either produces for its members on the bread-and-butter issues or doesn't survive. But the UFW has always been something more than a union, although it's never been dangerous, if you believe in the Bill of Rights. The UFW was the beginning. We attacked that historical source of shame and infamy that our people in this country lived with. We attacked that injustice, not by complaining, not by seeking handouts, not by becoming soldiers in the war on poverty; we organized.

Farm workers acknowledge we had allowed ourselves to become victims in a democratic society, a society where majority rules and collective bargaining are supposed to be more than academic theories and political rhetoric. And by addressing this historical problem, we created confidence and pride and hope in an entire people's ability to create the future. The UFW survival, its existence— were not in doubt in my mind when the time began to come. After the union became visible, when Chicanos started entering college in greater numbers, when Hispanics began running for public office in greater numbers, when our people started asserting their rights on a broad range of issues and in many communities across this land. The union survival, its very existence, sent out a signal to all Hispanics that we were fighting for our dignity. That we were challenging and overcoming injustice, that we were empowering the least educated among us, the poorest among us. The message was clear. If it could happen in the fields, it could happen anywhere: in the cities, in the courts, in the city councils, in the state legislatures. I didn't really appreciate it at the time, but the coming of our union signaled the start of great changes among Hispanics that are only now beginning to be seen.

I've traveled through every part of this nation. I have met and spoken with thousands of Hispanics from every walk of life, from every social and economic class. And one thing I hear most often from Hispanics, regardless of age or position, and from many non-Hispanics as well, is that the farm workers gave them the hope that they could succeed and the inspiration to work for change.

From time to time, you will hear our opponents declare that the union is weak, that the union has no support, that the union has not grown fast enough. Our obituary has been written many times. How ironic it is that the same forces that argue so passionately that the union is not influential are the same forces that continue to fight us so hard.

The union's power in agriculture has nothing to do with the number of farm workers on the union contract. It has nothing to do with the farm workers' ability to contribute to democratic politicians. It doesn't even have much to do with our ability to conduct successful boycotts. The very fact of our existence forces an entire industry, unionized and non-unionized, to spend millions of dollars year after year on increased wages, on improved working conditions and on benefits for workers. If we were so weak and unsuccessful, why do the growers continue to fight us with such passion? Because as long as we continue to exist, farm workers will benefit from our existence, even if they don't work under union contract. It doesn't really matter whether we have 100,000 or 500,000 members. In truth, hundreds of thousands of farm workers in California and in other states are better off today because of our work. And Hispanics across California and the nation who don't work in agriculture are better off today because of what the farm workers taught people about organization, about pride and strength, about seizing control over their own lives.

Tens of thousands of children and grandchildren of farm workers and the children and grandchildren of poor Hispanics are moving out of the fields and out of the barrio and into the professions and into business and into politics, and that movement cannot be reversed. Our union will forever exist as an empowering force among Chicanos in the Southwest. That means our power and our influence will grow and not diminish. Two major trends give us hope and encouragement. First, our union has returned to a tried and tested weapon in the farm workers non-violent arsenal: the boycott. After the Agricultural Labor Relations Act became law in California in 1975, we dismantled our boycott to work with the law. During the early and mid '70s millions of Americans supported our boycott. After 1975, we redirected our efforts from the boycott to organizing and winning elections under the law. That law helped farm workers make progress in overcoming poverty and injustice.

At companies where farm workers are protected by union contracts, we have made progress in overcoming child labor, in overcoming miserable wages and working conditions, in overcoming sexual harassment of women workers, in overcoming discrimination in employment, in overcoming dangerous pesticides, which poison our people and poison the food we all eat. Where we have organized these injustices soon passed in history, but under Republican Governor George Deukmejian, the law that guarantees our right to organize no longer protects farm workers; it doesn't work anymore.

In 1982, corporate growers gave Deukmejian $1 million to run for governor of California. Since he took office, Deukmejian has paid back his debt to the growers with the blood and sweat of California farm workers. Instead of enforcing the law as it was written against those who break it, Deukmejian invites growers who break the law to seek relief from governor's appointees. What does all this mean for farm workers? It means that the right to vote in free elections is a sham. It means the right to talk freely about the union among your fellow workers on the job is a cruel hoax. It means that the right to be free from threats and intimidation by growers is an empty promise. It means that the right to sit down and negotiate with your employer as equals across the bargaining table and not as peons in the fields is a fraud. It means that thousands of farm workers, who are owed millions of dollars in back pay because their employers broke the law, are still waiting for their checks. It means that 36,000 farm workers, who voted to be represented by the United Farm Workers in free elections, are still waiting for contracts from growers who refuse to bargain in good faith. It means that for farm workers child labor will continue. It means that infant mortality will continue. It means that malnutrition among children will continue. It means the short life expectancy and the inhuman living and working conditions will continue.

Are these make-believe threats? Are they exaggerations? Ask the farm workers who are waiting for the money they lost because the growers broke the law. Ask the farm workers who are still waiting for growers to bargain in good faith and sign contracts. Ask the farm workers who have been fired from their job because they spoke out for the union. Ask the farm workers who have been threatened with physical violence because they support the UFW, and ask the family of Rene Lopez, the young farm worker from Fresno who was shot to death last year because he supported the union as he came out of a voting booth. Ask the farm workers who watch their children go hungry in this land of wealth and promise. Ask the farm workers who see their lives eaten away by poverty and suffering.

These tragic events force farm workers to declare a new international boycott of California grapes, except the 3 percent of grapes produced under union contract. That is why we are asking Americans, once again, to join the farm workers by boycotting California grapes. The newest Harris Poll revealed that 17 million Americans boycotted grapes. We are convinced that those people and that good-will have not disappeared. That segment of the population which makes the boy-cotts work are the Hispanics, the Blacks, the other minorities, our friends in labor and the church. But it is also an entire generation of young Americans who matured politically and socially in the '60s and the '70s, millions of people for whom boycotting grapes and other products became a socially accepted pattern of behavior. If you were young, Anglo and/or near campers during the late '60s and early '70s, chances are you supported farm workers.

Fifteen years later, the men and women of that generation are alive and well. They are in their mid 30s and 40s. They are pursuing professional careers, their disposable incomes are relatively high, but they are still inclined to respond to an appeal from farm workers. The union's mission still has meaning for them. Only today, we must translate the importance of a union for farm workers into the language of the 1980s. Instead of talking about the right to organize, we must talk about protection against sexual harassment in the fields. We must speak about the right to quality food and food that is safe to eat. I can tell you that the new lan-guage is working, the 17 million are still there. They are responding not to picket lines and leafleting alone, but to the high-tech boycott of today, a boycott that uses computers and direct mail and advertising techniques, which has revolutionized business and politics in recent years. We have achieved more success with a boy-cott in the first 11 months of 1984 than we achieved in the last 14 years, since 1970.

The other trend that gives us hope is the monumental growth of Hispanic influ-ence in this country. And what that means: increased population, increased social and economic clout and increased political influence. South of the Sacramento River, Hispanics now make up now more than 25 percent of the population. That figure will top 30 percent by the year 2000. There are now 1.1 million Spanish-surnamed registered voters in California. In 1975, there were 200 Hispanic elected officials at all levels of government. In 1984, there are over 400 elected judges, city council members, mayors and legislators. In light of these trends, it's absurd to believe or to suggest that we are going to go back in time as a union or as a people.

The growers often try to blame the union for their problems, to lay their sins off on us, sins for which they only have themselves to blame. The growers only have themselves to blame as they begin to reap the harvest of decades of environmental damage they have brought upon the land: the pesticides, the herbicides, the soil fumigants, the fertilizers, the salt deposits from thoughtless irrigation, the ravages of years of unrestrained poisoning of our soil and water. Thousands of acres of land in California have already been irrevocably damaged by this wanton abuse of nature. Thousands more will be lost unless growers understand that dumping more and more poison from the soil won't solve their problems in the short or in the long term.

Health authorities in many San Joaquin Valley towns already warn young children and pregnant mothers not to drink the water, because of the nitrates from fertilizers which has poisoned the ground water. The growers have only themselves to blame for an increasing demand by consumers for higher-quality food, food that isn't tainted by toxics, food that doesn't result from plant mutations or chemicals that produce red luscious-looking tomatoes that taste like alfalfa. The growers are making the same mistakes American automakers made in the '60s and '70s when they refused to produce more economical cars and opened up the door to increased foreign competition.

Growers only have themselves to blame for increasing attacks on the publicly financed handouts and government welfare: water subsidies, mechanization research, huge subsidies for not growing crops. These special privileges came into being before the Supreme Court's "one person, one vote" decision, at a time when rural lawmakers dominated the legislature and the Congress. Soon, those handouts could be in jeopardy as government searches for more revenue and as urban taxpayers take a closer look at front programs and who they really benefit. The growers only have themselves to blame for the humiliation they have brought upon succeeding waves of immigrant groups that have sweated and sacrificed for a hundred years to make this industry rich.

For generations, they have subjugated entire races of dark-skinned farm workers. These are the sins of growers, not the farm workers. We didn't poison the land, we didn't open the door to imported produce, we didn't covet billions of dollars in government handouts, we didn't abuse and exploit the people who work the land. Today the growers are like a punch-drunk old boxer who doesn't know he's past his prime. The times are changing; the political and social environment has changed. The chickens are coming home to roost, and the time to account for past sins is approaching.

I am told these days farm workers should be discouraged and pessimistic. The Republicans control the governor's office and the White House. There is a conservative trend in the nation. Yet, we are filled with hope and encouragement. We have looked into the future and the future is ours. History and inevitability are on our side. The farm workers and their children and the Hispanics and their children are the future in California, and corporate growers are the past. Those politicians who ally themselves with the corporate growers and against farm workers and the Hispanics are in for a big surprise. They want to make their careers in politics, they want to hold power 20 and 30 years from now. But 20 and 30 years from now, in Modesto, in Salinas, in Fresno, in Bakersfield, in the Imperial Valley and in many of the great cities of California, those communities will be dominated by farm workers and not by growers, by the children and grandchildren of farm workers and not by the children and grandchildren of growers.

These trends are part of the forces of history which cannot be stopped. No person and no organization can resist them for very long; they are inevitable. Once social change begins it cannot be reversed. You cannot uneducate the person who has learned to read. You cannot humiliate the person who feels pride. You cannot oppress the people who are not afraid anymore. Our opponents must understand that it's not just the union we have built—unions like other institutions can come and go—but we're more than institutions. For nearly 20 years, our union has been on the cutting edge of a people's cause, and you cannot do away with an entire people and you cannot stamp out a people's cause. Regardless of what the future holds for the union, regardless of what the future holds for farm workers, our accomplishments cannot be undone. La causa, our cause, doesn't have to be experienced twice. The consciousness and pride that were raised by our union are alive and thriving inside millions of young Hispanics who will never work on a farm.

Like the other immigrant groups, the day will come when we win the economic and political rewards, which are in keeping with our numbers in society. The day will come when the politicians will do the right thing for our people out of political necessity and not out of charity or idealism. That day may not come this year. That day may not come during this decade, but it will come someday. And when that day comes, we shall see the fulfillment of that passage from the Book of Matthew in the New Testament: "The last shall be first, and the first shall be last." And on that day, our nation shall fulfill its creed, and that fulfillment shall enrich us all. Thank you very much.

Source: "What the Future Holds for Farm Workers and Hispanics." TM/© 2012 Cesar Chavez Foundation. http://chavez.cde.ca.gov/ModelCurriculum/teachers/ Lessons/resources/documents/Commonwealth_Club_SanFrancisco_11-9-84.pdf. Used by permission.

Extract from Interview with Guadalupe Gamboa, April 9, 2003

The son of Mexican American parents in Texas, Guadalupe Gamboa moved with his family in the late 1940s to the Yakima Valley in central Washington. Living mostly in labor camps, the family, along with Guadalupe, worked the fields. He graduated from high school and, unlike most of his farm worker friends, was able to go to college. At Yakima Valley Community College, he learned about the newly formed UFW. It was there that he met Tomas Villa-nueva, who would join him in the work of building a farm workers' move-ment in Washington state.

. . . I grew up my early years going from labor camp to labor camp. We would work in Washington cutting asparagus and then go and eventually we bought our own truck. [Then we would] get [in] our truck and drive down to Oregon to Wil-lamette Valley and pick beans and then drive down to California and pick cotton with the big companies in California during the winter and then come back in the spring and follow the same routine. So as a child I grew up going from school to school, and the first grade I think I started while I was here in Washington in the spring and I flunked the first grade 'cause I didn't know any English, and there were no programs or anything to make up for the fact that you couldn't understand what they were saying.

So anyway, like myself and our family, there were thousands of Mexican-American migrants from Texas in the early years, just working basically in the row crops, the asparagus, mainly with small growers or big packing houses, like Green Giant and Del Monte, or working in the sugar beets. At that time you had a lot of sugar beets; you had a big sugar processing plant run by U & I—Utah and Idaho Sugar Company in Toppenish. And then there was also a lot of mint, spearmint [and] peppermint that was grown and then distilled for the juices, where the oil was used to flavor candies. And then there was also hops that's used to fla-vor beer—[in the] hop yards. They were also picking potatoes and working in the carrots, so there were different jobs that people could do, but they pretty much all involved stooping over—very hard physical labor. There were a lot of orchards at that time, but interestingly enough, the orchard work was reserved more for the Anglo—the white farm worker. At that time, there were still a lot of white farm workers that had come from Oklahoma and Arkansas. They called them "Arkies" and "Okies" during the Dustbowl, the Depression. Some had moved on, but a lot had stayed. They were very poor, also, and they're the ones that worked in the orchards, because it was considered higher status work because you didn't have to be stooped over all day for low wages. So there was a real distinction between the Mexicans who did the stoop labor and the Anglos that did the orchard work—the pruning, the thinning, the picking. And orchard work was paid very well in comparison to today. It was done by piece-rate and people could make two, three times what the hourly wage was. So slowly, more and more Mexican workers started to come. I remember going to school and being one of a few in my school, but it would grow year by year.

Most of the work—at least the stoop labor—was either by piece rate, like in the asparagus, or by the hour, and the wage never was more than the minimum wage. It was just the minimum wage all the time. There were no benefits and at that time farm workers didn't have any unemployment or at least, in Washington, very few social services. So people worked, pooled their resources [and] tried to save money for periods when there was no employment. And it was hard work and there were a lot of indignities, because you could be fired at any time. There were no toilets in the fields or water provided for the workers. The worker basically had no say. So that's the background—a lot of hard work [and] very low pay. If the grower didn't like the work you were doing, he wouldn't pay you and you'd be fired.

Very few people went on to college. The farm workers had their Mexican culture; Anglos had their culture and social events and there was very little mixing of the two. Most farm workers dropped out of school, like my family, and became farm workers. It was in this type of background that we first started hearing about Cesar Chavez and the organizing efforts that were going on in California.

This was in the '60s. I was just finishing high school. I think I first heard about Cesar Chavez when I was junior college, which would have been about '65, '66. At that time, it was the '60s, when the civil rights movement had started. Lyndon Johnson was president [and] the War on Poverty had begun in the Yakima Valley because it was a poor area.

So I graduated from my high school in Sunnyside, and I was one of maybe ten or fifteen Latinos, and I remember I went through from first to the eighth grade in Outlook, which was a little town out in the country. It was a little country school. I remember in the sixth grade I had a very good teacher, a guy by the name [of] Mr. Williams. [He was] kind of an oddity. He was from out of town and used to drive a Volkswagen. I had never seen a Volkswagen in my life, but they were new at that time, in the '50s. So that showed he was pretty nonconformist. I really liked him and he really took an interest in me. I remember once him talking to me after school and asking me if I was planning on going to college and [I] said, "College—what's that?" because I had no idea what it was, you know, it just wasn't in my frame of reference. So he told me what it was. The reason he was asking was because at that time they started to track kids. You would put them in the smart classes or the vocational ed classes or the classes that are more academic to prepare you for college. He counseled me about going to college. Neither my father or mother had a single day of schooling when they were growing up. My father couldn't read [or] write and my mother could read but couldn't write in Spanish. She later learned when she was in her 60s how to write. My dad especially was always talking to me about the importance of having an education; because I hated school after I flunked the first grade. It was Anglo, hostile. But he was always telling me about the importance of going to school—that if you went to school you could get out of farm work and become a lawyer, a teacher, a doctor, and so I guess that stuck.

I didn't drop out. I kept going, and then I finally graduated and went on to junior college [at] Yakima Valley Junior College [YVC]. And it was at Yakima Valley College that I first met Tomás Villanueva, [with whom I] formed a long-term friendship and we both got involved with the United Farm Workers at the same time. He was an immigrant [but] more recent. I was born actually in Texas, in this country, and he was a recent immigrant from Mexico and had a real distinct Spanish accent, but a very smart guy. So then we met at YVC, and I started doing research on Cesar Chavez and writing papers about him. I remember going into the library and taking out *The Nation* and other leftist papers—I didn't know they were leftist at that time [laughter] and reading about the organizing efforts and the grape boycott—well, the grape strike—and the great organizing he was doing in California. So, both Tomás and I had a very deep interest in what was going on because of the situation of our families, and farm workers in general, and our own personal experiences and growing up and being cheated and being mistreated.

So we both got hired, we were both activists and we wanted to do something; so when the War on Poverty started, I believe in 1966, we both got employed by a War on Poverty program called Operation Grassroots, whose stated object was to go around interviewing people [to] find out why they were poor, you know, and what they needed to not be poor anymore [laughter]. It was very idealistic— that we thought that people were poor because they didn't know any better or needed a little fixing-up. Then people were saying, "Oh, we're poor because we don't get paid anything and our jobs don't last very long and we don't know how to speak English—very hard problems to solve. But it was through the War on Poverty, actually, that we first made contact with the United Farm Workers of America in the person of an organizer by the name of Nick Jones—[an] Anglo organizer who had been sent from Delano to look for people who had struck a grape ranch—I believe either Giumarra or DiGiorgio, one of the two. After pressure through our campaign from the union, the company had agreed to a secret-ballot election, and part of the deal was that anybody that had worked during [a] certain period of time could vote in the elections. So they had sent out organizers following the migrant stream all over the country looking for the strikers—a very, very thorough organizing campaign. [Nick] came and addressed the meeting—an anti–War on Poverty meeting. By that time both Tomás and I were pretty fed up with the War on Poverty, because they never talked about organizing workers or forming unions or forming political power—just nothing but services and stuff. So he gave a presentation at the end of a meeting which was like a real breath of fresh air. He talked about organizing and getting better wages and better working conditions in addition to looking for the strikers and former grape workers. We talked to him afterwards, and he invited us down to California, saying there was going to be an election that summer and they needed some help.

Both Tomás and I went down there. Tomás at that time had a 1958 or 1959 Pontiac and we took off and drove all night and got to Delano and it was pretty interesting. We arrived in Delano looking for Cesar Chavez, and in my mind, because I had been so conditioned by living in an Anglo world, Cesar Chavez was going to be a light-skinned, tall, debonair-looking guy in a suit, with a fancy car and having a nice, big, fancy office. So we arrived in Delano looking for such a guy, and couldn't find him and eventually got directed to a little run-down house in the barrio on the edge of town, which was the union headquarters and eventually Cesar Chavez showed up—this small, dark-skinned, Indian-looking guy with jet-black hair, dressed in jeans and a flannel shirt, in the middle of a bunch of workers. It was pretty amazing the first time that we saw him. Actually, the thing that made the most impact on me was, well, in addition to Cesar and his charisma, was the impact that he had obviously had on all the workers there. They were all really transformed, from the beaten-down workers in this state that lived in despair and didn't think they could do anything, and had been conditioned that they were inferior because they were farm workers, to workers that had been involved (at that time the grape strike had already occurred). They were all real fired up and determined and knew that they could win. They stuck together. It was an incredible transformation, and it had a really lasting impact on me. It showed the possibilities of what could be done.

So we were pretty much hooked after that [laughter], and we got put to work looking for people that we thought were being taken to work so that they could vote in the election. I was put in a bus, and Tomás was going to follow me, because we thought the bus might go to this farm, but it turned out that the bus went to a tomato field, instead of Giumarra or DiGiorgio. But again that was very symptomatic of the union. There were no hangers-on or people that just talked. People were put to work immediately. Then the election was held, and the UFW won by a huge majority. And so we were in Delano, we met Cesar Chavez, we were involved in the organizing, [and] we took part in the weekly Friday night meetings at the Filipino community hall that the workers had, where a report was given as to what was going on and the activities. I think we were introduced as representatives/visitors from Washington State. We were treated very cordially, very gracefully, and I think we spent two weeks there.

And then we came back to Washington and by that time—as I mentioned, we were both college students. This was our summer break and by that time we had decided we wanted to do something. I finished my two years at YVC and went another quarter—the fall of '66—and then transferred to the University of Washington in the spring of 1967. By that time the draft board was after me, because it was the height of the Vietnam War, [but] I managed to stay out of it. Tomás was married by that time and he decided not to go on to college. His dream was to become a doctor, and he started working with the War on Poverty and then eventually left it because they weren't doing very much. He formed the first farm workers union [and] the first farm workers health clinic in the Yakima Valley, after much opposition from the local politicians and the local medical association. [He] also started a co-op called the United Farm Workers Co-op that was supposed to be the base for organizing later on.

So that was the nucleus—the start of the contact and the relationship that's persisted to this day between Washington State and California . . .

We weren't getting very far through that winter and spring and then in the summer of I think it was '71, we were asked to go to California. The union had at that time—the United Farm Workers national office—had just moved into a new location called "La Paz." It was a headquarters in the foothills of the Tehachapi Mountains. It used to be a former TB sanitarium where they had sent people who had tuberculosis so that they could lie in bed and breathe the fresh country air, I guess, and the union had gotten it as a donation from one of the wealthy supporters. It was a big complex. It had over three hundred acres. So we went there and we were trained for about two or three—I think it was two days. Fred Ross, Sr., who is the person who trained Cesar on how to organize, and Cesar himself spent two days talking to us, just telling us the basics of organizing and giving us a history of how the organizing techniques that they had used very successfully in organizing farm workers had developed.

The main organizing technique that the union was using at that time and that we still use is called the house meeting—house meeting campaign drive, where you would rely on other workers themselves to help you organize a community. You would go and identify the leaders and then do a—we call them personal visit—explain to them what the idea was, what the concept of unionizing was and how you could help them and what the benefits potentially could be, economically and politically and then get them to buy in to agree it was a good thing. And then while they were excited, you would ask them then to hold a meeting at their house and invite four or five other people that they knew. That way the employers didn't know what was going on and the people would feel comfortable because it was at a friend's or relative's house. And then you would go in—you do reminding calls—and then you would go in and do your presentation and at the end—the main thing to get out of that meeting was to get other people to have other meetings. It was like a chain. So then you went to that person's and then you got two or three other meetings, and before too long, you covered a wide spectrum of the community. So Fred Ross demonstrated that for us how he did it and explained how Cesar had used it when he was first organizing and at the same time gave examples [and] gave a history of the union and got people involved in the whole process. It was very, very much like the popular education that's being used throughout Latin America now.

So we came back and you know then you would have meetings every morning. The people would go out in pairs for the first month or so and then they would do critiques afterwards and people would make suggestions on how to improve the presentation. So then we came back and then by that time Fred Ross, Jr., the son of Fred Ross, Sr., was assigned to work also in Washington State. So there were three of us then instead of just two and we started the house meeting campaigns and they worked. We no longer held the big meetings where nobody would come but instead had a series of meetings. And then at the end then we would call a big meeting and then everybody would come because they were people that we had organized and that knew each other and we used the networks to mobilize these other people, so in the space of a year, we had turned the thing completely around, and we were having actually a lot of success in terms of getting people involved . . .

Source: Guadalupe Gamboa. 2003. Interview by Anne O'Neill. Seattle Civil Rights and Labor History Project, University of Washington, April 9. http://depts.washington.edu/civilr/gGamboa-transcript.htm. Used by permission of Guadalupe Gamboa.

Annotated Bibliography

Bardacke, Frank. *Trampling Out the Vintage: Cesar Chavez and the Two Souls of the United Farm Workers*. New York: Verso, 2011. Exhaustively researched and authoritatively documented, this work is a reassessment of the rise, triumphs, internal turmoil, and ultimate decline of the United Farm Workers (UFW) as a labor union capable of wielding power on behalf of its constituents. Although the book does not fully frame Cesar Chavez's farm workers movement in the context of the growth of Latino pride and political power, it provides unique human-interest glimpses into the lives of scores of individuals involved in the complex events surrounding Chavez's achievements as well as his limitations.

Bender, Steven W. *One Night in America: Robert Kennedy, Cesar Chavez, and the Dream of Dignity*. Boulder, CO: Paradigm Publishers, 2008. The friendship and alliance that developed between Robert Kennedy and Cesar Chavez and their shared vision of fighting on behalf of society's poor deeply affected both men. This book skillfully captures the moments of both triumph and tragedy.

Chatfield, LeRoy, comp. *Farmworker Movement Documentation Project*. http://www.farmworkermovement.org/. LeRoy Chatfield was one of Chavez's close associates who had come to the farm workers movement from a Christian religious organization. Many years later, he created the Farmworker Movement Documentation Project, gathering oral histories, personal correspondence, published works, and other materials to provide an essential source for those researching the history of the UFW.

Chavez, Cesar, and Ilan Stavans, eds. *An Organizer's Tale*. New York: Penguin Classics, 2008. Ilan Stavans, one of the preeminent scholars of Latino history, edited Cesar Chavez's own reflections on the tactics and goals of the farm workers movement.

Cohen, Jerry. *Gringo Justice: The United Farm Workers Union, 1967–1981*. The Papers of Jerry Cohen, Amherst College Library, February 2008. https://www.amherst.edu/media/view/85629/original/Gringojustice.pdf. Lawyer Jerry Cohen, as head of the United Farmworkers legal team, participated in many of the most critical courtroom and legislative battles of the union. He wrote reminiscences of those battles in an unpublished tract called "Gringo Justice" that is housed in his papers at Amherst College Library.

Day, Mark. *Forty Acres: Cesar Chavez and the Farm Workers*. New York: Praeger Publishers, 1971. Franciscan Father Mark Day, who worked as an organizer and one of the editors of *El Malcriado*, the farm workers movement's newspaper, wrote this book in the midst of Cesar Chavez's continuing quest to enlist church members of all faiths in the farm workers' cause. His story is filled with unique, first-person accounts.

Dunne, John Gregory. *Delano: The Story of the California Grape Strike*. Reprint. Berkeley: University of California Press, 2007. Early in his estimable career, journalist and author John Gregory Dunne, who lived in California during the Delano grape strike, wrote a firsthand account that is still riveting in its depiction of the fast-moving events of the labor struggle.

Federal Bureau of Investigation. *File on Cesar Chavez and the United Farm Workers*. http://vault.fbi.gov/Cesar%20Chavez. From the early days of his organizing activities, the Federal Bureau of Investigation gave Cesar Chavez special scrutiny. Was he a member of an anti-American, subversive organization? The files on Chavez are now open online and provide valuable insight into the suspicions of the government investigators and what they actually found.

Ferriss, Susan, and Ricardo Sandoval. *The Fight in the Fields: Cesar Chavez and the Farm Workers Movement*. New York: Harcourt Brace, 1997. Containing many personal narratives from farm workers on the front lines of the union's struggles and many photographs, this book is a lively general history and standard reference work.

Ganz, Marshall. *Why David Sometimes Wins: Leadership, Organization, and Strategy in the California Farm Worker Movement*. New York: Oxford University Press, 2009. One of Chavez's closest political strategists, Marshall Ganz played a leading role in planning many of the marches, legislative fights, boycotts, and other battles of the movement. One of those who left the UFW after internal strife, Ganz later worked in the presidential campaign of Barack Obama in 2008. This book traces the tactical approaches that led to the surprising success of the drive toward a union of farm workers.

Griswold del Castillo, Richard, and Richard A. Garcia. *Cesar Chavez: A Triumph of Spirit*. Norman: University of Oklahoma Press, 1995. An examination of Cesar Chavez's life as it appears in the context of Mexican American and Chicano history, this biography also looks at the farm workers movement from the perspective of American liberalism and reform movements and the continuing struggles to grapple with such issues as immigration, nonviolent protest, and racial discrimination.

Hammerback, John, and Richard Jensen. *The Rhetorical Career of Cesar Chavez*. College Station: Texas A&M University Press, 2003. Although Cesar Chavez was not an eloquent orator or a masterful writer, this work shows how he was able to frame his message and vision into a powerful framework that inspired.

Jordane, Maurice "Mo." *The Struggle for the Health and Legal Protection of Farm Workers: El Cortito*. Houston, TX: Arte Publico Press, 2005. The fight against "El Cortito," the infamous short-handled hoe that farm workers were forced by the growers to use in the harvest fields, was one of the signal victories of the farm workers movement. California Rural Legal Assistance lawyer Maurice "Mo" Jourdane, along with the UFW, fought an aggressive legal and legislative war against those who would continue to force farm workers to use a tool that produced debilitating back injuries. This firsthand account chronicles Jordane's decade-long work to research and successfully advocate for a California state ban to protect the rights of field workers.

Levy, Jacques E. *Cesar Chavez: Autobiography of La Causa*. Paperback edition with foreword by Fred Ross Jr. Minneapolis: University of Minnesota Press, 2007. In 1969, journalist Jacques Levy met Cesar Chavez with an idea for a book on the farm workers movement. Reluctant at first, Chavez finally agreed to participate in the project, thus granting the writer unprecedented access not only to Chavez but to other UFW members. The book is largely composed of first-person accounts from those most directly involved in the union's struggles.

Martin, Philip. *Promise Unfulfilled: Unions, Immigration, and the Farm Workers*. Ithaca, NY: Cornell University Press, 2003. Despite the successes of the farm workers movement, especially the passage by the state of California in 1975 of the Agricultural Labor Relations Act (ALRA) granting field workers the right to organize, the plight of those workers in the twenty-first century remained grim. Wages remained low, working conditions barely tolerable, and only a small fraction of workers in the field unionized. This book examines the reasons that the movement and the ALRA left many challenges remaining.

Matthiessen, Peter. *Sal Si Puedes: Cesar Chavez and the New American Revolution*. Berkeley: University of California Press, 2000. The noted writer Peter Matthiessen spent three years working with Cesar Chavez. This account, featuring the author's elegant prose, is one of the most gripping firsthand looks into the many sides of the nonviolent movement for the rights of farm workers and the tactics of strikes, boycotts, marches, fasts, and community organizing that made real the improbable dream of a union for farm workers.

McWilliams, Carey, and Douglas C. Sackman. *Factories in the Fields: The Story of Migratory Farm Labor in California*. Berkeley: University of California Press, 2000. Long-time journalist, editor of *The Nation* magazine, and author of books and articles exploring pressing social issues, McWilliams first published *Factories in the Field* in 1939. McWilliams's book was the first broad expose of the economic and environmental ravages of corporate agriculture in California. Republished in 2000, the book remains a valuable source for understanding the origins of the farm workers' fight for a union in the 1960s.

Orosco, Jose-Antonio. *Cesar Chavez and the Common Sense of Nonviolence.* Albuquerque: University of New Mexico Press, 2008. The foundation and moral imperative of Cesar Chavez's farm workers movement was nonviolent protest. Derived not only from the reading and works of Gandhi and the tactics of the American civil rights movement, Chavez's concept of nonviolent social change was also steeped in the history of Latin American reform and Catholic teaching. This book explores Chavez's own ideas and contributions to nonviolence as a means of achieving social justice.

Pawell, Miriam. *The Union of Their Dreams: Power, Hope, and Struggle in Cesar Chavez's Farm Worker Movement.* New York: Bloomsbury Press, 2009. In 2006, *Los Angeles Times* reporter Miriam Pawel published a four-part series charging that the UFW had strayed from its original mission of helping farm workers and had suffered grievous decline not only in membership but in influence. This subsequent book focuses on eight individuals who clashed with Chavez over internal matters and left the union.

Prouty, Marco. *Cesar Chavez, the Catholic Bishops, and the Farmworkers' Struggle for Social Justice.* Tucson: University of Arizona Press, 2008. Like the black civil rights movement, the drive for a union of farm workers employed strong religious elements in its marches, writings, fasts, and use of religious symbols. Although Cesar Chavez and most of the farm workers were Catholics, it was not until 1969 that the American Catholic hierarchy responded to the movement by creating the Bishop' Ad Hoc Committee on Farm Labor.

Ross, Fred. *Conquering Goliath: Cesar Chavez at the Beginning.* Keene, CA: El Taller Grafico Press/United Farm Workers, 1989. Community organizer and founder of the Community Service Organization (CSO), Fred Ross became a close mentor, friend, and associate of Chavez. He gave Chavez, along with cofounder of the UFW Dolores Huerta, invaluable training in organizing that led to their drive and determination to found a union of farm workers. He was with Chavez and Huerta at the beginning and offers a unique perspective.

Scharlin, Craig, and Lilia V. Villanueva. *Philip Vera Cruz: A Personal History of Filipino Immigrants and the Farmworkers Movement.* Seattle: University of Washington Press, 2000. This oral memoir of the life of Philip Vera Cruz, a strong leader among Filipino farm workers, provides valuable insight into a largely ignored part of American labor history—the struggles of Filipino workers fighting against oppression and discrimination. It was Vera Cruz and other Filipino leaders of the Agricultural Workers Organizing Committee (AWOC) who convinced Cesar Chavez to align his own infant organization in the 1965 Delano grape strike that proved critical in the rise of the farm workers movement.

Shaw, Randy. *Cesar Chavez, the UFW, and the Struggle for Justice in the 21st Century.* Berkeley: University of California Press, 2008. Countering some recent studies that doubt the long-term impact of Cesar Chavez's work in establishing a union of farm workers, this book emphasizes the enormous influence that the movement brought to a wide-ranging number of activist enterprises and the rise of Latino economic and political empowerment.

Southwest Research and Information Center. "Voices from the Earth: An Interview with Dolores Huerta.' October 29, 2003. http://www.sric.org/voices/2004/v5n2/huerta.php. In October 2003, Dolores Huerta was in Albuquerque, New Mexico, to announce the launching of the Dolores Huerta Foundation, dedicated to training a new generation of grassroots organizers fighting for social change. While in Albuquerque, Huerta granted an interview to the University of New Mexico's Southwest Research and Information Center.

"The Story of Wendy Goepel Brooks, Cesar Chavez and La Huelga." http://www.farmworkermovement.us/essays/essays/007%20Brooks_Wendy.pdf. A young activist named Wendy Goepel, who had majored in sociology at Stanford, briefly worked for the California Department of Health, and had also been a consultant to Governor Pat Brown on the antipoverty VISTA program, joined the farm workers movement in its early days. Her recollections give extraordinary insight into the motivations and inspiration that led many young students to follow Chavez, Huerta, and the other leaders of the UFW.

United Farm Workers. "Veterans of Historic Delano Grape Strike Mark 40th Anniversary with Two-Day Reunion in Delano and La Paz." *El Malcriado*, Special Edition, September 17–18, 2005. http://www.ufw.org/_page.php?menu=research&inc=history/05.html. In 2005, the UFW held a reunion in California commemorating the 40th anniversary of the Delano grape strike. The various speeches and reminiscences delivered by such early participants in the farm workers movement as Dolores Huerta, Luis Valdez, Chris Hartmire, and others are unique personal perspectives.

Wells, Ronald A. "Cesar Chavez's Protestant Allies: The California Migrant Ministry and the Farm Workers." http://www.farmworkermovement.us/essays/essays/cec.pdf. From the beginning of Cesar Chavez's quest to form a farm workers union, the California Migrant Ministry (CMM) and its leaders Jim Drake and Chris Hartmire gave the movement a powerful religious presence. At synods, conventions, and other religious gatherings, they spoke of the rights of farm workers in terms of the ideals of Christian charity. Members of the Migrant Ministry remained staunch allies in the movement's drive for social justice and, as this article shows, Chavez gave great credit to the CMM for the creation and survival of the union.

Index

Page numbers in **boldface** refer to the main entries of the encyclopedia.

of 1975 (ALRA) and, 178; Burton, Philip, and, 177; Gallo Wine Company and, 176–78; march (*Peregrinación*) to Sacramento (1966) and, 177; Ross, Fred, and, 177; Teamsters Union and, 176

Molera Agricultural Group, 186

Mothers Against Chavez, 56

Murphy, Cathy, 186

Murphy, George, U.S. Senate Subcommittee on Migratory Labor Hearings (1966) and, 249

Nathan, Sandy, **179–81**; Agricultural Labor Relations Act of 1975 (ALRA) and, 179–80; arrest, 180; background, 179; and "The Game," 180; leaving United Farm Workers (UFW), 180–81

National Chavez Center, 38–39, 147. *See also* La Paz

National Farm Labor Union (NFLU): Chavez, Librado, and, 44; DiGiorgio Fruit Corporation and, 73; origin, 243

National Farm Workers Alliance (NFWA), 117–20

National Farm Workers Association (NFWA): Drake, Jim, and, 77; founding convention (1962), 93–94; Kircher, William, and, 142–43; Lyons, Mack, and, 153; McFarland tose grafters strike (1965) and, 165–67; merger with AWOC, xxiv–xxv; origin, xvi, 11–12, 244; Plan of Delano and, 196–98

National Farm Workers Service Center, Inc. (NFWSC), 90

National Labor Relations Act (NLRA), 20

National Migrant Ministry, 31

Neighbor to Neighbor, 57, 216

Nelson, Eugene, 237–38

Nonviolent protest, **181–84**; ethics, 182, 184; Gandhi, Mohandas Karamchand (Mahatma), and, 182–83; King, Martin Luther, Jr., and, 183; Oxnard organizing campaign (1958) and, 188–89; as traditional Latin American methods, 183; varieties, 181

North from Mexico: The Spanish-Speaking People of the United States (McWilliams), 170

Obama, Barack: Alinsky, Saul, and, 15; as director of DCP, 60; meeting with Chavez, Richard, 49

O'Hara, James G., 296–97

One Thousand Mile March (1975), **185–87**; Agricultural Labor Relations Act of 1975 (ALRA) and, 185; California Agricultural Labor Relations Act (CALRA) of 1975 and, 185; contract votes, 186–87; *Fighting for Our Lives* and, 186; Molera Agricultural Group and, 186

Oxnard Organizing Campaign (1958), **187–89**; Bracero Program and, 188; Community Service Organization (CSO) and, 187–89; nonviolent practices and, 188–89; United Packinghouse Workers of America and, 187–88

Padilla, Gilbert, **191–93**; Alinsky, Saul, and, 14; background, 191; and creation of United Farm Workers (UFW), 191; CSO and, 63; DiGiorgio Fruit Corporation

About the Author

Roger Bruns is a historian and former deputy executive director of the National Historical Publications and Records Commission at the National Archives in Washington, DC. He is the author of many books, including *Negro Leagues Baseball*, *Icons of Latino America: Latino Contributions to American Culture*, *Preacher: Billy Sunday and Big-Time American Evangelism*, and *Almost History: Close Calls, Plan B's, and Twists of Fate in America's Past*. He has written several biographies for young readers on such figures as Cesar Chavez and Martin Luther King Jr.